CBS Mini Dictionaries

ENGLISH-FRENCH
FRENCH-ENGLISH
DICTIONARY

CBS

CBS PUBLISHERS & DISTRIBUTORS

ISBN : 81-239-1015-0

First Indian Edition : 1989
Reprint : 2002
Reprint : 2003, 2006

Printed in India

Published by :
S.K. Jain for CBS Publishers & Distributors,
4596/1A, 11 Daryaganj, New Delhi-2 (India)

Printed at :
Asia Printograph,
Shahdara, Delhi - 110 032

ENGLISH-FRENCH DICTIONARY

ABBREVIATIONS

adj. adjective
adv. adverb
art. article
conj. conjunction
dem. demonstrative
f. feminine
fig. figurative
impers. impersonal
inf. infinitive
int. interjection
m. masculine
pers. person
pl. plural
poss. possessive
pp. past participle
pron. pronoun
qch. quelque chose
qn. qulqu'un
rel. relative
s. substantive
sing. singular
s.o. someone
sth. something
v.a. active verb
v.a. & n. active and neuter verb
v. aux. auxiliary verb
v.n. neuter verb
* irregular verb
prep. preposition

Pronunciation

We give below a short, simple guide to French pronunciation, giving the French sounds and their description. Vowels or consonants that are equivalent to the English ones are not indicated in this list.

Letters	*French key word*	*Description*
a, à, â	la, là, bâtir	between *bag* and *bug*
ai, aî	chaise, maître	resembles *ai* in *chair*
an	dans	between the vowels of *ah* and *oh* with *n* nasalised
au	pause	as in *oh* but with no final *u*
c	a) café	before *a, o, u* pronounced as *k*
	b) ici	before *e, i, y* pronounced *s* as in *say*
ç	français	as *s* in *say*
ch	chambre	as *sh* in *she*
e	a) le, petit	as the unstressed vowel of *the, standard*
	b) derriere, mer	(in a closed syllable) as *e* in *deck*
é	été	as in *day* but with no final *i*
è, ê	père, fête	resembles the vowels in *pear* or *mare* without diphthongization
eau	eau	as in *oh* but with no final *u*
en	enfant	between *ah* and *oh* with *n* nasalized
er	donner	as in *day* but with no final
eu	jeudi, leur	closer than *earth* or *sir* pronounced with the lips pouted
g	a) rouge	before *e, i, y* pronounced as *s* in *measure, usual*
	b) grand	as *g* in *grand, good*
gn	signe	as in *new* or *lenient*
h	homme	it is never pronounced in French
i	a) ici	tenser than English short *i*
	b) mise	as *ee* in *meet*
î	île	as *ee* in *meet*
ille	fille	as in *key* with *y* at the end
in	vin	resembles the sound in *ta* pronounced through the nose
o	jour	as *s* in *usual*
jô	mot, côte	as in *oh* but with no final *u*
œ	œil	closer than *earth* pronounced with the lips pouted
oi	moi	as in *memoir* (memwaa)

on	non, son	between *ah and oh* with *n* nasalized
ou, oû	rouge, goûter	short or long *oo* as in *foot* or
qu	quand, question	as *k* in English
r	rare	as a slightly rolled English *r*
s	a) son	usually *s* as in *say*
	b) maison	(between two vowels) *z* as in *zero*
th	thé	as *t* in English
tion	nation	always *sio*+nasal *n*
u, û	sur, sûr	no equivalent in English: round lips for *oo* and try to pronounce *ee*
un	brun	the vowel of *her, earth* with a nasal *n*
w	wagon	as *v* in English
x	a) deuxième	as *z* in *zero*
	b) six	as *s* in *say*
y	y	as short *i* in English

FRENCH GRAMMAR

L i a i s o n.—Final consonants are not usually pronounced, but in most cases, when a word begins with a vowel (or the mute *h*), it is linked with the last consonant of the preceding word. In such cases final *c* and *g* are pronounced as *k*, final *s* and *x* as *z*, e.g. les‿Anglais (lezangle).

S t r e s s.—In polysyllabic words stress usually falls on the last pronounced syllable, e.g. plusieurs, le docteur, la société.

The Article

The definite article is *le* (m.), *la* (f.), *les* (m. f. pl.). *Le*, *la* are shortened to *l'* before a vowel or mute *h*.

The indefinite article is *un* (m.), *une* (f.).

The Noun

The p l u r a l is generally formed in *s*. Nouns in *s*, *x*, and *z* do not change in the plural. Nouns in *au* and *eu* form their plurals in *x*, e.g. *joyau*, *joyaux*, *jeu*, *jeux*. Nouns in *al*, form their plurals in *aux*, e.g. *cheval*, *chevaux*.

There are two *genders* in French. Nearly all nouns ending in *e* mute are feminine, except those in *isme*, *age* and *iste*. Nearly all nouns ending in a consonant or a vowel other than *e* mute are masculine, except nouns in *tion* and *té*. Nouns in *er* form their f. in *ère* e.g. *laitier, laitière*. Nouns in *en, on* form their f. in *enne, onne*, e.g. *chien, chienne, lion, lionne*. Nouns in *eur* form their f. in *euse* except those in *ateur* which have *atrice*, e.g. *admirateur, admiratrice*.

The Adjective

The plural is generally formed in *s*. Adjectives in *s* or *x* do not change. Those in *al* usually form their plurals in *aux*, e.g. *principal, principaux*.

The feminine is generally formed by adding *e* to the masculine form, e.g. *élégant, élégante*. Adjectives in *f* change *f* into *ve*, e.g. *vif, vive*. Those in *x* change *x* into *se*, e.g. *heureux; heureuse*. Adj. in *er* form their f. in *ère*, e.g. *amer, amère*. Those in *el, eil, en, et, on* double the final consonant before adding *e*, e.g. *bel, belle, bon, bonne*.

Comparative.—'more . . . than' or '. . . er than' is to be translated by 'plus . . . que'; 'less . . . than' by 'moins . . . que'.

Superlative.—'the most . . .' or 'the . . . st' is to be translated by 'le plus . . .', 'la plus . . .' or 'les plus . . .'

The Pronoun

Personal pronouns: je, tu, il, elle; nous, vous, ils, elles.—*Accusative:* me, te, le, la; nous, vous, les. *Dative:* me, te, lui; nous, vous, leur.—

After prep.. moi, toi, lui, elle; nous, vous, eux, elles.

Reflexive pronouns: me, te, se; nous, vous, se.

Possessive pronouns: le mien (la mienne, les miens, les miennes), le tien (la tienne, les tiens, les tiennes), le sien (la sienne, les siens, les siennes); le nôtre (la nôtre, les nôtres), le vôtre (la vôtre, les vôtres), le leur (la leur, les leurs).

Relative pronouns: who = qui, whom = que, whose = dont, which = qui or que, to whom = a qui.

Interrogative pronoun: who, whom = qui; what = que.

The Adverb

Most French adverbs are formed by adding *ment*, to the feminine form of the corresponding adjective, e.g. *facile, facile+ment, heureux, heureuse + ment*. Those in *ant* and *ent* form their adverbs in *amment* and *emment*, respectively, e.g. *patient—patiemment*.

The Verb

We give here the conjugation of the two auxilliaries (*avoir, être*) and of the verbs in -er, -ir, and -re, giving only the principal simple forms:

avoir *Pres. Ind.* j'ai, tu as, il a, nous avons, vous avez, ils ont; *Impf.* j'avais, tu avais, il avait, nous avions, vous aviez, ils avaient; *Fut.* j'aurai, tu auras, il aura, nous aurons, vous aurez, ils auront; *Cond.* j'aurais, tu aurais, il aurait, nous aurions, vous auriez, ils auraient; *Pres. Subj.* que j'aie, que tu aies, qu'il ait, que nous ayons, que vous ayez, qu'ils aient; *Imp.* aie, ayons, ayez; *Pres. Part.* ayant; *Past.Part.* eu.

être *Pres. Ind.* je suis, tu es, il est, nous sommes, vous êtes, ils sont; *Impf.* j'étais, tu étais, il était, nous étions, vous étiez, ils étaient; *Fut.* je serai, tu seras, il sera, nous serons, vous serez, ils seront; *Cond.* je serais, tu serais, il serait, nous serions, vous seriez, ils seraient; *Pres. Subj.* que je sois, que tu sois, qu'il soit, que nous soyons, que vous soyez, qu'il soient; *Imp.* sois, soyons, soyez; *Pres. Part.* étant; *Past. Part.* été.

donner *Pres. Ind.* je donne, tu donnes, il donne, nous donnons, vous donnez, ils donnent; *Impf.* je donnais, tu donnais, il donnait, nous donnions, vous donniez, ils donnaient; *Fut.* je donnerai, tu donneras, il donnera, nous donnerons, vous donnerez, ils donneront; *Cond.* je donnerais, tu donnerais, il donnerait, nous donnerions, vous donneriez, ils donneraient; *Pres. Subj.* que je donne, que tu donnes, qu'il donne, que nous donnions, que vous donniez, qu'ils donnent; *Imp.* donne, donnons, donnez; *Pres. Part.* donnant; *Past. Part.* donné.

finir *Pres. Ind.* je finis, tu finis, il finit, nous finissons, vous finnissez, ils finissent; finis, il finit, nous finissons, vous finissez, ils finissent; *Impf.* je finissais, tu finissais, il finissait, nous finissions, vous finissiez, ils finissaïent; *Fut.* je finirai, tu finiras, il finira, nous finirons, vous finirez, ils finiront; *Cond.* je finirais, tu finirais, il finirait, nous finirions, vous finiriez, ils finiraient; *Pres. Subj.* que je finisse, que tu finisses, qu'il finisse, que nous finissions, que vous finissiez, qu'ils finissent; *Imp.* finis, finissons, finissez; *Pres. Part.* finissant; *Past Part.* fini.

rendre *Pres. Ind.* je rends, tu rends, il rend, nous rendons, vous rendez, ils rendent; *Impf.* je rendais, tu rendais, il rendait, nous rendions, vous rendiez, ils rendaient; *Fut.* je rendrai, tu rendras, il rendra, nous rendrons, vous rendrez, ils rendront; *Cond.* je rendrais, tu rendrais, il rendrait, nous rendrions, vous rendriez, ils rendraient; *Pres. Subj.* que je rende, que tu rendes, qu'il rende, que nous rendions, que vous rendiez, qu'ils rendent; *Imp*. rends, rendons, rendez; *Pres. Part.* rendant; *Past. Part*. rendu.

Irregular Verbs

Verbs in *-ger* add *e* before endings in *a* and *o*. Verbs in *-eler*, *-eter* double the *l* or *t* before a mute *e*. Verbs having an acute *é* in the last syllable but one change for a grave *e* when the ending begins with a mute *e*. Verbs in *-yer* change *y* into *i* before a mute *e*.

In the following list of the most frequent French irregular verbs (the root verbs only) the numbers indicate the principal tenses and forms in a fixed order: **1.** Present Indicative; **2.** Imperfect; 3. Future; **4.** Present Subjunctive; **5.** Imperative; **6.** Present Participle; **7.** Past Participle. (+ *être*, if *être* is used to form the past tenses e.g. je suis allé.)

absoudre 1. j'absous, tu absous, il absout, nous absolvons, vous absolvez, ils absolvent; **2.** j'absolvais; **3.** j'absoudrai; **4.** que j'absolve; **5.** absous, absolvons, absolvez; **6.** absolvant; **7.** absous, absoute.

acquérir 1. j'acquiers, tu acquiers, il acquiert, nous acquérons, vous acquérez, ils acquièrent; **2.** j'acquérais; **3.** j'acquerrai; **4.** que j'acquière; **5.** acquiers, acquérons, acquérez; **6.** acquérant; **7.** acquis.

aller 1. je vais, tu vas, il va, nous allons, vous allez, ils vont; **2.** j'allais; **3.** j'irai; **4.** que j'aille, que nous allions, qu'ils aillent; **5.** va, allons, allez; **6.** allant; **7.** allé (être).

assaillir 1. j'assaille, tu assailles, il assaille, nous assaillons, vous assaillez, ils assaillent; **2.** j'assaillais; **3.** j'assaillerai; **4.** que j'assaille; **5.** assaille, assaillons, assaillez; **6.** assaillant; **7.** assailli.

asseoir 1. j'assieds, tu assieds, il assied, nous asseyons, vous asseyez, ils asseyent *or* j'assois, tu assois, il assoit, nous assoyons, vous assoyez, ils assoient; **2.** j'assayais *or* j'assoyais; **3.** j'assiérai *or* j'assoierai; **4.** que j'asseye *or* que j'assoie; **5.** assieds, asseyons *or* assoyons, asseyez *or* assoyez; **6.** asseyant or assoyant; **7.** assis.

atteindre *as* **peindre.**

battre 1. je bats, tu bats, il bat, nous battons, vous battez, ils battent; **2.** je battais; **3.** je battrai; **4.** que je batte; **5.** bats, battons, battez; **6.** battant; **7.** battu.

boire 1. je bois, tu bois, il boit, nous buvons, vous buvez, ils boivent; **2.** je buvais; **3.** je boirai; **4.** que je boive; **5.** bois, buvons, buvez; **6.** buvant; **7.** bu.

bouillir 1. je bous, tu bous, il bout, nous bouillons, vous bouillez, ils bouillent; **2.** je bouillais; **3.** je bouillirai; **4.** que je bouille; **5.** bous, bouillons, bouillez; **6.** bouillant; **7.** bouilli.

clore 1. je clos, tu clos, il clôt; **3.** je clorai; **4.** que je close; **7.** clos.

concevoir 1. je çoncois, tu conçois, il conçoit, nous concevons, vous concevez, ils conçoivent; **2.** je concevais; **3.** je concevrai; **4.** que je conçoive; **5.** conçois, concevons, concevez; **6.** concevant; **7.** conçu.

conclure 1. je conclus, tu conclus, il conclut, nous concluons, vous concluez, ils concluent; **2.** je concluais; **3.** je conclurai; **4.** que je conclue; **5.** conclus, concluons, concluez; **6.** concluant; **7.** conclu.

conduire 1. je conduis, tu conduis, il conduit, nous conduisons, vous conduisez, ils conduisent; **2.** je conduisais; **3.** je conduirai; **4.** que je conduise; **5.** conduis, conduisons, conduisez; **6.** conduisant; **7.** conduit.

connaître 1. je connais, tu connais, il connaît, nous connaissons, vous connaissez, ils connaissent; **2.** je connaissais; **3.** je connaîtrai; **4.** que je connaisse; **5.** connais, connaissons, connaissez; **6.** connaissant; **7.** connu.

conquérir *as* **acquérir.**

construire *as* **conduire.**

contraindre 1. je contrains, tu contrains, il contraint, nous contraignons, vous contraignez, ils contraignent; **2.** je contraignais; **3.** je contraindrai; **4.** que je contraigne; **5.** contrains, contraignons, contraignez; **6.** contraignant; **7.** contraint.

coudre 1. je couds, tu couds, il coud, nous cousons, vous cousez, ils cousent; **2.** je cousais; **3.** je coudrai; **4.** que je couse; **5.** couds, cousons, cousez; **6.** cousant; **7.** cousu.

courir 1. je cours, tu cours, il court, nous courons, vous courez, ils courent; **2.** je courais; **3.** je courrai; **4.** que je coure; **5.** cours, courons, courez; **6.** courant; **7.** couru.

couvrir *as* **ouvrir.**

croire 1. je crois, tu crois, il croit, nous croyons, vous croyez, ils croient; **2.** je croyais; **3.** je croirai; **4.** que je croie; **5.** crois, croyons, croyez; **6.** croyant; **7.** cru.

croître 1. je crois, tu crois, il croit, nous croissons, vous croissez, ils croissent; **2.** je croissais; **3.** je croîtrai; **4.** que je croisse; **5.** crois, croissons, croissez; **6.** croissant; **7.** crû, crue.

cueillir 1. je cueille, tu cueilles, il cueille, nous cueillons, vous cueillez, ils cueillent; **2.** je cueillais; **3.** je cueillerai; **4.** que je cueille; **6.** cueillant; **7.** cueilli.

cuire 1. je cuis, tu cuis, il cuit, nous cuisons, vous cuisez, ils cuisent; **2.** je cuisais; **3.** je cuirai; **4.** que je cuise; **5.** cuis, cuisons, cuisez; **6.** cuisant; **7.** cuit.

déchoir 1. je déchois, tu déchois, il déchoit, nous déchoyons, vous déchoyez, ils déchoient; **2.** je déchoyais; **3.** je décherrai; **4.** que je déchoie; **7.** déchu.

déconfire *as* **confire.**

découvrir *as* **ouvrir.**

déduire, détruire *as* **conduire.**

devoir 1. je dois, tu dois, il doit, nous devons, vous devez, ils doivent; **2.** je devais; **3.** je devrai; **4.** que je doive; **5.** dois, devons, devez; **6.** devant; **7.** du, due.

dire 1. je dis, tu dis, il dit, nous disons, vous dites, ils disent; **2.** je disais; **3.** je dirai; **4.** que je dise; **5.** dis, disons, dites; **6.** disant **7.** dit.

dissoudre 1. je dissous, tu dissous, il dissout, nous dissolvons, vous dissolvez, ils dissolvent; **2.** je dissolvais; **3.** je dissoudrai; **4.** que je dissolve; **5.** dissous, dissolvons, dissolvez; **6.** dissolvant; **7.** dissous, dissoute.

dormir 1. je dors, tu dors, il dort, nous dormons, vous dormez, ils dorment; **2.** je dormais; **3.** je dormirai; **4.** que je dorme; **5.** dors, dormons, dormez; **6.** dormant; **7.** dormi.

échoir *or* **écheoir 1.** il échoit *or* il échet, ils échoient; **2.** il échoyait; **3.** il écherra, ils écherront; **4.** qu'il échoie; **6.** échéant; **7.** échu.

écrire 1. j'écris, tu écris, il écrit, nous écrivons, vous écrivez, ils écrivent; **2.** j'écrivais; **3.** j'écrirai; **4.** que j'écrive; **5.** écris, écrivons, écrivez; **6.** écrivant; **7.** écrit.

envoyer 1. j'envoie, tu envoies, il envoie, nous envoyons, vous envoyez, ils envoient; **2.** j'envoyais; **3.** j'enverrai; **4.** que j'envoie; **5.** envoie, envoyons, envoyez; **6.** envoyant; **7.** envoyé.

éteindre *as* **peindre.**

étreindre *as* **peindre.**

exclure *as* **conclure.**

faire 1. je fais, tu fais, il fait nous faisons, vous faites, ils font; **2.** je faisais; **3.** je ferai; **4.** que je fasse; **5** fais, faisons, faites; **6.** faisant; **7.** fait.

falloir 1. il faut; **2.** il fallait **3.** il faudra; **4.** qu'il faille **7.** fallu.

feindre as peindre.

frire 1. je fris, tu fris, il frit **3.** je frirai; **5.** fris; **7.** frit

fuir 1. je fuis, tu fuis, il fuit nous fuyons, vous fuyez, il fuient; **2.** je fuyais; **3.** je fuirai; **4.** que je fuie; **5.** fuis fuyons, fuyez; **6.** fuyant **7.** fui.

gésir 1. il gît, nous gisons

vous gisez, ils gisent; **2.** je gisais; **6.** gisant.

haïr 1. je hais, tu hais, il hait, nous haïssons, vous haïssez, ils haïssent; **2.** je haïssais; **3.** je haïrai; **4.** que je haïsse; **5.** hais, haïssons, haïssez; **6.** haïssant, **7.** haï.

instruire *as* **conduire.**

joindre 1. je joins, tu joins, il joint, nous joignons, vous joignez, ils joignent; **2.** je joignais; **3.** je joindrai; **4.** que je joigne; **5.** joins, joignons, joignez; **6.** joignant; **7.** joint.

lire 1. je lis, tu lis, il lit, nous lisons, vous lisez, ils lisent; **2.** je lisais; **3.** je lirai; **4.** que je lise; **5.** lis, lisons, lisez; **6.** lisant; **7.** lu.

luire *as* **nuire.**

maudire 1. je maudis, tu maudis, il maudit, nous maudissons, vous maudissez, ils maudissent; **2.** je maudissais; **3.** je maudirai; **4.** que je maudisse; **5.** maudis, maudissons, maudissez; **6.** maudissant; **7.** maudit.

mentir *as* **sentir.**

mettre 1. je mets, tu mets, il met, nous mettons, vous mettez, ils mettent; **2.** je mettais; **3.** je mettrai; **4.** que je mette; **5.** mets, mettons, mettez; **6.** mettant. **7.** mis.

moudre 1. je mouds, tu mouds, il moud, nous moulons, vous moulez, ils moulent; **2.** je moulais; **3.** je moudrai; **4.** que je moule; **5.** mouds, moulons, moulez; **6.** moulant; **7.** moulu.

mourir 1. je meurs, tu meurs, il meurt, nous mourons, vous mourez, ils meurent; **2.** je mourais; **3.** je mourrai; **4.** que je meure; **5.** meurs, mourons, mourez; **6.** mourant; **7.** mort (être.)

mouvoir 1. je meus, tu meus, il meut, nous mouvons, vous mouvez, ils meuvent; **2.** je mouvais; **3.** je mouvrai; **4.** que je meuve; **5.** meus, mouvons, mouvez; **6.** mouvant; **7.** mû, mue.

naître 1. je nais, tu nais, il nait, nous naissons, vous naissez, ils naissent; **2.** je naissais; **3.** je naîtrai; **4.** que je naisse; **5.** nais, naissons, naissez; **6.** naissant; **7.** né, née (être.)

nuire 1. je nuis, tu nuis, il nuit, nous nouisons, vous nuisez, ils nuisent; **2.** je nuisais; **3.** je nuirai; **4.** que je nuise; **5.** nuis, nuisons, nuisez; **6.** nuisant; **7.** nui.

offrir *as* **ouvrir.**

ouvrir 1. j'ouvre, tu ouvres, il ouvre, nous ouvrons, vous ouvrez, ils ouvrent; **2.** j'ouvrais; **3.** j'ouvrirai; **4.** que j'ouvre; **5.** ouvre, ouvrons, ouvrez; **6.** ouvrant; **7.** ouvert.

paître 1. je pais, tu pais, il paît, nous paissons, vous paissez, ils paissent; **2.** je paissais; **3.** je paîtrai; **4** que je paisse; **5.** pais, paissons, paissez; **6.** paissant.

paraître 1. je parais, tu parais, il paraît, nous paraissons, vous paraissez, ils paraissent; **2.** je paraissais; **3.** je paraîtrai; **4.** que je paraisse; **5.** parais, paraissons, paraissez; **6.** paraissant; **7.** paru.

partir 1. je pars, tu pars, il part, nous partons, vous partez, ils partent; **2.** je partais; **3.** je partirai; **4.** que je parte; **5.** pars, partons, partez; **6.** partant; **7.** parti (être.)

peindre 1. je peins, tu peins, il peint, nous peignons, vous peignez, ils peignent; **2.** je peignais; **3.** je peindrai; **4.** que je peigne; **5.** peins, peignons, peignez; **6.** peignant; **7.** peint.

plaire 1. je plais, tu plais, il plaît, nous plaisons, vous plaisez, ils plaisent; **2.** je plaisais; **3.** je plairai; **4.** que je plaise; **5.** plais, plaisons, plaisez; **6.** plaisant; **7.** plu.

pouvoir 1. je peux *or* je puis, tu peux, il peut, nous pouvons, vous pouvez, ils peuvent; **2.** je pouvais; **3.** je pourrai; **4.** que je puisse; **6.** pouvant; **7.** pu.

prendre 1. je prends, tu prends, il prend, nous prenons, vous prenez, ils prennent; **2.** je prenais; **3.** je prendrai; **4.** que je prenne; **5.** prends, prenons, prenez: **6.** prenant; **7.** pris.

prescrire *as* **écrire.**

produire *as* **conduire.**

proscrire *as* **écrire.**

recevoir *as* **concevoir.**

reconstruire *as* **conduire.**

réduire *as* **conduire.**

repartir *as* **partir.**

reproduire *as* **conduire.**

résoudre 1. je résous, tu résous, il résout, nous résolvons, vous résolvez, ils résolvent; **2.** je résolvais; **3.** je résoudrai; **4.** que je résolve; **5.** résous, résolvons, résolvez; **6.** résolvant; **7.** résolu.

restreindre *as* **peindre.**

rire 1. je ris, tu ris, il rit, nous rions, vous riez, ils rient; **2.** je riais; **3.** je rirai; **4.** que je rie; **5.** ris, rions, riez; **6.** riant; **7.** ri.

savoir 1. je sais, tu sais, il sait, nous savons, vous savez, ils savent; **2.** je savais; **3.** je saurai; **4.** que je sache; **5.** sais, sachons, sachez; **6.** sachant; **7.** sus.

sentir 1. je sens, tu sens, il sent, nous sentons, vous sentez, ils sentent; **2.** je sentais; **3.** je sentirai; **4.** que je sente; **5.** sens, sentons, sentez; **6.** sentant; **7.** senti.

servir 1. je sers, tu sers, ils sert, nous servons, vous servez, ils servent; **2.** je servais; **3.** je servirai; **4.** que je serve; **5.** sers, servons, servez; **6.** servant; **7.** servi.

sortir 1. je sors, tu sors, il sort, nous sortons, vous sortez, ils sortent; **2.** je sortais; **3.** je sortirai; **4.** que je sorte; **5.** sors, sortons, sortez; **6.** sortant; **7.** sorti

(**être**).
souffrir *as* **ouvrir.**
se souvenir *as* **venir.**
suffire 1. je suffis, tu suffis, il suffit, nous suffisons, vous suffisez, ils suffisent; **2.** je suffisais; **3.** je suffirai; **4.** que je suffise; **5.** suffis, suffisons, suffisez; **6.** suffisant; **7.** suffi.
suivre 1. je suis, tu suis, il suit, nous suivons, vous suivez, ils suivent; **2.** je suivais; **3.** je suivrai; **4.** que je suive; **5.** suis, suivons, suivez; **6.** suivant; **7.** suivi.
surseoir 1. je sursois, tu sursois, il sursoit, nous sursoyons, vous sursoyez, ils sursoient; **2.** je sursoyais; **3.** je surseoirai; **4.** que je sursoie; **5.** sursois, sursoyons, sursoyez; **6.** sursoyant; **7.** sursis.
taire *as* **plaire.**
teindre *as* **peindre.**
tenir 1. je tiens, tu tiens, il tient, nous tenons, vous tenez, ils tiennent; **2.** je tenais; **3.** je tiendrai; **4.** que je tienne; **5.** tiens, tenons, tenez; **6.** tenant; **7.** tenu.
traduire *as* **conduire.**
traire 1. je trais, tu trais, il trait, nous trayons, vous trayez, ils traient; **2.** je trayais; **3.** je trairai; **4.** que je traie; **5.** trais, trayons, trayez; **6.** trayant; **7.** trait.
vaincre 1. je vaincs, tu vaincs, il vainc, nous vainquons, vous vainquez, ils vainquent; **2.** je vainquais; **3.** je vaincrai; **4.** que je vainque; **5.** vaincs, vainquons, vainquez; **6.** vainquant; **7.** vaincu.
valoir 1. je vaux, tu vaux, il vaut, nous valons, vous valez, ils valent; **2.** je valais, **3.** je vaudrai; **4.** que je vaille; **6.** valant; **7.** valu.
venir 1. je viens, tu viens, il vient, nous venons, vous venez, ils viennent; **2.** je venais; **3.** je viendrai; **4.** que je vienne; **5.** viens, venons, venez; **6.** venant; **7.** venu (être.)
vêtir 1. je vêts, tu vêts, il vêt, nous vêtons, vous vêtez, ils vêtent; **2.** je vêtais; **3.** je vêtirai; **4.** que je vête; **5.** vêts, vêtons, vêtez; **6.** vêtant; **7.** vêtu.
vivre 1. je vis, tu vis, il vit, nous vivons, vous vivez, ils vivent; **2.** je vivais; **3.** je vivrai; **4.** que je vive; **5.** vis, vivons, vivez; **6.** vivant; **7.** vécu.
voir 1. je vois, tu vois, il voit, nous voyons, vous voyez, ils voient; **2.** je voyais; **3.** je verrai; **4.** que je voie; **5.** vois, voyons, voyez; **6.** voyant; **7.** vu.
vouloir 1. je veux, tu veux, il veut, nous voulons, vous voulez, ils veulent; **2.** je voulais; **3.** je voudrai; **4.** que je veuille, que nous voulions; **5.** veuille, veuillons, veuillez *or* voulez; **6** voulant; **7.** voulu.

FRENCH PHRASES

Good morning. Good evening. Good-bye.	Bonjour. Bonsoir. Au revoir.
I beg your pardon. Excuse me.	Je vous demande pardon. Pardon.
How are you? Very well — and you?	Comment allez-vous? Très bien — et vous?
How do you do (delighted to meet you).	Enchanté (de faire votre connaissance) monsieur (madame, mademoiselle).
Allow me! You are very kind.	Permettez-moi! Vous etes très gentil.
It's all the same to me.	Cela m'est égal.
Your good health.	A votre santé.
Allow me to introduce you to . . .	Permettez-moi de vous présenter à . . .
It is fine (bad) weather.	Il fait beau (mauvais) temps.
You are right. You are wrong.	Vous avez raison. Vous avez tort.
It is not my fault.	Ce n'est pas ma faute.
To do one's best.	Faire son possible.
It is very annoying.	C'est très ennuyeux.
You're pulling my leg.	Vous vous moquez de moi.
So much the better (worse).	Tant mieux (pis).
He's a jolly nice fellow.	C'est un chic type.
To put one's foot in it.	Mettre les pieds dans le plat.
Things are going badly.	Rien ne va bien. Tout va mal.
I am an Englishmen (Englishwoman).	Je suis anglais (anglaise).
I cannot speak French.	Je ne parle pas, français.
I am looking for . . .	Je cherche . . .
I don't understand you.	Je ne vous comprends pas.
Please speak slowly!	Parlez lentement, s'il vous plaît!
Is there anyone here who speaks English?	Y-a-t-il quelque'un qui parle anglais?
Where is the British Consulate?	Où est le consulat britannique?

It is wonderful, splendid !	C'est épatant, formidable !
No . . . Trespassers will be prosecuted.	Défense de . . . sous peine d'amende.
No entry.	Entrée interdite.
Lavatory.	Les toilettes, les lavabos, les cabinets.
What time is it?	Quelle heure est-il?
It is five past one.	Il est une heure cinq.
We are in a hurry.	Nous sommes pressés.
How long does it take to . . . ?	Combien de temps faut-il pour . . .?
This evening, tonight. Last night.	Ce soir. Hier soir.
How long have you been here?	Depuis quand êtes-vous ici?
I have been here a month.	Je suis ici depuis un mois.
Can we lunch (dine) here?	Est-ce qu'on peut déjeuner (dîner) ici?
There are four of us.	Nous sommes quatre.
We only want a snack.	Nous voudrions seulement un casse-croûte.
Please give us the menu.	Voulez-vous nous donner le menu, s'il vous plaît.

NOMBRES CARDINAUX

ET ORDINAUX

1 *one*, un.	**1st** *first*, premier.
2 *two*, deux.	**2nd** *second*, deuxième.
3 *three*, trois.	**3rd** *third*, troisième.
4 *four*, quatre.	**4th** *fourth*, quatrième.
5 *five*, cinq.	**5th** *fifth*, cinquième.
6 *six*, six.	**6th** *sixth*, sixième.
7 *seven*, sept.	**7th** *seventh*, septième.
8 *eight*, huit.	**8th** *eighth*, huitième.
9 *nine*, neuf.	**9th** *ninth*, neuvième.
10 *ten*, dix.	**10th** *tenth*, dixième.
11 *eleven*, onze.	**11th** *eleventh*, onzième.
12 *twelve*, douze.	**12th** *twelfth*, douzième.
13 *thirteen*, treize.	**13th** *thirteenth*, treizième.
14 *fourteen*, quatorze.	**14th** *fourteenth*, quatorzième.
15 *fifteen*, quinze.	**15th** *fifteenth*, quinzième.
16 *sixteen*, seize.	**16th** *sixteenth*, seizième.

A

a, an, *art.* un, -e.
abandon, *v. a.* abandonner.
abate, *v. a. & n.* diminuer; se calmer, s'apaiser.
abbey, *s.* abbaye *f.*
abbot, *s.* abbé *m.*
abbreviate, *v. a.* abréger.
abbreviation, *s.* abréviation *f.*
abdicate, *v.a. & n.* abdiquer.
abdomen, *s.* abdomen *m.*
abhor, *v. a.* détester, abhorrer.
ability, *s.* capacité *f.*, habilité *f.*
able, *adj.* capable.
aboard, *adv.* à bord.
abode, *s.* demeure *f.*
abolish, *v.a.* abolir; supprimer.
abominable, *adj.* abominable.
abound, *v.n.* abonder (de).
about, *adv. & prep.* autour (de); environ, presque; au sujet de.
above, *adv. & prep.* au-dessus (de); *(in book)* ci-dessus.
abroad, *adv.* à l'étranger.
absence, *s.* absence *f.*, éloignement *m.*
absent, *adj.* absent.
absolute, *adj.* absolu.
absolve, *v.a.* absoudre; relever de; remettre, pardonner.
absorb, *v. a.* absorber.
abstain, *v.n.* s'abstenir de.
abstract, *adj.* abstrait.
abstraction, *s.* abstraction *f.*
absurd, *adj.* absurde; ridicule.
abundance, *s.* abondance *f.*
abundant, *adj.* abondant.
abusive, *adj.* abusif; injurieux; offensant.
academic, *adj.* académique.
academy, *s.* académie *f.*
accelerate, *v.a.* accélérer; *v.n.* s'accélérer.
accent, *s.* accent *m.*
accept, *v.a.* accepter
access, *s.* accès *m.*
accessible, *adj.* accessible.
accessory, *s. & adj.* accessoire *(m.).*
accident, *s.* accident *m.*
accidental, *s.* accidentel.
accommodate, *v. a.* accommoder; loger; ~ *oneself to* s'accommoder à.
accommodation, *s.* ajustement *m.*, adaptation *f.*; commodité *f.*; logement *m.*
accompany, *v.a.* accompagner.
accomplish, *v.a.* accomplir, achever.
accomplishment, *s.* accomplissement *m.*; talent *m.*
accord, *s.* accord *m.*, consentement *m.*
according: ~ *to* selon, d'après.
accordingly, *adv.* donc; en conséquence.

account, *s.* compte *m.; (narration)* récit *m.; on ~ of* à cause de; *on no ~* dans aucun cas; *take into ~* tenir compte de; — *v.n. ~ for* expliquer; rendre compte de.
accuracy, *s.* exactitude *f.*
accusation, *s.* accusation *f.*
accuse, *v.a.* accuser; incriminer.
accustom, *v.a.* accoutumer (à).
ache, *s.* douleur *f.*
achieve, *v.a.* accomplir, achever; atteindre.
acknowledge, *v.a.* reconnaitre; accuser réception de.
acquaint, *v.a.* informer (de); faire part à.
acquaintance, *s.* connaissance *f.*
acquire, *v.a.* acquérir.
acre, *s.* arpent *m.*
across, *prep.* à travers; en croix.
act, *s.* action *f.*; *(law)* loi *f.; (theatre)* acte *m.*; — *v.n.* agir; *v.a.* jouer.
action, *s.* action *f.*; acte *m.*; *(war)* combat *m.*
active, *adj.* actif.
activity, *s.* activité *f.*
actor, *s.* acteur *m.*
actress, *s.* actrice *f.*
actual, *adj.* réel.
actually, *adv.* en fait.
adapt, *v.a.* adapter.
add, *v.a.* ajouter; additionner.
addition, *s.* addition *f.*; *in ~ to* en plus de.
additional, *adj.* additionnel; supplémentaire.
address, *s.* adresse *f.*; — *v.a.* adresser.
adequate, *adj.* suffisant.
adjust, *v.a.* ajuster, régler.
administer, *v.a.* & *n.* administrer.
administration, *s.* administration *f.*
admirable, *adj.* admirable.
admiral, *s.* amiral *m.*
admiration, *s.* admiration *f.*
admire, *v.a.* admirer.
admission, *s.* admission *f.*; entrée *f.*
admit, *v.a.* admettre; laisser entrer.
adopt, *v.a.* adopter.
adoption, *s.* adoption *f.*
adore, *v.a.* adorer.
adult, *adj.* & *s.* adulte *(m.f.)*
advance, *v. n.* avancer; — *s.* avance *f.*; pr[illegible] *m.*
advantage, *s.* avantage *m.*
adventure, *s.* aventure *f.*
adversary, *s.* adversaire *m.*
adverse, *adj.* adverse.
adversity, *s.* adversité *f.*
advertise, *v.a.* annoncer; faire de la réclame (pour).
advertisement, *s.* annonce *f.*; réclame *f.*
advice, conseil *m.*; avis *m.*
advise, *v.a.* conseiller.
aerial, *s.* antenne *f.*
aerodrome, *s.* aérodrome *m.*
aeroplane, *s.* avion *m.*
affair, *s.* affaire *f.*

affect, *v.a.* affecter.
affection, *s.* affection *f.*
affectionate, *adj.* affectueux.
affirmative, *adj.* affirmatif; — *s.* affirmative *f.*
afford, *v.a.* donner, fournir, accorder; *can* ~ avoir les moyens de.
afraid, *adj.* effrayé; *be* ~ *of* avoir peur de.
African, *adj.* africain; — *s.* Africain, -e.
after, *prep.* & *adj.* après.
afternoon, *s.* après-midi *m.* or *f.*
afterwards, *adv.* après, ensuite.
again, *adv.* encore une fois, de nouveau.
against, *prep.* contre.
age, *s.* âge *m.*
agency, *s.* agence *f.*
agent, *s.* agent *m.*
aggression, *s.* agression *f.*
ago, *adv.* il y a.
agony, *s.* agonie *f.*
agree, *v.n.* s'accorder, être d'accord; ~ *(up-) on* convenir sur; ~ *to* consentir à; ~ *with* entrer dans les idées de.
agreeable, *adj.* agréable.
agreement, *s.* accord *m.*
agricultural, *adj.* agricole.
agriculture, *s.* agriculture *f.*
ahead, *adv.* en avant.
aid, *s.* aide *f.*; — *v.a.* aider, assister.
aim, *s.* but *m.*; objectif *m.*; visée *f.*; — *v.a.* & *n.* viser.
air. *s.* air *m.*
air-conditioning, *s.* conditionnement d'air *m.*; climatisation *f.*
aircraft, *s.* avion *m.*
air-line, *s.* ligne *f.* aérienne.
air-mail *s.* poste aérienne; *by* ~ par avion.
airport, *s.* aéroport *m.*,
alarm, *v.a.* alarmer; —*s.* alarme *f.*
alcoholic, *adj.* alcoolique.
ale, *s.* bière *(f.)* anglaise.
alike, *adj.* semblable; — *adv.* également.
alive, *adj.* vivant.
all, *pron. s., adv.* & *adj.* tout; *not at* ~ pas du tout.
allege, *v.a.* alléguer.
alley, *s.* ruelle *f.*
allow, *v.a.* permettre; laisser; admettre.
allude, *v.n.* faire allusion.
ally, *v.a.* allier; *v.n.* s'allier; — *s.* allié, -e.
almost, *adv.* presque; à peu près.
alone, *adj.* & *adv.* seul.
along, *prep.* le long de.
aloud, *adv.* à haute voix.
already, *adv.* déjà.
also, *adv.* aussi.
altar, *s.* autel *m.*
alter, *v.a.&n.* changer.
alternate, *adj.* alternatif; — *v.n.* alterner.
although, *conj.* quoique; bien que.
altitude, *s.* altitude *f.*, élévation *f.*
altogether, *adv.* tout à fait; entièrement.
always, *adv.* toujours.

amaze, *v.a.* frapper d'étonnement, frapper de stupeur.
amazing, *adj.* étonnant.
ambassador, *s.* ambassadeur *m.*
ambassadress, *s.* ambassadrice *f.*
ambition, *s* ambition *f.*
ambitious, *adj.* ambitieux.
ambulance, *s.* ambulance (automobile) *f.*
amend, *v.a.* amender.
amends: *make* ~ *for* dédommager de.
American, *adj.* américain; — *s.* Américain, -e.
among, *prep.* parmi; chez.
amount, *s.* somme *f.*; *(total)* montant *m.*; — *v.n.* ~ *to* monter à.
ample, *adj.* ample.
amplifier, *s.* amplificateur *m.*
amuse, *v.a.* amuser; divertir.
amusement, *s.* amusement *m.*; divertissement *m.*
an *see* **a.**
analogy, *s.* analogie *f.*
analyse, *v.a.* analyser.
analysis, analyse *f.*
anarchy, *s.* anarchie *f.*
anatomy, *s.* anatomie *f.*
ancestor, *s.* ancêtre *m.* *f.*
anchor, *s.* ancre *f.*
ancient, *adj.* ancien; antique.
and, *conj.* et.
anecdote, *s.* anecdote *f.*
angel, *s.* ange *m.*
anger, *s.* colère *f.*
angle, *s.* angle *m.*
angler, *s.* pêcheur *m.*
Anglican, *adj.* anglican.
angry, *adj.* fâché, irrité.
animal, *s.* animal *m.* *(pl.* -aux).
ankle, *s.* cheville *f.*
anniversary, *s.* anniversaire *m.*
announce, *v.a.* annoncer.
announcement, *s.* annonce.
announcer, *s.* speaker *m.*
annoy, *v.a.* ennuyer; contrarier; gêner.
annoying, *adj.* contrariant; ennuyeux.
annual, *adj.* annuel.
annul, *v.a.* annuler.
another, *pron.* & *adj.* un autre, une autre.
answer, *s.* réponse *f.*; — *v.a.&n.* répondre.
ant, *s.* fourmi *f.*
antelope, *s.* antilope *f.*
antibiotic, *s.* antibiotique *m.*
anticipate, *v.a.* anticiper.
antipathy, *s.* antipathie *f.*
antiquated, *adj.* vieilli.
antiquity, *s.* antiquité *f.*
anvil, *s.* enclume *f.*
anxiety, *s.* anxiété *f.*
anxious, *adj.* inquiet; désireux; *be* ~ *to* désirer faire qch.
any, *adj.* & *pron.* quelque; *(at all)* n'importe quoi/qui/quel; *(some, in question)* du, de la; *have you* ~? en avez vous; *not* ~ ne . . . pas de; ~ *more* encore du.
anybody, *pron.* quelqu'un; *(at all)* n'importe qui.
anyhow, *adv.* n'importe comment.
anyone *see* **anybody.**

anything, *pron.* quelque chose; *(at all)* n'importe quoi.
anyway, *see* **anyhow.**
anywhere, *adv.* n'importe où.
apart, *adv.* à part; de côté; ~ *from* en dehors de.
apartment, *s.* logement *m.;* appartement *m.*
apologize, *v.n.* faire des excuses, s'excuser.
apology, *s.* excuse *f.*
apostle, *s.* apôtre *m.*
appalling, *adj.* épouvantable.
apparatus, *s.* appareil *m.*
apparent, *adj.* manifeste.
appeal, *s.* appel *m.;* — *v.n.* en appeler (à).
appear, *v.n.* (ap)paraître; *(seem)* sembler.
appearance, *s.* apparition *f.; (look)* air *m.*
appendicitis, *s.* appendicite *f.*
appendix, *s.* appendice *m.*
appetite, *s.* appétit *m.*
applaud, *v.n.* applaudir.
applause, *s.* applaudissement *m.*
apple, *s.* pomme *f.*
appliance, *s.* appareil *m.*
applicant, *s.* postulant, -e.
application, *s.* demande *f.; (use)* application *f.*
apply, *v.a.* appliquer; — *v.n.* avoir rapport à; ~ *for* solliciter.
appoint, *v.a.* nommer; désigner.
appointment, *s.* nomination *f.;* emploi *m.;* rendez-vous *m.*
appreciate, *v.a.* apprécier.
appreciation, *s.* appréciation *f.*
apprehend, *v.a.* appréhender; *(understand)* comprendre.
apprentice, *s.* apprenti *m.*
approach, *s.* approche *f.;* — *v. a. & n.* (s')approcher (de).
appropriate, *adj.* approprié, convenable.
approval, *s.* approbation *f.*
approve, *v.a. & n.* approuver.
approximate, *adj.* approximatif.
approximation, approximation *f.*
apricot, *s.* abricot *m.*
April, *s.* avril *m.*
apron, *s.* tablier *m.*
aptitude, *s.* aptitude *f.*
Arab, *s.* Arabe *m.*
Arabian, *adj.* arabe.
arbitrary, *adj.* arbitraire.
arcade, *s.* arcade *f.*
arch, *s.* arche *f.;* arc *m.*
archaeology, *s.* archéologie *f.*
archbishop, *s.* archevêque *m.*
architect, *s.* architecte *m.*
architecture, *s.* architecture *f.*
area, *s.* surface *f.;* aire *f.*
Argentine, *adj.* argentine.
argue, *v.n.* argumenter; *v.a.* discuter.
argument, *s.* argument *m.;* discussion *f.*
arise, *v. n.* se lever; *(emerge)* surgir; *(come from)* résulter de.

aristocratic, *adj*. aristocratique.
arm¹, *s*. bras *m*.
arm², *s.(pl)*. arme(s) *f*.
armament, *s*. armement *m*.
armchair, *s*. fauteuil *m*.
armour, *s*. armure *f*.
army, *s*. armée *f*.
around, *adv*. & *prep*. autour (de).
arouse, *v.a*. réveiller.
arrange, *v.a*. arranger.
arrangement, *s*. arrangement *m*.; ~*s* mesures *f*. *pl*.
array, *s*. ordre *m*.
arrears, *s*. *pl*. arriéré *m*.
arrest, *v.a*. arrêter; — *s*. arrestation *f*.
arrival, *s*. arrivée *f*.
arrive, *v.n*. arriver.
arrow, *s*. flèche *f*.
art, *s*. art *m*.
artery, *s*. artère *f*.
article, *s*. article *m*.
artificial, *adj*. artificiel.
artillery, *s*. artillerie *f*.
artist, *s*. artiste *m*.
artistic, *adj*. artistique.
as, *adv*. & *conj*. comme; *(like a)* en; *(when)* comme; ~ . . . ~ aussi . . . que.
ascend, *v.n*. monter.
ash(es), *s*. *(pl.)* cendre *f*.
ashamed, *adj*. honteux; *be* ~ *of* avoir honte de.
ashore, *adv*. à terre.
ash-tray, *s*. cendrier *m*.
Asiatic, *adj*. asiatique.
aside, *adv*. de côté.
ask, *v*. *a*. demander (à + qn., de + *inf*.); ~ *about* se renseigner sur; ~ *for* demander.
asleep, *adj*. endormi; *fall* ~ s'endormir.
aspect, *s*. aspect *m*.; *(look)* air *m*.
aspire, *v.n*. aspirer à.
ass, *s*. âne *m*.
assail, *v*. *a*. assaillir.
assault, *s*. assaut *m*.
assemble, *v*. *a*. assembler; *v.n*. s'assembler.
assembly, *s*. assemblée *f*.; ~ *hall* halle *f*. de montage; ~ *line* chaîne *f*. de montage.
assert, *v.a*. affirmer.
assess, *v.a*. cotiser.
assets, *s*. *pl*. actif *m*.
assign, *v*. *a*. assigner; céder.
assignment, *s*. cession *f*.
assist, *v.a*. aider.
assistance, *s*. aide *f*.
associate, *v.a*. associer; — *s*. associé, -e *m*. *f*.
association, *s*. association *f*.
assume, *v.a*. prendre; assumer; supposer.
assumption, *s*. supposition *f*.
assurance, *s*. assurance *f*.
assure, *v.a*. assurer.
astonish, *v*. *a*. étonner.
astonishment, *s*. étonnement *m*.
astronomy, *s*. astronomie f.
at, *prep*. *(place, time)* à; *(house, shop)* chez.
athletic, *adj*. athlétique.
athletics, *s*. athlétisme *m*.
at-home, *s*. réception *f*.
atlas, *s*. atlas *m*.
atmosphere, *s*. atmosphère *f*.
atom, *s*. atome *m*.
atomic, *adj*. atomique; ~

bomb bombe *f.* atomique; **~** *energy* énergie *f.* atomique.
attach, *v.a.* attacher.
attaché, *s.* attaché *m.*; **~** *case* petite valise *f.*
attachment, *s.* attachement *m.*
attack, *v.a.* attaquer; — *s.* attaque *f.*
attain, *v.a.* atteindre.
attainment, *s.* réalisation *f.*; connaissances *f. pl.*
attempt, *s.* tentative *f.*; — *v.a.* tenter; entreprendre.
attend, *v.a.* suivre; *(look after)* soigner; — *v.i.* faire attention à; assister.
attendance, *s.* présence *f.*; *(persons present)* assistance *f.*
attendant, *s.* serviteur *m.*; employé *m.*; ouvreuse *f.*
attention, *s.* attention *f.*
attitude, *s.* attitude *f.*
attorney, *s.* avoué *m.*
attract, *v.a.* attirer.
attraction, *s.* attraction *f.*
attractive, *adj.* attrayant.
attribute, *v.a.* attribuer.
auction, *s.* vente *f.*
audience, *s.* auditoire *m.*
audio-visual, *adj.* audiovisuel.
auditorium, *s.* salle *f.* (de cours).
August, *s.* août *m.*
aunt, *s.* tante *f.*
Australian, *adj.* australien — *s.* Australien, -ne *m. f.*
Austrian, *adj.* autrichien; — *s.* Autrichien, -enne *m. f.*
authentic, *adj.* authentique.
author, *s.* auteur *m.*
authority, *s.* autorité *f.*
authorize, *v.a.* autoriser.
automatic, *adj.* automatique.
autonomy, *s.* autonomie *f.*
autumn, *s.* automne *m.*
avail, *s.* *be of no* **~** ne servir à rien; — *v.a.* **~** *oneself of* profiter de.
available, *adj.* disponible; sous la main.
avalanche, *s.* avalanche *f.*
avenge, *v.a.* venger.
avenue, *s.* avenue *f.*
average, *s.* moyenne *f.*; — *adj.* moyen.
aversion, *s.* aversion *f.*
avoid, *v.a.* éviter.
await, *v.a.* attendre.
awake, *v. a.* éveiller; *v. n.* s'éveiller; — *adj.* éveillé.
awaken, *v.a.* éveiller.
award, *v.a.* accorder.
aware, *adj.* *be* **~** *of* avoir conscience de, savoir bien.
away, *adv.* (au) loin; *carry* **~** enlever; *go* **~** partir.
awful, *adj.* terrible.
awhile, *adv.* pendant quelque temps, un moment.
awkward, *adj.* *(pers.)* gauche; maladroit; *(things)* gênant, embarrassant.
axe, *s.* hache *f.*
axis. *s.* axe *m.*

axle, *s.* essieu *m.*

B

babble, *s.* babil *m.*; — *v.n.* babiller.
baby, *s.* bébé *m.*
baby-sitter, *s.* garde-bébé *m.*
bachelor, *s.* célibataire; *(arts)* licencié *m.*
back, *s.* dos *m.*; *(hand)* revers *m.*; *(football)* arrière *m.*; — *adj.* de derrière; arriéré; — *adv.* en arrière; *be ~* être de retour; — *v.a.* soutenir, seconder; *(bet)* parier pour; *v.n.* reculer.
background, *s.* fond *m.*; arrière-plan *m.*
backstairs, *s. pl.* escalier *m.* de service.
backward, *adj.* arriéré.
backwards, *adv.* en arrière; à reculons.
bacon, *s.* lard *m.*
bad, *adj.* mauvais.
badge, *s.* insigne *m.*
badger, *s.* blaireau *m.*
badly, *adv.* mal.
bag, *s.* sac *m.*; *(large)* valise *f.*
baggage, *s.* bagage *m.*
bait, *s.* amorce *f.*
bake, *v.a.* cuire; faire cuire.
baker, *s.* boulanger *m.*
bakery, *s.* boulangerie *f.*
balance, *s.* *(weighing, account)* balance *f.*; *(bank)* solde *m.*; *(equilibrium)* équilibre *m.*; *v.a.* balancer; *v.n.* se balancer.
balcony, *s.* balcon *m.*
bald, *adj.* chauve; plat.
ball, *s.* *(games)* balle *f.* ballon *m.*; *(bowl)* boule *f.*; *(dance)* bal *m.*
ball-bearings, *s. pl.* roulement *m.* à billes.
ballet, *s.* ballet *m.*
balloon, *s.* ballon *m.*
ball(-point) pen, *s.* stylo *m.* à bille.
bamboo, *s.* bambou *m.*
banana, *s.* banane *f.*
band, *s.* *(people)* troupe *f.*; bande *f.*; orchestre *m.*; *(ribbon, tie)* ruban *m.*; lien *m.*
bandage, *s.* bandage *m.*
bandit, *s.* bandit *m.*
bang, *s.* coup *m.*; claquement *m.*
banish, *v.a.* bannir.
banister, rampe *f.*
bank[1], *s.* *(river)* rive *f.*; *(earth)* talus *m.*
bank[2], *s.* banque *f.*
bank-holiday, *s.* (jour *m.* de) fête *f.* légale.
banknote, *s.* billet *m.* (de banque).
bankruptcy, *s.* banqueroute *f.*; faillite *f.*
banner, *s.* bannière *f.*
banquet, *s.* banquet *m.*
baptism, *s.* baptême *m.*
baptize, *v.a.* baptiser.
bar, *s.* *(iron, tribunal, music)* barre *f.*; *(railway)* barrière *f.*; *(obstacle)* obstacle *m.*; *(lawyers)* barreau *m.*; *(counter place for drink)* comptoir *m.*, débit *m.* (de boissons), bar *m.*
barber, *s.* coiffeur *m.*
bare, *adj.* nu; *(mere)* seul.

barefoot, *adj.* nu-pieds.
barely, *adv.* à peine.
bargain, *s.* marché *m.*; — *v.n.* marchander.
bark, *s.* aboiement *m.*; — *v.n.* aboyer.
barley, *s.* orge *f.*
barmaid, *s.* demoiselle *f.* de comptoir, barmaid *f.*
barman, *s.* garçon *m.* de comptoir, barman *m.*
barn, *s.* grange *f.*
barometer, *s.* baromètre *m.*
baron, *s.* baron *m.*
baroness, *s.* baronne *f.*
barracks, *s. pl.* caserne *f.*
barrel, *s.* tonneau *m.*
barren, *adj.* stérile.
barrier, *s.* barrière *f.*
barrister, *s.* avocat *m.*
bartender *see* **barman.**
barter, *s.* échange *m.*; — *v.a.* échanger.
base, *s.* fondement *m.*; base *f.*
basement, *s.* sous-sol *m.*
bashful, *adj.* timide.
basic, *adj.* fondamental; basique.
basin, *s.* bassin *m.*; cuvette *f.*
basis, *s.* base *f.*
basket, *s.* panier *m.*
basket-ball, *s.* basket-ball *m.*
bass, *s.* basse *f.*
bat[1], *s.* chauve-souris *f.*
bat[2], *s.* batte *f.*
bath, *s.* bain *m.*; *(tub)* baignoire *f.*
bathe, *v.n.* se baigner; *v.a.* baigner.
bathing-costume, *s.* costume *m.* de bain(s).
bathroom, *s.* salle *f.* de bain.
battery, *s.* *(military)* batterie *f.*; *(electr.)* pile *f.*
battle, *s.* bataille *f.*
bay, *s.* baie *f.*
be, *v. n.* être; *(be situated)* se trouver; *there is* il y a.
beach, *s.* plage *f.*
bead, *s.* *(string of)* collier *m.*
beak, *s.* bec *m.*
beam, *s.* *(timber)* poutre *f.*; *(light)* rayon *m.*
bean, *s.* fève *f.*
bear[1], *s.* ours *m.*
bear[2], *v.a.* porter; soutenir; supporter.
beard, *s.* barbe *f.*
bearing, *s.* rapport *m.*
beast, *s.* bête *f.*
beat, *v.a.* battre; frapper; — *s.* battement *m.*
beautiful, *adj.* beau, bel, belle.
beauty, *s.* beauté *f.*
beaver, *s.* castor *m.*
because, *conj.* parce que; ~ *of* à cause de.
beckon, *v.n.* faire signe (à).
become, *v. n.* devenir.
bed, *s.* lit *m.*
bed-clothes, *s. pl.* couvertures *f. pl.*
bedroom, *s.* chambre *f.* à coucher.
bee, *s.* abeille *f.*
beech, *s.* hêtre *m.*
beef, *s.* bœuf *m.*
beef-steak, *s.* bifteck *m.*
beer, *s.* bière *f.*
beetle, *s.* scarabée *m.*
beetroot, *s.* betterave *f.*
before, *prep.* *(time)* avant;

(space) devant; — *adv.* avant; *(in front)* en avant.
beforehand, *adv.* d'avance; en avance.
beg, *v.a.* demander, prier; *v. n.* mendier; *I ~ your pardon!* excusez-moi!; pardon!
beget, *v.a.* engendrer.
beggar, *s.* mendiant, -e.
begin, *v. a.* & *n.* commencer.
beginner, *s.* commençant, -e *m. f.*
beginning, *s.* commencement *m.*
behalf, *s. on ~ of* de la part de; *in ~ of* en faveur de.
behave, *v.n.* se conduire.
behaviour, *s.* conduite *f.*
behind, *prep.* derrière.
Belgian, *adj.* belge; — *s.* Belge *m. f.*
belief, *s.* croyance *f.*
believe, *v.a.* & *n.* croire.
bell, *s.* cloche *f.*
belly, *s.* ventre *m.*
belong, *v.n. ~ to* appartenir à.
belongings, *s. pl.* effets *m.;* biens *m.*
below, *adv.* au-dessous; en bas; — *prep.* au-dessous de.
belt, *s.* ceinture *f.*
bench, *s.* banc *m.; (working)* établi *m.*
bend, *v. a.* courber; tendre fléchir; *v.n.* se courber; — *s.* courbure *f.; (road)* tournant *m.*
beneath *see* **below.**
benefit, *s.* bienfait *m.; (gain)* bénéfice *m.*
bent, *s.* penchant *m.*
berry, *s.* baie *f.; (coffee)* grain *m.*
berth, *s.* couchette *f.; (for ship)* mouillage *m.*
beseech, *v. a.* supplier.
beside, *prep.* auprès de, à côté de.
besides, *adv.* en outre.
best, *adj.* le meilleur; *do one's ~* faire tout son possible (pour).
bestow, *v. a.* conférer (à).
bet, *v.a.* parier.
betray, *v. a.* trahir.
better, *adj.* meilleur; *adv.* mieux.
between, *prep* entre.
beyond, *prep.* au delà de.
bias, *s.* biais *m.; (fig.)* préjugé *m.*
Bible, *s.* bible *f.*
bibliography, *s.* bibliographie *f.*
bicycle, *s.* bicyclette *f.*
big, *adj.* grand; gros.
bill, *s. (hotel)* note *f.; (restaurant)* addition *f.; (invoice)* facture *f.; (of exchange)* lettre *f.* de change; *(of fare)* carte *f.*, menu *m.; (poster)* affiche *f.; (parliament)* projet *m.* de loi.
bin, *s.* huche *f.*, coffre *m.*
bind, *v.a.* lier; *(book)* relier.
biological, *adj.* biologique.
biology, *f.* biologie *f.*
birch, *s.* bouleau *m.*
bird, *s.* oiseau *m.*
birth, *s.* naissance *f.*
birthday, *s.* anniversaire *m.*
birth-place, *s.* lieu *m.* de

naissance.
biscuit, *s.* biscuit *m.*
bishop, *s.* évêque *m.*
bit[1], *s.* morceau *m.; (drill)* mèche *f.; a* ~ un peu (de).
bit[2], *s. (horse)* mors *m.*
bite, *v. a.* & *n.* mordre.
bitter, *adj.* amer; mordant; *(cold)* âpre.
bitterness, *s.* amertume *f.*
black, *adj.* noir.
blackbird, *s.* merle *m.*
blackmail, *s.* chantage *m.*
blacksmith, *s.* forgeron *m.*
bladder, *s.* vessie *f.*
blade, *s.* lame *f.*
blame, *s.* blâme *m.*; — *v. a.* blâmer, accuser qn.
blameless, *adj.* innocent.
blank, *adj.* blanc; nu; — *s.* blanc *m.*
blanket, *s.* couverture *f.*
blast, *s.* rafale *f.*; coup *m.* de vent; souffle *m.*; — *v.a.* faire sauter; détruire.
blaze, *s.* flamme *f.*; — *v.n.* flamber.
bleak, *adj.* lugubre.
bleed, *v.a.* & *n.* saigner.
blend, *s.* mélange *m.*; — *v.a.* fondre; mêler.
bless, *v.a.* bénir.
blessing, *s.* bénédiction *f.*
blind[1], *adj.* aveugle.
blind[2], *s.* store *m.*
blindness, *s.* cécité *f.*
blink, *v. n.* clignoter.
bliss, *s.* félicité *f.*
blister, *s.* ampoule *f.*
block, *s.* bloc *m.*; *(wood)* billot *m.*; *(buildings)* pâté *m.*; *(traffic)* encombrement *m.*
blond *adj.* blond.
blood, *s.* sang *m.*
bloody, *adj.* sanglant.
bloom, *s.* fleur *f.*; — *v. n.* fleurir.
blossom, *s.* fleur *f.*
blot, *s.* tache *f.*; pâté *m.*
blouse, *s.* blouse *f.*
blow[1], *v. a. (trumpet)* sonner; *(glass)* souffler; ~ *out* éteindre; ~ *up* faire sauter; *v.n. (wind)* souffler.
blow[2], *s.* coup *m.*
blue, *adj.* bleu.
blunder, *s.* bévue *f.*; — *v. n.* faire une bévue
blunt, *adj.* émoussé; *(person)* brusque.
blush, *v.n.* rougir.
board, *s.* planche *f.*; *(meals)* pension *f.*; *(council)* conseil *m.*; *(paper)* carton *m.*; *(theatre)* ~*s* planches; ~ *and lodging* pension *f.* et chambre(s); *on* ~ *(ship)* à bord d'un navire; — *v.n.* prendre pension chez; *v.a.* monter à bord de.
boarder, *s.* pensionnaire *m. f.*
boarding-house, *s.* pension *f.*
boarding-school, *s.* pensionnat *m.*
boast, *s.* vanterie *f.*; — *v. n.* se vanter (de).
boat, *s.* bateau *m.*
body, *s.* corps *m.*
bog, *s.* marécage *m.*
boil[1], *v.a.* faire bouillir; *(cook)* faire cuire; *v. n.* bouillir.
boil[2], *s.* furoncle *m.*
boiler, *s.* chaudière *f.*

bold, *adj.* hardi; effronté.
boldness, *s.* hardiesse *f.*; effronterie *f.*
bolt, *s.* verrou *m.*; — *v. a.* verrouiller; *v. n.* filer.
bomb, *s.* bombe *f.*
bond, *s.* lien *m.*
bone, *s.* os *m.*; *(fish)* arête *f.*
bonnet, *s.* chapeau *m.*; bonnet *m.*; *(motor)* capot *m.*
bony, *adj.* osseux; maigre.
book, *s.* livre *m.*; — *v.a* prendre (un billet); retenir.
bockcase, *s.* bibliothèque *f.*
booking-office, *s.* guichet *m.*
book-keeper, *s.* teneur *m.* de livres.
book-keeping, *s.* compatibilité *f.*
booklet, *s.* livret *m.*
bookseller, *s.* libraire *m.*
bookshelf, *s.* rayon *m.*
bookshop, *s.* librairie *f.*
book-stall, *s.* bibliothèque (de gare) *f.*
boot, *s.* bottine *f.*; brodequin *m.*
booth, *s.* baraque *f.*
booty, *s.* butin *m.*
border, *s.* bord *m.*; frontière *f.*
bore, *v. a.* ennuyer, raser; —*s.* raseur *m.*
boring, *adj.* ennuyeux, assommant.
born, *pp.* né; *be* ~ naître.
borrow, *v. a.* emprunter.
bosom, *s.* sein *m.*
boss, *s.* patron *m.*
botanical, *adj.* botanique.
botany, *s.* botanique *m.*
both, *pron. & adj.* l'un(e) et l'autre; tous (les) deux; ~ ... *and* et ... et ...
bother, *v.a.* tracasser.
bottle, *s.* bouteille *f.*
bottom, *s.* bas *m.*; fond *m.*; derrière *m.*
bough, *s.* rameau *m.*
bound, *pp.* ~ *for* à destination de, en route pour.
boundary, *s.* borne *f.*
bounty, *s.* générosité *f.*
bouquet, *s.* bouquet *m.*
bow[1], *s.* arc *m.*; *(violin)* archet *m.*; *(knot)* nœud *m.*
bow[2], *v.a.* incliner; courber; *v.n.* s'incliner; se courber; — *s.* salut *m.*; *(ship)* avant *m.*
bowels, *s. pl.* entrailles *f.*
bowl, *s.* bol *m.*, jatte *f.*
box, *s.* boîte *f.*, caisse *f.*; *(horse)* stalle *f.*; *(theatre)* loge *f.*; *(on the ears)* soufflet *m.*; — *v. n.* boxer.
box-office, *s.* bureau *m.* de location.
boy, *s.* garçon *m.*; ~ *scout* boy-scout *m.*, éclaireur *m.*
bra, *s.* soutien-gorge *m.*
brace, *s.* couple *f.*; lien *m.*; ~*s* bretelles *f. pl.*
bracelet, *s.* bracelet *m.*
brain, *s.* cerveau *m.*; ~*s* cervelle *f.*
brainy, *adv.* intelligent.
brake, *s.* frein *m.*
branch, *s.* branche *f.*
brand, *s.* tison *m.*; marque *f.*; — *v.a.* marquer.

brandy, *s.* cognac *m.*
brass, *s.* cuivre jaune *m.*
brave, *adj.* brave.
brawl, *s.* querelle *f.*
bread, *s.* pain *m.*
breadth, *s.* largeur *f.*
break, *v.a.* briser, casser; *(law)* violer; *(promise)* manquer; *(news)* apprendre à; *v. n.* se casser; se briser; ~ *down* abattre; s'effondrer; *(motor)* avoir une panne; ~ *in* dresser; ~ *up* lever; — *s.* interruption *f.*; pause *f.*
break-down, *s.* *(motor)* panne *f.*; *(health)* débâcle; ~ *lorry* dépanneuse *f.*
breakfast, *s.* déjeuner *m.*
breast, *s.* poitrine *f.*, sein *m.*
breath, *s.* haleine *f.*; souffle *m.*
breathe, *v.a.* & *n.* respirer.
breathless, *adj.* essoufflé; sans souffle.
breeches, *s. pl.* culotte *f.*
breed, *s.* race *f.*; — *v.a.* élever.
breeze, *s.* brise *f.*
breezy, *adj.* venteux.
brew, *v.a.* brasser.
bribe, *s.* pot-de-vin *m.*; — *v.a.* corrompre.
brick, *s.* brique *f.*
bricklayer, *s.* maçon *m.*
bride, *s.* mariée *f.*
bridegroom. *s.* marié *m.*
bridge, *s.* pont *m.*
bridle, *s.* bride *f.*
brief, *adj.* bref.
briefcase, *s.* serviette *f.*
briefly, *adv.* brièvement.
briefs, *s. pl.* slip *m.*
bright, *adj.* brillant; vif; clair; éclatant.
brighten, *v.a.* faire briller; égayer.
brightness, *s.* éclat *m.*
brilliant, *s.* brillant *m.*
brim, *s.* bord *m.*
bring, *v.a.* amener; apporter; ~ *about* amener; ~ *back* rapporter; ~ *forth* produire; ~ *up* élever.
brink, *s.* bord *m.*
brisk, *adj.* vif; actif.
bristle, *s.* *(brush)* poil *m.*
British, *adj.* britannique.
brittle, *adj.* cassant.
broad, *adj.* large; vaste.
broadcast, *v.a.* radiodiffuser.
broadcasting, *s.* radiodiffusion *f.*
broken, *adj.* brisé.
bronze, *s.* bronze *m.*
brooch, *s.* broche *f.*
brood, *s.* couvée *f.*; *v.n.* couver.
brook, *s.* ruisseau *m.*
broom, *s.* balai *m.*
brother, *s.* frère *m.*
brother-in-law, *s.* beau-frère *m.*
brow, *s.* sourcil *m.*
brown, *adj.* brun.
bruise, *s.* contusion *f.*; — *v.a.* meurtrir.
brush, *s.* brosse *f.*; pinceau *m.*; balai *m.*; — *v.a.* brosser; ~ *up* donner un coup de brosse à.
brutal, *adj.* brutal, cruel.
brutality, *s.* brutalité *f.*
bubble, *s.* bulle *f.*; — *v. n.* bouillonner.
buck, *s.* daim *m.*

bucket, *s.* seau *m.*
buckle, *s.* boucle *f.*
bud, *s.* bourgeon *m.*
budget, *s.* budget *m.*
buffet, *s.* soufflet *m.*
bug, *s.* punaise *f.*
build, *v.a.* bâtir; construire; sur; ~ *up* établir.
builder, *s.* entrepreneur *m.* de bâtiments; constructeur *m.*
building, *s.* bâtiment *m.*
bulb, *s.* bulbe *m.; (lamp)* ampoule *f.*
bulge, *v.n.* bomber.
bulk, *s.* masse *f.;* volume *m.*
bull, *s.* taureau *m.*
bullet, *s.* balle *f.*
bulletin, *s.* bulletin *m.*
bump, *s.* bosse *f.;* collision *f.;* coup *m.*
bumper, *s.* pare-choc *m.*
bun, *s.* brioche *f.*
bunch, *s.* bouquet *m.;* botte *f.;* grappe *f.*
bundle, *s.* botte *f.;* paquet *m.;* fagot *m.*
bunk, *s.* couchette *f.*
buoy, *s.* bouée *f.*
burden, *s.* charge *f.;* fardeau *m.*
burglar, *s.* cambrioleur *m.*
burial, *s.* enterrement *m.*
burn, *v.a.* & *n.* brûler.
bursary, *s.* bourse *f.*
burst, *v.n.* éclater; crever; exploser; *v.a.* faire éclater; rompre; crever; — *s.* éclat *m.*; explosion *f.*
bury, *v.a.* enterrer.
bus, *s.* autobus *m.*
bush, *s.* buisson *m.*
business, *s.* affaires *f. pl.;* profession *f.;* **on ~** pour affaires; ~ ***hours*** heures *(f. pl.)* d'ouverture.
businessman, *s.* homme *m.* d'affaires.
bus-stop, *s.* arrêt *m.* d'autobus.
busy, *adj.* occupé, affairé.
but, *conj.* mais.
butcher, *s.* boucher *m.; ~'s (shop)* boucherie *f.*
butter, *s.* beurre *m.*
butterfly, *s.* papillon *m.*
buttock, *s.* fesse *f.,* derrière *m.*
button, *s.* bouton *m.*
buy, *v.a.* acheter.
buyer, *s.* acheteur *m.*
by, *prep.* par; *de*; ~ ***Monday*** d'ici à lundi.
bystander, *s.* spectateur, -trice *m. f.*

C

cab, *s.* taxi *m.;* fiacre *m.*
cabbage, *s.* chou *m.*
cabin, *s.* cabane *f.; (ship)* cabine *f.*
cabinet, *s. (politics)* cabinet *m.*
cable, *s.* câble *m.*
cablegram, *s.* câblogramme *m.*
café, *s.* café(-restaurant) *m.*
cage, *s.* cage *f.*
cake, *s.* gâteau *m.*
calculate, *v.a.&n.* calculer.
calculation, *s.* calcul *m.*
calendar, *s.* calendrier *m.*
calf, *s.* veau *m.; (leg)* mollet *m.*
call, *v. a. & n.* appeler; ~ *for.* réclamer; ~ ***on*** faire visite à; — *s.*

appel *m.*; cri *m.*; *(visit)* visite *f.*
call-box, *s.* cabine *f.* téléphonique.
calm, *adj.* calme.
calorie, *s.* calorie *f.*
camel, *s.* chameau, -elle *m. f.*
camera, *s.* appareil *m.* (photographique).
camp, *s.* camp *m.*
campaign, *s.* campagne *f.*
camping, *s.* camping *m.*
can[1], *s.* broc *m.*; pot *m.*
can[2], *v. aux.* pouvoir; savoir.
canal, *s.* canal *m.*
canary, *s.* canari *m.*
cancel, *v.a.* annuler.
cancer, *s.* cancer *m.*
candle, *s.* chandelle *f.*; bougie *f.*
cannon, *s.* canon *m.*
canoe, e *s.* canoë *m.*
canteen, *s.* cantine *f.*
canvas, *s.* toile *f.*
cap, *s.* bonnet *m.*; casquette *f.*
capable, *adj.* capable (de).
capacity, *s.* capacité *f.*
cape, *s.* *(land)* cap *m.*; *(cloak)* pèlerine *f.*; cape *f.*
capital, *s.* *(city)* capitale *f.*; *(letter)* majuscule *f.* *(commerce)* capital *m*;
capsule, *s.* capsule *f.*
captain, *s.* capitaine *m.*
caption, *s.* sous-titre *m.*
captivate, *v.a.* captiver.
capture, *v.a.* capturer; — *s.* capture *f.*
car, *s.* voiture *f.*, auto *f.*
caravan, *s.* roulotte *f.* (de camping), caravane *f.*
carbon-paper, *s.* papier *m.* carbone.
carburetter, *s.* carburateur *m.*
card, *s.* carte *f.*
cardboard, *s.* carton *m.*
cardinal, *adj. m.* cardinal *m.*
care, *s.* attention *f.*; soin *m.*; souci *m.*; ~ *of* aux bons soins de; *take* ~ *of* prendre soin de; *v.n.* ~ *for* se soucier de; ~ *to* aimer.
career, *s.* carrière *f.*
careful, *adj.* soigneux.
careless, *adj.* insouciant, négligent.
caress, *v.a.* caresser.
cargo, *s.* cargaison *f.*
caricature, *s.* caricature *f.*
carnation, *s.* œillet *m.*
carpenter, *s.* charpentier *m.*
carpet, *s.* tapis *m.*
carriage, *s.* voiture *f.*; *(transport)* transport *m.*
carriage-way, *s.* chaussée *f.*
carrier, *s.* voiturier *m.*
carrot, *s.* carotte *f.*
carry, *v.a.* porter; transporter; ~ *on* exercer; ~ *out* mettre à exécution.
cart, *s.* charrette *f.*
cartridge, *s.* cartouche *f.*
carve, *v. a.& n.* sculpter; *(meat)* découper.
case, *s.* *(box)* étui *m.*, caisse *f.*; *(instance)* cas *m.*; cause *f.*
casement, *s.* croisée *f.*
cash, *s.* espèces *f. pl.*

cash-book, *s.* livre *m.* de caisse.
cashier, *s.* caissier, -ère *m. f.*
cash-register, *s.* caisse *f.* enregistreuse.
cask, *s.* tonneau *m.*
cast, *v.a.* jeter; *(metal)* fondre; — *s.* coup *m.*; *(theatre)* distribution *f.*
castle, *s.* château *m.*
casual, *adj.* casuel.
casualty, *s.* accident *m.*
cat, *s.* chat, -te *m. f.*
catalogue, *s.* catalogue *m.*
catastrophe, *s.* catastrophe *f.*
catch, *v.a.* saisir; attraper; *(eye)* frapper; ~ *up* rattraper; — *s.* prise *f.*; attrape *f.*
category, *s.* catégorie *f.*
cater, *v.n.* pourvoir à.
caterpillar, *s.* chenille *f.*
cathedral, *s.* cathédrale *f.*
catholic, *adj.* catholique.
catholicism, *s.* catholicisme *m.*
cattle, *s.* bétail *m.* *(pl.* bestiaux).
cauliflower, *s.* chou-fleur *m.*
cause, *s.* cause *f.*; motif *m.*; — *v.a.* causer.
caution, *s.* prudence *f.*
cautious, *adj.* prudent.
cave, *s.* caverne *f.*
cavity, *s.* cavité *f.*
cease, *v.a.* & *n.* cesser.
ceiling, *s.* plafond *m.*
celebrate, *v.a.* célébrer.
celebration, *s.* célébration *f.*; commémoration *f.*
celery, *s.* céleri *m.*
cell, *s.* cellule *f.*
ellar, *s.* cave *f.*
cello, *s.* violoncelle *m.*
cellophane, *s.* cellophane *f.*
cement, *s.* ciment *m.*; — *v.a.* cimenter.
cemetery, *s.* cimetière *m.*
centenary, *s.* centenaire *m.*
central, *adj.* central.
centre, *s.* centre *m.*
century, *s.* siècle *m.*
cereal, *s.* céréale *f.*
ceremony, *s.* cérémonie *f.*
certain, *adj.* certain.
certainly, *adj.* certainement; sans doute
certainty, *s.* certitude *f.*
certificate, *s.* certificat *m.*
certify, *v.a.* certifier.
chain, *s.* chaîne *f.*
chair, *s.* chaise *f.*; *(professorship)* chaire *f.*; *take the* ~ présider.
chairman, *s.* président *m.*
chalk, *s.* craie *f.*
challenge, *s.* défi *m.*; — *v.a.* défier; provoquer.
chamber, *s.* chambre *f.*; ~*s* étude *f.*; appartement *m.*
champagne, *s.* champagne *m.*
champion, *s.* champion *m.*
championship, *s.* championnat *m.*
chance, *s.* chance *f.*; *by* ~ par hasard.
chancellor, *s.* chancelier *m.*
chancery, *s.* chancellerie *f.*
change, *s.* changement *m.*; *(money)* monnaie *f.*; — *v.a.&n.* changer.
channel, *s.* canal *m.*;

m.; the English Channel la Manche.
chap, *s.* type *m.*
chapel, *s.* chapelle *f.*
chaplain, *s.* chapelain *m.*
chapter, *s.* chapitre *m.*
character *s.* caractère *m.; (theatre)* personnage *m.*
characteristic, *adj.* caractéristique; — *s.* trait *m.* caractéristique.
charcoal, *s.* charbon *m.* de bois
charge, *s.* charge *f.; (price)* prix *m.; (accusation)* accusation *f.;* — *v.a.* charger (de); *(price)* demander; faire payer; *(accuse)* accuser (de).
charity, *s.* charité *f.*
charm, *s.* charme *m.*
charming, *adj.* charmant.
chart, *s.* carte *f.* marine.
charter, *s.* charte *f.*
charwoman, *s.* femme *f.* de ménage.
chase, *v.a.* chasser; poursuivre; — *s.* chasse *f.*
chassis, *s.* châssis *m.*
chat, *s.* causette *f.;* — *v. n.* causer.
chatter, *v.n.* babiller; *(teeth)* claquer.
cheap, *adj.* bon marché.
cheat, *v.a.* tromper; tricher; — *s.* tromperie *f.;* tricherie; *(pers.)* fourbe *m.*
check, *v.a.* contrôler, vérifier; *(stop)* arrêter; — *s.* vérification *f.*, contrôle *m.*
checkmate, *s.* échec et mat *m.*
check-up, *s.* examen *m.* médical.
cheek, *s.* joue *f.*
cheeky, *adj.* impertinent.
cheer, *v.a.* réjouir, encourager; acclamer; *v.n.* ~ *up* reprendre sa gaieté ; courage!; — *s.* joie *f.;* ~*s* acclamations *f.*
cheerful, *adj.* joyeux.
cheese, *s.* fromage *m.*
chemical, *adj.* chimique.
chemist, *s.* chimiste *m.;* pharmacien *m.;* ~*'s (shop)* pharmacie *f.*
chemistry, *s.* chimie *f.*
cheque, *s.* chèque *m.; traveller's* ~ chèque *m.* de voyage.
cheque-book, *s.* carnet *m.* de chèques.
cherish, *v. a.* soigner; *(hope)* caresser.
cherry, *s.* cerise *f.*
chess, *s.* échecs *m. pl.*
chess-board, *s.* échiquier *m.*
chest, *s.* coffre *m.; (part of body)* poitrine *f.;* ~ *of drawers* commode *f.*
chestnut, *s.* châtaigne *f.*
chew, *v.a.* mâcher.
chicken, *s.* poulet *m.*
chief, *adj.* principal; — *s.* chef *m.*
chiefly, *adv.* principalement.
child, *s.* enfant *m.f.*
childhood, *s.* enfance *f.*
childish, *adj.* enfantin.
childless, *adj.* sans enfant.
chill, *s.* coup *m.* de froid; — *v.a.* refroi-

dir, glacer.
chilly, *adj. (weather)* frais; (un peu) froid.
chimney, *s.* cheminée *f.*
chin, *s.* menton *m.*
china, *s.* porcelaine *f.*
Chinese, *adj.* chinois; — *s.* Chinois, -e.
chip, *s.* éclat *m.;* copeau *m.; ~s* frites *f. pl.*
chirp, *v.n.* gazouiller.
chisel, *s.* ciseau *m.;* — *v.a.* ciseler.
chivalry, *s.* chevalerie *f.*
chocolate, *s.* chocolat *m.*
choice, *s.* choix *m.*
choir, *s.* chœur *m.*
choke, *v.a. & n.* étouffer.
choose, *v.a.* choisir.
chop, *s.* côtelette *f.*
chorus, *s.* chœur *m.*
Christian, *adj.* chrétien; *~ name* prénom *m.*
Christianity, *s.* christianisme *m.*
Christmas, *s.* Noël *m.; ~ eve* veille *f.* de Noël.
chuckle, *v.n.* rire tout bas; — *s.* rire étouffé.
church, *s.* église *f.*
churchyard, *s.* cimetière *m.*
cider, *s.* cidre *m.*
cigar, *s.* cigare *m.*
cigarette, *s.* cigarette *f.*
cigarette-case, *s.* étui *m.* à cigarettes.
cigarette-holder, *s.* porte-cigarette *m.*
cinders, *s.pl.* cendres *f.*
cine-camera, *s.* camera *f.*
cinema, *s.* cinéma *m.*
cinerama, *s.* cinérama *m.*
circle, *s.* cercle *m.*
circuit, *s.* circuit *m.;* détour *m.;* tournée *f.*
circular, *adj.* circulaire.
circulate, *v.n.* circuler; *v.a.* faire circuler.
circulation, *s.* circulation *f.*
circumstance, *s.* circonstance *f.*
circus, *s.* cirque *m.*
cistern, *s.* citerne *f.*
citation, *s.* citation *f.*
cite, *v. a.* citer.
citizen, *s.* citoyen, -ne *m. f.*, habitant *m.*
citizenship, *s.* droit *m.* de cité.
city, *s.* ville *f.; the City* Cité *f.*
civil, *adj.* civil; *(polite)* poli; *~ servant* fonctionnaire *m.*
civilization, *s.* civilisation *f.*
civilize, *v.a.* civiliser.
claim, *s.* demande *f.*, réclamation *f.;* droit *m.;* — *v.a.* revendiquer, réclamer.
clamp, *s.* crampon *m.*
clang, *s.* bruit *m.* métallique; — *v.n.* retentir.
clap, *s.* battement *m.;* applaudissements *m. pl.;* — *v.n.* applaudir.
clash, *v.a.* choquer; *v.n.* s'entre-choquer.
clasp, *s.* agrafe *f.;* fermoir *m.;* — *v.a.* agrafer; joindre.
class, *s.* classe *f.*
classic(al), *adj.* classique.
classify, *v.a.* classifier.
class-room, *s.* classe *f.*
clatter, *s.* bruit *m.;* fracas *m.;* — *v.n.* faire

du bruit.
clause, *s.* clause *f.*, article *m.*
claw, *s.* griffe *f.;* serre *f.;* ongle *m.*
clay, *s.* glaise *f.;* argile *f.*
clean, *adj.* propre; blanc; pur; — *v.a.* nettoyer.
cleanse, *v.a.* nettoyer.
clear, *adj.* clair; — *v.a.* déblayer; éclaircir; *v.n.* s'éclaircir; ~ *away* enlever; ~ *out* filer.
clearly, *adv.* clair, clairement; évidemment.
cleave, *v.a.* fendre; *v.n.* se fendre.
clergy, *s.* clergé *m.*
clergyman, *s.* ministre *m.*
clerk, *s.* employé *m.*, commis *m.*
clever, *adj.* habile, adroit; intelligent.
client, *s.* client *m.*
cliff, *s.* falaise *f.*
climate, *s.* climat *m.*
climb, *v.a.* & *n.* grimper.
cling, *v.n.* ~ *to* se cramponner à.
clinic, *s.* clinique *f.*
clip, *s.* pince; — *v.a.* tondre; couper; rogner; *(tickets)* poinçonner.
cloak, *s.* manteau *m.*
cloak-room, *s.* consigne *f.;* vestiaire *m.*
clock, *s.* horloge *f.;* pendule *f.; it is 10 o'clock* il est dix heures.
close, *v.a.* *(shut)* fermer; *(end)* terminer; *v.n.* (se) fermer; se terminer; — *adj.* fermé; *(narrow)* étroit; *(relations)* proche; intime; — *adv.* tout près; — *s.* enclos *m.; (end)* fin *f.*
closely, *adv.* de près; étroitement.
closet, *s.* cabinet *m.;* armoire *f.*
cloth, *s.* drap *m.; (table)* nappe *f.*
clothe, *v.a.* vêtir.
clothes, *s.pl.* habits *m.pl.*
clothing, *s.* vêtements *m. pl.*
cloud, *s.* nuage *m.*
cloudy, *adj.* couvert.
clover, *s.* trèfle *m.*
club, *s.* *(stick)* massue *f.; (people)* cercle *m.*, club *m.*, société *f.; (cards)* trèfle *m.*
clue, *s.* fil *m.; (crossword)* définition *f.*
clumsy, *adj.* gauche.
cluster, *s.* grappe *f.*
clutch, *v.a.* empoigner; *m.* pour empoigner; *(motor)* embrayage *m.*
coach, *s.* voiture *f.;* wagon *m.;* autocar *m.; (sports)* entraineur *m.*
coal, *s.* charbon *m.*
coal-mine, *s.* mine *f.* de houille.
coarse, *adj.* grossier; vulgaire.
coast, *s.* côte *f.*
coat, *s.* *(jacket)* veston *m.; (top)* pardessus *m.*, manteau *m.*
cock, *s.* coq *m.*, mâle *m.; (gun)* chien *m.; (tap)* robinet *m.*
cocktail, *s.* cocktail *m.*
cocoa, *s.* cacao *m.*
cod, *s.* morue *f.*

code, *s.* code *m.*
coffee, *s.* café *m.*
coffee-pot, *s.* cafetière *f.*
coffin, *s.* cercueil *m.*
cog-wheel, *s.* roue *f.* dentée.
coil, *s.* rouleau *m.*; bobine *f.*; — *v.a.* lover; enrouler.
coin, *s.* pièce *f.*
coincidence, *s.* coïncidence *f.*
coke, *s.* coke *m.*
cold, *adj.* froid; *be* ~ *(pers.)* avoir froid; *(weather)* faire froid; — *s.* froid *m.*; *(in the head)* rhume *m.*; *catch a* ~ s'enrhumer.
collaborate, *v. n.* collaborer.
collaborator, *s.* collaborateur, -trice *m.f.*
collapse, *v.n.* s'effondrer; *(pers.)* s'affaisser; — *s.* effondrement *m.*; *(pers.)* affaissement *m.* subit.
collar, *s.* col *m.*; collet *m.*
colleague, *s.* collègue *m. f.*
collect, *v.a.* rassembler; recueillir.
collection, *s.* collection *f.*; collecte *f.*; *(mail)* levée *f.*
college, *s.* collège *m.*
collide, *v.n.* se heurter (contre), entrer en collision.
colliery, *s.* houillère *f.*; mine *f.*
collision, *s.* collision *f.*
colon, *s.* deux points *m. pl.*
colonel, *s.* colonel *m.*
colony, *s.* colonie *f.*
colour, *s.* couleur *f.*
colourful, *adj.* coloré.
colourless, *adj.* terne, pâle.
column, *s.* colonne *f.*
comb, *s.* peigne *m.*; — *v.a.* peigner.
combat, *s.* combat *m.*
combination, *s.* combinaison *f.*
combine, *v.a.* combiner.
come, *v.n.* venir, arriver; ~ *across* rencontrer; ~ *back* revenir; ~ *by* obtenir; passer; ~ *down* descendre; ~ *in* entrer; ~ *off* avoir lieu; se détacher; ~ *out* sortir; ~ *up* monter.
comedian, *s.* comédien *m.*
comedy, *s.* comédie *f.*
comely, *adj.* avenant, bienséant.
comfort, *s.* consolation *f.*; bien-être *m.*; — *v.a.* consoler.
comfortable, *adj.* confortable; commode; *be* ~ être à l'aise.
comic, *adj.* comique.
comma, *s.* virgule *f.*
command, *s.* ordre *m.*; — *v.a.* commander.
commander, *s.* commandant *m.*
commandment, *s.* commandement *m.*
commemorate, *v.a.* commémorer.
commence, *v.a.& n.* commencer.
commend, *v.a.* recommander; louer.
comment, *s.* commentai-

re *m.*; — *v.n.* commenter.
commentary, *s.* commentaire *m.*
commerce, *s.* commerce *m.*
commercial, *adj.* commercial; ~ *traveller* voyageur *m.* de commerce.
commission, *s.* commission *f.*; commande *f.*
commissioner, *s.* commissaire *m.*
commit, *v.a.* commettre; confier; ~ *oneself* se compromettre.
commitment, *s.* engagement *m.*
committee, *s.* comité *m.*
commodity, *s.* marchandise *f.*, article *m.*
common, *adj.* commun.
commonwealth, *s.* *the British Commonwealth* commonwealth *m.*
communicate, *v. a.* & *n.* communiquer.
communication, *s.* communication *f.*
communication-cord, *s.* signal *m.* d'alarme.
communion, *s.* communion *f.*
communiqué, *s.* communiqué *m.*
community, *s.* communauté *f.*
compact, *s.* pacte *m.*; poudrier *m.*; — *adj.* compact; concis.
companion, *s.* compagnon, -agne *m. f.*
company, *s.* compagnie *f.*; société *f.*
comparatively, *adv.* comparativement.
compare, *v.a.* comparer (*to* à, *with* avec).
comparison, *s.* comparaison *f.*
compartment, *s.* compartiment *m.*
compass, *s.* *(mariner's)* boussole *f.*; *(pair of)* ~*es* compas *m.*
compassion, *s.* compassion *f.*
compel, *v.a.* forcer.
compete, *v.n.* faire concurrence (à); concourir.
competence, *s.* compétence *f.*; capacité *f.*
competent, *adj.* capable.
competition, *s.* concurrence *f.*; concours *m.*; compétition *f.*
competitor, *s.* concurrent *m.*
compilation, *s.* compilation *f.*
compile, *v.a.* compiler.
complain, *v.n.* se plaindre
complaint, *s.* plainte *f.*; maladie *f.*; réclamation *f.*
complement, *s.* complément *m.*
complete, *v.a.* compléter, achever; — *adj.* complet.
complicated, *adj.* compliqué.
complication, *s.* complication *f.*
compliment, *s.* compliment *m.*
comply, *v.n.* ~ *with* se conformer à.
component, *adj.* & *s.* composant *(m.)*.
compose, *v.a.* composer; *be* ~*d of* se compo-

ser de.
:omposer, *s.* compositeur *m.*
:omposition, *s.* composition *f.*; dissertation *f.*
:ompound, *s. & adj.* composé *(m.)*; — *v.a.* composer.
omprehend, *v.a.* comprendre.
omprehension, *s.* compréhension *f.*
ompress, *v.a.* comprimer.
ompromise, *s.* compromis *m.*; — *v.a.* compromettre.
compulsory, *adj.* obligatoire.
compute, *v.a.* calculer, computer.
computer, *s.* calculateur *m.* (électronique).
omrade, *s.* camarade *m.*
onceal, *v. a.* cacher.
onceit, *s.* vanité *f.*
onceive, *v.a.* concevoir.
oncept, *s.* concept *m.*
oncern, *v.a.* concerner; regarder; *be ~ed (in, with)* s'intéresser (à); *(about)* s'inquiéter (de); — *s.* affaire *f.*; entreprise *f.*; anxiété *f.*
oncerning, *prep.* concernant.
oncert, *a.* concert *m.*
oncession, *s.* concession *f.*
onciliation, *s.* réconciliation *f.*
oncise, *adj.* concis.
:onclude, *v.a. &n.* conclure.
onclusion, *s.* conclusion *f.*; *in ~* pour conclure.
concrete, *s.* béton *m.*; — *adj.* concret.
condemn, *v.a.* condamner.
condense, *v.a.* condenser.
condition, *s.* condition *f.*; état *m.*; *on ~ that* à condition que.
conduct, *s.* conduite *f.*; — *v. a.* conduire; diriger.
conductor, *s.* receveur *m.*; chef *m.* d'orchestre.
cone, *s.* cône *m.*
confederacy, *s.* confédération *f.*
confer, *v.a. & n.* conférer.
conference, *s.* conférence *f.*
confess, *v.a.* avouer; confesser.
confession, *s.* confession *f.*
confidence, *s.* confiance *f.*
confident, *adj.* confiant.
confidential, *adj*. confidentiel.
confine, *v.a.* confiner, enfermer; *be ~d to bed* être alité.
confirm, *v. a.* confirmer.
confirmation, *s.* confirmation *f.*
conflict, *s.* conflit *m.*
confound, *v. a.* confondre.
confront, *v.a.* être en face; confronter.
confuse, *v.a.* brouiller, mettre en désordre.
confusion, *s.* confusion *f.*
congratulate, *v.a.* féliciter (de).
congratulation, *s.* félicitations *f. pl.*
congregation, *s.* assemblée *f.*, congrégation *f.*
congress, *s.* congrès *m.*

conjunction, *s.* conjonction *f.*
connect, *v.a.* joindre, lier; associer.
connection, *s.* connexion *f.;* rapport *m.; (railw.)* correspondance *f.*
conquer, *v.a.* vaincre; conquérir.
conqueror, *s.* vainqueur *m.;* conquérant *m.*
conscience, *s.* conscience *f.*
conscious *adj. be* ~ (= *not fainting)* avoir connaissance; *be* ~ *of* avoir la conscience de.
consciousness, *s.* connaissance *f.;* conscience *f.*
conscript, *adj.* & *s.* conscrit *(m.).*
consent, *s.* consentement; — *v.n.* consentir.
consequence, *s.* conséquence *f.*
consequent, *adj.* conséquent.
consequently, *adv.* par conséquent.
conservation, *s.* conservation *f.*
consider, *v.a.* considérer.
considerable, *adj.* considérable.
considerate, *adj.* attentif; réfléchi.
consideration, *s.* considération *f.; (money)* rémunération *f.*
consign, *v.a.* livrer; consigner, expédier.
consignment, *s.* expédition *f.;* envoi *m.*
consist, *v. n.* ~ *of* se composer de, consister en.
consistent, *adj.* conséquent.
consolation, *s.* consolation *f.*
consonant, *s.* consonne *f.*
conspicuous, *adj.* en vue; frappant.
conspiracy, *s.* conspiration *f.*
conspire, *v. a.* & *n.* conspirer.
constable, *s.* agent *m.* (de police).
constant, *adj.* continuel; constant.
constipation, *s.* constipation *f.*
constitute, *v.a.* constituer.
constitution, *s.* constitution *f.*
constrain, *v.a.* contraindre (à).
constraint, *s.* contrainte *f.*
construct, *v. a.* construire.
construction, *s.* construction *f.*
consul, *s.* consul *m.*
consulate, *s.* consulat *m.*
consult, *v.a.* & *n.* consulter.
consultation, *s.* consultation *f.;* ~ *room* cabinet *m.* (de consultation).
consume, *v.a. (destroy)* consumer; *(use up)* consommer.
consumer, *s.* consommateur, -trice *m.f.;* ~ *goods* articles *m.* de grande consommation.
consumption, *s.* consommation *f.; (disease)* phtisie *f.,* tuberculose *f.*
contact, *s.* contact *m.;* — *v.a.* entrer en relations avec.
contain, *v.a.* contenir.
container, *s.* récipient *m.*

contemplate, *v.a.* contempler; projeter.
contemplation, *s.* contemplation *f.*
contemporary, *adj.* & *s.* contemporain *(m.).*
contempt, *s.* mépris *m.*
contemptuous, *adj.* méprisant.
contend, *v.n.* lutter contre (pour).
content, *s.* contentement *m.*; *~s* contenu *m.*; *table of ~s* table *f.* des matières; — *adj.* content.
contest, *s.* lutte *f.*; *(sport)* rencontre *f.*, match *m.*; *(dispute)* contestation *f.*; — *v. a.* contester.
continent, *s.* continent *m.*
continental, *adj.* continental.
continual, *adj.* continuel.
continuation, *s.* continuation *f.*; suite *f.*
continue, *v.a.* & *n.* continuer.
continuous, *adj.* continu.
contract, *s.* contrat *m.*; — *v.a.* contracter.
contractor, *s.* entrepreneur *m.*
contradiction, *s.* contradiction *f.*
contrary, *adj.* contraire; — *adv.* contrairement.
contrast, *s.* contraste *m.*; — *v.a.* mettre en contraste.
contribute, *v. a.* & *n.* contribuer.
contribution, *s.* contribution *f.*; article *m.*
contributor, *s.* contribuant *m.*; collaborateur *m.*
contrive, *v.a.* inventer.
control, *s.* autorité *f.*; maîtrise *f.*; direction *f.*, commande *f.*; — *v.a.* gouverner, commander, maîtriser, diriger; contrôler.
controversy, *s.* polémique *f.*, controverse *f.*
convenience, *s.* commodité *f.*, convenance *f.*; *public ~* cabinets *m. pl.* d'aisances.
convenient, *adj.* commode; *be ~ to s.o.* convenir à qn.
conversation, *s.* conversation *f.*
converse, *v.n.* converser; causer.
convert, *v.a.* convertir.
convey, *v.a.* transporter; transmettre; présenter.
conveyance, *s.* transport *m.*; voiture *f.*, véhicule *m.*
conveyer, *s.* porteur *m.*; *~ belt* bande *f.* transporteuse.
convict, *s.* forcat *m.*; — *v.a.* convaincre (de), condamner.
convince, *v. a.* convaincre (de).
convoy, *s.* convoi *m.*
cook, *s.* cuisinier, -ière *m. f.*; *head ~* chef *m.*; — *v.a.* faire cuire; *v.n.* cuire.
cooking, *s.* cuisine *f.*
cool, *adj.* frais *(f.* fraîche); *(fig.)* calme; — *v.a.* rafraîchir.
co-operate, *v.n.* coopérer.
co-operation, *s.* coopération *f.*

copper, *s.* cuivre *m.*
copy, *s.* copie *f.;* exemplaire *m.;* numéro *m.* — *v. a.* copier.
copy-book, *s.* cahier *m.*
copyright, *s.* droit *m.* d'auteur.
coral, *s.* corail *m.*
cord, *s.* corde *f.*
cordial, *adj.* cordial.
cork, *s.* bouchon *m.*
corkscrew, *s.* tire-bouchon *m.*
corn, *s.* grain *m.;* grains *m. pl.; (wheat)* blé *m; (maize)* maïs *m.*
corner, *s.* coin *m.*
corporal, *adj.* corporel; — *s.* caporal *m.*
corporation, *s.* corporation *f.*
corps, *s.* corps *m.*
corpse, *s.* cadavre *m.*
correct, *adj.* correct; exact; — *v.a.* corriger, rectifier.
correction, *s.* correction *f.;* rectification *f.*
correspond, *v.n.* correspondre; être conforme (à).
correspondence, *s.* correspondance *f.*
correspondent, *s.* correspondant *m.*
corresponding, *adj.* correspondant.
corridor, *s.* corridor *m.;* couloir *m.*
corridor-train, *s.* train *m.* à couloir.
corrupt, *adj.* corrompu.
cosmetics, *s. pl.* cosmétiques *m. pl.*, produits *m.pl.* de beauté.
cosmonaut, *s.* cosmonaute *m.*
cost, *s.* coût *m.*, frais *m. pl.;* prix *m.; ~ of living* coût de la vie; *at the ~ of* au prix de; — *v.n.* coûter.
costly, *adj.* coûteux.
costume, *s.* costume *m.*
cosy, *adj.* confortable.
cottage, *s.* chaumière *f.*
cotton, *s.* coton *m.*
couch, *s.* canapé *m.*, divan *m.*
cough, *s.* toux *f.;* — *v.n.* tousser.
council, *s.* conseil *m.*
councillor, *s.* conseiller *m.*
counsel, *s.* conseil *m.;* avocat *m.*
count[1], *s.* compte *m.; (title)* comte *m.*
count[2], *v.a.* & *n.* compter.
countenance, *s.* visage *m.;* air *m.*
counter, *s.* comptoir *m.*, guichet *m.;* jeton *m.*
counterfoil, *s.* souche *f.*
countersign, *v.a.* contresigner.
countess, *s.* comtesse *f.*
countless, *adj.* innombrable.
country, *s.* pays *m.; (not town)* campagne *f.*
countryman, *s.* campagnard *m.*
countryside, *s.* (les) campagnes *f.pl.*
countrywoman, *s.* paysanne *f.*
county, *s.* comté *m.*
couple, *s.* couple *f.*
courage, *s.* courage *m.*
courageous, *adj.* courageux.

course, *s.* cours *m.; route f.; (meal)* service *m.*, plat *m.*; *of* ~ bien entendu.
court, *s.* cour *f.*; tribunal *m.*; court *m.* (de tennis); — *v.a.* faire la cour à.
courteous, *adj.* courtois.
courtesy, *s.* courtoisie *f.*
courtship, *s.* cour *f.*
courtyard, *s.* cour *f.*
cousin, *s.* cousin, -e *m. f.*
cover, *s.* couverture *f.*; couvercle *m.*; *(meal)* couvert *m.*; *(post)* enveloppe *f.*; — *v.a.* couvrir.
cow, *s.* vache *f.*
coward, *s.* & *adj.* lâche *m.*
crab, *s.* crabe *m.*
crack, *s.* craquement *m.*; — *v.a.* faire craquer; *v.n.* craquer; se fêler.
cradle, *s.* berceau *m.*
craft, *s.* habileté *f.*; embarcation *f.*; métier *m.*; profession *f.*
craftsman, *s.* artisan *m.*
cram, *v.a.* fourrer; bourrer.
crane, *s.* grue *f.*
crash, *s.* fracas *m.*; débâcle; atterrissage brutal, collision; *v.n.* tomber avec fracas; s'écraser sur le sol.
crash-helmet, *s.* serre-tête *m.*
crave, *v.n.* ~ *for* désirer ardemment.
crawl, *v.n.* ramper; *(pers.)* se traîner.
crayon, *s.* crayon *m.*
craze, *s.* manie *f.*
crazy, *adj.* fou, toqué
creak, *s.* cri *m.*, grincement *m.*; — *v. n.* crier grincer.
cream, *s.* crème *f.*
crease, *s.* (faux) pli *m.*
create, *v.a.* créer.
creation, *s.* création *f.*
creature, *s.* créature *f.*
credit, *s.* crédit *m.*; mérite *m.*; honneur *m.*; *on* ~ à terme; *give* ~ *to* ajouter foi à; — *v.a.* ajouter foi à, créditer.
creditor, *s.* créancier *m.*
creek, *s.* crique *f.*
creep, *v.n.* ramper; se glisser.
crew, *s.* équipage *m.*; équipe *f.*
crib, *s.* mangeoire *f.*; lit *m.* d'enfant; berceau *m.*
cricket, *s.* *(game)* cricket *m.*
crime, *s.* crime *m.*
criminal, *adj.* & *s.* criminel, -elle.
cripple, *s.* estropié *m.*
crisis, *s.* crise *f.*
crisp, *adj.* croquant, croustillant; *(air)* vif.
critic, *s.* critique *m.*
critical, *adj.* critique.
criticize, *v.a.* critiquer.
critique, *s.* critique *f.*
croak, *v.n.* croasser.
crochet, *s.* crochet *m.*
crop, *s.* récolte *f.*; cueillette *f.*
cross, *s.* croix *f.*; — *v.a.* croiser, traverser.
crossing, *s.* passage *m.*;

(*sea*) traversée *f.*; *level* ~ passage à niveau.
cross-question, *s.* contre-interrogatoire *m.*; — *v.a.* contre-interroger.
cross-reference, *s.* renvoi *m.*
crossroad, *s.* chemin *m.* de traverse; ~*s* carrefour *m.*
cross-section, *s.* coupe *f.* en travers.
cross-word (puzzle) *s.* mots *m.pl.* croisés.
crouch, *v. n.* se blottir.
crow, *s.* corneille *f.*
crowd, *s.* foule *f.*; tas *m.*
crowded, *adj.* encombré, comble.
crown, *s.* couronne *f*; — *v.a.* couronner.
crucial, *adj.* décisif.
crude, *adj* brut; cru; grossier.
cruel, *adj.* cruel.
cruelty, *s.* cruauté *f.*
cruet, *s.* burette *f.*
cruise, *v.n.* croiser; — *s.* voyage *m.*
cruising, *adj.* ~ *speed* vitesse *f.* de croisière.
crumb, *s.* mie *f.*; miette *f.*
crumble, *v.a.* émietter; *v.n.* s'émietter.
crusade, *s.* croisade *f.*
crush, *s.* écrasement *m.*; cohue *f.*; — *v.a.* écraser.
crust, *s.* croûte *f.*
crutch, *s.* béquille *f.*
cry, *s.* cri *m.*; — *v.a.* crier; ~ *down* décrier; *v.n.* crier; (*weep*) pleurer.
crystal, *s.* cristal *m.*
cub, *s.* petit *m.*; (*boy scout*) louveteau *m.*
cube, *s.* cube *m.*
cuckoo, *s.* coucou *m.*
cucumber, *s.* concombre *m.*
cue, *s.* réplique *f.*
cuff, *s.* poignet *m.*, manchette *f.*
cuff-links, *s. pl.* boutons *m.pl.* de manchette.
culminate, *v.n.* se terminer.
culprit, *s.* accusé, -e *m. f.*
cultivate, *v.a.* cultiver.
cultural, *adj.* cultural.
culture, *s.* culture *f.*
cunning, *s.* ruse *f.*, finesse *f.*; — *adj.* rusé.
cup, *s.* tasse *f.*; gobelet *m.*
cupboard, *s.* armoire *f.*; placard *m.*
curate, *s.* vicaire *m.*
curb, *s.* gourmette *f.*
curd, *s.* (lait) caillé *m.*
curdle, *v.a.* cailler; *v.n.* se cailler.
cure, *s.* guérison *f.*; cure *f.*; remède *m.*; — *v.a.* guérir.
curiosity, *s.* curiosité *f.*
curious, *adj.* curieux.
curl, *s.* boucle *f.*; — *v.a.* & *n.* boucler, friser; ~ *up* s'enrouler.
curly, *adj.* bouclé, frisé.
currant, *s.* *black* ~ cassis *m.*; *red* ~ groseille *f.* rouge.
currency, *s.* circulation *f.*, cours *m.*; terme *m.* d'échéance; unité *f.* monétaire, monnaie *f.*; *foreign* ~ monnaie étrangère.
current, *adj.* courant, en

cours; *in ~ use* d'usage courant; *~ events* actualités *f.*; *~ account* compte *m.* courant; — *s.* courant *m.*; cours *m.*

curse, *s.* malédiction *f.*; — *v.a.* maudire; *v.n.* blasphémer.

curtain, *s.* rideau *m.*

curve, *s.* courbe *f.*

cushion, *s.* coussin *m.*

custom, *s.* coutume *f.*; *~s* douane *f.*; *~s duties* droits *m.* de douane; *~s declaration* déclaration *f.* de douane; *~s formalities* la visite de la douane.

customary, *adj.* coutumier; accoutumé.

customer, *s.* client *m.*, acheteur *m.*

custom-house, *s.* douane *f.*; *~ officer* douanier *m.*

cut, *v.a.* couper; trancher; tailler; hacher; *~ down* abattre, couper; réduire; *~ off* couper; *~ out* tailler; *~ up* couper, débiter; — *s.* *(knife)* coup *m.*; *(wound)* coupure *f.*; *(clothes)* coupe *f.*; *(meat)* morceau *m.*; *(in wages)* réduction *f.*

cutlery, *s.* coutellerie *f.*

cutlet, *s.* côtelette *f.*

cutter, *s.* tailleur *m.*; coupeur *m.*

cycle, *s.* cycle *m.*; bicyclette *f.*; — *v.n.* pédaler.

cycling, *s.* cyclisme *m.*

cylinder, *s.* cylindre *m.*

cynic, *adj.* & *s.* cynique *m.*

Czech, *adj.* tchèque; — *s.* Tchèque *m.*

D

dad, daddy, *s.* papa *m.*

dagger, *s.* poignard *m.*

daily, *adj.* journalier, quotidien; — *s.* (journal) quotidien *m.*

dainty, *adj.* friand, délicat; gentil; — *s.* friandise *f.*

dairy, *s.* laiterie *f.*

daisy, *s.* marguerite *f.*

dam, *s.* barrage *m.*; digue *f.*

damage, *s.* dommage *m.*; préjudice *m.*; *~s* dommages-intérêts *m.*

damn, *v.a.* condamner; — *s.* juron *m.*

damp, *adj.* humide; — *s.* humidité *f.*; — *v.a* mouiller, humecter.

dance, *s.* danse *f.*; bal *m.*; *v.n.* & *a.* danser.

dancer, *s.* danseur, -euse *m. f.*

dancing-hall, *s.* salle *f.* de danse; dancing *m.*

dancing-shoes, *s.pl.* souliers *m.* de bal, escarpins *m.*

Dane, *s.* Danois, -e *m. f.*

danger, *s.* danger *m.*

dangerous, *adj.* dangereux.

Danish, *adj.* danois; — *s.* *(language)* danois *m.*

dare, *v. aux.* & *a.* oser.

daring, *adj.* audacieux.

dark, *adj.* obscur, sombre; *(colour)* foncé; *(fig.)* triste; *be ~* faire som-

bre; — *s.* obscurité *f.*; *in the* ~ dans l'obscurité.
darken, *v.a.* obscurcir.
darkness, *s.* obscurité *f.*
darling, *adj.* & *s.* chéri, -e.
darn, *v.a.* repriser.
darning, *s.* reprise *f.*
dart, *s.* dard *m.*; ~*s (game)* fléchettes *f.pl.*
dash, *v.a.* lancer; flanquer (par terre); ~ *to pieces* briser en morceaux; *v.n.* ~ *against* se heurter contre; ~ *at* se précipiter sur — *s. (with pen)* trait *m.*, tiret *m.*; *(vigour)* élan *m.*, fougue *f.*; attaque *f.* soudaine.
dash-board, *s.* tablier *m*; tableau *m.* de bord.
data, *s. pl.* données *f.*
date[1], *s.* date *f.*; millésime *m.*; *be up to* ~ être à la page; — *v.a.* & *n.* dater.
date[2], *s.* datte *f.*
daughter, *s.* fille *f.*
daughter-in-law, *s.* belle-fille *f.*
dawn, *s.* point *m.* du jour; aube *f.*
day, *s.* jour *m.*; *(whole day)* journée *f.*
daylight, *s.* jour *m.*
daytime, *s.* jour *m.*, journée. *f.*
daze, *v.a.* étourdir; éblouir.
dazzle, *v.a.* éblouir.
deacon, *s.* diacre *m.*
dead, *adj.* mort; *the* ~ les morts *m.pl.*
deadly, *adj.* mortel.
deaf, *adj.* sourd; ~ *and dumb* sourd-muet.
deal, *v.a.* ~ *out* distribuer; donner; *v.n.* ~ *with* traiter qn; commercer, traiter avec qn; traiter (d'un sujet); ~ *in* commercer de; — *s. (cards)* donne *f.*; *(commerce)* affaire *f.*, *a good* ~, *a great* ~ beaucoup (de).
dealer, *s.* marchand *m.* *(in* de).
dean, *s.* doyen *m.*
dear, *s.* & *adj.* cher *m.*, chère *f.*
death, *s.* mort *f.*
debate, *s.* débat *m.*, discussion *f.*; — *v.a.* discuter, mettre en discussion.
debt, *s.* dette *f.*
debtor, *s.* débiteur, -trice *m. f.*
decay, *s.* décadence *f.*; — *v.n.* tomber en décadence; pourrir.
decease, *s.* décès *m.*; — *v.n.* décéder.
deceit, *s.* déception *f.*; tromperie *f.*
deceive, *v.a.* tromper; décevoir.
December, *s.* décembre *m.*
decent, *adj.* décent; assez bon.
deception, *s.* déception *f.*
decide, *v.a.* décider.
decision, *s.* décision *f.*
decisive, *adj.* décisif.
deck, *s.* pont *m.*
deck-chair, *s.* transatlantique *f.*
declaration, *s.* déclaration *f.*

declare, *v.a.* déclarer.
decline, *s.* décadence *f.*; — *v.a.* décliner; *v.n.* baisser.
decorate, *v.a.* décorer (de).
decoration, *s.* décoration *f.*
decrease, *v.a.* & *n.* diminuer; — *s.* diminution *f.*
decree, *s.* décret *m.*
dedicate, *v.a.* dédier.
deed, *s.* action *f.*; acte *m.*
deem, *v.a.* juger.
deep, *adj.* profond; *ten feet* ~ dix pieds de profondeur.
deer, *s.* cerf *m.*
deface, *v.a.* défigurer.
defeat, *s.* défaite *f.*; — *v.a.* vaincre.
defect, *s.* défaut *m.*
defence, *s.* défense *f.*
defend, *v.a.* défendre.
defender, *s.* défenseur *m.*
defer, *v.a.* retarder, ajourner; ~ *to* déférer à.
defiance, *s.* défi *m.*; *set at* ~ défier.
deficiency, *s.* manque *m.*
deficient, *adj.* insuffisant.
defile, *s.* défilé *m.*; — *v.n.* défiler; *v.a.* souiller.
define, *v.a.* définir.
definite, *adj.* déterminé, défini.
definition, *s.* définition *f.*
defy, *v.a.* défier; braver.
degrade, *v.a.* dégrader.
degree, *s.* degré *m.*; *(university)* grade m.; diplôme *m.*
delay, *s.* retard *m.*, délai *m.*; — *v.a.* retarder; différer; *v.n.* tarder.
delegate, *s.* délégué *m.*
delegation, *s.* délegation *f.*
deliberate, *adj.* délibéré; — *v.a.* & *n.* délibérer.
delicacy, *s.* délicatesse *f.*
delicate, *adj.* délicat.
delicious, *adj* délicieux.
delight, *v.a.* *be* ~*ed at* être enchanté dé.
delightful, *adj.* déliceux.
delinquent, *s.* délinquant *m.*
deliver, *v.a.* *(letters)* distribuer, *(goods etc.)* livrer, *(message)* remettre; *(speech)* faire, prononcer; *(free)* délivrer; *be* ~*ed of* accoucher de.
delivery, *s.* *(letters)* distribution *f.*, *(message)* remise *f.*, *(goods)* livraison *f.*; *(speech)* prononciation *f.*, débit *m.*
delusion, *s.* illusion *f.*
demand, *s.* demande, *f.* réclamation *f.*; — *v. a.* demander, réclamer.
democracy, *s.* démocratie *f.*
democrat, *s.* démocrate *m.*
democratic, *adj.* démocratique.
demolish, *v.a.* démolir.
demonstrate, *v.a.* démontrer.
demonstration, *s.* démonstration *f.*
den, *s.* antre *m.*; repaire *m.*
denial, *s.* dénégation *f.*
denomination, *s.* dénomination *f.*; secte *f.*
denote, *v.a.* dénoter.
denounce, *v.a.* dénoncer.
dense, *adj.* dense, épais.
density, *s.* densité *f.*

dentist, *s.* dentiste *m.*
denture, *s.* *(artificial)* dentier *m.*
deny, *v.a.* nier.
depart, *v.n.* partir.
department, *s.* département *m.*
departure, *s.* départ *m.*
depend, *v.n.* dépendre (de), compter (sur).
dependence, *s.* dépendance *f.*
dependent, *adj.* dépendant.
deplore, *v.a.* déplorer.
deposit, *s.* dépôt *m.*; — *v.a.* déposer.
depot, *s.* dépôt *m.*
depression *s.* abattement *m.*
deprive, *v.a.* priver (de).
depth, *s.* profondeur *f.*
deputy, *s.* délégué *m.*; vice-, sous-.
derive, *v.a.* retirer (de); *be* ~*d from* dériver de.
descend, *v.n.* descendre.
descendant, *s.* descendant, -e *m. f.*
descent, *s.* descente *f.*
describe, *v.a.* décrire.
description, *s.* description *f.*; sorte *f.*
desert, *s.* désert *m.*; — *v.a.* déserter.
deserve, *v.a.* mériter.
design, *s.* dessein *m.*; projet *m.*; dessin *m.*; — *v.a.* dessiner.
desirable, *adj.* désirable.
desire, *s.* désir *m.*; — *v.a.* désirer.
desk, *s.* bureau *m.*
desolation, *s.* désolation *f.*
despair, *s.* désespoir *m.*; — *v.n.* désespérer.
despatch *see* **dispatch.**
desperate, *adj.* **désespéré.**
despise, *v.a.* **mépriser.**
despite, *prep.* ~ *(of)* **en** dépit de.
dessert, *s.* dessert *m.*
destination, *s.* destination *f.*
destine, *v.a.* destiner.
destiny, *s.* destin *m.* destinée *f.*
destroy, *v.a.* **détruire.**
destruction, *s.* **destruction** *f.*
detach, *v.a.* **détacher.**
detachment, *s.* **détachement** *m.*
detail, *s.* détail *m.*
detain, *v.a.* **retenir;** détenir.
detect, *v.a.* découvrir.
detective, *s.* détective *m.*
detention, *s.* détention *f.*
detergent, *s.* détergent *m.*
deteriorate, *v.n.* se détériorer.
determination, *s.* détermination *f.*
determine, *v.a.* & *n.* déterminer, décider.
detrimental, *adj.* préjudiciable.
develop, *v.a.* développer; *v.n.* se développer.
development, *s.* développement *m.*
deviation, *s.* déviation *f.*
device, *s* expédient *m.*; invention *f.*
devil, *s.* diable *m.*
devilish, *adj.* diabolique.
devise, *v.a.* combiner; tramer.
devote, *v.a.* consacrer.
devoted, *adj.* dévoué.
devotion, *s.* dévotion *f.*;

dévouement *m*.
devour, *v.a.* dévorer.
dew, *s.* rosée *f*.
diagnosis, *s.* diagnostic *m*.
diagram, *s.* diagramme *m*.
dial, *s.* cadran *m.*; — *v.a.* composer un numéro.
dialogue, *s.* dialogue *m*.
diameter, *s.* diamètre *m*.
diamond, *s.* diamant *m.*; *(cards)* carreau *m*.
diaper, *s.* couche *f*.
diarrhoea, *s.* diarrhée *f*.
diary, *s.* journal *m.*; agenda *m*.
dictate, *v.a.* dicter; *v.n.* **~ *to*** donner des ordres à.
dictation, *s.* dictée *f*.
dictator, *s.* dictateur *m*.
dictionary, *s.* dictionnaire *m*.
die[1], *s.* dé *m*.
die[2], *v.n.* mourir.
Diesel engine, *s.* moteur *m.* Diesel; diesel *m*.
diet, *s.* alimentation *f.*; régime *m*.
differ, *v.n.* différer.
difference, *s.* différence *f*.
different, *adj.* différent.
difficult, *adj.* difficile.
difficulty, *s.* difficulté *f*.
diffuse, *adj.* diffus.
dig, *v.a.* bêcher.
digest, *v.a.* digérer.
digestion, *s.* digestion *f*.
dignity, *s.* dignité *f*.
diligent, *adj.* diligent.
dim, *adj.* faible, pâle, obscur.
dimension, *s.* dimension *f*.
diminish, *v. a. & n.* diminuer.
dimple, *s.* fossette *f*.
dine, *v.n.* dîner.
dining-car, *s.* wagon-restaurant *m*.
dining-hall, *s.* salle *f.* à manger; réfectoire *m*.
dining-room, *s.* salle *f.* à manger.
dinner, *s.* dîner *m*.
dinner-jacket, *s.* smoking *m*.
dip, *v.a. & n.* plonger.
diploma, *s.* diplôme *m*.
diplomacy, *s.* diplomatie *f*.
diplomat, *s.* diplomate *m*.
diplomatic, *adj.* diplomatique.
direct, *adj.* direct; — *v. a.* diriger; commander; adresser.
direction, *s.* direction *f*; instructions *f. pl.*
directly, *adv.* directement; tout de suite.
director, *s.* directeur *m*.
directory, *s.* annuaire *m.*; Bottin *m*.
dirt, *s.* saleté *f.*; boue *f.*, crotte *f.*; crasse *f*.
dirty, *adj.* sale; crotté; crasseux.
disadvantage, *s.* désavantage *m*.
disagree, *v.n.* différer; se brouiller; ne pas convenir (à).
disagreeable, *adj.* désagréable.
disappear, *v. n.* disparaître
disappearance, *s.* disparition *f*.
disappoint, *v.a.* désappointer; tromper.
disappointment, *s.* désappointement *m*.

disapprove, *v.n.* ~ *of* désapprouver qch.
disaster, *s.* désastre *m.*
disastrous, *adj.* désastreux.
disc *see* **disk.**
discern, *v.a.* discerner.
discharge, *v. a.* décharger; *(employee)* congédier; renvoyer; *(prisoner)* élargir; *(gas)* dégager; *(debt)* liquider; *(duty)* s'acquitter de; — *s.* décharge *f.*; *(employee)* congé *m.*; *(prison)* élargissement *m.*
discipline, *s.* discipline *f.*
disclose, *v.a.* découvrir.
discontented, *adj.* mécontent (de).
discourage, *v. a.* décourager.
discouragement, *s.* découragement *m.*
discourse, *s.* discours *m.*
discover, *v.a.* découvrir.
discovery, *s.* découverte *f.*
discredit, *s.* discrédit *m.*; — *v.a.* discréditer.
discreet, *adj.* discret.
discretion, *s.* discrétion *f.*; prudence *f.*
discuss, *v.a.* discuter.
discussion, *s.* discussion *f.*
disdain, *v.a.* dédaigner; — *s.* dédain *m.*
disease, *s.* maladie *f.*
disembark *v.a.* & *n.* débarquer.
disgrace, *s.* disgrâce *f.*; — *v.a.* disgracier.
disgraceful, *adj.* honteux.
disguise, *s.* déguisement; — *v.a.* déguiser.
disgust, *s.* dégoût *m.*; — *v.a.* dégoûter.
disgusting, *adj.* dégoûtant
dish, *s.* plat *m.*; mets *m.*; *wash up the ~es* laver la vaisselle.
dishonest, *adj.* malhonnête.
dishonour, *s.* déshonneur *m.*; — *v.a.* déshonorer *(bill)* ne pas honorer.
disinfect, *v. a.* désinfecter.
disk, *s.* disque *m.*
dislike, *s.* aversion *f.*, dégoût *m.*; — *v.a.* ne pas aimer.
dismal, *adj.* lugubre, sombre.
dismay, *s.* consternation *f.*
dismiss, *v.a.* congédier; bannir, écarter.
disobedience, *s.* désobéissance *f.*
disobedient, *adj.* désobéissant.
disobey, *v. a.* désobéir (à).
disorder, *s.* désordre *m.*
dispatch, *s.* expédition *f.*; dépêche *f.*
dispensary, *s.* pharmacie *f.*
dispense, *v.a.* dispenser; préparer; *v.n.* ~ *with* se disposer de.
disperse, *v.a.* disperser.
displaced, *adj.* ~ *person* personne *f.* déplaeée.
displacement, *s.* déplacement *m.*
display, *v.a.* exposer; étaler; déployer, faire preuve de; — *s.* exposition *f.*; étalage *m.*; parade *f.*
displease, *v.a.* déplaire à
disposal, *s.* *at s.o.'s* ~ à la disposition de qn.

dispose, *v.n.* ~ *of* disposer de; vendre.
disposition, *s.* disposition *f.*
dispute, *s.* dispute *f.* discuission *f.*; — *v.a* discuter; *v. n.* se disputer.
disqualify, *v.a.* disqualifier.
dissatisfy, *v.a.* mécontenter.
dissolve, *v.a.* dissoudre; *v.n.* se dissoudre.
distance, *s.* distance *f.*
distant, *adj.* lointain; éloigné.
distil, *v. a.* & *n.* distiller.
distinct, *adj.* distinct (de); marqué.
distinction, *s.* distinction *f.*
distinguish, *v.a.* distinguer.
distract, *v.a.* distraire.
distraction, *s.* distraction *f.*; confusion *f.*
distress, *s.* détresse *f.*; — *v.a.* affliger.
distribute, *v. a.* distribuer.
distribution, *s.* distribution *f.*
district, *s.* région *f.*, contrée *f.*; district *m.*
disturb, *v.a.* troubler; déranger.
disturbance, *s.* trouble *m.*, dérangement *m.*
ditch, *s.* fossé *m.*
dive, *v.n.* plonger (*into* dans).
diver, *s.* plongeur *m.*, scaphandrier *m.*
divergent, *adj.* divergent.
diversion, *s.* déviation *f.*
divide, *v.a.* divider.
dividend, *s.* dividende *m.*
divine, *adj.* divin.
divinity, *s.* théologie *f.*
division, *s.* division *f.*
divorce, *s.* divorce *m.*; — *v. a.* divorcer (d'avec).
dizzy, *adj. feel* ~ avoir le vertige.
do, *v.. a.* faire; finir; ~ *away with* supprimer; ~ *up* envelopper; ~ *with* se contenter de.
dock, *s.* bassin *m.*
doctor, *s.* docteur *m.*; médecin *m.*
doctrine, *s.* doctrine *f.*
document, *s.* document *m.*
dog, *s.* chien *m.*
dogma, *s.* dogme *m.*
doll, *s.* poupée *f.*
dollar, *s.* dollar *m.*
domestic, *adj.* & *s.* domestique (*m. f.*).
domicile, *s.* domicile *m.*
dominate, *v.a.* &. *n.* dominer.
dominion, *s.* domination *f.*; ~*s* colonies *f.*
donkey, *s.* âne *m.*
doom, *s.* sentence *f.*; — *v.a.* condamner; ~*ed to* voué à.
door, *s.* porte *f.*; (*vehicle*) portière *f.*
dormitory, *s.* dortoir *m.*
dose, *s.* dose *f.*
dot, *s.* point *m.*
double, *adj.* & *s.* double (*m.*).
doubt, *s.* doute *m.*; *no* ~ sans doute; — *v.a.* & *n.* douter.
doubtful, *adj.* douteux.
doubtless, *adj.* sans doute.

dough, *s.* pâte *f.*

dove, *s.* colombe *f.*

down, *adv.* à bas, en bas, par en bas; *be* ~ *with (illness)* être au lit avec; *fall* ~ tomber à terre; *go* ~ aller en bas; — *prep.* le long de; ~ *the river* en aval; ~ *the street* plus bas dans la rue.

downhill, *s.* pente *f.*; — *adv.* en pente, en descendant.

downstairs, *adv.* en bas.

downwards, *adv.* en bas.

dozen, *s.* douzaine *f.*

draft, *s.* projet *m.*; *(letter)* minute *f.*; *(troops)* détachement *m.*; *(drawing)* esquisse *f.*

drag, *v.a.* traîner; tirer.

drain, *s.* égout *m.*, canal *m.*; — *v.a.* drainer; vider.

drama, *s.* drame *m.*; théâtre *m.*

dramatic, *adj.* dramatique.

draper, *s.* marchand *m.* d'étoffes, (marchand) drapier *m.*; ~'s magasin *m.* de nouveautés.

draught, *s.* tirage *m.*; *(drink)* trait *m.*; *(air)* courant *m.* d'air.

draw, *v.a.* *(pull)* tirer, traîner; *(tooth)* arracher; *(sketch)* dessiner; ~ *down* baisser; ~ *on* tirer; ~ *out* prolonger; — *v. n.* tirer; ~ *near* s'approcher.

drawer, *s.* **tiroir** *m.*

drawing, *s.* **dessin** *m.*

drawing-pin, *s.* punaise *f.*

drawing-room, *s.* **salon** *m.*

dread, *v.a.* redouter.

dreadful, *adj.* **redoutable.**

dream, *s.* rêve *m.*; — *v.a.* & *n.* rêver.

dress, *s.* habits *m.pl.*; robe *f.*; — *v. a.* **habiller**; *v.n.* s'habiller; ~ *a wound* panser.

dress-circle, *s.* **(premier)** balcon *m.*

dressing-gown, *s.* *(woman)* peignoir *m.*, *(man)* **robe** *f.* de chambre.

dressmaker, *s.* couturière *f.*

drift, *v.n.* **flotter**; **dériver**; — *s.* dérive *f.*; amoncellement *m.*

drill, *s.* foret *m.*; *(soldiers)* exercice *m.*

drink, *s.* boisson *f.*; — *v.a.* boire.

drip, *v.n.* dégoutter.

drive, *v.a.* conduire; ~ *in (nail)* enfoncer; *v.n.* conduire; aller en voiture.

driver, *s.* *(engine)* mécanicien *m.*; *(bus)* conducteur *m.*; *(car)* chauffeur *m.*

driving, *s.* conduite *f.*; ~ *licence* permis *m.* de conduire.

drop, *s.* goutte *f.*; — *v.a.* laisser tomber; **abandonner**; *v.n.* (dé)-goutter; ~ *in* entrer en passant.

drown, *v.a.* noyer; *v.n.* se noyer.

drug, *s.* drogue *f.*

druggist, *s.* **droguiste** *m.*

drum, *s.* tambour *m.*

drunk, *adj.* ivre.

dry, *adj.* sec, sèche; aride; tari; — *v.a.* sécher.
dry-clean, *v.a.* nettoyer à sec.
dual, *adj.* double.
dub, *v.a.* doubler.
duchess, *s.* duchesse *f.*
duck, *s.* cane *f.*; canard *m.*
due, *adj.* *(proper)* dû; *(owing)* exigible; échéant, payable; *in ~ form* en bonne et due forme; *in ~ time* en temps voulu; *~ to* causé par, par suite de; *the train is ~ at* le train arrive à; — *s.* dû *m.*; droit *m.*
duke, *s.* duc *m.*
dull, *adj.* borné; ennuyeux; *(colour)* terne; *(weather, sad)* triste.
dumb, *adj.* muet.
dummy, *s.* mannequin *m.*; *(cards)* mort *m.*
dung, *s.* fumier *m.*
dupe, *s.* dupe *f.*; — *v.a.* duper.
duplicate, *s.* duplicata *m.*; — *adj.* en double; — *v.a.* faire en double.
during, *adv.* pendant, au cours de.
dusk, *s.* crépuscule *m.*
dust, *s.* poussière *f.*
dustbin, *s.* poubelle *f.*
dusty, *adj.* poussiéreux, poudreux.
Dutch, *adj.* hollandais.
Dutchman, *s.* Hollandais *m.*
duty, *s.* devoir *m.*; *(customs)* droit *m.*; *(task)* tâche *f.*, fonction(s) *f.(pl.)*; *be on ~* être de service.
duty-free, *adj.* exempt de droits, en franchise.
dwarf, *s.* nain, -e *m. f.*
dwell, *v.n.* habiter; *~ (up)on* s'appesantir sur.
dwelling, *s.* habitation *f.*
dwelling-house *s.* maison *f.* d'habitation.
dwindle, *v.n.* diminuer.
dye, *s.* teinte *f.*, teinture *f.*; — *v.a.* teindre.
dynasty, *s.* dynastie *f.*

E

each, *pron.* chacun, -e; *~ other* l'un l'autre; — *adj.* chaque.
eager, *adj.* ardent.
eagle, *s.* aigle *m.*
ear, *s.* oreille *f.*
earl, *s.* comte *m.*
early, *adv.* de bonne heure — *adj.* précoce; premier.
earn, *v. a.* gagner; mériter
earnest, *adj.* sérieux.
earnings, *s.pl.* salaire *m.*
earth, *s.* terre *f.*
earthenware, *s.* poterie *f.*
earthquake, *s.* tremblement *m.* de terre.
ease, *s.* aise *f.*; repos *m.*; *at one's ~* à son aise; *with ~* avec facilité.
east, *s.* est *m.*; — *adj.* d'est, de l'est; — *adv.* à l'est (de).
Easter, *s.* Pâques *m. pl.*
eastern, *adj.* (de l')est, oriental.
eastwards, *adv.* vers l'est.
easy, *adj.* facile.

easy-chair, *s.* fauteuil *m.*
easy-going, *adj.* nonchalant.
eat, *v.a.* manger; *~ up* finir; dévorer.
ebb, *s.* reflux *m.*
ecclesiastic, *adj.* & *s.* ecclésiastique *(m.).*
economic, *adj.* économique.
economical, *adj.* économe.
economics, *s.* économie *f.* politique.
economize, *v.n.* faire des économes.
economy, *s.* économie *f.*
ecstasy, *s.* extase *f.*
edge, *s.* tranchant *m.*, fil *m.*; bord *m.*
edition, *s.* édition *f.*
editor, *s.* rédacteur *m.*
editorial, *s.* article *m.* de fond.
educate, *v.a.* élever.
education, *s.* éducation *f.*
effect, *s.* effet *m.*
effective, *adj.* efficace; effectif.
efficiency, *s.* efficacité *f.*
efficient, *adj.* capable.
effort, *s.* effort *m.*
egg, *s.* œuf *m.*; *boiled ~* œuf à la coque; *fried ~* œuf sur le plat.
Egyptian, *adj.* égyptien; — *s.* Egyptien, -enne *m. f.*
eight, *adj.* & *s.* huit.
eighteen, *adj.* & *s.* dix-huit.
eighteenth, *adj.* dix-huitième.
eighth, *adj.* huitième.
eighty, *adj.* & *s.* quatre-vingt(s).
either, *pron.* & *adj.* l'un ou l'autre; chacun; chaque; *~ ... or* ou ... ou.
elaborate, *v.a.* élaborer; — *adj.* minutieux.
elastic, *adj.* élastique.
elbow, *s.* coude *m.*
elderly, *adj.* d'un certain âge.
elect, *v.a.* choisir; élire.
election, *s.* élection *f.*
electric(al), *adj.* électrique; *~al engineer* (ingénieur) électricien *m.*
electricity, *s.* électricité *f.*
electron, *s.* électron *m.*
electronic, *adj.* électronique.
elegance, *s.* élégance *f.*
elegant, *adj.* élégant.
element, *s.* élément *m.*
elementary, *adj.* élémentaire.
elephant, *s.* éléphant *m.*
elevate, *v.a.* élever.
eleven, *adj.* & *s.* onze.
eleventh, *adj.* onzième.
elm, *s.* orme *m.*
else, *adj.* autre; *anything ~, madam?* encore quelque chose, Madame?; — *adv. or ~* ou bien, autrement.
elsewhere, *adv.* ailleurs.
embankment, *s.* remblai *m.*
embark, *v.a.* embarquer; *v.n.* s'embarquer.
embarrass, *v.a.* embarrasser.
embassy, *s.* ambassade *f.*
embrace, *v.a.* embrasser.
embroidery, broderie *f.*

emerge, *v.n.* émerger; apparaître.
emergency, *s.* circonstance *f.* critique; *in case of* ~ en cas d'accident *or* d'urgence; ~ *exit* sortie *f.* de secours.
emigrant, *s.* émigrant, -e *m. f.*
emigrate, *v.n.* émigrer.
emigration, *s.* émigration *f.*
eminent, *adj.* éminent.
emit, *v.a.* émettre.
emotion, *s.* émotion *f.*
emphasis, *s.* accent *m.*, force *f.*; *lay* ~ *on* appuyer sur.
emphasize, *v. a.* appuyer sur.
empire, *s.* empire *m.*
employ, *v.a.* employer.
employee, *s.* employé *m.*
employer, *s.* employeur *m.*
employment, *s.* emploi *m.*
empty, *adj.* vide.
enable, *v. a.* rendre capable.
enclose, *v.a.* entourer (de); joindre (à une lettre).
encounter, *v.a.* affronter; rencontrer.
encourage, *v.a.* encourager.
encouragement, *s.* encouragement *m.*
encyclopaedia, *s.* encyclopédie *f.*
end, *s.* bout *m.*; fin *f.*; — *v.a.&n.* finir; ~ *in* finir en.
endeavour, *s.* effort *m.*; — *v. n.* s'efforcer (à *or* de).
ending, *s.* terminaison *f.*; fin *f.*
endless, *adj.* sans fin.
endorse, *v.a.* endosser.
endorsement, *s.* endossement *m.*
endow, *v.a.* doter (de).
endure, *v.a.* supporter, endurer.
enemy, *s.* ennemi, -e *m. f.*
energetic, *adj.* énergique.
energy, *s.* énergie *f.*
enforce, *v.a.* imposer; *(law)* faire exécuter.
engage, *v.a.* engager; fiancer; *be* ~*d* être occupé; être fiancé(e).
engagement, *s.* engagement *m.*; fiançailles *f. pl.*
engine, *s.* machine *f.*
engine-driver, *s.* mécanicien *m.*
engineer, *s.* ingénieur *m.*
English, *adj.* anglais.
Englishman, *s.* Anglais *m.*
Englishwomen, *s.* Anglaise *f.*
enjoy, *v. a.* jouir de; trouver bon; ~ *oneself* s'amuser.
enjoyment, *s.* jouissance *f.*
enlarge, *v.a.* agrandir.
enlist, *v.a.* enrôler.
enormous, *adj.* énorme.
enough, *adj.* & *adv.* assez (de).
enquire *see* **inquire.**
enrage, *v.a.* exaspérer.
enrol(l), *v.a.* enrôler.
ensign, *s.* *(flag)* drapeau *m.*, pavillon *m.*; *(pers.)* porte-drapeau *m.*
ensue, *v.n.* s'ensuivre.
enter, *v.a.* entrer (d[illegible]

(in list) inscrire.
enterprise, *s.* entreprise *f.*
entertain, *v.a.* amuser; recevoir; avoir (une opinion).
entertainment, *s.* divertissement *m.;* amusement *m.;* hospitalité *f.*
enthusiasm, *s.* enthousiasme. *m.*
enthusiastic, *adj.* enthousiaste.
entire, *adj.* entier.
entirely, *adv.* entièrement.
entitle, *v.a. be ~d to* avoir droit à.
entrance, *s.* entrée *f.; ~ examination* examen d'entrée *m.*
entreat, *v.a.* supplier.
entry, *s.* entrée *f.;* inscription *f.*
enumerate, *v.a.* énumérer.
envelope, *s.* enveloppe *f.*
envious, *adj.* envieux (de).
enviromment, *s.* milieu *m.*
envy, *s.* envie *f.;* — *v.a.* envier.
epidemic, *s.* épidémie *f.*
equal, *adj.* égal.
equality, *s.* égalité *f.*
equation, *s.* équation *f.*
equip, *v.a.* équiper.
equipment, *s.* équipement *m.*
erase *v.a.* effacer.
erect, *adj.* droit ; — *v.a.* dresser; ériger.
err, *v.n.* errer.
error, *s.* erreur *f.*
escalator, *s.* escalator *m.*, escalier *m.* roulant.
escape, *v. n.* (s')échapper; — *s.* fuite *f.*
escort, *s.* escorte *f.;* — *v.a.* escorter.
essay, *s.* essai *m.*, composition *f.*
essential, *adj.* essentiel.
establish, *v.a.* établir.
establishment, *s.* établissement *m.*
estate, *s.* propriété *f.*; biens *m. pl.*
esteem, *s.* estime *f.;* — *v.a.* estimer.
estimate, *s.* estimation *f.;* évaulation *f.;* — *v.a.* estimer.
eternal, *adj.* éternel.
eucharist, *s.* eucharistie *f.*
European, *adj.* européen.
evacuate, *v.a.* évacuer.
even, *adj.* uni; égal; pair; — *adv.* même; *~ if* même si.
evening, *s.* soir *m.; (party)* soirée *f.*
event, *s.* événement *m.*
eventual, *adj.* éventuel.
ever, *adv.* toujours; *(any time)* jamais.
evermore, *adv.* toujours.
every, *adj. (all)* tous; *(each)* chaque; *~ day* tous les jours.
everybody, *pron.* tout le monde.
everyday, *adj.* de tous les jours.
everyone *see* **everybody.**
everything, *pron.* tout *m.*
everywhere, *adv.* partout.
evidence, *s.* évidence *f.*
evident, *adj.* évident.
evil, *s.* mal *m.;* — *adj.* mauvais.
evolution, *s.* évolution *f.*
ewe, brebis *f.*

exact, *adj.* exact.
exactly, *adv.* exactement.
exaggerate, *v.a.* exagérer.
exaggeration, *s.* exagération *f.*
examination, *s.* examen *m.*
examine, *v.a.* examiner; vérifier; *(customs)* visiter.
example, *s.* exemple *m.*; *for* ~ par exemple.
excavation, *s.* fouille *f.*
exceedingly, *adv.* excessivement.
excel, *v. a.* surpasser; *v. n.* exceller à.
excellent, *adj.* excellent.
except, *v.a.* excepter; — *prep.* excepté; sauf; ~ *for* exception faite pour.
exception, *s.* exception *f.*
exceptional, *adj.* exceptionnel.
excess, *s.* excès *m.*; ~ *luggage* excédent *m.* de bagages.
excessive, *adj.* excessif.
exchange, *s.* échange *m.*; *(telephone)* bureau central *m.*; *foreign* ~ change *m.*; — *v.a.* échanger.
excite, *v.a.* exciter.
excitement, *s.* excitation *f.*
exclaim, *v.n.* s'écrier.
exclamation, *s.* exclamation *f.*
exclude, *v.a.* exclure.
exclusive, *adj.* exclusif.
excursion, *s.* excursion *f.*
excuse, *s.* excuse *f.*; — *v.a.* excuser.
execute, *v.a.* exécuter.
execution, *s.* exécution *f.*
executive, *adj.* & *s.* exécutif *m.*; agent *m.* d'exécution
exempt, *adj.* exempt (de); *v.a.* exempter (de).
exercise, *s.* exercice *m.*; — *v.a.* exercer.
exertion, *s.* effort *m.*
exhaust, *v.a.* épuiser.
exhaust-pipe, *s.* tuyau *m.* d'échappement.
exhibit, *v. a.* présenter, exhiber; exposer.
exhibition, *s.* exhibition *f.*; exposition *f.*
exist, *v.n.* exister.
existense, *s.* existence *f.*
exit, *s.* sortie *f.*
expand, *v.a.* étendre; dilater.
expansion, *s.* expansion *f.*
expect, *v.a.* attendre, s'attendre à; *(think)* croire.
expedient, *s.* expédient *m.*
expedition, *s.* expédition *f.*
expel, *v.a.* expulser.
expense, *s.* dépense *f.*
expensive, *adj.* coûteux, cher.
experience, *s.* expérience *f.*; — *v.a.* éprouver.
experiment, *s.* expérience *f.*; — *v.n.* faire des expériences, expérimenter.
experimental, *adj.* expérimental.
expert, *s.* expert *m.*
expire, *v.n.* expirer.
explain, *v.a.* expliquer.
explanation, *s.* explication *f.*
exploration, *s.* exploration.
explore, *v.a.* explorer.

explosion, *s.* explosion *f.*
export, *s.* exportation *f.*; **~s** articles *m.pl.* d'exportation; — *v.a.* exporter.
exporter, *s.* exportateur *m.*
expose, *v.a.* exposer.
exposure, *s.* exposition *f.*; révélation *f.*
express, *adj.* exprès; formel; exact; ~ *letter* lettre *f.* par exprès; — *s.* *(train)* express *m.*; — *v.a.* exprimer.
expression, *s.* expression *f.*
exquisite, *adj.* exquis.
extend, *v.a.* étendre; prolonger.
extension, *s.* extension *f.*; prolongation *f.*
extensive, *adj.* étendu, vaste.
extent, *s.* étendue *f.*
extinguish, *v.a.* éteindre.
extra, *adj.* supplémentaire.
extract, *s.* extrait *m.*; — *v.a.* extraire.
extraordinary, *adj.* extraordinaire.
extravagant, *adj.* extravagant.
extreme, *adj.* & *s.* extrême *(m.)*.
extremely, *adv.* extrêmement.
extremity, *s.* extrèmité *f.*
eye, *s.* œil *m.*
eyebrow, *s.* sourcil *m.*
eyelid, *s.* paupière *f.*
eyepiece, *s.* oculaire *m.*

F

fable, *s.* fable *f.*
fabric, *s.* tissu *m.*; textile *m.*
face, *s.* visage *m.*; face *f.*; figure *f.*; *in ~ of* devant; — *v.a.* affronter, faire face à, braver.
facility, *s.* facilité *f.*
fact, *s.* fait *m.*; *in ~* de fait; en effet.
factor, *s.* facteur *m.*; élément *m.*
factory, *s.* fabrique *f.*; usine *f.*
faculty, *s.* faculté *f.*
fade, *v.n.* se faner; ~ *away* s'évanouir.
fail, *v.n.* manquer (de); *(not succeed)* échouer, *(in an exam)* être refusé.
failure, *s.* insuccès *m.*
faint, *v.n.* s'évanouir.
fair, *adj.* beau; bel, belle; *(hair)* blond; *(just)* juste; *(weather)* clair; ~ *play* jeu loyal *m.*
fairly, *adv.* assez bien.
faith, *s.* foi *f.*
faithful, *adj.* fidèle.
falcon, *s.* faucon *m.*
fall, *v.n.* tomber; baisser; ~ *back on* avoir recours à; ~ *in* s'effondrer; ~ *off* se déprécier; ~ *under* être compris dans; — *s.* chute *f.*; baisse *f.*
false, *adj.* faux; artificiel.
falter, *v.n.* hésiter.
fame, *s.* réputation *f.*; renommée *f.*
familiar, *adj.* familier, intime (avec).
family, *s.* famille *f.*
famous, *adj.* célèbre, fa-

meux.

fan[1], *s.* éventail *m.*; ventilateur *m.*

fan[2], *s.* passionné, -e *m. f.*, fervent *m.*

fancy, *s.* fantaisie *f.*, imagination *f.*

fantastic, *adj.* fantastique; fantasque.

far, *adv.* loin; ~ *off* au loin; *as* ~ *as* autant que; *by* ~ de beaucoup; *how* ~ *is it?* à quelle distance est-ce?; — *adj.* lointain.

fare, *s.* prix de (la) place *m.*; *(taxi)* prix de la course *m.*; *(food)* chère *f.*

farewell, *s.* adieu *m.*; *bid* ~ *to* dire adieu à.

farm, *s.* ferme *f.*

farmer, *s.* fermier *m.*

farming, *s.* agriculture *f.*

farmyard, *s.* cour *f.* de ferme.

farther, *adv.* plus loin (que).

fashion, *s.* mode *f.*; manière *f.*

fashionable, *adj.* élégant.

fast, *adj.* vite, rapide; *be* ~ *(clock)* avancer; — *adv.* vite.

fasten, *v.a.* attacher.

fastener, *s.* attache *f.*; agrafe *f.*; *zip* ~ fermeture éclair *f.*

fat, *adj.* gros, gras; — *s.* gras *m.*; graisse *f.*

fatal, *adj.* fatal.

fate, *s.* destin *m.*, sort *m.*

father, *s.* père *m.*

father-in-law, *s.* beau-père *m.*

fatigue, *s.* fatigue *f.*

fault, *s.* défaut *m.*; faute *f.*

faultless, *adj.* sans faute.

faulty, *adj.* défectueux.

favour, *s.* faveur *f.*; *in* ~ *of* en faveur de; *do a* ~ rendre un service (à).

favourable, *adj.* favorable.

favourite, *adj.* favori.

fear, *s.* crainte *f.*; — *v.a.& n.* craindre.

fearful, *adj.* affreux, effrayant.

feast, *s.* fête *f.*; festin *m.*

feat, *s.* exploit *m.*

feather, *s.* plume *f.*

feature, *s.* trait *m.*; caractéristique *f.*; ~ *film* le grand film.

February, *s.* février *m.*

federal, *adj.* fédéral.

federation, *s.* fédération *f.*

fee, *s.* honoraires *m. pl.*; *(school)* ~*s* frais *m. pl.*

feeble, *adj.* faible.

feed, *v. a.* nourrir; paître

feel, *v.n.&a.* (se) sentir éprouver, ressentir *(with hand)* toucher tâter; ~ *cold* avoir froid.

feeling, *s.* sentiment *m*

fellow, *s.* camarade *m.*, compagnon *m.*; garçon *m.*; *(of a society)* membre *m.*, *(university)* agrégé *m.*

fellowship, *s.* camaraderie *f.*; communauté *f.*

female, *adj.* féminin; *(animal)* femelle; — *s.* femme *f.*; femelle *f.*

feminine, *adj.* féminin.

fence, *s.* clôture *f.*; palissade *f.*; — *v.a.* enclore; *v. n.* faire de

l'escrime.
fencing, *s.* escrime *f.*
fender, *s.* pare-choc(s) *m.*
ferry, *s.* (passage *m.* en) bac *m.*
ferry-boat, *s.* bac *m.*
fertile, *adj.* fertile.
fertilize, *v.a.* fertiliser.
festival, *s.* festival *m.*
fetch, *v.a.* aller chercher; apporter.
feudal, *adj.* féodal.
fever, *s.* fièvre *f.*
few, *pron.* & *adj.* peu (de); *a* ~ quelques(-uns).
fiancé, -e, *s.* fiancé, -e *m. f.*
fibre, *s.* fibre *f.*
fiction, *s.* fiction *f.*; *(novels)* romans *m. pl.*
field, *s.* champ *m.*; *(sport)* terrain *m.*
fierce, *adj.* cruel, violent, féroce.
fiery, *adj.* de feu; ardent.
fifteen, *adj.* & *s.* quinze *(m.)*.
fifteenth, *adj.* quinzième.
fifth, *adj.* cinquième; cinq.
fiftieth, *adj.* cinquantième.
fifty, *adj.* & *s.* cinquante *(m.)*.
fig, *s.* figue *f.*
fight, *s.* combat *m.*; lutte *f.*
fighter, *s.* combattant *m.*; avion *m.* de chasse.
figure, *s.* figure *f.*; *(arithm.)* chiffre *m.*
file[1], *s.* *(tool)* lime *f.*; — *.a.* limer.
file[2], *s.* classeur *m.*, dossier *m.*; liasse *f.*; *(people)* file *f.*; — *v.a.* **classer**; enregistrer.
filing-cabinet, *s.* **cartonnier** *m.*, fichier *m.*
fill, *v.a.* remplir; **occuper**; ~ *in*, *up* remplir.
film, *s.* *(photo)* **pellicule** *f.*; *(cinema)* **film** *m.*
filter, *s.* filtre *m.*; — *v.a.* filtrer.
filthy, *adj.* sale; *(fig.)* obscène.
fin, *s.* nageoire *f.*
final, *adj.* final.
finally, *adv.* enfin.
finance, *s.* finance *f.*
financial, *adj.* financier.
find, *v.a.* trouver; ~ *out* inventer, découvrir.
fine[1], *s.* *(penalty)* amende *f.*; — *v.a.* mettre à l'amende.
fine[2], *adj.* fin; beau.
finger, *s.* doigt *m.*; *first* ~ index *m.*
finger-print, *s.* empreinte *f.* digitale.
finish, *v. a.* finir; terminer.
Finnish, *adj.* finlandais.
fir, *s.* sapin *m.*
fire, *s.* feu *m.*; *on* ~ en feu; — *v.a.* mettre feu à; *(gun)* tirer; *v.n.* tirer.
fire-arm, *s.* arme *f.* à feu.
fire-brigade, *s.* les pompiers *m. pl.*
fire-engine, *s.* pompe *f.* à incendie.
fire-escape, *s.* escalier *m.* de sauvetage.
fireplace, *s.* cheminée *f.*
fire-station, *s.* poste *m.*

d'incendie.
fireworks, *s.pl.* feu *m.* d'artifice.
firm¹, *s.* maison *f.* (de commerce).
firm², *adj.* ferme.
firmament, *s.* firmament *m.*
firmness, *s.* fermeté *f.*
first, *adj.* premier; — *adv.* premièrement; d'abord; *(railway)* en première; *at* ~ d'abord.
firstly, *adv.* premièrement.
first-rate, *adj.* de premier ordre.
fish, *s.* poisson *m.*; — *v. a. & n.* pêcher.
fisher(man), *s.* pêcheur *m.*
fishmonger, *s.* poissonnier *m.*
fist, *s.* poing *m.*
fit¹, *s.* attaque *f.*; accès *m.*
fit², *adj.* convenable, bon, propre; en état (de), capable (de).
five, *adj. & s.* cinq *(m.)*.
fix, *v.a.* fixer; ~ *up* arranger.
flag, *s.* drapeau *m.*; *(navy)* pavillon *m.*
flagrant, *adj.* flagrant.
flake, *s.* flocon *m.*
flame, *s.* flamme *f.*
flannel, *s.* flanelle *f.*
flap, *s.* coup *m.*, tape *f.*
flare, *v.n.* flamboyer.
flash, *s.* éclair *m.*; — *v.n.* jeter des éclairs, étinceler.
flashlight, *s.* flash (électronique) *m.*
flat¹, *adj.* plat; insipide; *(postitive)* formel, net; — *s.* plat *m.*; *(music)* bémol *m.*
flat², *s.* appartement *m.*; étage *m.*
flatter, *v.a.* flatter.
flattery, *s.* flatterie *f.*
flavour, *s.* saveur *f.*, goût *m.*, arome *m.*
flax, *s.* lin *m.*
flea, *s.* puce *f.*
flee, *v.a. & n.* **fuir, se** sauver.
fleece, *s.* toison *f.*
fleet, *s.* flotte *f.*
flesh, *s.* chair *f.*; viande *f.*
flexible, *adj.* flexible.
flight, *s.* vol *m.* *(birds, stairs)* volée *f.*; *(fleeing)* fuite *f.*
flimsy, *adj.* ténu; **fragile;** frivole.
fling, *v.a.* jeter.
flirt, *s.* coquette *f.*; — *v.n.* flirter.
float, *v.n.* flotter; *v.a.* faire flotter.
flock, *s.* troupeau *m.*, troupe *f.*
flood, *s.* inondation *f.*; *(tide)* flux *m.*; — *v.a.* inonder.
flood-light, *v.a.* illuminer par projecteurs.
floor, *s.* plancher *m.*, parquet *m.*; *(storey)* étage *m.*
flour, *s.* farine *f.*
flourish, *v.n.* fleurir; prospérer.
flow, *v.n.* couler, s'écouler; — *s.* flux *m.*; **cours** *m.*
flower, *s.* fleur *f.*
flower-bed, *s.* plate-bande *f.*
flu, *s.* grippe *f.*

flue, *s.* tuyau *m.*
fluent, *adj.* facile, coulant.
fluid, *adj.* & *s.* fluide *(m.)*.
fluorescent, *adj.* ~ *lamp* tube *m.* fluorescent.
flush, *v.a.* inonder; nettoyer avec une chasse d'eau; *v. n.* rougir.
flute, *s.* flûte *f.*
flutter, *s.* voltigement *m.*; — *v. a.* agiter; *v. n.* voltiger.
fly[1], *s.* mouche *f.*
fly[2], *v.n.* voler; prendre l'avion (pour).
foam, *s.* écume *f.*; *(beer)* mousse *f.*
focus, *s.* foyer *m.*
fodder, *s.* fourrage *m.*
fog, *s.* brouillard *m.*
foil[1], *s.* feuille *f.*; tain *m.*
foil[2], *s.* *(fencing)* fleuret *m.*
fold, *s.* pli *m.*; — *v.a.* plier; envelopper; *(arms)* croiser; ~ *up* replier.
folding, *adj.* pliant.
foliage, *s.* feuillage *m.*
folk, *s.* gens *m. pl.*
follow, *v.a.* suivre; accompagner; *v.n.* suivre; s'ensuivre; *as* ~*s* comme suit.
follower, *s.* suivant *m.*, compagnon *m.*, partisan *m.*
following, *adj.* suivant; *the* ~ ce qui suit.
folly, *s.* sottise *f.*
fond, *adj. be* ~ *of* aimer.
food, *s.* nourriture *f.*, aliments *m. pl.*
fool, *s.* sot *m.*
foolish, *adj.* sot; fou.
foot, *s.* pied *m.*; *on* ~ à pied.
football, *s.* football *m.*; ballon *m.*
foot-brake, *s.* frein *m.* à pied
foot-note, *s.* note *f.* (au bas de la page).
footstep, *s.* pas *m.*
for[1], *prep.* pour; *(in exchange for)* contre; *(because of)* à cause de; *(time)* pendant; *(in spite of)* malgré.
for[2], *conj.* car.
forbid, *v.a.* défendre; interdire.
force, *s.* force *f.*; violence *f.*; — *v.a.* forcer.
forearm, *s.* avant-bras *m.*
forecast, *s.* prévision *f.*; — *v.a.* prévoir.
forefinger, *s.* index *m.*
foreground, *s.* premier plan *m.*
forehead, *s.* front *m.*
foreign, *adj.* étranger.
foreigner, *s.* étranger, -ère *m. f.*
foremost, *adj.* premier; — *adv. first and* ~ tout d'abord.
foresee, *v.a.* prévoir.
forest, *s.* forêt *f.*
foretell, *v.a.* prédire.
foreword, *s.* avant-propos *m.*
orge, *v.a.* forger.
forgery, *s.* contrefaçon *f.*; faux *m.*
forget, *v.a.* oublier.
forgetful, *adj.* oublieux.
forgive, *v.a.* pardonner.
fork, *s.* fourchette *f.*; *(hay)* fourche *f.*

form, *s.* forme *f.; (bench)* banc *m.; (class)* classe *f.; (paper)* formule *f.;* **~** *of government* régime *m.;* — *v.a.* former.
formal, *adj.* formel.
formality, *s.* formalité *f.*
former, *pron.* le premier, la première; celui-là, celle-là; — *adj.* premier, -ère; précédent.
formerly, *adv.* autrefois.
formula, *s.* formule *f.*
forsake, *v. a.* abandonner.
fortieth, *adj.* quarantième.
fortification, *s.* fortification *f.*
fortify, *v.a.* fortifier.
fortnight, *s.* quinze jours *m. pl.*
fortress, *s.* forte sse *f.*
fortunate, *adj.* ureux.
fortunately *ad* heureusement
fortune, *s.* fortune *f*
forty, *adj.* & *s.* quarante *(m.).*
forward, *adv.* en avant; *go* **~** (s')avancer; — *adj.* avancé; — *v.a.* faire suivre; expédier.
forwarding, *s.* expédition *f.;* **~** *agency* entreprise *f.* de transport.
forwards, *adv.* en avant.
foul, *adj.* sale; impure; *(language)* ordurier.
found, *v. a.* fonder.
foundation, *s.* fondation *f.*
founder, *s.* fondateur *m.*
fountain, *s.* fontaine *f.*
fountain-pen, *s.* stylo(graphe) *m.*
four, *adj.* & *s.* quatre *(m.).*
fourteen, *adj.* & *s.* quatorze *(m.).*
fourth, *adj.* quatrième; quatre.
fowl, *s.* poule *f.*
fox, *s.* renard *m.*
fraction, *s.* fraction *f.*
fracture, *s.* fracture *f.*
fragile, *adj.* fragile.
fragment, *s.* fragment *m.*
fragrant, *adj.* parfumé.
frame, *s. (picture)* cadre *m.; (structure)* charpente *f.; (window)* châssis *m.*
framework, *s.* charpente *f.*
frank, *adj.* franc.
frankness, *s.* franchise *f.*
fraud, *s.* fraude *f.*
free, *adj.* libre; **~** *of, from* exempt de.
freedom, *s.* liberté *f.*
freely, *adv.* librement; gratis.
freeze, *v.a.* geler.
freight, *s.* fret *m.*
French, *adj.* français; — *s. (language)* le français; *the* **~** les Français *m. pl.*
French-bean(s), *s. (pl.)* haricots *m. pl.* verts.
Frenchman, *s.* Français *m.*
Frenchwoman, *s.* Française *f.*
frequent, *adj.* fréquent; — *v. a.* fréquenter.
frequently, *adv.* fréquemment.
fresh, *adj.* frais, fraîche; nouveau, nouvel, -elle.
friar, *s.* moine *m.*
fricassee, *s.* fricassée *f.*
friction, *s.* friction *f.*
Friday, *s.* vendredi *m.*
fridge, *s.* frigo *m.*

friend, *s.* ami, -e *m. f.*
friendly, *adj.* aimable; ami; amical.
friendship, *s.* amitié *f.*
fright, *s.* peur *f.; take* ~ prendre peur.
frighten, *v.a.* effrayer.
frightful, *adj.* affreux; effrayant.
frock, *s.* robe *f.*
frog, *s.* grenouille *f.*
frolic, *s.* ébats *m. pl.;* — *v.n.* folâtrer, gambader.
from, *prep. (place)* de; *(time)* depuis; *(separation)* de, à; *(change)* de.
front, *s.* front *m.;* devant *m.;* façade *f.; in* ~ *of* en face de, en avant de; — *adj.* de devant.
front-door, *s.* porte *f.* d'entrée.
frontier, *s.* frontière *f.*
frost, *s.* gelée *f.*
frosty, *adj.* de gelée; *fig.* froid.
frown, *v.a. & n.* froncer les sourcils.
frozen, *adj.* gelé.
fruit, *s.* fruit *m.*
fruitful, *adj.* fructueux.
fruit-tree, *s.* arbre fruitier *m.*
frustrate, *v.a.* déjouer; décevoir; contrecarres.
fry, *v. a. & n.* (faire) frire.
frying-pan, *s.* poêle (à frire) *f.*
fuel, *s.* combustible *m.*
fulfil, *v.a.* accomplir.
full, *adj.* plein; complet; ~ *name* les nom et prénoms *m. pl.;* ~ *stop* point *m.*
full-time, *adj.* de toute la journée.
fully, *adv.* pleinement.
fume, *s.* fumée *f.*
fun, *s.* amusement *m.; for* ~ pour rire.
function, *s.* fonction *f.*
fund, *s.* fonds *m.*
fundamental, *adj.* fondamental.
funeral, *s.* funérailles *f. pl.*
funnel, *s.* entonnoir *m.; (steamer)* cheminée *f.*
funny, *adj.* drôle.
fur, *s.* fourrure *f.*
fur-coat, *s.* manteau *m.* de fourrure.
furious. *adj.* furieux.
furnace, *s.* fourneau *m.*
furnish, *v. a.* pourvoir (de), fournir; meubler (de).
furniture, *s.* meubles *m. pl.,* ameublement *m.; piece of* ~ meuble *m.*
furrier, *s.* fourreur *m.*
furrow, *s.* sillon *m.*
further, *adv.* plus loin; *(any longer)* davantage; — *adj.* ultérieur; autre; plus lointain; supplémentaire, nouveau.
furthermore, *adv.* en outre, de plus.
fury, *s.* fureur *f.; (pers.)* furie *f.*
fuss, *s.* embarras *m.;* bruit *m.; make a* ~ faire des embarras; — *v. n.* faire des embarras; ~ *about* faire l'affairé.
future, *s.* avenir *m.; (gramm.)* futur *m.; in the* ~ à l'avenir; — *adj.* futur.

G

gain, *s.* gain *m.;* — *v.a.*

gagner.
gait, *s.* allure *f.*
gala, *s.* gala *m.*
gale, *s.* grand vent *m.*
gall, *s.* bile *f.*; fiel *m*; amertume *f.*
gallant, *adj.* brave; galant.
gallery, *s.* galerie *f.*
gallon, *s.* gallon *m.*
gallop, *s.* galop *m.*; — *v.n.* galoper.
gamble, *v. n.* jouer; — *s.* jeu *m.*
game, *s.* jeu *m.*; partie *f.*; *(animal)* gibier *m.*
gamekeeper, *s.* garde-chasse *m.*
gang, *s.* bande *f.*; équipe *f.*
gangway, *s.* passage *m.*
gaol *see* **jail.**
gap, *s.* trou *m.*; brèche *f.*; vide *m.*
gape, *v.n.* bâiller; *stand gaping* gober des mouches; *~ at* regarder bouche bée.
garage, *s.* garage *m.*
garden, *s.* jardin *m.*
gardener, *s.* jardinier *m.*
garlic, *s.* ail *m.*
garment, *s.* vêtement *m.*
garnish, *s.* garniture *f.*; — *v.a.* garnir.
garter, *s.* jarretière *f.*
gas, *s.* gaz *m.*
gasp, *s.* soupir *m.*
gas-works, *s. pl.* usine *f.* à gaz.
gate, *s.* porte *f.*
gateway, *s.* portail *m.*
gather, *v.a.* réunir; amasser; cueillir; *(understand)* conclure; *v.n.* s'assembler.
gathering, *s.* rassemblement *m.*; abcès *m.*
gauge, *s.* jauge *f.*; calibre *m.*; indicateur *m.*; — *v.a.* jauger; calibrer.
gauze, *s.* gaze *f.*
gay, *adj.* gai.
gear, *s.* attirail *m.*, appareil *m.*; *(motorcar)* vitesse *f.*
gear-box, *s.* boîte *f.* des vitesses.
gear-lever, *s.* levier *m.* des vitesses.
general, *adj.* général; — *s.* général *m.* *(pl.* généraux).
generation, *s.* génération *f.*
generator, *s.* générateur *m.*
generosity, *s.* générosité *f.*
generous, *adj.* généreux.
genial, *adj.* doux, douce; bienfaisant.
genius *s.* génie *m.*
gentle, *adj.* doux, douce.
gentleman, *s.* gentleman *m.*
genuine, *adj.* authentique; vrai.
geographical, *adj.* géographique.
geography, *s.* géographie *f*
geology, *s.* géologie *f.*
geometric(al), *adj.* géométrique.
geometry, *s.* géométrie *f.*
germ, *s.* germe *m.*
German, *adj.* allemand; — —*s.* Allemand, -e *m.f.*
gesticulate, *v.n.* gesticuler.
gesture, *s.* geste *m.*
get, *v.a.* obtenir, procurer, trouver, recevoir; — *v.n.* arriver; *(become)* devenir; *~ at* parvenir (à); *~ in* entrer;

~ *off* partir; ~ *on* prospérer; *(agree)* s'accorder (avec); ~ *out of* sortir (de); ~ *over* surmonter; *(illness)* se remettre; ~ *up* se lever.
geyser, *s.* chauffe-bain *m.*
ghost, *s.* esprit *m.;* revenant *m.*, fantôme *m.*
giant, *s.* géant *m.*
gift, *s.* don *m.*
gifted, *adj.* bien doué.
gills, *s. pl.* ouïes *f.*
gin, *s.* genièvre *m.;* gin *m.*
giraffe, *s.* girafe *f.*
girdle, *s.* ceinture *f.;* — *v.a.* ceinturer.
girl, *s.* jeune fille *f.*
give, *v. a.* donner; ~ *up* renoncer à; livrer; *v.n.* ~ *in* céder (à).
glacier, *s.* glacier *m.*
glad, *adj.* heureux; content; joyeux.
gladness, *s.* joie *f.*
glance, *s.* coup *m.* d'œil,; — *v. n.* ~ *at* jeter un regard sur.
glare, *s.* lumière *f.* éblouissante; clinquant *m.;* — *v.n.* briller d'un éclat éblouissant.
glass, *s.* verre *m.; (pane)* vitre *f.;* ~*es* lunettes *f. pl.*
glazier, *s.* vitrier *m.*
gleam, *s.* lueur *f.;* — *v. n.* luire.
glide, *v. n.* glisser; planer.
glider, *s.* planeur *m.*
glimmer, *s.* lueur *f.;* — *v.n.* jeter une lueur faible.
glimpse, *s.* coup *m.* d'œil (rapide).
glitter, *v.n.* étinceler.
globe, *s.* globe *m.*
gloomy, *adj.* sombre.
glorious, *adj.* glorieux.
glory, *s.* gloire *f.*
glove, *s.* gant *m.*
glow, *v.n.* luire rouge; *(joy)* rayonner; *(coal)* être rouge; — *s.* chaleur *f.;* lumière *f.; fig.* ardeur *f.*
glue, *s.* colle (forte) *f.;* — *v.a.* coller.
gnat, *s.* cousin *m.;* moustique *f.*
gnaw, *v.a. & n.* ronger.
go, *v. n.* aller; ~ *away* s'en aller; ~ *back* retourner; ~ *back on one's word* reprendre sa parole; ~ *down* descendre; baisser; ~ *in for* s'occuper de, s'adonner à, faire (de); ~ *into* entrer dans; ~ *off* s'en aller; ~ *on* continuer; *(happen)* se passer; ~ *out* sortir; ~ *over, through* traverser; *(read)* parcourir; ~*up* monter; ~ *with* accompagner; ~ *without* se passer de; *let* ~ lâcher prise.
goal, *s.* but *m.*
goalkeeper, *s.* gardien (de but) *m.*
goat, *s.* bouc *f.*, chèvre *f.*
God, *s.* Dieu *m.*
god-child, *s.* filleul, -e *m. f.*
godfather, *s.* parrain *m.*
godmother, *s.* marraine *f.*
goggles, *s. pl.* bésicles *f.*
gold, *s.* or *m.*
golden, *adj.* d'or, en or.

golf, *s.* golf *m.*
good, *adj.* bon; *~ evening!* bonsoir!; *~ morning!* bonjour!; *be so ~ as to* avoir la bonté de; *make ~* remplir; indemniser de; – *s.* bien *m.*; *~s* marchandise *f.*; *~s station* gare *f.* de marchandises; *~s train* train *m.* de marchandises.
good-bye, *int.* & *s.* adieu *(m.)*.
good-looking, *adj.* de belle mine, beau.
goodness, *s.* bonté *f.*
good-tempered, *adj.* de caractère facile, de bonne humeur.
goodwill, *s.* bonne volonté *f.*
goose, *s.* oie *f.*
gooseberry, *s.* groseille *f.* à maquereau.
gospel, *s.* évangile *m.*
gossip, *s.* bavardage *m.*; racontar *m.*, cancan *m.*; *(pers.)* compère *m.*; commère *f.*; – *v.n.* bavarder.
Gothic, *adj.* gothique.
govern, *v.a.* & *n.* gouverner.
governess, *s.* gouvernante *f.*
government, *s.* gouvernement *m.*
governor, *s.* gouverneur *m.*
gown, *s.* robe *f.*
grace, *s.* grâce *f.*
graceful, *adj.* gracieux.
gracious, *adj.* gracieux.
grade, *s.* grade *m.*; classe *f.*
gradual, *adj.* graduel.
graduate, *s.* gradué, -e *m. f.*; – *v.a.* graduer; *v.n.* prendre ses diplômes.
grain, *s.* grain *m.*
grammar, *s.* grammaire *f.*
grammar-school, *s.* lycée *m.*, collège *m.*
grammatical, *adj.* grammatical.
gram(me), *s.* gramme *m.*
gramophone, *s.* gramophone *m.*, phonographe *m.*
gramophone-record, *s.* disque *m.*
grand, *adj.* grand; magnifique; *~ stand* tribune *f.*
grandchild, *s.* petit-fils *m.*, petite-fille *f.* *(pl.* petits-enfants *m.)*
granddaughter, *s.* petite-fille *f.*
grandfather, *s.* grand-père *m.*
grandmother, *s.* grand'mère *f.*
grandson, *s.* petit-fils *m.*
granite, *s.* granit *m.*
granny, *s.* grand'maman *f.*
grant, *v.a.* accorder, concéder; accéder; *~ that* admettre que; – *s.* don *m.*, concession *f.*; subside *m.*
grape, *s.* grain *m.* de raisin; *bunch of ~s* grappe *f.* de raisin.
grape-fruit, *s.* pamplemousse *f.*
graph, *s.* graphique *m.*, courbe *f.*
graphic, *adj.* graphique.

grasp, *v.a.* saisir; comprendre; — *s.* prise *f.*, étreinte *f.*
grass, *s.* herbe *f.*; gazon *m.*
grasshopper, *s.* sauterelle *f.*
grate, *s.* grille *f.*; — *v.a.* râper; faire grincer; *v.n.* grincer.
grateful, *adj.* reconnaissant (à).
gratitude, *s.* reconnaissance *f.*
grave[1], *s.* tombe *f.*, tombeau *m.*
grave[2], *adj.* grave.
gravel, *s.* gravier *m.*
gravy, *s.* jus *m.*
gray, *adj.* gris.
graze, *v.n.* paître.
grease, *s.* graisse *f.*; — *v.a.* graisser.
great, *adj.* grand; *a* ~ *many* beaucoup (de).
greatly, *adj.* très; beaucoup.
greatness, *s.* grandeur *f.*
greed, *s.* avidité *f.*
greedy, *adj.* avide.
Greek, *adj.* grec, grecque; —*s.* Grec *m.*, Grecque *f.*
green, *adj.* vert.
greengrocer, *s.* fruitier, -ère *m. f.*
greenhouse, *s.* serre *f.*
greet, *v.a.* saluer.
greeting, *s.* salutation *f.*
grey, *adj.* gris.
grief, *s.* chagrin *m.*
grieve, *v.a.* affliger; *v.n.* s'affliger.
grill, *s.* gril *m.*; — *v.a.* griller.
grim, *adj.* sévère, menaçant, sinistre.
grin, *v.n.* grimacer; ~ *at* faire des grimaces à; — *s.* rire *m.*; grimace *f.*
grind, *v.a.* moudre.
grinder, *s.* *(tooth)* molaire *f.*
grindstone, *s.* meule *f.*
grip, *s.* étreinte *f.*; prise *f.*; — *v.a.* saisir, étreindre.
groan, *v. n.* gémir; — *s.* gémissement *m.*
grocer, *s.* épicier, -ère *m. f.*; ~*'s (shop)* épicerie *f.*
grocery, *s.* épicerie *f.*
groove, *s.* rainure *f.*
gross, *adj.* gros; grossier; *(weight)* brut.
ground, *s.* terre *f.*; terrain *m.*; *(reason)* raison *f.*; ~*s* jardins *m. pl.*; — *v.a.* fonder.
group, *s.* groupe *m.*
grow, *v.a.* cultiver; *v.n.* *(pers.)* grandir; *(plant)* croître; *(become)* devenir.
growl, *s.* grondement *m.*; — *v.n.* gronder.
grown-up, *s.* grande personne *f.*
growth, *s.* croissance *f.*; culture *f.*; récolte *f.*
grudge, *s.* rancune *f.*; — *v.a.* donner à contrecœur à.
grumble, *v.n.* grommeler; — *s.* grognement *m.*
grunt, *s.* grognement *m.*; — *v.n.* grogner.
guarantee, *s.* garantie *f.*; *(pers.)* garant, -e *m. f.*; — *v.a.* garantir.
guard, *s.* garde *f.*; *(train)* conducteur *m.*; — *v.a.* garder; *v.n.* ~ *against*

se garder.
guardian, *s.* gardien, -enne *m. f.*
guess, *v.a.* & *n.* deviner; conjecturer; — *s.* conjecture *f.*
guest, *s.* invité *m.*, convive *m.;* hôte, -esse *m. f.*
guide, *s.* guide *m.;* — *v. a.* guider.
guide-book, *s.* guide *m.*
guilt, *s.* culpabilité *f.*
guilty, *adj.* coupable (de).
guitar, *s.* guitare *f.*
gulf, *s.* golfe *m.*
gull, *s.* mouette *f.*
gullet, *s.* gosier *m.*
gum[1], *s.* gomme *f.;* — *v.a.* gommer.
gum[2], *s.* *(teeth)* gencive *f.*
gun, *s.* fusil *m.;* canon *m.*
gush, *v.i.* jaillir; — *s.* jaillissement *m.*
gutter, *s.* *(street)* ruisseau *m.*
gymnasium, *s.* gymnase *m.*
gymnastics, *s.* gymnastique *f.*

H

haberdashery, *s.* mercerie *f.*
habit, *s.* habitude *f.*
hail, *s.* grêle *f.;* — *v.n.* grêler.
hair, *s.* *(single)* cheveu *m.; (whole)* cheveux *m. pl.; (animal)* poil *m.*
hairdresser, *s.* coiffeur, -euse *m. f.*
half, *s.* moitié *f.;* demi *m.;* — *adj.* demi; ~ *an hour* une demi-heure *f.*
half-time, *s.* mi-temps *m.*
half-way, *adv.* à mi-chemin; à moitié chemin; à mi-distance.
hall, *s.* (grande) salle *f.; (college)* réfectoire *m.; (house)* vestibule *m.; (hotel)* hall *m.*
halt, *s.* halte *f.; v.a.* faire arrêter; *v.n.* faire halte; boiter.
ham, *s.* jambon *m.*
hammer, *s.* marteau *m.*
hand, *s.* main *f.; (pers.)* ouvrier *m.; (clock)* aiguille *f.; on the one* ~ ...*on the other* d'une part ... d'autre part.
handbag, *s.* sac (à main) *m.*
handbook, *s.* manuel *m.*
handkerchief, *s.* mouchoir *m.*
handle, *s.* manche *m.*, anse *f.;* poignée *f.;* bras *m.;* — *v.a.* manier; traiter.
hand-made, *adj.* fait à la main.
handsome, *adj.* joli.
handwriting, *s.* écriture *f.*
handy, *adj.* *(pers.)* adroit; *(thing)* commode.
hang, *v.a.* pendre; *(with tapestry)* tendre; ~ *up* accrocher; *v. n.* pendre; dépendre (de).
hanger, *s.* crochet *m.;* cintre *m.*
happen, *v.n.* arriver; se trouver; *I ~ed to be present* je me trouvais là par hasard.
happiness, *s.* bonheur *m.*
happy, *adj.* heureux.
harbour, *s.* port *m.*

hard, *adj.* dur; difficile; sévère; ~ *up* gêné; — *adv.* durement; *work* ~ travailler dur.
hardly, *adv.* à peine.
hardware, *s.* quincaillerie *f.*
hare, *s.* lièvre *m.*
harm, *s.* mal *m.*; tort *m.*; *do* ~ *to* nuire à.
harmful, *adj.* nuisible.
harmless, *adj.* inoffensif.
harmony, *s.* harmonie *f.*
harness, *s.* harnais *m.*
harp, *s.* harpe *f.*
harsh, *adj.* revêche; âpre; rigoureux.
hart, *s.* cerf *m.*
harvest, *s.* moisson *f.*; *(crop)* récolte *f.*
haste, *s.* hâte *f.*; *make* ~ se dépêcher.
hasten, *v.a.* hâter; *v. n.* se dépêcher.
hasty, *adj.* précipité.
hat, *s.* chapeau *m.*
hate, *v. a.* haïr; — *s.* haine *f.*
hateful, *adj.* odieux.
hatred, *s.* haine *f.*
haul, *v.a.* traîner; haler; — *s.* traction *f.*
haulage, *s.* roulage *m.*; frais *m.pl.* de roulage.
haunch, *s.* hanche *f.*
haunt, *v.a.* fréquenter; hanter.
have, *v.a.* avoir; *(food)* prendre; ~ *to* il faut que, il faut (+ *inf.*); *had rather* préférer (+ *inf.*); ~ *on (clothes)* porter.
haversack, *s.* havresac *m.*
hawk, *s.* faucon *m.*
hay, *s.* foin *m.*
hazard, *s.* hasard *m.*
hazy, *adj.* brumeux; *(fig.)* vegue.
he, *pron.* il, *(alone)* lui; ~ *who* celui qui
head, *s.* tête *f.*; *chief)* chef *m.*; *(river)* source *f.*; — *v.a.* être en tête de; — *adj.* principal.
headache, *s.* mal *m.* de tête.
heading, *s.* en-tête *m.*
headlight, *s.* phare *m.*, projecteur *m.*
headline, *s.* manchette *f.*
headmaster, *s.* directeur *m.*
headquarters, *s. pl* quartier *m.* général.
heal, *v.a.* guérir; *v.n.* se guérir.
health, *s.* santé *f.*
healthy, *adj.* bien portant; sain.
heap, *s.* amas *m.*, tas *m.*; — *v.a.* ~ *up* entasser.
hear, *v.a.* entendre; *(listen to)* écouter; *v. n.* entendre; ~ *from* recevoir une lettre de; ~ *of* avoir des nouvelles de; entendre parler de.
heart, *s.* cœur *m.*; *by* ~ par cœur.
hearth, *s.* foyer *m.*
hearty, *adj.* cordial.
heat, *s.* chaleur *f.*; *(anger)* colère *f.*; — *v.a.&n.* chauffer.
heating, *s.* chauffage *m.*
heave, *v.a.* lever; pousser; jeter; *v.n.* se soulever.
heaven, *s.* ciel *m.*
heavy, *adj.* pesant; lourd.
hedge, *s.* haie *f.*

hedgehog, *s.* hérisson *m.*
heed, *s.* attention *f.; take ~ to* faire attention à.
heedless, *adj.* insouciant; inattentif.
heel, *s.* talon *m.*
height, *s.* hauteur *f.*
heir, *s.* héritier *m.*
heiress, *s.* héritière *f.*
helicopter, *s.* hélicoptère *m.*
hell, *s.* enfer *m.*
hello, *int.* allô!
helm, *s.* barre (du gouvernail) *f.*
helmet, *s.* casque *m.*
help, *v.a.* aider; secourir; *~ oneself* se servir; — *s.* aide *f.*
helpful, *adj. (pers.)* serviable; *(thing)* utile.
helping, *s.* portion *f.*
helpless, *adj.* sans secours.
hem, *s.* ourlet *m.;* bord *m.*
hen, *s.* poule *f.*
hence, *adv. (place, time)* d'ici; *(reason)* de là.
her, *pron. (acc.)* la; *(dat.)* lui; *(alone)* elle.
herb, *s.* herbe *f.*
herd, *s.* troupeau *m.*
here, *adv.* ici; *from ~* d'ici; *look ~!* dites donc!; *~ he is!* le voici!
heritage, *s.* héritage *m.*
hermit, *s.* ermite *m.*
hero, *s.* héros *m.*
heroic, *adj.* héroïque.
heroine, *s.* héroïne *f.*
herring, *s.* hareng *m.*
hers, *pron.* à elle; le sien, la sienne, les siens, les siennes.
herself, *pron.* elle-même; *(reflex.)* se.
hesitate, *v.n.* hésiter.
hew, *v.a.* couper.
hiccough, hiccup, *s.* hoquet *m.*
hide, *v.a.* cacher; *v.n.* se cacher.
hideous, *adj.* hideux; horrible.
high, *adj.* haut; *(speed)* grand; *(price)* élevé; — *adv.* haut.
highness, *s.* altesse *f.*
highroad, highway, *s.* grande route *f.*
hike, *v.n.* faire du tourisme à pied.
hiker, *s.* touriste *f.*, randonneur, -euse (à pied) *m. f.*
hill, *s.* colline *f.*
hilly, *adj.* montueux.
him, *pron. (acc.)* le; *(dat.)* lui; *(alone)* lui.
himself, *pron.* lui-même; *(reflex.)* se; *by ~* tout seul.
hinder, *v.a.* empêcher.
hindrance, *s.* empêchement *m.*
hinge, *s.* gond *m.;* charnière *f.;* — *v.n.* tourner (sur).
hint, *s.* allusion *f.;* avis *m.;* — *v.n. ~ at* faire allusion à.
hip, *s.* hanche *f.*
hire, *s.* louage *m.; for ~* à louer; — *v.a. & n.* louer.
his, *pron.* son, sa; ses.
hiss, *s.* sifflement *m.;* — *v. a. & n.* siffler.
historic(al), *adj.* historique.
history, *s.* histoire *f.*
hit, *v.a.* frapper; atteindre; trouver; —

s. coup *m.*; succès *m.*
hitch-hike, *v.n.* faire de l'auto-stop.
hive, *s.* ruche *f.*
hoard, *s.* magot *m.*, amas *m.*; — *v. a.* thésauriser; entasser.
hoarse, *adj.* raque.
hobby, *s.* dada *m.*
hockey, *s.* hockey *m.*
hoe, *s.* houe *f.*
hog, *s.* porc *m.*
hoist, *v.a.* hisser; —*s.* monte-charge *m.*
hold, *v.a.* tenir; retenir; maintenir; contenir; *(consider)* tenir (pour); ~ *back* retenir; ~ *out* tendre; offrir ; ~ *that* soutenir que; — *v.n.* tenir; *(be true)* être vrai; ~ *on* ne pas lâcher prise; ~ *out* durer.
holder, *s.* possesseur *m.*
hole, *s.* trou *m.*
holiday, *s.* fête *f.*, jour *m.* férié; *(holidays)* vacances *f. pl.*, congé *m.*; *be on* être en congé, en vacance(s).
hollow, *adj.* creux, -euse; *fig.* faux, fausse.
holy, *adj.* saint; bénit.
home, *s.* foyer *m.*, demeure *f.*; *at* ~ chez soi, à la maison; — *adv.* chez soi; *come, go* ~ rentrer; — *adj.* domestique; de l'intérieur.
homeless, *adj.* sans asile.
homely, *adj.* simple; modeste.
homesickness, *s.* mal du pays *m.*
homeward, *adv.* vers la maison; ~ *bound* en retour.
honest, *adj.* honnête.
honesty, *s.* honnêteté *f.*
honey, *s.* miel *m.*
honeymoon, *s.* lune *f.* de miel.
honour, *s.* honneur *m.*; — *v.a.* honorer.
hood, *s.* capuchon *m.*; capeline *f.*; *(motor)* capote *f.*
hoof, *s.* sabot *m.*
hook, *s.* crochet *m.*, croc *m.*; *(fishing)* hameçon *m.*
hoop, *s.* cercle *m.*
hoot, *v.a.* huer; *v.n.* corner; — *s.* huée *f.*
hooter, *s.* sirène *f.*; corne *f.*, trompe *f.*
hop, *v.n.* sautiller.
hope, *s.* espérance *f.*; espoir *m.*; — *v.n.* espérer.
hopeful, *adj.* plein d'espoir.
hopeless, *adj.* sans espoir
horizon, *s.* horizon *m.*
horizontal, *adj.* horizontal.
horn, *s.* corne *f.*; trompe *f.*
horrible, *adj.* affreux, -euse.
horse, *s.* cheval *m.* *(pl.* chevaux).
horseback: *on* ~ à cheval.
horseman, *s.* cavalier *m.*
horse-race, *s.* course *f.* de chevaux.
horseshoe, *s.* fer *m.* à cheval.
hose, *s.* bas *m. pl.*
hospitable, *adj.* hospitalier.
hospital, *s.* hôpital *m.*
hospitality, *s.* hospita-

lité *f*.
host, *s*. hôte *m*.
hostel, *s*. pension *f*. pour étudiants, hôtellerie *f*.
hostess, *s*. hôtesse *f*.
hostile, *adj*. hostile (à).
hostility, *s*. hostilité *f*.
hot, *adj*. chaud.
hotel, *s*. hôtel *m*.
hour, *s*. heure *f*.
house, *s*. maison *f*.; *(theatre)* salle *f*.
household, *s*. ménage *m*.
housekeeper, *s*. gouvernante *f*.
housekeeping, *s*. ménage *m*.
housewife, *s*. ménagère *f*.
housework, *s*. travaux *(m. pl.)* domestiques; *do the* ~ faire le ménage.
how, *adv*. comment; ~ *many, much?* combien de?; ~ *long?* combien de temps?; ~ *are you?* comment allez-vous?
however, *adv*. de quelque manière que...; toutefois, cependant.
howl, *v. a.* & *n*. hurler; — *s*. hurlement *m*.
hue, *s*. couleur *f*.; cri *m*.
hug, *v.a.* serrer dans les bras.
huge, *adj*. énorme.
hullo, *int*. holà!; allô!
hum, *v. n.* bourdonner; — *s*. bourdonnement *m*.
human, *adj*. humain.
humanity, *s*. humanité *f*.
humble, *adj*. humble.
humorous, *adj*. amusant; humoristique; drôle.
humour, *s*. humour *m*.; *be in a* ~ *to* être d'humeur à.
hundred, *s*. cent *m*.
hundredth, *adj*. centième.
hundredweight, *s*. quintal *m*.
Hungarian, *adj*. hongrois; — *s*. Hongrois, -e *m*. *f*.
hunger, *s*. faim *f*.; — *v.n.* avoir faim.
hungry, *adj*. affamé; *be* ~ avoir faim.
hunt, *v.a.* & *n*. chasser; *(with hounds)* chasser à courre; — *s*. chasse (à courre) *f*.
hunter, *s*. chasseur *m*.
hurl, *v.a.* jeter; lancer.
hurry, *s*. hâte; *be in a* ~ *to* être pressé de; — *v.n.* se presser; ~ *up!* pressez-vous!; *v.a.* presser, hâter.
hurt, *v.a.* faire mal à; blesser; *(feelings)* froisser.
husband, *s*. mari *m*.
hush, *int*. chut!; — *s*. calme *m*.; — *v.a.* calmer.
husk, *s*. cosse *f*.; glume *f*.; — *v. a.* écosser, monder.
hut, *s*. cabane *f*.
hydrogen, *s*. hydrogène *m*.
hygiene, *s*. hygiène *f*.
hymn, *s*. hymne *m*.
hyphen, *s*. trait d'union *m*.
hypnotize, *v.a.* hypnotiser.
hypocrisy, *s*. hypocrisie *f*.
hysterical, *adj*. hystérique.

I

I, *pron*. je; moi.

ice, *s.* glace *f.*
ice-cream, *s.* glace *f.*
icy, *adj.* glacial.
idea, *s.* idée *f.*
ideal, *adj.* & *s.* idéal *(m.)*.
identical, *adj.* identique.
identity, *s.* identité *f.*; *~ card* carte *f.* d'identité.
idle, *adj.* désœuvré; *(lazy)* paresseux; — *v.a.* *~ away* perdre.
idleness, *s.* oisiveté *f.*; paresse *f.*
if, *conj.* si; *as ~* comme si.
ignition, *s.* ignition *f.*; *(motor)* allumage *m.*
ignorant, *adj.* ignorant; *be ~ of* ignorer.
ignore, *v.a.* refuser de connaître.
ill, *adj.* malade; *(bad)* mauvais; *be taken ~* tomber malade; *~ luck* malheur *m.*; — *adv.* mal; — *s.* mal *m.*
illegal, *adj.* illégal.
illegitimate, *adj.* illégitime.
illicit, *adj.* illicite.
illness, *s.* maladie *f.*
illusion, *s.* illusion *f.*
illustrate, *v.a.* illustrer.
illustration, *s.* illustration *f.*; exemple *m.*
image, *s.* image *f.*
imagination, *s.* imagination *f.*
imagine, *v. a.* imaginer; se figurer.
imitate, *v.a.* imiter.
immediate, *adj.* immédiat.
immense, *adj.* immense.
immigrant, *adj.* & *s.* immigrant, -e *(m. f.)*.
immigrate, *v. n.* immigrer
immigration, *s.* immigration *f.*
immoral, *adj.* immoral.
immortal, *adj.* immortel.
impatience, *s.* impatience *f.*
impatient, *adj.* impatient.
impediment, *s.* obstacle *m.*
impel, *v.a.* forcer; pousser.
imperfect, *adj.* & *s.* imparfait *(m.)*.
imperial, *adj.* impérial.
impertinent, *adj.* impertinent.
implement, *s.* outil *m.*, ustensile *m.*
implication, *s.* implication *f.*
implore, *v.a.* implorer.
imply, *v.a.* impliquer; donner à entendre.
import, *v.a.* importer; *(mean)* signifier; — *s.* *(usu. pl.)* importation(s) *f.*
importance, *s.* importance *f.*
important, *adj.* important.
importer, *s.* importateur *m.*
impose, *v.a.* imposer (à).
impossibility, *s.* impossibilité *f.*
impossible, *adj.* impossible.
impression, *s.* impression *f.*
imprison, *v.a.* emprisonner.
imprisonment, *s.* emprisonnement.
improbable, *adj.* improbable.
improper, *adj.* impropre;

inconvenant.
improve, *v.a.* améliorer; perfectionner; *v.n.* s'améliorer.
improvement, *s.* amélioration *f.;* progrès *m.*
impulse, *s.* impulsion *f.*
in, *prep.* dans; en; à; *~ the morning* le matin; *~ the evening* le soir; *~ time* à temps; *~ spring* au printemps.
inadequate, *adj.* insuffisant.
incapable, *adj.* incapable (de).
incense, *s.* encens *m.*
inch, *s.* pouce *m.*
incident, *s.* incident *m.*
incidental, *adj.* fortuit; incidental.
incline, *v. a.* & *n.* incliner.
include, *v.a.* comprendre; renfermer.
inclusive, *adj.* inclusif; *~ of* y compris.
income, *s.* revenu *m.*
income-tax, *s.* impôt *m.* sur (le) revenu.
incompatible, *adj.* incompatible.
incompetent, *adj.* incompétent.
inconsistent, *adj.* inconséquent.
inconvenient, *adj.* incommode, gênant.
increase, *v.a.&n.* augmenter; — *s.* augmentation *f.*
incredible, *adj.* incroyable.
incur, *v. a.* contracter; encourir; s'attirer.
incurable, *adj.* incurable.
indebted, *adj.* endetté.
indeed, *adv.* de fait; vraiment.
independence, *s.* indépendance *f.*
independent, *adj.* indépendant.
index, *s.* index *m.; (on dial)* aiguille *f.*; *(math.)* exposant *m.; ~ finger* index *m.*
Indian, *adj.* indien; des Indes; *~ corn* maïs *m.* — *s.* Indien, -enne *m. f.*
india-rubber, *s.* gomme *f.*
indicate, *v.a.* indiquer.
indicator, *s.* indicateur *m.*
indifference, *s.* indifférence *f.*
indifferent, *adj.* indifférent (à).
indigestion, *s.* indigestion *f.*
indignant, *adj.* indigné.
indirect, *adj.* indirect.
indiscreet, *adj.* indiscret.
indiscretion, *s.* indiscrétion *f.;* imprudence *f.*
indispensable, *adj.* indispensable.
individual, *adj.* individuel; — *s.* individu *m.*
indoor, *adj.* d'intérieur.
indoors, *adv.* à la maison; *stay ~* ne pas sortir.
induce, *v.a.* persuader; *(cause)* occasionner.
inducement, *s.* encouragement *m.* *~s* attraits *m. pl.*
indulge, *v. a.* se livrer (à); caresser; *v.n.* *~ in* s'abandonner à; se laisser aller à.
indulgence, *s.* indulgence *f.;* laisser-aller *m.*
industrial, *adj.* industriel.

industrious, *adj.* travailleur.
industry, *s.* industrie *f.*
inefficient, *adj.* incapable; inefficace.
inestimable, *adj.* inestimable.
inevitable, *adj.* inévitable.
inexpensive, *adj.* peu coûteux, peu cher, bon marché.
inexperienced, *adj.* inexpérimenté.
inexplicable, *adj.* inexplicable.
infallible, *adj.* infaillible.
infamous, *adj.* infâme.
infant, *s.* enfant *m. f.*
infantry, *s.* infanterie *f.*
infant-school, *s.* école *f.* maternelle.
infection, *s.* infection *f.*
infer, *v.a.* conclure, déduire.
inferior, *adj.* inférieur.
infinitive, *s.* infinitif *m.*
infirm, *adj.* infirm.
infirmary, *s.* infirmerie *f.*
inflame, *v.a.* enflammer
inflammable, *adj.* inflammable.
inflate, *v.a.* gonfler.
inflexion, *s.* inflexion *f.*
inflict, *v.a.* infliger; imposer à.
influence, *s.* influence *f.*; — *v.a.* influencer.
influenza, *s.* grippe *f.*
inform, *v.a.* informer.
informal, *adj.* sans cérémonie.
information, *s.* information *f.*; renseignements *m. pl.*
ingenious, *adj.* ingénieux.
ingenuity, *s.* ingéniosité *f.*
ingredient, *s.* ingrédient *m.*
inhabit, *v.a.* habiter.
inhabitant, *s.* habitant *m.*
inherit, *v.a.* & *n.* hériter (de).
inheritance, *s.* héritage *m.*
initial, *s.* initiale *f.*
initiative, *s.* initiative *f.*
injection, *s.* injection *f.*
injure, *v.a.* nuire à; blesser.
injury, *s.* préjudice *m.*; dommage *m.*; blessure *f.*
injustice, *s.* injustice *f.*
ink, *s.* encre *f.*
inland, *s.* & *adj.* intérieur *(m.)*.
inn, *s.* auberge *f.*; taverne *f.*
inner, *adj.* intérieur.
innocence, *s.* innocence *f.*
innocent, *adj.* innocent.
innumerable, *adj.* innombrable.
inoculate, *v.a.* inoculer.
inquire, *v.n.* ~ *about* s'enquérir, se renseigner sur; ~ *after* demander après, demander des nouvelles de.
inquiry, *s.* demande *f.*; recherche *f.*; *make inquiries about* s'informer de; ~ *office* bureau *m.* des renseignements.
insane, *adj.* fou, fol, folle.
inscription, *s.* inscription *f*
insect, *s.* insecte *m.*
insecure, *adj.* peu sûr, mal assuré.
insensible, *adj.* sans connaissance; insensible.
inseparable, *adj.* inséparable.

insert, *v. a.* insérer (dans).
inside, *s. & adj.* intérieur *(m.)*; — *adv.* à l'intérieur.
insignificant, *adj.* insignifiant.
insist, *v.n.* insister *(on* sur).
insistence, *s.* insistance *f.*
inspect, *v.a.* inspecter.
inspection, *s.* inspection *f.*
inspector, *s.* inspecteur *m.*
inspiration, *s.* inspiration *f.*
inspire, *v.a.* inspirer.
install. *v.a.* installer.
instalment, *s.* fraction *f.*, acompte *m.*
instance, *s.* exemple *m.*; cas *m.*; *for* ~ par exemple.
instant, *adj.* urgent; — *s.* instant *m.*
instead, *adv.* ~ *of* au lieu de.
instinct, *s.* instinct *m.*
institute, *s.* institut *m.*; — *v.a.* instituer.
institution, *s.* institution *f.*
instruct, *v. a.* instruire.
instruction, *s.* instruction *f.*
instructive, *adj.* instructif.
instrument, *s.* instrument *m.*
instrumental, *adj.* instrumental.
insufficiency, *s.* insuffisance *f.*
insufficient, *adj.* insuffisant.
insult, *s.* insulte *f.*; — *v.a.* insulter.
insurance, *s.* assurance *f.*
insure, *v. a.* (faire) assurer.
integral, *adj.* intégral; — *s.* intégrale *f.*
integrity, *s.* intégrité *f.*
intellectual, *adj.* intellectuel.
intelligence, *s.* intelligence *f.*; *(information)* renseignements *m.pl.*
intelligent, *adj.* intelligent.
intend, *v. a.* avoir l'intention de (faire qch.), se proposer de; destiner qn., qch. (à); vouloir dire.
intense, *adj.* intense.
intensity, *s.* intensité *f.*
intent, *s.* intention *f.*; — *adj.* ~ *on* absorbé dans.
intention, *s.* intention *f.*
intercontinental, *adj.* intercontinental.
interest, *s.* intérêt *m.*; — *v.a.* intéresser.
interesting, *adj.* intéressant.
interfere, *v. n.* intervenir; ~ *with* gêner; se mêler de.
interior, *adj. & s.* intérieur *(m.)*.
intermediate, *adj.* intermédiaire.
intermission, *s.* interruption *f.*, pause *f.*
internal, *adj.* interne; intérieur.
international, *adj.* international.
interpret, *v.a.* interpréter.
interpretation, *s.* interprétation *f.*
interpreter, *s.* interprète *m.*
interrogation, *s.* interrogation *f.*
interrupt, *v.a.* interrompre.
interruption, *s.* interrup-

tion *f.*
interval, *s.* intervalle *m.*
intervention, *s.* intervention *f.*
interview, entrevue *f.*; interview *m. f.*
intimate, *adj.* intime.
into, *prep.* dans; en.
intolerable, *adj.* intolérable.
introduce, *v.a.* introduire; *(pers.)* présenter.
introduction, *s.* introduction *f.*; *(pers.)* présentation *f.*
invade, *v.a.* envahir.
invalid[1], *s.* malade *m. f.*
invalid[2], *adj.* invalide.
invasion, *s.* invasion *f.*
invent, *v.a.* inventer.
invention, *s.* invention *f.*
inverted, *adj.* ~ *commas* guillemets *m.*
invest, *v.a.* *(money)* placer.
investigate, *v.a.* rechercher.
investigation, *s.* investigation *f.*
investment, *s.* placement *m.*
invisible, *adj.* invisible.
invitation, *s.* invitation *f.*
invite, *v.a.* inviter.
invoice, *s.* facture *f.*
involuntary, *adj.* involontaire.
involve, *v.a.* envelopper (dans); impliquer (dans); entraîner.
inward, *adj.* intérieur; interne.
inwards, *adv.* intérieurement; en dedans.
Irish, *adj.* irlandais
iron, *s.* fer *m.* — *v.a.* repasser.
ironical, *adj.* ironique.
ironware, *s.* quincaillerie *f.*
ironworks, *s.* ferronnerie *f.*
irony, *s.* ironie *f.*
irregular, *adj.* irrégulier.
irrelevant, *adj.* non pertinent; hors de la question; inapplicable (à).
irresolute, *adj.* irrésolu.
irritate, *v.a.* irriter.
island, *s.* île *f.*; *(street)* refuge *m.*
isle, *s.* île *f.*
isolate, *v.a.* isoler.
isotope, *s.* isotope *m.*
issue, *s.* *(way out)* sortie *f.*; *(end)* issue *f.*, fin *f.*, résultat *m.*; *(publication)* publication *f.*, édition, *(paper)* numéro *m.*, *(money)* émission *f.*; — *v. a.* émettre; publier.
it, *pron.* il, elle; *(acc.)* le, la; *of it* en; *to* ~ y.
Italien, *adj.* italien; — *s.* Italien, -enne *m.f.*
itch, *s.* démangeaison *f.*; — *v.n.* démanger.
itchy, *adj.* galeux.
item, *s.* article *m.*, détail *m.*
its, *pron.* son, sa, *pl.* ses.
itself, *pron.* lui-même, elle-même; se; *(emphatic)* même.
ivory, *s.* ivoire *m.*
ivy, *s.* lierre *m.*

J

jack, *s.* *(cards)* valet *m.*;

(lifting) cric *m.*, lève-auto *m.*
jackal, *s.* chacal *m.*
jacket, *s.* veston *m.*
jail, *s.* prison *f.*
jam¹, *s.* confiture *f.*
jam², *v.a.* serrer; coincer; encombrer; — *s.* encombrement *m.*
January, *s.* janvier *m.*
Japanese, *adj.* japonais.
jar, *s.* jarre *f.*; bocal *m.*
javelin, *s.* javeline *f.*
jaw, *s.* mâchoire *f.*
jealous, *adj.* jaloux.
jealousy, *s.* jalousie *f.*
jelly, *s.* gelée *f.*
jerk, *s.* saccade *f.*; secousse *f.*
jersey, *s.* jersey *m.*
jet, *s.* jet *m.*; *(gas)* bec *m.*; *~ plane* avion *m.* à réaction.
Jew, *s.* Juif *m.*
jewel, *s.* bijou *m.*
jeweller, *s.* bijoutier *m.*; *~'s shop* bijouterie *f.*
jewellery, *s.* bijouterie *f.*
jib, *s.* foc *m.*
job, *s.* tâche *f.*; travail *m.* *(pl.* -aux*)*; emploi *m.*; *odd ~s* petits travaux *m.*
join, *v.a.* joindre; unir; se joindre (à); *v.n.* se joindre; s'unir; *~ in* prendre part à.
joiner, *s.* menuisier *m.*
joint, *s.* joint *m.*; articulation *f.*; *(meat)* gros morceau *m.*; — *adj.* commun; indivis; co-; *~-stock company* société *f.* par actions.
joke, *s.* plaisanterie *f.*
jolly, *adj.* joyeux; jovial.
journal, *s.* journal *m.* *(pl.* -aux*)*.
journalist, *s.* journaliste *m.*
journey, *s.* voyage *m.*
joy, *s.* joie *f.*
joyful, *adj.* joyeux.
judge, *s.* juge *m.*; — *v.a.&n.* juger.
judg(e)ment, *s.* jugement *m.*
jug, *s.* cruche *f.*; pot *m.*
juggler, *s.* jongleur *m.*
Jugoslav, *adj.* yougoslave.
juice, *s.* jus *m.*
July, *s.* juillet *m.*
jump, *s.* saut *m.*; — *v.n.* & *a.* sauter.
junction, *s.* jonction *f.*; (gare *f.* d')embranchement. *m.*
June, *s.* juin *m.*
jungle, jungle *f.*
junior, *adj.* jeune.
jury, *s.* jury *m.*
juryman, *s.* juré *m.*
just, *adj.* juste; — *adv.* *(exactly)* juste; *(barely)* à peine; *~ now* il n'y a qu'un instant; *~ so* précisément.
justice, *s.* justice *f.*
justification, *s.* justification *f.*
justify, *v.a.* justifier.
jut, *v.n.* *~ out* faire saillie.
juvenile, *adj.* juvénile; d'enfants.

K

kangaro, *s.* kangourou *m.*
keel, *s.* quille *f.*
keen, *adj.* aigu; tranchant; *(mind)* péné-

trant; *be ~ on* être enthousiaste de, avoir la passion de.

keep, *v.a.* tenir; garder; maintenir; observer; ~ *back* retenir; ~ *up* soutenir; — *v. n.* rester; ~ *on* continuer à.

keeper, *s.* gardien *m.*

kerb, *s.* bordure *f.*

kernel, *s.* amande *f.*

kettle, *s.* bouilloire *f.*

key, *s.* clé *f.*; *(piano)* touche *f.*; *(music)* ton *m.*

keyboard, *s.* clavier *m.*

kick, *v.a.* donner un coup de pied (à); *v.n.* ruer; — *s.* coup *m.* de pied.

kid, *s.* chevreau *m.*; *(child)* gosse *m. f.*

kidney, *s.* rein *m.*; *(food)* rognon *m.*

kill, *v.a.* & *n.* tuer; abattre.

kilogram(me), *s.* kilogramme *m.*

kilometre, *s.* kilomètre *m.*

kind, *adj.* bon; bienveillant; aimable.

kindle, *v.a.* allumer; exciter; enflammer; *v.n.* s'enflammer.

kindly, *adj.* bon; doux.

kindness, *s.* bonté *f.*; bienveillance *f.*

kindred, *s.* parenté *f.*; parents *m.pl.*

king, *s.* roi *m.*

kingdom, *s.* royaume *m.*

kinsman, *s.* parent *m.*

kiss, *s.* baiser *m.*; *v.a.* embrasser; baiser.

kit, *s.* fourniment *m.*

kitchen, *s.* cuisine *f.*

kite, *s.* cerf-volant *m.*

kitten, *s.* petit chat *m.*

knapsack, *s.* havresac *m.*

knee, *s.* genou *m.* *(pl.* -x).

kneel, *v.n.* s'agenouiller; ~ *down* se mettre à genoux.

knife, *s.* couteau *m.*

knight, *s.* chevalier *m.*; *(chess)* cavalier *m.*

knit, *v. a.* tricoter; *(brow)* froncer.

knob, *s.* bosse *f.*; bouton *m.*

knock, *s.* coup *m.*; — *v.a.* & *n.* frapper; ~ *down* renverser.

knocker, *s.* marteau *m.*

knot, *s.* nœud *m.*; — *v.a.* nouer; *v.n.* se nouer.

know, *v.a.* savoir; connaître; reconnaître; ~*n for* connu pour; — *v.n.* savoir; ~ *of* avoir connaissance de; *let* ~ prévenir.

knowledge, *s.* connaissance *f.*; *(acquired)* savoir *m.*

knuckle, *s.* articulation *f.* de doigt.

L

label, *s.* étiquette *f.*; — *v.a.* étiqueter.

laboratory, *s.* laboratoire *m.*

labour, *s.* travail *m.*; ~ *(e)exchange* bureau *m.* de placement; — *v.n.* travailler.

labourer, *s.* travailleur *m.*

lace, *s.* dentelle *f.*

lack, *s.* manque; — *v.a.* & *n.* ~ *(for)* manquer (de).
lad, *s.* jeune garçon *m.*
ladder, *s.* échelle *f.*
lading, *s.* chargement *m.*
ladle, *s.* louche *f.*
lady, *s.* dame *f.*; *young* ~ jeune dame *f.*; demoiselle *f.*, jeune fille *f.*
lag, *v.n.* ~ *behind* rester en arrière.
lake, *s.* lac *m.*
lamb, *s.* agneau *m.*
lame, *adj.* boiteux.
lamp, *s.* lampe *f.*
lamp-shade, *s.* abat-jour *m.*
land, *s.* *(not sea)* terre *f.*; *(country)* pays *m.*; — *v.n.* & *a.* débarquer; *(plane)* atterrir.
landing, *s.* débarquement *m*; *(plane)* atterrissage *m.*
landing-strip, *s.* piste *f.* d'atterrissage.
landlady, *s.* propriétaire *f.*; aubergiste *f.*
landlord, *s.* propriétaire *m.*; aubergiste *m.*
landscape, *s.* paysage *m.*
lane, *s.* ruelle *f.*; chemin *m.*
language, *s.* langue *f.*; *(expression)* langage *m.*
lap[1], *s.* genoux *m. pl.*; *(coat)* pan *m.*; *(sports)* tour (de piste) *m.*
lap[2], *v. a.* envelopper (de); laper.
lapse, *s.* faute *f.*; chute *f.*; lapsus *m.*; *(time)* laps *m.*; — *v.n.* retomber (dans); *(time)* s'écouler; *(fail)* faire un faux pas.
lard, *s.* saindoux *m.*
larder, *s.* dépense *f.*
large, *adj.* gros, grand; considérable; *at* ~ en liberté, en général.
lark, *s.* alouette *f.*
last, *adj.* dernier; — *adv.* dernièrement, en dernier lieu; — *v.n.* durer.
lasting, *adj.* durable.
latch, *s.* loquet *m.*
latch-key, *s.* clef *f.* de porte.
late, *adj.* tardif; *be* ~ être en retard; — *adv.* tard; ~*r on* par la suite; plus tard.
lately, *adv.* dernièrement, recemment.
latest, *adj.* récent, le dernier; *at (the)* ~ au plus tard.
lathe, *s.* tour *m.*
lather, *s.* mousse *f.*
Latin, *adj.* latin; — *s.* latin *m.*
latter, *adj.* dernier; *the* ~ ce dernier; celui-ci, celle-ci, ceux-ci.
laugh, *v.n.* rire *(at* de); — *s.* rire *m.*
laughter, *s.* rire *m.*
launch, *v.a.* lancer.
launching, *adj.* ~ *site* rampe *f.* à fusées.
laundry, *s.* buanderie *f.*, blanchisserie *f.*
lavatory, *s.* lavabo *m.* cabinet *m.* de toilette.
lavish, *adj.* prodigue (de). — *v.a.* prodiguer.
law, *s.* loi *f.*; droit *m.*
law-court, *s.* cour *f.* de justice, tribunal *m.*

lawful, *adj*. légal; permis; légitime.
lawn, *s*. pelouse *f*.
lawn-mower, *s*. tondeuse *f*.
lawsuit, *s*. procès *m*.
lawyer, *s*. homme *m*. de loi avoué *m*.; avocat *m*.
lay, *v.a*. coucher, poser, étendre; ~ *aside, by* mettre de côté; *(money)* réserver; ~ *down* poser; ~ *on* appliquer; *be laid up* être alité.
lay-by, *s*. refuge *m*., garage *m*.
layer, *s*. couche *f*.
lazy, *adj*. paresseux.
lead[1], *s*. *(metal)* plomb *m*.
lead[2], *v.a*. & *n*. mener, conduire; ~ *the way* montrer le chemin.
leader, *s*. conducteur *m*.; *(newspaper)* éditorial *m*.
leadership, *s*. conduite *f*.; direction *f*.
leaf, *s*. feuille *f*.; *(book)* feuillet *m*.; page *f*.
leak, *s*. fuite *f*.; voie d'eau *f*.; — *v.n*. fuir.
lean, *adj*. maigre.
leap, *v*. *n*. & *a*. sauter; — *s*. saut *m*.
learn, *v.a*. & *n*. apprendre.
learning, *s*. savoir *m*., science *f*.
leash, *s*. laisse *f*.
least, *adj*. le plus petit; le moindre; — *adv*. le moins; — *s*. moins *m*.; *at* ~ au moins, à tout le moins; *not in the* ~ pas le moins du monde.
leather, *s*. cuir *m*.
leave, *v*. *a*. laisser; quitter; *be left* rester; — *s*. permission *f*.; congé *m*.; *on* ~ en congé.
lecture, *s*. conférence *f*. *(on* sur); — *v.n*. faire des conférences.
lecturer, *s*. conférencier *m*.; *(univ.)* professeur *m*. (de faculté).
left, *adj*. & *s*. gauche *(f.)*
left-luggage office, *s* consigne *f*.
leg, *s*. jambe *f*.; patte *f*
legal, *adj*. légal.
legislature, *s*. législature *f*.
legitimate, *adj*. légitime
leisure, *s*. loisir *m*.; *be at* ~ être de loisir
lemon, *s*. citron *m*.
lemonade. *s*. limonade *f*
lend, *v.a*. prêter.
length, *s*. longueur *f*. *(time)* durée *f*.
lengthen, *v.a*. allonger prolonger.
lens, *s*. lentille *f*.
leopard, *s*. léopard *m*
less, *adj*. moindre; moins de; — *adv*. moins; ~ *than* moins de.
lessen, *v*. *a*. & *n*. diminuer
lesson, *s*. leçon *f*.
lest, *conj*. de peur que.
let, *v.a*. laisser, permettre à; *(house)* louer; ~ *me go* laisse-moi aller; ~ *down* laisser tomber (à); ~ *in* laisser entrer
letter, *s*. lettre *f*.; ~s belles-lettres *f. pl*.
lettuce, *s*. laitue *f*.
level, *s*. niveau *m*.; — *adj*. uni; plat; horizontal;

— *v.a.* niveler; pointer:
lever, *s.* levier *m.*
levy, *s.* levée *f.;* — *v.a.* lever.
lexicon, *s.* lexique *m.*
liability, *s.* responsabilité *f.; liabilities* passif *m.*
liable, *adj.* responsable (de); sujet (à).
liar, *s.* menteur, *m.*
liberal, *adj.* libéral; généreux.
liberty, *s.* liberté *f.*
librarian, *s.* bibliothécaire *m. f.*
library, *s.* bibliothèque *f.*
licence, *s.* permission *f.;* permis *m.,* patente *f.; (excess of liberty)* licence *f.*
license, *v.a.* accorder un permis (à).
lick, *v.a.* lécher.
lid, *s.* couvercle *m.*
lie[1], *s.* mensonge *m.;* — *v.n.&a.* mentir.
lie[2], *v.n.* être couché; *(dead)* reposer; *(be situated)* se trouver; *~ down* se coucher; *it ~s with you* cela dépend de vous.
lieutenant, *s.* lieutenant *m.*
life, *s.* vie *f.*
life-insurance, *s.* assurance *f.* sur la vie.
lifeless, *adj.* inanimé.
lift, *v.a.* lever; *fig.* élever; *~ up* soulever; — *s. (apparatus)* ascenseur *m.; give s. o. a ~* faire monter qn (dans sa voiture).
light[1], *s.* lumière *f.;* éclairage *f.;* jour *m.;* lampe *f.; (fire)* feu *m.; come to ~* se révéler; — *v. a.* allumer; éclairer; *v.n.* s'éclairer; — *adj.* clair; éclairé.
light[2], *adj.* léger; *make ~ of* faire peu de cas de.
lighten[1], *v.a.* éclairer; *v.n.* faire des éclairs.
lighten[2], *v.a.* alléger.
lighter, *s.* briquet *m.*
lighthouse, *s.* phare *m.*
lighting, *s.* éclairage *m.*
lightning, *s.* éclair *m.*
like[1], *adj.* semblable, pareil, ressemblant; — *prep.* comme.
like[2], *v.a.* aimer; *I should ~ to* je voudrais + *inf.*
likely, *adv.* probable.
likeness, *s.* ressemblance *f.;* portrait *m.*
lily, *s.* lis *m.*
limb, *s.* membre *m.*
limit, *s.* limite *f.; v.a.* limiter.
limited, *adj. ~ liability company* société anonyme *f.*
line, *s.* ligne *f.; (poetry)* vers *m.; railw.)* voie *f.;* — *v.a. (garment)* doubler; *v.n. ~ up* s'aligner; faire la queue.
linen, *s.* toile *f.;* ligne *m.*
lining, *s.* doublure *f.*
link, *s.* chaînon *m., fig.* lien *m.;* — *v.a.* lier; unir.
lion, *s* lion *m.*
lip, *s.* lèvre *f.*
lipstick, *s.* rouge *m.* à lèvres.
liquid, *adj.. & s.* liquide *(m.).*

list, *s*. liste *f*.; — *v.a.* enregistrer.
listen, *v.n.* (also ~ *in*) écouter.
listener, *s*. auditeur, -trice *m. f.*
literary, *adj*. littéraire.
literature, *s*. littérature *f*.
litter, *s*. litière *f*.
little, *adj*. petit; peu de.
live, *v.n.* vivre; *(reside)* habiter, demeurer; ~ *on* vivre de.
lively, *adv*. vivant, gai.
liver, *s*. foie *m*.
living-room, *s*. salle *f*. de séjour.
load, *s*. charge *f*.; fardeau *m*.; — *v.a.* charger.
loaf, *s*. pain *m*.
loan, *s*. prêt *m*.; emprunt *m*.
loathe, *v.a.* détester.
lobby, *s*. couloir *m*., vestibule *m*.
lobster, *s*. homard *m*.
local, *adj*. local.
location, *s*. emplacement *m*.; situation *f*.
lock[1], *s*. serrure *f*.
lock[2], *s*. *(hair)* boucle *f*.
locksmith, *s*. serrurier *m*.
lodger, *s*. locataire *m. f.*
lodging, *s*. logement *m*. *furnished* ~*s* garni *m*.
log, *s*. bûche *f*.; bille *f*.
logical, *adj*. logique.
loin, *s*. *(pork)* longe *f*.; *(beef)* aloyau *m*.; rein *m*.
lonely, *adj*. solitaire.
long[1], *adj*. long; *a* ~ *time (since)* depuis longtemps; *be* ~ *in* être long à; — *adv*. longtemps; *how* ~*?* combien de temps?; ~ *ago* il y a longtemps.
long[2], *v.n.* ~ *for* désirer qch., soupirer après.
long-distance, *adj*. à (longue) distance.
long-play(ing), *adj*. ~ *record* microsillon *m*.
look, *v. n. & a.* regarder; ~ *after* soigner; ~ *at* regarder; ~ *back* regarder en arrière; ~ *for* chercher; ~ *into* examiner; ~ *out* être sur ses gardes, *int*. gare!; ~ *over* parcourir; ~ *up* chercher; — *s*. regard *m*.; air *m*.; aspect *m*.
looking-glass, *s*. miroir *m*.
loom, *s*. métier *m*. de tisserand.
loop, *s*. boucle .
loose, *adj*. lâche; délié, détaché; vague.
loosen, *v.a.* desserrer.
lord, *s*. maître *m*.; seigneur *m*.
lorry, *s*. camion *m*.
lose, *v.a. & n.* perdre.
loss, *s*. perte *f*.
lot, *s*. sort *m*.; *(portion)* partage *m*.; *a* ~ *of* beaucoup de.
lottery, *s*. loterie *f*.
loud, *adj*. fort; bruyant.
loud-speaker, *s*. haut-parleur *m*.
lounge, *s*. (grand) vestibule *m*.; foyer *m*., hall *m*.; — *v.n.* flâner.
lounge-suit, *s*. complet veston *m*.
love, *s*. amour *m*.; — *v.a.* aimer.

lovely, *adj.* beau, bel, belle; charmant.
lover, *s.* amoureux *m.*; amant *m.*
low, *adj.* & *adv.* bas.
lower, *adj.* inférieur; *(deck)* premier (pont); — *v.a.* baisser; *(flags, sails)* amener.
loyal, *adj.* loyal; fidèle.
loyalty, *s.* loyauté *f.*
lubricate, *v.a.* lubrifier.
luck, *s.* chance *f.*; *bad* ~ malchance *f.*
lucky, *adj.* heureux.
luggage, *s.* bagages *m. pl.*
luggage-van, *s.* fourgon *m.* (aux bagages).
lump, *s.* morceau *m.*
lunch, *s.* déjeuner *m.*; — *v.n.* déjeune .
lung, *s.* poumon *m.*
lute, *s.* luth *m.*
luxurious, *adj.* luxueux.
luxury, *s.* luxe *m.*
lyre, *s.* lyre f.
lyric, *adj.* lyrique.

M

machine, *s.* machine *f.*
machinery, *s.* machines *f.pl.*; *fig.* mécanisme *m.*
mackintosh, *s.* imperméable *m.*
mad, *adj.* fou, fol, folle.
madam, *s.* madame *f.*
magazine, *s.* revue *f.*; *(rifle)* magasin *m.*
magic, *adj.* magique.
magistrate, *s.* magistrat *m.*
magnet, *s.* aimant *m.*
magnetic, *adj.* magnétique.
magnificent, *adj.* magnifique.
maid, *s.* (jeune) fille *f.*; bonne *f.*
mail, *s.* courrier *m.*
mail-boat, *s.* paquebot-poste *m.*
mail-van, *s.* wagon-poste *m.*
main, *adj.* principal.
mainland, *s.* terre *f.* ferme.
mainly, *adv.* principalement.
mains, *s.* secteur (de courant) *m.*
maintain, *v.a.* maintenir; soutenir.
maintenance, *s.* entretien *m.*
majesty, *s.* majesté *f.*
major, *s.* commandant *m.*; — *adj.* majeur.
majority, *s.* majorité *f.*; plupart *f.*
make, *v.a.* & *n.* faire; rendre; ~ *away with* détruire; ~ *for* se diriger vers; ~ *off* décamper; ~ *out* comprendre; prouver; ~ *over* céder; ~ *up (list)* dresser; *(invent)* inventer; ~ *up for* compenser; — *s.* forme *f.*, fabrication *f.*
male, *adj.* mâle; masculin; — *s.* mâle *m.*
malice, *s.* méchanceté *f.*
man, *s.* homme *m.*
manage, *v. a.* conduire, diriger, gérer, gouverner; *I shall* ~ *it* j'en

viendrai à bout.
management, *s.* direction *f.*; gérance *f.*
manager, *s.* directeur *m.*; gérant *m.*
manicure, *s.* manicure *n. f.*
manifest, *adj.* manifeste; — *v.a.* manifester.
manipulate, *v.a.* manipuler.
manner, *s.* manière *f.*; air *m.*; ~s manières *f. pl.*; *(morals)* mœurs *f. pl.*
manœuvre, *s.* manœuvre *f.*; — *v.a.* faire manœuvrer.
manor, *s.* manoir *m.*
manual, *adj.* & *s.* manuel *(m.)*.
manufacture, *s.* manufacture *f.*; — *v.a.* fabriquer.
manufacturer, *s.* manufacturier *m.*; fabricant *m.*
manure, *s.* fumier *m.*
manuscript, *s.* manuscrit *m.*
many, *adj.* beaucoup de.
map, *s.* carte *f.* géographique.
marble, *s.* marbre *m.*
march, *s.* marche *f.*; — *v.n.* marcher.
March, *s.* mars *m.*
mare, *s.* jument *f.*
margarine, *s.* margarine *f.*
marine, *s.* marine *f.*; — *adj.* marin; maritime.
mariner, *s.* marin *m.*
mark, *s.* marque *f.*; *(aim)* but *m.*; *(school)* point *m.*; *(coin)* marc *m.*; — *v.a.* marquer; souligner.
market, *s.* marché *m.*
market-price, *s.* prix *m.* courant.
marmalade, *s.* marmelade *f.* (d'oranges).
marriage, *s.* mariage *m.*
married, *adj.* marié.
marry, *v. a.* épouser; *v. n.* *(get married)* se marier.
marsh, *s.* marais *m.*
marshal, *s.* maréchal *m.*; — *v.a.* ranger; conduire.
martial, *adj.* martial.
martyr, *s.* martyr *m.*
marvel, *s.* merveille *f.*; — *v.n.* s'étonner (de).
marvellous, *adj.* merveilleux.
masculine, *adj.* mâle; masculin.
mask, *s.* masque *m.*
mason, *s.* maçon *m.*
mass[1], *s.* masse *f.*; majorité *f.*
mass[2], *s.* *(eccles.)* messe *f.*
mast, *s.* mât *m.*
master, *s.* maître *m.*; — *v. a.* maîtriser
mat, *s.* *(door)* paillasson *m.*; *(table)* dessous de plat, *m.*
match[1], *s.* égal, -e *m. f.*, pareil, -le *m. f.*, mariage *m.*; *(pers.)* parti *m.*; *(sport)* match *m.*; — *v.a.* assortir; *v.n.* s'assortir.
match[2], *s.* allumette *f.*
mate, *s.* camarade *m.*; *(birds)* mâle *m.*, femelle *f.*; *(chess)* mat *m.*; *(ship)* second *m.*; — *v.a.* marier (à); *v.n.*

s'accoupler.
material, *s.* matière *f.*; — *adj.* matériel.
maternal, *adj.* maternel.
mathematical, *adj.* mathématique.
mathematics, *s.* mathématiques *f. pl.*
matinée, *s.* matinée *f.*
matron, *s.* mère de famille, *f.*; *(hospital)* infirmière-en-chef *f.*; surveillante *f.*
matter, *s.* matière *f.*; affaire *f.*; sujet *m.*; chose *f.*; *as a ~ of fact* en fait; *what is the ~?* qu'est-ce qu'il y a?; — *v.n.* importer; *it does not ~* n'importe.
mattress, *s.* matelas *m.*; *spring ~* sommier *m.*, matelas *m.* à ressort.
mature, *adj.* mûr; — *v.a. & n.* mûrir.
maturity, *s.* maturité *f.*
May, *s.* mai *m.*
may, *v. aux.* pouvoir; *~ I?* vous permettez?
maybe, *adv.* peut-être.
mayor, *s.* maire *m.*
me, *pron.* *(acc.)* me; *(alone, with prep.)* moi.
meadow, *s.* pré *m.*
meal, *s.* repas *m.*
mean[1], *s.* moyen terme, *m.*; *(math.)* moyenne *f.*; *~s* moyens *m. pl.*, *(way to do)* moyen *m.*; *by ~s of* au moyen de; *by all ~s* mais certainement; *by no ~s* en aucune façon; — *adj.* moyen.
mean[2], *v.a.* *(signify)* vouloir dire, signifier; *(wish)* vouloir (faire), avoir l'intention (de); destiner; *what does that word ~?* que signifie ce mot?; *what do you ~ by that?* qu'entendez-vous par là?
mean[3], *adj.* misérable, pauvre; bas, vil; ladre.
meaning, *s.* intention *f.*; sens *m.*
meantime, -while, *adv.* *(in the ~)* dans l'intervalle, pendant ce temps-là.
measure, *s.* mesure *f.*; — *v.a.* mesurer.
meat, *s.* viande *f.*; *(food)* nourriture *f.*
mechanic, *s.* artisan *m.*, mécanicien *m.*
mechanical, *adj.* mécanique.
mechanics, *s.* mécanique *f.*
mechanism, *s.* mécanisme *m.*
mechanize, *v.a.* mécaniser.
medal, *s.* médaille *f.*
medical, *adj.* médical; *~ student* étudiant *m.* en médicine.
medicine, *s.* médecine *f.*
meditate, *v.a. & n.* méditer.
medium, *s.* moyen terme *m.*; milieu *m.*; — *adj.* moyen.
meet, *v.a.* rencontrer (qn.), se rencontrer avec (qn.); *(face)* affronter; *(expenses)* faire face à; *~ sy at the station* aller recevoir

qn. à la gare; — *v. n.* se rencontrer; ~ *with* rencontrer; éprouver.
meeting, *s.* rencontre *f.*; réunion *f.*
mellow, *adj.* mûr; moelleux.
melody, *s.* mélodie *f.*
melon, *s.* melon *m.*
melt, *v.a.* fondre.
member, *s.* membre *m.*
memorial, *s.* monument *m.*; mémorial *m.*
memory, *s.* mémoire *f.*; souvenir *m.*
mend, *v. a.* raccommoder; réparer; corriger.
mental, *adj.* mental.
mention, *v. a.* mentionner; citer; *don't ~ it* il n'y a pas de quoi.
merchandise, *s.* marchandise *f.*
merchant, *s.* négociant *m.*; commerçant *m.*
merciful, *adj.* miséricordieux.
mercy, *s.* pitié *f.*; miséricorde *f.*
mere, *adj.* seul.
merely, *adv.* purement; simplement.
merit, mérite *m.*; — *v.a.* mériter.
merry, *adj.* gai.
mess, *s.* gâchis *m.*; *make a ~ of* gâcher.
message, *s.* message *m.*
messenger, *s.* messager *m.*
metal, *s.* métal *m.*
meteorology, *s.* météorologie *f.*
method, *s.* méthode *f.*
metre, *s.* mètre *m.*
microphone, *s.* microphone *m.*
microscope, *s.* microscope *m.*
middle, *s.* milieu *m.*; — *adj.* du milieu; moyen.
midnight, *s.* minuit *m.*
might, *s.* force *f.*; puissance *f.*
mighty, *adj.* fort; puissant
migrate, *v.n.* émigrer.
mild, *adj.* doux; bénin.
mile, *s.* mille *m.*
mileage, *s.* parcours *m.*; *(expense)* prix *m.* par mille.
military, *adj.* militaire.
milk, *s.* lait *m.*
milkman, *s.* laitier *m.*
mill, *s.* moulin *m.*; fabrique *f.*
miller, *s.* meunier *m.*
milliner, *s.* modiste *f.*
million, *s.* million *m.*
mince, *s.* hachis *m.*; — *v.a.* hacher.
mind, *s.* esprit *m.*; *(remembrance)* souvenir *m.*; *(opinion)* pensée *f.*, avis *m.*; *change one's ~* changer d'avis; *make up one's ~ to* se décider à, se résigner à; — *v.a.* faire attention à, prendre garde à; écouter; *(look after)* garder; *(trouble about)* s'inquiéter de; *do you ~ my smoking?* est-ce que cela vous gêne que je fume?; *I don't ~* cela m'est égal; *never ~* ça ne fait rien.
mine[1], *s.* mine *f.*; — *v.a.* miner.
mine[2], *pron.* à moi; le mien.

miner, *s.* mineur *m.*
mineral, *adj.* & *s.* minéral (*m.*).
minister, *s.* ministre *m.*
ministry, *s.* ministère *m.*
minor, *adj.* mineur.
minority, *s.* minorité.
mint, *s.* Hôtel *m.* de la Monnaie; *(plant)* menthe *f.*
minus, *adj.* en moins; — *adv.* moins.
minute, *s.* minute *f.*; petit moment, *m.*; *~ hand* grande aiguille *f.*
miracle, *s.* miracle *m.*
mirror, *s.* miroir *m.*
miscarry, *v.n.* avorter.
miscellaneous, *adv.* divers.
mischief, *s.* mal *m.*; méchanceté *f.*
miser, *s.* avare *m.*
miserable, *adj.* misérable; malheureux.
misery, *s.* misère *f.*
misfortune, *s.* malheur *m.*
miss[1], *v.a.* manquer; ne pas entendre; ne pas voir; s'apercevoir de l'absence (de); *~ out* omettre; *be ~ing* manquer.
miss[2], *s.* mademoiselle *f.*
missile, *s.* projectile *m.*
mission, *s.* mission *f.*
missionary, *s.* missionnaire *m. f.*
mist, *s.* brouillard *m.*, brume *f.*
mistake, *s.* erreur *f.*, méprise *f.*; faute *f.*; — *v.a.* se tromper de; *~ for* prendre pour; *be ~n* se tromper.
mistress, *s.* maîtresse *f.* (de maison).
mistrust, *s.* méfiance *f.*
misty, *adj.* brumeux.
misunderstand, *v. a.* comprendre mal.
mitten, *s.* mitaine *f.*
mix, *v.a.* mêler; mélanger; *be ~ed up in* être mêlé à.
mixture, *s.* mélange *m.*; mixture *f.*
moan, *v.n.* gémir; — *s.* gémissement *m.*
mob, *s.* foule *f.*, populace *f.*
mobilization, *s.* mobilisation *f.*
mobilize, *v.a.* mobiliser.
mock, *s.* moquerie *f.*; — *adj.* faux; — *v.a.* railler.
mockery, *s.* moquerie *f.*
model, *s.* modèle *m.*
moderate, *adj.* modéré; — *v.a.* modérer.
moderation, *s.* modération *f.*
modern, *adj.* moderne.
modest, *adj.* modeste.
modesty *s.* modestie *f.*
modify, *v.a.* modifier.
moist, *adj.* moite, humide.
moisten, *v.a.* humecter.
moisture, *s.* humidité *f.*
molecule, *s.* molécule *f.*
moment, *s.* moment *m.*
momentary, *adj.* momentané.
monarch, *s.* monarque *m.*
monarchy, *s.* monarchie *f.*
Monday, *s.* lundi *m.*
money, *s.* argent *m.*; monnaie *f.*
money-order, *s.* mandat *m.*

monk, *s.* moine *m.*
monkey, *s.* singe *m.*
monopolize, *v.a.* monopoliser.
monopoly, *s.* monopole *m.*
monotonous, *adj.* monotone.
monstrous, *adj.* monstrueux.
month, *s.* mois *m.*
monthly, *adj.* mensuel; — *adv.* mensuellement.
monument, *s.* monument *m.*
monumental, *adj.* monumental.
mood, *s.* humeur *f.*; mode *m.*
moon, *s.* lune *f.*
moonlight, *s.* clair *m.* de lune
moor, *s.* bruyère *f.*
mop, balai *m.*: — *v.a.* (**also** ~ *up*) éponger, essuyer.
moral, *s.* morale *f.*; ~*s* moeurs *f. pl.*; — *adj.* moral; de morale.
more, *adj.* & *pron.* plus de; davantage de; ~ *than* plus que; *some* ~ en ... davantage; *no* ~ n'en ... pas davantage, ne ... plus; — *adv.* plus; davantage; ~ *and* ~ de plus en plus.
moreover, *adv.* de plus.
morning, *s.* matin *m.*; *in the* ~ le matin; — *adj.* du matin.
mortal, *adj.* & *s.* mortel (*m.*, *f.*).
mortality, *s.* mortalité *f.*
mortgage, *s.* hypothèque *f.*; — *v. a.* hypothéquer.
mosquito, *s.* moustique *f.*
moss, *s.* mousse *f.*
most, *adj.* & *pron.* le plus (de), la plupart (de); *at the* ~ tout au plus; ~ *people* la plupart des gens; *make the* ~ *of* tirer le meilleur parti de; — *adv.* très, fort, bien.
mostly, *adv.* pour la plupart; principalement; la plupart du temps.
motel, *s.* motel *m.*
moth, *s.* mite *f.*
mother, *s.* mère *f.*
mother-in-law, *s.* belle-mère *f.*
mother-tongue, *s.* langue *f.* maternelle.
motion, *s.* mouvement *m.*: signe *m.*; (*proposal*) motion *f.*
motionless, *adj.* immobile.
motive, *s.* motif *m.*
motor, *s.* moteur *m.*
motor-bus, *s.* autobus *m.*
motor-car, *s.* auto(mobile) *f.*
motor-coach, *s.* autocar *m.*
motor-cycle, *s.* motocyclette *f.*
motor-scooter, *s.* scooter *m.*
motorway,, *s.* autoroute *f.*
mould, *s.* moule *m.*; — *v.a.* mouler.
mount, *s.* mont *m.*; — *v.a.* & *n.* monter.
mountain, *s.* montagne *f.*
mountaineering, *s.* alpinisme *m.*

mountainous, *adj.* montagneux.
mourn, *v. n.* & *a.* pleurer, (se) lamenter.
mouse, *s.* souris *f.*
moustache, *s.* moustache *f.*
mouth, *s.* bouche *f.*; *(beast)* gueule *f.*
move, *s.* mouvement *m.*; *(chess)* coup *m.*; — *v.a.* remuer; déplacer; *(goods)* transporter; *(affect)* émouvoir; *(motion)* proposer ~ *house (also:* ~*)* déménager; — *v.n.* se mouvoir, se déplacer; s'avancer; *(chess)* jouer; ~ *forward* s'avancer; ~ *in* emménager; ~ *out* déménager; ~ *on* avancer; *int.* circulez!
movement, *s.* mouvement *m.*
mow, *v.a.* faucher; tondre.
mower, *s.* faucheur *m.*; faucheuse (à moteur) *f.*
much, *adj.* & *pron.* beaucoup; — *adv.* beaucoup; très; *too* ~ trop.
mud, *s.* boue *f.*
muddle, *s.* fouillis *m.*; — *v.a.* embrouiller.
muddy, *adj.* boueux.
mug, *s.* timbale *f.*
mule, *s.* mulet *m.*, mule *f.*
multiple, *adj.* multiple.
multiplication, *s.* multiplication *f.*
multiply, *v.a.* multiplier.
multitude, *s.* multitude *f.*
municipal, *adj.* municipal.
murder, *s.* meurtre *m.*
murderer, *s.* meurtrier *m.*
murmur, *s.* murmure *m.*
muscle, *s.* muscle *m.*
museum, *s.* musée *m.*
mushroom, *s.* champignon *m.*
music, *s.* musique *f.*
musical, *adj.* musical; ~ *instrument* instrument *m.* de musique.
music-hall, *s.* café *m.* concert.
musician, *s.* musicien, -enne *m. f.*
must, *v. aux.* il faut que; devoir.
mustard, *s.* moutarde *f.*
mute, *adj.* muet.
mutter, *s.* murmure *m.*; — *v. n.* murmurer.
mutton, *s.* mouton *m.*
mutual, *adj.* mutuel.
my, *pron.* mon, ma; mes *(pl.)*.
myself, *pron.* moi-même; *by* ~ seul.
mysterious, *adj.* mystérieux.
mystery, *s.* mystère *m.*
mystic, *adj.* mystique.
myth, *s.* mythe *m.*

N

nail, *s.* *(to hammer)* clou *m.*; *(on fingers)* ongle *m.*; — *v.a.* clouer.
nail-brush, *s.* brosse *f.* à ongles.

naked, *adj.* nu; dénudé.
name, *s.* nom *m.*; — *v.a.* nommer; désigner.
namely, *adv.* savoir.
nap, *s.* somme *m.*
napkin, *s.* serviette *f.*; *(infant)* couche *f.*
narrate, *v. a.* raconter.
narrow, *adj.* étroit.
nation, *s.* nation *f.*
national, *adj.* national.
nationality, *s.* nationalité *f.*
nationalize, *v.a.* nationaliser.
native, *adj.* & *s.* natif, -ive *(m. f.)*.
natural, *adj.* naturel.
naturalize, *v.a.* naturaliser.
nature, *s.* nature *f.*
naughty, *adj.* méchant.
naval, *adj.* naval
navigate, *v.n.* naviguer.
navigator, *s.* navigateur *m.*
navy, *s.* marine *f.*
near, *adv.* près, proche; — *prep.* près de, auprès de; — *adj.* proche.
nearly, *adv.* *(almost)* presque.
neat, *adj.* propre; élégant.
necessary, *adj.* nécessaire.
necessity, *s.* néccesité *f.*
neck, *s.* cou *m.*
necklace, *s.* collier *m.*
necktie, *s.* cravate *f.*
need, *s.* besoin; — *v.a.* avoir besoin (de); demander.
needle, *s.* aiguille *f.*
needless, *adj.* inutile.
needy, *adj.* nécessiteux.
negative, *adj.* négatif; — *s.* négative *f.*; *(photo)* cliché *m.*; *in the* ~ négativement.
neglect, *v. a.* négliger (de).
negligence, *s.* négligence *f.*
negotiation, *s.* négociation *f.*
negro, -ess s. nègre *m.*, négresse *f.*
neighbour, *s.* voisin, -e *m. f.*
neighbourhood, *s.* voisinage *m.*
neither, *pron.* & *adj.* ni l'un ni l'autre.
nephew, *s.* neveu *m.*
nerve, *s.* nerf *m.*
nervous, *adj.* nerveux.
nest, *s.* nid *m.*
net[1], *s.* filet *m.*
net[2], *adj.* net.
network, *s.* réseau *m.*
neutral, *adj.* neutre.
never, *adj.* (ne . . .) jamais.
nevertheless, *adv.* néanmoins.
new, *adj.* neuf, neuve; nouveau, -el, -elle; *New Year* Nouvel An.
news, *s.* nouvelle *f.*
newspaper, *s.* journal *m.*
next, *adj.* le plus proche; prochain, suivant; ~ *door to* à côté de; *adv.* ensuite, après; — *prep.* ~ *to* à côté de.
nice, *adj.* agréable, bon; gentil.
niece, *s.* nièce *f.*
night, *s.* nuit *f.*; soir *m.*; *by* ~ de nuit; *good* ~! bonne nuit!
nightingale, *s.* rossignol *m.*
nine, *adj.* & *s.* neuf *(m.)*.
nineteen, *adj.* & *s.* dix-

neuf *(m.)*.
ninety, *adj.* & *s.* quatre--vingt-dix *(m.)*.
ninth, *adj.* neuvième; neuf.
nip, *v.a.* pincer.
nitrogen, *s.* azote *m.*
no, *adj.* ne ... pas (de), ne ... aucun.
noble, *adj.* noble.
nobleman, *s.* gentilhomme *m.*
nobody, no one, *pron.* personne ne (+ *verb*).
noise, *s.* bruit *m.*
noisy, *adj.* bruyant.
none, *pron.* ne ... aucun; personne ne (+ *verb.*)
nonsense, *s.* bêtise; *m. no* ~ pas de bêtises
non-smoker, *s.* compartiment *m.* pour non-fumeurs.
non-stop, *adj.* & *adv.* sans arrêt; sans escale.
noon, *s.* midi *m.*
nor, *conj.* ni; *(and ... not)* et ne ... pas, non plus.
normal, *adj.* normal.
north, *s.* nord *m.*; — *adj.* du nord.
north-east, *adj.* & *s.* nord-est *m.*
northern, *adj.* du nord.
north-west, *adj.* & *s.* nord-ouest *m.*
nose, *s.* nez *m.*
nostril, *s.* narine *f.*
not, *adv.* ne ... pas, ne ... point.
notable, *adj.* notable.
note, *s.* note *f.*; *(letter and money)* billet *m.*; *(tone)* ton *m.*; — *v.a.* noter; remarquer.
note-book, *s.* carnet *m.*
noted, *adj.* distingué.
nothing, *pron.* rien; ne ... rien.
notice, *s.* avis *m.*; attention *f.*; connaissance *f.*; *take* ~ *of* faire attention à.
notify, *v.a.* avertir, notifier.
notion, *s.* idée *f.*
noun, *s.* nom *m.*
nourish, *v.a.* nourrir.
novel, *s.* roman *m.*
novelist, *s.* romancier *m.*
novelty, *s.* nouveauté *f.*
November, *s.* novembre *m.*
now, *adv.* maintenant.
nowadays, *adv.* de nos jours.
nowhere, *adv.* ne ... nulle part.
nuclear, *adj.* nucléaire; ~ *energy* énergie *f.* nucléaire; ~ *physics* physique *f.* nucléaire; ~ *power station* centrale *f.* nucléaire.
nuisance, *s.* *(pers.)* peste *f.*; *(thing)* ennui *m.*
number, *s.* nombre *m.*, numéro *m.*
number-plate, *s.* plaque *f.* matricule.
numerous, *adj.* nombreux.
nun, *s.* religieuse *f.*
nurse, *s.* nourrice *f.*, bonne (d'enfant) *f.*; *(hospital)* infirmier, -ère *m. f.*; — *v.a.* *(suckle)* allaiter; *(the sick)* soigner.
nursery, *s.* chambre *f.* des enfants.
nut, *s.* noix *f.*, noisette *f.*

nylon, *s.* nylon *m.; ~ stockings (*or *~s)* bas nylons *m. pl.*

O

oak, *s.* chêne *m.*
oar, *s.* rame *f.*
oat(s) *s. (pl).* avoine *f.*
oath, *s.* serment *m.*
obedience, *s.* obéissance *f.*
obedient, *adj.* obéissant.
obey, *v.a.* & *n.* obéir (à).
object, *s.* objet *m.;* but *m.; (gramm.)* régime *m.; — v.a.* objecter; *v.n.* s'opposer (à).
objection, *s.* objection *f.*
objective, *adj.* & *s.* objectif *(m.).*
obligation, *s.* obligation *f.*
oblige, *v.a.* obliger.
obscure, *adj.* obscur.
observation, *s.* observation *f.*
observe, *v.a.*& *n.* observer.
obstacle, *s.* obstacle *m.*
obstinate, *adj.* obstiné.
obtain, *v.a.* obtenir.
obvious, *adj.* évident.
occasion, *s.* occasion *f.*
occasional *adj.* occasionnel.
occasionally, *adv.* de temps en temps.
occupation, *s.* occupation *f.*
occupy, *v.a.* occuper; *~ oneself with* s'occuper de.
occur, *v.n.* arriver; se trouver; *it ~red to me* il m'est venu à l'idée que.
occurrence, *s.* événement *m.*
ocean, *s.* océan *m.*
October, *s.* octobre *m.*
odd, *adj.* impair; dépareillé, déparié; *(strange)* non usuel, bizarre.
odds, *s. pl.* avantage *m.;* chances *f. pl.*
of, *prep.* de.
off, *adv.* à . . . de distance; *be ~* s'en aller; *be well ~* être à l'aise; *— prep.* de.
offence, *s* offense *f.*
offend, *v. a.* & *n.* offenser.
offensive, *s.* offensive *f.*
offer, *s.* offre *f.; — v.a.* offrir.
office, *s.* bureau *m.; (of pers.)* charge *f.;* fonction *f.*
officer, *s.* officer *m.; (police)* agent *m.*
official, *adj.* officiel; *— s.* fonctionnaire *m. f.*
often, *adv.* souvent.
oil, *s.* huile *f.;* pétrole *m.*
ointment, *s.* onguent *m.*
old, *adj.* vieux, -eil, -eille; âgé; ancien; *how ~ are you?* quel âge avez-vous?; *~ age* vieillesse *f.; grow ~* vieillir.
old-fashioned, *adj.* à l'ancienne mode.
omission, *s.* omission *f.*
omit, *v.a.* omettre (de).
on, *prep.* sur; *(prep. omitted with days etc.); ~ Monday* lundi; *~ time* à la minute.
once, *adv.* une fois; autrefois; *at ~* tout de suite.
one, *adj.* & *s.* un, une; *— pron. (~, ~s omitted if*

preceded by adj.); (people, they) on; *this* ~ celui-ci; *that* ~ celui-là; ~'*s* son, sa, ses; *which* ~? lequel ...?
oneself, *pron*, soi-même; *by* ~ tout seul.
onion, *s.* oignon *m.*
onlooker, *s.* spectateur, -trice *m. f.*
open, *adj.* ouvert; découvert; public; franc; — *v.a.* ouvrir; *v.n.* s'ouvrir.
opening, *s.* ouverture *f.*
opera, *s.* opéra *m.*
operate, *v.a.* & *n.* opérer; ~ *on* opérer (qn).
operating-theatre, *s.* salle *f.* d'opération.
operation, *s.* opération *f.*
operative, *adj.* actif.
opinion, *s.* opinion *f.*; *in my* ~ à mon avis.
opponent, *s.* adversaire *m.*
opportunity, *s.* occasion *f.*
oppose, *v.a.* s'opposer à; ~*d to* opposé à.
opposition, *s.* opposition *f.*
optional, *adj.* facultatif.
or, *conj.* ou; *whether* ... ~ ou ... ou.
oral, *adj.* oral.
orange, *s.* orange *f.*
orchard, *s.* verger *m.*
orchestra, *s.* orchestre *m.*
order, *s.* ordre *m.*; *(commerce)* commande *f.*; *(ruling)* règlement *m.*; — *v.a.* ordonner; *(goods)* commander.
order-form, *s.* bon *m.* commande.
ordinary, *adj.* ordinaire *m.*
ore, *s.* minerai *m.*
organ, *s.* organe *m.*; *(music)* orgue *m.*
organic, *adj.* organique.
organization, *s.* organisation. *f*
organize, *v.a.* organiser.
oriental, *adj.* oriental.
origin, *s.* origine *f.*
original, *adj.* original.
ornament, *s.* ornement *m.*; — *v.a.* orner.
ornamental, *adj.* ornemental.
orphan, *adj.* & *s.* orphelin, -e *(m. f.)*.
other, *adj.* & *pron.* autre.
otherwise, *adv.* autrement.
ought, *v. aux.* devoir.
ounce, *s.* once *f.*
our, *adj.* notre, *(pl.)* nos.
ours, *pron.* le, la nôtre; les nôtres.
ourself, *pron.* nous(-mêmes); *ourselves* nous(-mêmes); *by ourselves* seul, -s.
out, *adv.* dehors; — *prep.* ~ *of* hors de.
outdoors, *adv.* dehors, en plein air.
outfit, *s.* trousseau *m.*
outing, *s.* excursion *f.*
outline, *s.* contour *m.*; aperçu *m.*; — *v.a.* esquisser.
outlive, *v.a.* survivre à.
outlook, *s.* perspective *f.*
output, *s.* production *f.*
outrageous, *adj.* outrageant; atroce.
outset, *s.* début *m.*; *at the* ~ dès le commence-

ment.
outside, *adv.* au dehors; — *prep.* en dehors de; — *adj.* du dehors; — *s.* extérieur.
outskirts, *s. pl.* banlieue *f.*; lisière *f.*
outstanding, *adj.* non réglé, à payer; saillant; éminent.
outward, *adj.* extérieur.
outwards, *adv.* à l'extérieur, en dehors.
oven, *s.* four *m.*
over, *prep.* au-dessus de; *(motion)* par dessus; *(superior)* sur; *(more than)* plus de; *(across)* par; — *adv.* *(more)* davantage; *(finished)* fini, passé; *(too)* trop.
overcoat, *s.* pardessus *m.*
overcome, *v.a.* surmonter; vaincre.
overcrowded, *adj.* surpeuplé.
overdo, *v.a.* faire trop cuire; exagérer.
overexpose, *v.a.* surexposer.
overflow, *s.* débordement *m.*; — *v.a.* inonder; *v.n.* déborder.
overlook, *v.a.* *(look on to)* avoir vue sur; *(neglect)* négliger; *(superintend)* surveiller.
overpower, *v.a.* accabler; subjuguer.
oversea, *adj.* d'outre-mer; **~s** *(adv.)* outre-mer.
oversight, *s.* inadvertence *f.*
overtake, *v.a.* rattraper; surprendre (par).
overthrow, *s.* renversement *m.*; — *v.a.* renverser.
overtime, *s.* heures *f. pl.* supplémentaires.
overwhelming, *adj.* accablant.
owe, *v.a.* devoir (à); être redevable (à).
owing, *adj.* ~ *to* à cause de.
owl, *s.* hibou *m.*
own, *adj.* propre; *of my* ~ à moi; — *v.a.* posséder.
owner, *s.* propriétaire *m. f.*
ox, *s.* bœuf *m.*
oxygen, *s.* oxygène *m.*
oyster, *s.* huître *f.*

P

pace, *s.* pas *m.*; *v.a.* arpenter; *v.n.* aller au pas.
pack, *s.* paquet; *(cards)* jeu *m.*; *(wool)* balle; *(hounds)* meute *f.*; — *v.a.* emballer; faire: ~ *off* expédier.
package, *s.* colis *m.*; paquet *m.*
packet, *s.* paquet *m.*
pact, *s.* pacte *m.*
pad, *s.* bourrelet *m.*; tampon *m.*; bloc *m.*; *blotting* ~ buvard *m.*
paddle, *v.n.* pagayer.
page, *s.* page *f.*
pail, *s.* seau *m.*
pain, *s.* douleur *f.*; *take* ~*s* se donner de la peine.
painful, *adj.* douloureux.
paint, *s.* peinture *f.*; — *v. a.* peindre.

painter, *s.* peintre *m.*
painting, *s.* peinture *f.*
pair, *s.* paire *f.*; couple *m.*
palace, *s.* palais *m.*
palate, *s.* palais *m.*
pale, *adj.* pâle; *grow* ~ pâlir.
palm, *s.* palme *f.*
pan, *s.* poêle *f.*
pane, *s.* vitre *f.*
panel, *s.* panneau *m.*
panorama, *s.* panorama *m.*
pansy, *s.* pensée *f.*
pantry, *s.* office *f.*
pants, *s.pl.* caleçon *m.*; pantalon *m.*
paper, *s.* papier *m.*; *(newspaper)* journal *m.*; *(essay)* étude *f.*; *(exam)* composition *f.*
parade, *s.* parade *f.*; — *v.n.* parader.
paraffin, *s.* pétrole *m.*
paragraph, *s.* paragraphe *m.*
parallel, *s.* *(line)* parallèle *f.*; *(comparison)* parallèle *m.*; — *adj.* parallèle.
paralysis, *s.* paralysie *f.*
parcel, *s.* paquet *m.*
pardon, *s.* pardon *m.*; *I beg your* ~ je vous demande pardon; *(I beg your)* ~? comment (dites-vous)?, pardon?; — *v.a.* pardonner.
parents, *s. pl.* père *m.* et mère *f.*, parents.
parish, *s.* paroisse *f.*
Parisian, *adj.* parisien; — *s.* Parisien, -enne *m.f.*
park, *s.* parc *m.*; *(car)* (parc de) stationnement *m.*; — *v.a.* garer; stationner; *no* ~*ing* stationnement interdit.
parliament, *s.* parlement *m.*
parliamentary, *adj.* parlementaire.
parlour, *s.* petit salon *m.*
parrot, *s.* perroquet *m.*
part, *s.* part *f.*; partie *f.*; *(theatre)* rôle *m.*; *(region)* région *f.*; *on my* ~ de ma part; *take* ~ *in* prendre part à; — *v.a.* diviser; séparer; *v.n.* se diviser; *(pers.)* se séparer (de).
partial, *adj.* *(unfair)* partial; *(incomplete)* partiel.
participant, *s.* participant *m.*
participate, *v.n.* ~ *in* prendre part à.
participation, *s.* participation *f.*
participle, *s.* participe
particular, *adj.* particulier; — *s.* détail
partly, *adv.* en partie.
partner, *s.* associé, *m. f.*; partenaire *m*
partridge, *s.* perdrix *f.*
party, *s.* parti *m.*; partie *f.*; groupe *m.*; réception *f.*, soirée *f.*
pass, *v.a.* passer; dépasser; surpasser; *(law)* voter; *(resolution)* prendre; *(exam)* être reçu (à); — *v. n.* passer; — *s.* défilé *m.*; laisser-passer *m.*
passage, *s.* passage *m.*; couloir *m.*
passenger, *s.* voyageur,

-euse *m. f.*; passager, -ère *m. f.*
passer-by, *s.* passant *m.*
passion, *s.* passion *f.*
passionate, *adj.* passionné.
passive, *adj.* & *s.* passif *(m.).*
passport, *s.* passeport *m.*
past, *adj.* passé; dernier; — *s.* passé *m.*
paste, *s.* pâte *f.*
pastime, *s.* passe-temps *m*
pastry, *s.* pâtisserie *f.*
patch, *s.* pièce *f.*
patent, *s.* brevet *m.* d'invention.
path, -way, *s.* sentier *m.*
patience, *s.* patience *f.*
patient, *s.* malade *m. f.*; — *adj.* patient.
patriot, *s.* patriote *m. f.*
patrol, *s.* patrouille; — *v.n.* aller en patrouille.
patron, *s.* patron *m.*; client *m.*
pattern, *s.* modèle *m.*
pause, *s.* pause *f.*; — *v.n.* faire une pause.
pave, *v.a.* paver.
pavement, *s.* trottoir *m.*
pavilion, *s.* pavillon *m.*
paw, *s.* patte *f.*
pay, *v.a.* payer; *(visit)* faire; ~ *off* acquitter; — *v.n.* payer; — *s.* paye *f.*, salaire *m.*
payable, *adj.* payable (à).
payment, *s.* payement *m.*
pea, *s.* pois *m.*
peace, *s.* paix *f.*
peaceful, *adj.* paisible.
peach, *s.* pêche *f.*
peacock, *s.* paon *m.*
peak, *s.* pic *m.*, cime *f.*
pear, *s.* poire *f.*
pearl, *s.* perle *f.*
peasant, *s.* **paysan, -anne** *m. f.*
pebble, *s.* caillou *m.*
peck, *s.* coup *m.* de bec.
peculiar, *adj.* particulier.
pedestrian, *s.* piéton *m.*
peel, *s.* pelure *f.*; — *v.a.* peler.
peer, *s.* pair *m.*
peg, *s.* pince *f.*; piquet *m.*
pen, *s.* stylo *m.*
penalty, *s.* peine *f.*
pencil, *s.* crayon *m.*
penicillin, *s.* pénicilline *f.*
penknife, *s.* canif *m.*
penny, *s.* penny *m.*
pension, *s.* pension *f.*
people, *s.* peuple *m.*; gens *m. pl.* [*f.* with *adj.* before it]; famille *f.*
pepper, *s.* poivre *m.*
per, *prep.* **par**; ~ *cent* pour cent.
perceive, *v.a.* percevoir.
perch, *s.* perchoir *m.*; — *v.n.* se percher.
perfect, *adj.* parfait; — *v.a.* rendre **parfait**; achever.
perform, *v.a.* accomplir, exécuter.
performance, *s.* représentation *f.*
perfume, *s.* parfum *m.*
perhaps, *adv.* peut-être.
peril, *s.* péril *m.*
period, *s.* période *f.*
periodical, *s.* périodique *m.*
perish, *v.n.* périr.
perishable, *adj.* périssable.
permanent, *adj.* permanent.
permission, *s.* permission

f.
permit, *s.* permis *m.*; — *v.a.* permettre.
persecution, *s.* persécution *f.*
Persian, *adj.* persan.
persist, *v.n.* persister.
person, *s.* personne *f.*
personal, *adj.* personnel.
personality, *s.* personnalité *f.*
perspiration, *s.* transpiration *f.*
persuade, *v.a.* convaincre (de), persuader.
pertain, *v.n.* appartenir (à).
pet, *s.* enfant *m.f.* gâté, -e; — *adj.* favori; ~ *dog* chien *m.* familier.
petrol, *s.* essence *f.*
petroleum, *s.* pétrole *m.*
petticoat, *s.* jupon *m.*
phase, *s.* phase *f.*
pheasant, *s.* faisan, -e *m. f.*
phenomenon, *s.* phénomène *m.*
philosopher, *s.* philosophe *m.*
philosophy, *s.* philosophie *f.*
phone, *s.* téléphone *m.*; — *v.a.* & *n.* téléphoner.
photo(graph), *s.* photographie *f.* — *v.a.* photographier.
phrase, *s.* phrase *f.*
physical, *adj.* physique.
physician, *s.* médecin *m.*
physicist, *s.* physicien *m.*
physics, *s.* physique *f.*
pianist, *s.* pianiste *m. f.*
piano, *s.* piano *m.*
pick, *v. a.* cueillir; picoter; *(teeth)* curer; *(bone)* ronger; *(choose)* choisir; ~ *out* choisir; ~ *up* ramasser; prendre.
pickle, *s.* marinade *f.* ~*s* pickles *m.*
picnic, *s.* pique-nique *m.*
picture, *s.* tableau *m.*; portrait *m.*; film *m.*; ~*s* cinéma *m.*
pie, *s.* pâté *m.*
piece, *s.* morceau *m.*; partie *f.*; pièce *f.*; ~ *of news* nouvelle *f.*; ~ *of work* ouvrage *m.*
pier, *s.* jetée *f.*
pierce, *v.a.* percer.
pig, *s.* cochon *m.*
pigeon, *s.* pigeon *m.*
pile[1], *s.* tas *m.*; — *v.a.* (also ~ *up*) entasser, amasser.
pile[2], *s.* pieu *m.*, pilot *m.*
pill, *s.* pillule *f.*
pillar, *s.* pilier *m.*
pillar-box, *s.* boîte *f.* aux lettres.
pillow, *s.* oreiller *m.*
pilot, *s.* pilote *m.*
pin, *s.* épingle *f.*
pinch, *v.a.* pincer.
pine, *s.* pin *m.*
pineapple, *s.* ananas *m.*
pink, *adj.* & *s.* rose *(m.)*.
pint, *s.* pinte *f.*
pious, *adj.* pieux.
pipe, *s.* tuyau *m.*; *(smoking)* pipe *f.*
pistol, *s.* pistolet *m.*
pit, *s.* fosse *f.*; creux *m.*; *(theatre)* parterre *m.*
pitch, *s.* degré *m.*; ton *m.*; *v.a.* *(tent)* dresser; *(camp)* asseoir.
pity, *s.* pitié *f.*; dommage *m.*

place, *s.* lieu *m.*, endroit *m.*; place *f.*; emploi *m.*; — *v.a.* mettre.
plain, *adj.* uni; simple; évident; ordinaire.
plait, *s.* tresse *f.*
plan, *s.* plan *m.*; projet *m.*; — *v.a.* faire le plan (de).
plane, *s.* plan *m.*; *(tool)* rabot *m.*; *(aero-)* avion *m.*; — *v.a.* raboter.
planet, *s.* planète *f.*
plank, *s.* planche *f.*
plant, *s.* plante *f.*; *(works)* usine *f.*, fabrique *f.*; — *v.a.* planter.
plantation, *s.* plantation *f.*
plaster, *s.* (em)plâtre *m.*
plastic, *adj.* plastique; *~s* plastiques *m. pl.*
plate, *s.* plaque *f.*; planche *f.*; *(china)* assiette *f.*; *(silver)* vaisselle *f.*
platform, *s.* quai *m.*
platinum, *s.* platine *m.*
platter, *s.* plat *m.*
play, *s.* jeu *m.*; pièce *f.* de théâtre; — *v.a.* & *n.* jouer.
player, *s.* joueur, -euse *m. f.*
playground, *s.* cour *f.* de récréation.
plea, *s.* excuse *f.*; défense *f.*
plead, *v.a.&n.* plaider
pleasant, *adj.* agréable.
please, *v.a.* & *n.* plaire (à); *be ~ed with, to* être content de; *as you ~* comme vous voulez; *if you ~* s'il vous plaît.
pleasure, *s.* plaisir *m.*
pledge, *s.* gage *m.*; — *v.a.* mettre en gage.
plenty, *s.* abondance *f.*; *~ of* quantité de, beaucoup de.
plot, *s.* *(land)* terrain *m.*; *(story)* intrigue *f.*; *(conspiracy)* complot *m.*; *v. n.* conspirer.
plough, *s.* charrue *f.*; — *v.a.&n.* labourer.
plug, *s.* tampon *m.*; prise *f.* de courant; — *v.a.* tamponner.
plum, *s.* prune *f.*
plume, *s.* plume *f.*; plumet *m.*
plunder, *v.a.* piller; — *s.* pillage *m.*
plunge, *v.a.* & *n.* plonger; — *s.* plongeon *m.*
plural, *s.* & *adj.* pluriel *(m.)*.
plus, *prep.* plus.
ply, *v.a.* manier; s'appliquer (à); *v.n.* faire le service (entre).
pocket, *s.* poche *f.*
pocket-book, *s.* carnet *m.*; portefeuille *m.*
poem, *s.* poème *m.*
poet, *s.* poète *m.*
poetic(al), *adj.* poétique
poetry, *s.* poésie *f.*
point, *s.* point *m.*; pointe *f.*; — *v.a.* & *n.* *~ out* montrer du doigt; faire valoir (un fait); *~ to* indiquer.
poison, *s.* poison *m.*; — *v.a.* empoisonner.
poisonous, *adj.* vénéneux.
pole, *s.* pôle *m.*
Pole, *s.* Polonais, -e *m. f.*

police, *s.* police *f.*
policeman, -officer, *s.* agent (de police) *m.*
police-station, *s.* poste (de police) *m.*
policy, *s.* politique *f.*; *(insurance)* police *f.*
polish, *s.* poli *m.*; *fig.* politesse *f.*; — *v. a.* polir.
Polish, *adj.* polonais.
polite, *adj.* poli.
political, *adj.* politique.
politician, *s.* politique *m.*; politicien *m.*
politics, *s.* politique *f.*
poll, *s.* vote *m.*; liste *f.* (électorale); scrutin *m.*
pool[1], *s.* mare *f.*
pool[2], *s.* pool *m.*
poor, *adj.* pauvre; *(bad)* mauvais.
pope, *s.* pape *m.*
popular, *adj.* populaire.
popularity, *s.* popularité *f.*
population, *s.* population *f.*
pork, *s.* porc *m.*; ~ *butcher* charcutier *m.*
port, *s.* port *m.*; *(ship)* bâbord *m.*
portable, *adj.* portatif.
porter, *s.* portier *m.*; *(railw.)* porteur *m.*
portfolio, *s.* serviette *f.*
portion, *s.* portion *f.*; — *v.a.* partager.
portrait, *s.* portrait *m.*
Portuguese, *adj.* portugais; — *s.* Portugais, -e *m. f.*
position, *s.* position *f.*
positive, *adj.* & *s.* positif *(m.)*.
possess, *v.a.* posséder.
possession, *s.* possession *f.*
possibility, *s.* possibilité *f.*
possible, *adj.* possible.
post[1], *s.* poteau *m.*; — *v.a.* afficher, placarder.
post[2], *s.* poste *f.*; courrier *m.* — *v.a.* mettre à la poste.
postage, *s.* port *m.*, affranchissement; ~ *paid* port payé.
postal, *adj.* postal; ~ *order* mandat (de poste) *m.*
poster, *s.* affiche *f.*
post-free, *adj.* franco.
postman, *s.* facteur *m.*
post(-)office, *s.* bureau *m.* de poste
postpone, *v.a.* remettre.
postscript, *s.* post-scriptum *m.*
pot, *s.* pot *m.*
potato, *s.* pomme *f.* de terre.
pottery, *s.* poterie *f.*
pouch, *s.* blague *f.*
poultry, *s.* volaille *f.*
pound, *s.* livre *f.*
pour, *v.a.* verser.
pouring, *adj.* torrentiel.
poverty, *s.* pauvreté *f.*
powder, *s.* poudre *f.*
power, *s.* pouvoir *m.*; puissance *f.*; force *f.*
powerful, *adj.* puissant.
power-plant, -station, *s.* centrale *f.* électrique.
practical, *adv.* pratique.
practice, *s.* pratique *f.*; exercise *m.*
practise, *v.a.* pratiquer, exercer; étudier.
praise, *s.* louange *f.*; — *v.a.* louer.
pray, *v.a.* & *n.* prier.

prayer, *s.* prière *f.*
preach, *v.a.* & *n.* prêcher.
preacher, *s.* prédicateur *m.*
precede, *v.a.* précéder.
preceding, *adj.* précédent.
precious, *adj.* précieux.
precision, *s.* précision *f.*
predecessor, *s.* prédécesseur *m.*
predict, *v.a.* prédire.
prefabricated, *adj.* préfabriqué.
preface, *s.* préface *f.*
prefer, *v.a.* préférer *(to* à), aimer mieux.
preferable, *adj.* préférable (à).
preference, *s.* préférence *f.*
pregnant, *adj.* enceinte.
prejudice, *s.* préjugé *m.*
preliminary, *adj.* préliminaire.
premature, *adj.* prématuré.
premier, *s.* premier ministre *m., (in France)* président *m.* du conseil.
premises, *s. pl.* lieux *m. pl.;* local *m.,* immeuble *m.*
premium, *s.* prime *f.*
preparation, *s.* préparation *f.*
prepare, *v.a.* préparer, apprêter; — *v.n.* se préparer.
preposition, *s.* préposition *f.*
Presbyterian, *adj.* presbytérien.
prescribe, *v.a.* prescrire, ordonner; *v.n.* ~ *for* faire une ordonnance pour.
prescription, *s.* prescription *f.; (medical)* ordonnance *f.*
presence, *s.* présence *f.*
present[1], *adj.* présent; actuel; — *s.* présent *m.; at* ~ à présent.
present[2], *s. (gift)* cadeau *m.,* présent *m.;* — *v.a.* présenter; donner.
presently, *adv.* tout à l'heure.
preserve, *v.a.* préserver; *(fruits)* conserver; — *s.* confiture *f.;* conserve *f.*
president, *s.* président *m.*
press, *s.* presse *f.;* — *v.a.* presser; serrer.
pressure, *s.* pression *f.*
presume, *v.a.* présumer.
presumption, *s.* présomption *f.*
pretend, *v. a.* & *n.* feindre, faire semblant; prétendre (à).
pretention, *s.* prétension *f.*
pretty, *adj.* joli.
prevail, *v.n.* prévaloir; prédominer.
prevent, *v.a.* empêcher.
prevention, *s.* empêchement *m.*
previous, *adj.* antérieur (à).
prey, *s.* proie *f.*
price, *s.* prix *m.;* cours *m.*
price-list, *s.* prix-courant *m.,* tarif *m.*
prick, *v.a.* piquer; — *s.* piqûre *f.*
pride, *s.* orgueil *m.*
priest, *s.* prêtre *m.*

primary, *adj.* primaire.
prime, *adj.* ~ *minister see* **premier.**
primitive, *adj.* primitif.
prince, *s.* prince *m.*
princess, *s.* princesse *f.*
principal, *adj.* principal; — *s.* directeur *m.*, patron, -ne *m.f.*, principal *m.*
principle, *s.* principe *m*
print, *s.* empreinte *f.*; impression *f.*; *out of* ~ épuisé; — *v.a.* imprimer; faire une empreinte (sur); *(photo)* tirer; ~*ed matter* imprimés *m. pl.*
printing-office, *s.* imprimerie *f.*
prison, *s.* prison *f.*
prisoner, *s.* prisonnier, -ère *m. f.*
private, *adj.* particulier; personel; privé.
privilege, *s.* privilège *m.*
prize, *s.* prix *m.*
probability, *s.* probabilité *f.*
probable, *adj.* probable.
probably, *adv.* probablement.
problem, *s.* problème *m.*
procedure, *s.* procédé *m.*
proceed, *v.n.* aller (à); se mettre (à); avancer; passer (à); procéder; ~ *with* continuer.
process, *s.* développement *m.*; méthode *f.*, procédé *m.*; — *v.n.* aller en procession.
procession, *s.* cortège *m.*; procession *f.*
proclaim, *v. a.* proclamer.
proclamation, *s.* proclamation *s.*
produce, *v.a.* produire.
producer, *s.* producteur, -trice *m. f.*
product, *s.* produit *m.*
production, *s.* production *f.*
profess, *v.a.* professer, déclarer.
profession, *s.* profession *f.*
professional, *adj.* professionnel; de profession.
professor, *s.* professeur *m.*
profit, *s.* profit *m.*; — *v.n.* ~ *by* profiter de.
profitable, *adj.* profitable.
profound, *adj.* profond.
programme, *s.* programme *m.*
progress, *s.* progrès *m.*; marche *f.*; — *v.n.* s'avancer, faire des progrès.
prohibit, *v.a.* défendre.
prohibition, *s.* prohibition *f.*, défense *f.*
project, *s.* projet *m.*; — *v.a.* projeter; *v.n.* saillir.
projector, *s.* projecteur *m.*
prolong, *v.a.* prolonger.
prominent, *adj.* (pro)éminent.
romise, *s.* promesse *f.*; — *v.a.* promettre.
promote, *v.a.* donner de l'avancement (à); encourager.
promotion, *s.* promotion *f.*, avancement *m.*
prompt, *adj.* prompt; — *v.a.* *(rheatre)* souffler; inspirer.
pronoun, *s.* pronom *m.*

pronounce, *v.a.* prononcer.
pronunciation, *s.* prononciation *f.*
proof, *s.* preuve *f.*; épreuve *f.*
propeller, *s.* hélice *f.*
proper, *adj.* propre; convenable.
property, *s.* propriété *f.*
prophet, *s.* prophète *m.*
proportion, *s.* proportion *f.*
propose, *v.a.* proposer.
proposition, proposal, *s.* proposition *f.*
prose, *s.* prose *f.*
prospect, *s.* prospective *f.*
prospectus, *s.* prospectus *m.*
prosper, *v.n.* prospérer.
prosperity, *s.* prospérité *f.*
prosperous, *adj.* prospère.
protest, *s.* protestation *f.*; protêt *m.*; — *v.a.* protester.
Protestant, *adj.* & *s.* protestant, -e *(m. f.)*.
proud, *adj.* fier, -ère.
prove, *v.a.* prouver; éprouver.
proverb, *s.* proverbe *m.*
provide, *v.a.* pourvoi de; fournir de; *v.n.* ~ *for* pourvoir à; ~*d that* pourvu que.
providence, *s.* prévoyance *f.*
province, *s.* province *f.*
provincial, *adj.* provincial.
provision, *s.* provision *f.*
provoke, *v. a.* provoquer (à).
prudent, *adj.* prudent.
psalm, *s.* psaume *m.*
psychological, *adj.* psychologique.
psychology, *s.* psychologie *f.*
public, *adj.* & *s.* public *m.*
publication, *s.* publication *f.*
publicity, *s.* publicité *f.*
publish, *v.a.* publier.
publisher, *s.* éditeur *m.*
pudding, *s.* pouding *m.*
pull, *v.a.* tirer; ~ *down* démolir; ~ *out* arracher; ~ *up* arrêter; *v. n.* tirer; ~ *through* s'en tirer; — *s.* traction *f.*, tirage *f.*
pulpit, *s.* chaire *f.*
pulse, *s.* pouls *m.*
pump, *s.* pompe *f.*; — *v. a.* pomper.
punch[1], *s.* poinçon *m.*; — *v.a.* poinçonner, percer.
punch[2], *s.* punch *m.*
punctual, *adj.* ponctuel.
puncture, *s.* piqûre *f.*; *(tyre)* crevaison *f.*; — *v.a.& n.* crever.
punish, *v.a.* punir.
punishment,, *s.* punition *f.*
pupil[1], *s.* élève *m. f.*
pupil[2], *s.* *(eye)* pupille *f.*
puppy, *s.* petit chien *m.*
purchase, *s.* achat *m.*; — *v.a.* acheter.
pure, *adj.* pur.
purge, *v.a.* purger.
purify, *v.a.* purifier.
purity, *s.* pureté *f.*
purpose, *s.* but *m.*
purse, *s.* porte-monnaie

m., bourse *f.*
pursue, *v.a.* (pour)suivre.
pursuit, *s.* poursuite *f.*
push, *v.a.* & *n.* pousser; ~ *back* repousser; ~ *on* faire avancer; pousser (jusqu'à); — *s.* poussé *f.*; allant *m.*
puss, *s.* minet *m.*
put, *v.a.* mettre; *(express)* dire; ~ *back* remettre; ~ *down* déposer; attribuer; inscrire; ~ *off* remettre; ôter; ~ *on* mettre; ~ *out* tendre; éteindre; ~ *up* ouvrir; loger; ~ *up with* s'accommoder.
puzzle, *v.a.* embarrasser.
pyjamas, *s. pl.* pyjama *m.*
pyramid, *s.* pyramide *f.*

Q

quadrangle, *s.* quadrilatère *m.*; cour *f.*
quake, *v.n.* trembler.
qualification, *s.* qualification *f.*; compétence *f.*
qualify, *v.a.* qualifier; *v.n.* ~ *for* passer l'examen de.
quality, *s.* qualité *f.*
quantity, *s.* quantité *f.*
quarrel, *s.* querelle *f.*; brouille *f.*; — *v.n.* se brouiller; ~ *with* se quereller avec.
quarter, *s.* quartier *m.*; quart *m.*; ~*s* quartiers *m.pl.*
quartet(te), *s.* quatuor *m.*
quay, *s.* quai *m.*
queen, *s.* reine *f.*; *(cards)* dame *f.*
queer, *adj.* bizarre.
quench, *v.a.* éteindre.
question, *s.* question *f.*; — *v.a.* interroger.
queue, *s.* queue *f.*; — *v.n.* ~ *up* faire (la) queue.
quick, *adj.* prompt, rapide; vif.
quick(ly), *adv.* vite.
quiet, *adj.* tranquille; calme; *be* ~ se taire.
quilt, *s.* courtepointe *f.*
quit, *v.a.* quitter.
quite, *adv.* tout à fait.
quiver, *v.n.* trembler.
quiz, *s.* mystification *f.*; persifleur *m.*; *v.a.* railler.
quotation, *s.* citation *f.*
quote, *v.a.* citer.

R

rabbi, *s.* rabbin *m.*
rabbit, *s.* lapin, -e *m. f.*
race[1], *s.* course *f.*; — *v.n.* faire la course; courir; lutter de vitesse.
race[2], *s.* race *f.*
rack, *s.* râtelier *m.*
racket, *s.* raquette *f.*
radiate, *v.n.* rayonner, irradier; *v.a.* dégager.
radiator, *s.* radiateur *m.*
radical, *adj.* radical.
radio, *s.* radio *f.*
radioactive, *adj.* radioactif.

radish, *s.* radis *m.*
rag, *s.* chiffon *m.*
rage, *s.* rage *f.*
raid, *s.* razzia *f.*, rafle *f.*; raid *m.*
rail, *s.* barre *f.*, rampe *f.*; rail *m.*; *by* ~ par chemin de fer.
railway, *s.* chemin *m.* de fer.
rain, *s.* pluie *f.*; — *v.n.* pleuvoir.
rainy, *adj.* pluvieux.
raise, *v.a.* lever, élever; soulever; *(plants)* faire pousser, cultiver.
rake, *s.* râteau *m.*
rally, *v.n.* se rallier; — *s.* ralliement *m.*
ramify, *v.n.* ramifier.
random, *s. at* ~ par hasard.
range, *s.* rangée *f.*; *(mountains)* chaîne *f.*; *(extent)* étendue *f.*; *(kitchen)* fourneau *m.*; — *v.a.* ranger.
rank, *s.* rang *m.*; grade *m.*
ransom, *s.* rançon *f.*; — *v.a.* payer rançon pour.
rap, *s.* tape *f.*; coup *m.*; — *v.a.* frapper.
rapid, *adj.* rapide.
rare, *adj.* rare.
rascal, *s.* coquin *m.*
rash, *adj.* téméraire; inconsidéré.
raspberry, *s.* framboise *f.*
rat, *s.* rat *m.*
rate, *s.* taux *m.*, cours *m.*, tarif *m.*; *(speed)* vitesse *f.*, allure *f.*; *(tax)* taxe *f.*; *at the* ~ *of* à la vitesse de; *at any* ~ en tout cas, quoi qu'il en soit; — *v.a.* estimer; taxer.
rather, *adv.* plutôt; un peu.
ratify, *v.a.* ratifier.
ration, *s.* ration *f.*
rational, *adj.* raisonnable.
rattle, *s.* bruit *m.*; — *v.n.* faire du bruit.
raven, *s.* corbeau *m.*
raw, *adj.* cru; ~ *material* matière *f.* première.
ray, *s.* rayon *m.*
razor, *s.* rasoir *m.*; *safety* ~ rasoir de sûreté; *electric* ~ rasoir électrique.
razor-blade, *s.* lame *f.* de rasoir.
reach, *v.a.* arriver (à); atteindre; *v. n.* atteindre; parvenir (à); — *s.* étendue *f.*; portée *f.*; *within* ~ à portée.
react, *v.n.* réagir.
reaction, *s.* réaction *f.*
reactor, *s.* réacteur *m.*
read, *v.a.* lire; *(study)* étudier; ~ *for (exam)* préparer.
reader, *s.* lecteur, -trice *m. f.*
reading, *s.* lecture *f.*
ready, *adj.* prêt (à); prompt (à); près (de); *get* ~ (se) préparer.
real, *adj.* réel; véritable.
reality, *s.* réalité *f.*
realization, *s.* réalisation *f.*
realize, *v.a.* réaliser.
really, *adv.* vraiment.
realm, *s.* royaume *m.*; *fig.* domaine *m.*

reap, *v.a.* & *n.* moissonner.
reaper, *s.* moissonneur *m.*
rear, *adj.* de derrière; — *s.* arrière *m.;* queue *f.;* — *v.a.* élever; *v. n.* se cabrer.
reason, *s.* raison *f.;* — *v. a.* & *n.* raisonner.
reasonable, *adj.* raisonnable.
reasoning, *s.* raisonnement *m.*
rebellion, *s.* rébellion *f.*
rebuke, *s.* réprimande *f.;* — *v.a.* réprimander.
recall, *v.a.* rappeler; *(remember)* se rappeler.
receipt, *s.* reçu *m.*, quittance *f.;* recette *f.*
receive, *v.a.* recevoir.
receiver, *s.* destinataire *m. f.; (phone, wireless)* écouteur *m.*, récepteur *m.*, poste *m.*
recent, *adj.* récent.
recently, *adv.* récemment.
reception, *s.* réception *f.*
receptionist, *s.* portier *m.* d'auberge; employé à la réception.
recipe, *s.* recette *f.*
recital, *s.* récit *m.;* récital *m.*
recite, *v.a.* & *n.* réciter.
reckless, *adj.* insouciant.
reckon, *v.a.* compter.
recognize, *v.a.* reconnaître.
recollect, *v. a.* se rappeler.
recommend, *v.a.* recommander.
recommendation, *s.* recommandation *f.*
reconcile, *v. a.* réconcilier.
record, *s.* rapport *m.* officiel; souvenir *m.;* mention *f.;* archives *f. pl.; (gramophone)* disque *m.; (sport)* record *m.;* — *v.a.* enrégistrer; rapporter.
recount, *v.a.* raconter.
recover, *v.a.* recouvrer; *v.n.* se remettre.
recreation, *s.* récréation *f.*
recruit, *s.* recrue *f.;* — *v.a.* recruter.
rectangle, *s.* rectangle *m.*
rector, *s.* recteur *m.;* curé *m.*
recur, *v. n.* revenir.
red, *adj.* rouge; roux.
redress, *v.n.* réparer; redresser.
reduce, *v.a.* réduire.
reduction, *s.* réduction *f.*
reed, *s.* roseau *m.*
reef, *s.* ris *m.*; récif *m.*
reel, *s.* dévidoir *m.;* bobine *f.;* — *v.n.* tourner.
refer, *v.a.* référer; renvoyer; *v.n.* ~ *to* se rapporter à, s'en rapporter à, se référer à.
referee, *s.* arbitre *m.;* — *v.a.* arbitrer.
reference, *s.* renvoi *m.*, référence *f.;* rapport *m.;* allusion *f.; with ~ to* à propos de; *have ~ to* se rapporter à.
refill, *s.* recharge *f.*
reflect, *v.a.* réfléchir; *v.n.* méditer (sur).
reflection, *s.* réflexion

f.; image *f.*
reform, *s.* réforme *f.*; — *v.a.* réformer.
Reformation, *s.* Réforme *f.*
refrain, *v.n.* ~ *from* se retenir de.
refresh, *v.a.* refraîchir.
refreshment, *s.* rafraîchissement *m.*; ~ *room* buffet *m.*
refrigerator, *s.* réfrigérateur *m.*
refuge, *s.* refuge *m.*; *take* ~ se réfugier.
refugee, *s.* réfugié, -e *m. f.*
refusal, refus *m.*
refuse, *v.a.* refuser.
refute, *v.a.* réfuter.
regain, *v.a.* reconquérir; regagner; reprendre.
regard, *s.* égard *m.*; *with* ~ *to* à l'égard de; *kind(est)* ~*s* meilleurs amitiés *f. pl.*; — *v.a.* regarder; tenir compte (de); considérer.
regent, *s.* régent *m.*
regime, *s.* régime *m.*
regiment, *s.* régiment *m.*
region, *s.* région *f.*
register, *v. a.* enregistrer.
regret, *v.a.* regretter; — *s.* regret *m.*
regular, *adj.* régulier.
regulate, *v.a.* régler.
regulation, *s.* ordonnance *f.*; réglementation *f.*
rehearsal, *s.* répétition *f.*
rehearse, *v.a.* répéter.
reign, *s.* règne *m.*; — *v. a.* régner
rein, *s.* rêne *f.*
reject, *v.a.* rejeter; refuser.
relate, *v.a.* raconter; *be* ~*ed to* être apparenté à; *v.n.* ~ *to* se rapporter à; *relating to* relatif à.
relation, *s.* relation *f.*, rapport *m.* (à); *(relative)* parent, -e *m f.*
relative, *s.* parent, -e *m. f.*; — *adj.* relatif; ~ *to* au sujet de.
relax, *v.n.* se relâcher; *v. a.* relâcher.
relay, *s.* relais *m.*
release, *s.* délivrance *f.*; — *v.a.* libérer; décharger (de).
reliable, *adj.* digne de confiance.
relic, *s.* relique *f.*
relief[1], *s.* délivrance *f.*; soulagement *m.*; secours *m.*
relief[2], *s.* relief *m.*
relieve, *v.a.* soulager; secourir; délivrer.
religion, *s.* religion *f.*
religious, *adj.* religieux.
rely, *v.n.* ~ *upon* compter sur.
remain, *v.n.* rester.
remark, *s.* remarque *f.*; — *v.a.* remarquer; *v.n.* faire une remarque.
remarkable, *adj.* remarquable.
remedy, *s.* remède *m.*
remember, *v.a.* se souvenir (de), se rappeler.
remembrance, *s.* souvenir *m.*
remind, *v. a.* ~ *of* rappeler (à), faire souvenir (de).
remit, *v.a.* remettre.

remittance, *s.* remise *f.*
remorse, *s.* remords *m.*
remote, *adj.* reculé.
removal, *s.* déménagement *m.;* enlèvement; *(dismissal)* renvoi *m.*
remove, *v.a.* déménager; enlever; *(dismiss)* renvoyer, *(from school)* retirer; *v.n.* déménager; s'en aller.
Renaissance, *s.* Renaissance *f.*
render, *v.a.* rendre.
renew, *v.a.* renouveler.
renounce, *v.a.* renoncer (à); dénoncer; répudier.
rent, *s. (house)* loyer *m.;* — *v.a.* louer.
repair, *s.* réparation *f.;* — *v.a.* réparer.
repay, *v.a.* rembourser.
repeat, *v.a.* répéter.
repentance, *s.* repentir *m.*
repetition, *s.* répétition *f.*
replace, *v.a.* replacer.
reply, *s.* réponse *f.;* — *v.a. & n.* répondre.
report, *s.* rapport *m.,* compte *m.* rendu; bruit *m.;* bulletin *m.;* — *v.a.* rapporter; rendre compte (de).
reporter, *s.* reporter *m.*
represent, *v.a.* représenter.
representation, *s.* représentation *f.*
representative, *s.* représentant *m.*
reproach, *s.* reproche *m.*
reproduce, *v.a.* reproduire.
reproduction, *s.* reproduction *f.*
reprove, *v.a.* réprimander.
republic, *s.* république *f.*
repulsion *s.* répulsion *f.*
repulsive, *adj.* repoussant.
reputation, repute, *s.* réputation *f.*
request, *s.* requête *f.;* — *v.a.* demander.
require, *v. a.* demander; exiger.
requirement, *s.* besoin *m.;* exigence *f.*
rescue, *s.* délivrance *f.;* secours *m.;* — *v.a.* délivrer; secourir.
research, *s.* recherche *f.*
resemble, *v.a.* ressembler (à).
resent, *v.a.* être froissé (de); ressentir.
reserve, *s.* réserve *f.;* — *v.a.* réserver.
reside, *v.n.* résider.
residence, *s.* résidence *f.*
resident, *s.* habitant *m.;* — *adj.* résidant.
resign, *v.a.* résigner, se démettre (de); *v.n.* donner sa démission.
resignation, *s.* résignation *f.;* démission *f.*
resist, *v. a.* résister (à).
resistance, *s.* résistance *f.*
resolution, *s.* résolution *f.*
resolve, *v.a.* résoudre; *v.n.* se résoudre (à), se décider (à faire).
resort, *s.* recours *m.;* ressource *f.;* — *v.n.* ~ *to* avoir recours à.
resource, *s.* ressource *f.*
respect, *s.* respect *m.;* rapport *m.; **in this ~*** sous ce rapport; ***with ~** to* concernant ...;

— *v.a.* respecter.
respectful, *adj.* respectueux.
respective, *adj.* respectif.
respond, *v.n.* répondre.
response, *s.* réponse *f.*
responsibility, *s.* responsabilité *f.*
responsible, *adj.* responsable (de).
rest[1], *s.* reste *m.; the* ~ les autres.
rest[2], *s.* repos *m.;* pause *f.;* — *v.n.* se reposer.
restaurant, *s.* restaurant *m.*
restless, *adj.* sans repos; inquiet; agité.
restoration, *s.* restauration *f.*
restore, *v.a.* restaurer.
restrain, *v.a.* retenir; ~ *from* empêcher de.
restraint, *s.* contrainte *f.;* retenue *f.*
restrict, *v.a.* restreindre.
restriction, *s.* restriction *f.*
result, *s.* résultat *m.;* — *v.n.* ~ *from* résulter de; ~ *in* avoir pour résultat.
resume, *v.a.* reprendre.
retain, *v.a.* retenir.
retire, *v.n.* se retirer.
retreat, *s.* retraite *f.*
return, *v.n.* revenir, retourner; *v.a.* rendre; renvoyer; *(answer)* faire; — *s.* retour *m*; renvoi *m.;* ~ *ticket* billet *m.* d'aller et retour.
reveal, *v.a.* révéler.
revenge, *s.* vengeance *f.;* — *v.a.* venger.
revenue, *s.* revenu *m.*
reverend, *adj.* révérend.
reverse, *adj.* inverse; — *s.* revers *m.*
review, *s.* revue *f.; (of book)* compte *m.* rendu, critique *f.;* — *v.a.* revoir; *(book)* faire la critique (d'un livre).
revision, *s.* révision *f.*
revolt, *s.* révolte *f.*
revolution, *s.* révolution *f.; (motor)* tour *m.*
reward, *s.* récompense *f.;* — *v.a.* récompenser.
rheumatism, *s.* rhumatisme *m.*
rhyme, *s.* rime *f.*
rhythm, *s.* rythme *m.*
rib, *s.* côte *f.*
rice, *s.* riz *m.*
rich, *adj.* riche.
rid, *v.a. get* ~ *of* se débarrasser de.
riddle, *s.* énigme *f.*
ride, *v.n.* monter; aller à cheval *or* à bicyclette; *(bus)* voyager; aller (en autobus); *v.a.* monter; — *s.* promenade *f.*
ridge, *s.* crête *f.*
ridiculous, *adj.* ridicule.
rifle, *s.* fusil *m.*
right, *adj.* droit; correct, exact; juste, bon; bien; ~ *side* endroit *m.; be* ~ avoir raison; *that's* ~ c'est ça; — *s.* droit *m.; (opposed to left)* droite *f.;* — *adv.* droit; bien; *(very)* très.
rim, *s.* bord *m.*
ring[1], *s.* anneau *m.;* cercle *m.; (sport)* ring *m.*
ring[2], *v.n.* & *a.* sonner;

~ up appeler (au téléphone); — *s.* son *m.; coup m.* de sonnette; *there is a ~ at the door* on sonne (à la porte).
rinse, *v.a.* rinser.
riot, *s.* émeute *f.*
rip, *v.a.* déchirer; *~ up* arracher; *v.n.* aller à toute vitesse.
ripe, *adj.* mûr.
rise, *v. n.* se lever; *(revolt)* se soulever; *(prices)* hausser; *(originate)* naître (de); — *s.* montée *f.; (salary)* augmentation *f.; give ~ to* donner lieu à.
risk, *s.* risque *m.;* — *v.a.* risquer.
rival, *adj.* & *s.* rival, -e *(m. f.);* — *v.a.* rivaliser (avec).
rivalry, *s.* rivalité *f.*
river, *s.* fleuve *m.*, rivière *f.*
road, *s.* route *f.*, chemin *m.*
road-map, *s.* carte *f.* routière. *f.*
roar, *s.* rugissement *m.;* — *v.n.* rugir; hurler.
roast, *v.a.* & *n.* rôtir; — *s.* rôti *m.*
rob, *v.a.* voler.
robber, *s.* voleur *m.*
robbery, *s.* vol *m.*
robe, *s.* robe *f.*
robin, *s.* rouge-gorge *m.*
rock, *s.* rocher *m.*, roc *m.*
rocket, *s.* fusée *f.*
rocky, *adj.* rocheux.
rod, *s.* baguette *f.*
rogue, *s.* coquin, -e *m. f.*
roll, *s.* rouleau *m.;* liste *f.;* — *v. a.* rouler.
roller-towel, *s.* essuie-mains *m.* à rouleau.
Roman, *adj.* romain; — *s.* Romain, -e *m. f.*
romantic, *adj.* romanesque; romantique.
roof, *s.* toit *m.*
room, *s.* chambre *f.;* salle *f.; (space)* place *f.*
root, *s.* racine *f.;* source *f.*
rope, *s.* corde *f.*
rose, *s.* rose *f.*
rotten, *adj.* pourri, carié.
rough, *adj.* rude; grossier; brut; *(sea)* gros.
roughly, *adv.* approximativement.
round, *adj.* rond; — *adv.* de tour, en rond, autour; *hand ~* faire circuler; *go ~* tourner; *turn ~* tourner, se retourner; — *prep.* autour de; — *s.* rond *m.*, cercle *m.*; tournée *f.;* tour *m.*
rouse, *v.a.* réveiller.
route, *s.* route *f.*
routine, *s.* routine *f.*
row[1], *s.* rang *m.*, rangée *f.;* ligne *f.*
row[2], *v.n.* ramer; *v.a.* faire aller (à la rame); — *s.* promenade *f.* en canot.
row[3], *s.* chahut *m.*, vacarme *m.*, querelle *f.;* réprimande *f.*
royal, *adj.* royal.
rub, *v.a.* frotter.
rubber, *s.* caoutchouc *m.*
rubbish, *s.* décombres *m. pl.;* ordure(s) *f. (pl),* immondices *f. pl.*

ruby, *s.* rubis *m.*
rudder, *s.* gouvernail *m.*
rude, *adj.* rude.
ruffian, *s.* bandit *m.*
ruffle, *s.* ride *f.*; — *v.a.* rider; ébouriffer.
rug, *s.* couverture *f.*; tapis *m.*
ruin, *s.* ruine *f.*; — *v. a.* ruiner.
rule, *s.* autorité *f.*; règle *f.*; *(of the road)* code *m.*; *as a* ~ généralement; — *v.a.* gouverner; régler; guider; ~ *out* exclure.
ruler, *s.* gouverneur *m.*, souverain *m.*; *(for lines)* règle *f.*
rum, *s.* rhum *m.*
Rumanian, *adj.* roumain; — *s.* Roumain, -e *m. f.*
rumour, *s.* rumeur *f.*
run, *v.n.* courir; fuir, se sauver; *(flow)* couler; *(veh.)* marcher, faire le service; *(engine)* fonctionner; *(play in theatre)* se jouer; *v.a.* faire fonctionner; mettre en service; faire marcher, faire aller; ~ *after* courir après; ~ *away* s'enfurir; ~ *down* descendre en courant; *(health)* s'affaiblir; ~ *in (motor)* roder; ~ *into* heurter, rencontrer; ~ *off* s'enfuir; s'écouler; ~ *out* se terminer; ~ *over* passer dessus; ~ *up (debts)* entasser; — *s.* course *f.*; voyage *m.*
runner, *s.* coureur, -euse *m. f.*
runway, *s.* piste (d'envol) *f.*
rupture, *s.* rupture *f.*
rural, *adj.* rural.
rush, *v.n.* se précipiter, se jeter; *v.a.* entraîner à toute vitesse; — *s.* ruée *f.*, hâte *f.*; ~ *hours* heures *f.pl.* d'affluence, coup *m.* de feu.
Russian, *adj.* russe; — *s.* Russe *m. f.*
rust, *s.* rouille *f.*
rustic, *adj.* rustique.
rustle, *s.* bruissement *m.*
rye, *s.* seigle *m.*

S

sabre, *s.* sabre *m.*
sack, *s.* sac *m.*
sacrament, *s.* sacrement *m.*
sacrifice, *s.* sacrifice *m.*
sad, *adj.* triste.
saddle, *s.* selle *f.*
sadness, *s.* tristesse *f.*
safe, *adj.* sûr, en sûreté. sans danger; — *s.* coffre-fort *m.*
safely, *adv.* sain et sauf; en sûreté.
safety, *s.* sûreté *f.*
sail, *s.* voile *f.*; — *v.n.* faire voile, naviguer.
sailor, *s.* marin *m.*, matelot *m.*
saint, *s.* saint, -e *m. f.*
sake: *for the* ~ *of* pour l'amour de.
salad, *s.* salade *f.*
salary, *s.* traitement *m.*, appointements *m. pl.*

sale, *s.* vente *f.*; *(auction)* vente *f.* aux enchères.
salesman, *s.* vendeur *m.*
saleswoman, *s.* vendeuse *f.*
salmon, *s.* saumon *m.*
saloon, *s.* salon *m.*; *~ bar* bar *m.*
salt, *s.* sel *m.*
salt-cellar, *s.* salière *f.*
salvation, *s.* salut *m.*
same, *adj.* & *pron.* même.
sanatorium, *s.* sanatorium *m.*
sanction, *s.* sanction *f.*; — *v.a.* sanctionner.
sand, *s.* sable *m.*; *the ~s* la plage.
sandal, *s.* sandale *f.*
sandwich, *s.* sandwich *m.*
sanitary, *adj.* sanitaire.
sarcastic, *adj.* sarcastique.
sardine, *s.* sardine *f.*
Satan, *s.* Satan *m.*
satellite, *s.* satellite *m.*
satire, *s.* satire *f.*
satisfaction, *s.* satisfaction *f.*
satisfactory, *adj.* satisfaisant.
satisfy, *v.a.* satisfaire.
Saturday, *s.* samedi *m.*
sauce, *s.* sauce *f.*
sausage, *s.* saucisse *f.*
save, *v. a.* sauver; *(spare)* épargner, gagner; *v.n.* économiser.
savings-bank, *s.* caisse *f.* d'épargne.
Saviour, *s.* Sauveur *m.*
saw, *s.* scie *f.*; — *v.a.* & *n.* scier.
say, *v. a.* dire; *that is to ~* c'est-à-dire.
scale¹, *s.* plateau (de balance) *m.*; *(pair of) ~s* balance *f.*; — *v. a.* peser.
scale², *s.* échelle *f.*; *(music)* gamme *f.*
scale³, *s.* *(fish)* écaille *f.*
scanty, *adj.* maigre.
scar, *s.* cicatrice *f.*
scarce, *adj.* rare.
scarcely, *adv.* à peine.
scare, *s.* panique *f.*; — *v.a.* effrayer.
scarf, *s.* écharpe *f.*, foulard *m.*
scarlet, *adj.* écarlate.
scatter, *v.a.* disperser; éparpiller; dissiper.
scene, *s.* scène *f.*; *behind the ~s* dans les coulisses.
scenery, *s.* paysage *m.*; *(theatre)* décor *m.*
scent, *s.* odeur *f.*; parfum *m.*; *(dog)* flair *m.*
schedule, *s.* liste *f.*; cédule *f.*
scheme, *s.* plan *m.*; projet *m.*
scholar, *s.* *(child)* écolier, -ère *m. f.*; *(learned)* savant *m.*
scholarship, *s.* bourse *f.*
school, *s.* école *f.*; classe *f.*
schoolboy, -girl, *s.* écolier, -ère *m. f.*
schoolmaster, *s.* instituteur *m.*, maître *m.* d'école.; *(secondary)* professeur *m.*
schoolmistress, *s.* maîtresse *f.* d'école; *(secondary)* professeur *m.*
schoolroom, *s.* (salle de) classe *f.*
science, *s.* science *f.*
scientific, *adj.* scientifi-

que.
scientist, *s.* savant *m.*
scissors, *s. pl.* ciseaux *m. pl.*
scold, *v.a.* gronder.
scoop, *s.* écope *f.*
scooter, *s.* scooter *m.*
scope, *s.* portée *f.*; envergure *f.*; carrière *f.*
scorch, *v.a.* roussir, brûler.
score, *s.* entaille *f.*; *(sum)* compte *m.*; *(games)* points *m. pl.*, marque *f.*, score *m.*; *(twenty)* vingtaine *f.*; *(music)* partition *f.*; — *v.a.* marquer; ~ *out* rayer.
scorn, *s.* mépris *m.*
Scotch, Scottish, Scots, *adj.* écossais.
Scotsman, *s.* Écossais *m.*
scout, *s.* éclaireur *m.*
scrambled: ~ *eggs* œufs *m. pl* brouillés.
scrap, *s.* morceau *m.*; bout *m.*
scrape, *v.a.* gratter; râcler; ~ *off* décrotter.
scratch, *v.a.* gratter; égratigner; *v. n.* griffer gratter; — *s.* égratignure *f.*; *m.* coup d'ongle.
scream, *v.n.* & *a.* crier; — *s.* cri *m.*
screen, *s.* écran *m.*
screw, *s.* vis *f.*
scrub, *v.a.* frotter; nettoyer à la brosse.
scrupulous, *adj.* scrupuleux.
sculptor, *s.* sculpteur *m.*
sculpture, *s.* sculpture *f.*; — *v.a.* sculpter.
scythe, *s.* faux *f.*
sea, *s.* mer *f.*; *by* ~ par (voie de) mer.
seal[1], *s.* *(animal)* phoque *m.*
seal[2], *s.* sceau *m.*; — *v.a.* sceller; cacheter.
seam, *s.* couture *f.*
seaport, *s.* port *m.* de mer.
search, *v.a.* chercher; — *s.* recherche *f.*
search-light, *s.* projecteur *m.*
seasickness, *s.* mal *m.* de mer.
seaside, *s.* bord *m.* de la mer.
season, *s.* saison *f.*
seat, *s.* siège *m.*; — *v.a.* asseoir; placer.
second, *adj.* second; deux; deuxième; — *s.* seconde *f.*
secondary, *adj.* secondaire; ~ *school* école *f.* secondaire.
second-hand, *adj.* de seconde main, d'occasion.
secret, *adj.* & *s.* secret *(m.)*.
secretary, *s.* secrétaire *m. f.*
section, *s.* section *f.*
secular, *adj.* séculier.
secure, *adj.* en sûreté, sûr; — *v.a.* mettre en sûreté; obtenir; fixer.
security, *s.* sécurité *f.* caution *f.*; sûreté *f.* *securities* valeurs *f. pl.*, *social* ~ sécurité *f.* socialé.
sediment, *s.* sédiment *m.*
see, *v.a.* voir; *(under-*

stand) comprendre; *(make sure)* s'assurer; *(accompany)* accompagner; ~ *about* s'occuper de; ~ *out* accompagner jusqu'à la porte; ~ *through* voir à travers, pénétrer; mener à bonne fin; ~ *to* veiller à, s'occuper de.

seed, *s.* semence *f.*; graine *f.*

seek, *v.a.* chercher.

seem, *v.n.* sembler, paraître.

seize, *v.a.* saisir; prendre.

seldom, *adv.* rarement.

select, *v.a.* choisir.

selection, *s.* choix m.

self, *s.* moi *m.*

self-conscious, *adj.* gêné.

self-control, *s.* maîtrise *f.* de soi-même.

selfish, *adj.* égoïste.

selfishness, *s.* égoïsme *m.*

self-respect, *s.* respect *m.* de soi.

self-service, *adj.* ~ *restaurant* restaurant à libre service.

sell, *v.a.* vendre; ~ *out* vendre tout son stock; *v. n.* se vendre.

seller, *s.* vendeur, -euse *m. f.*

semaphore, *s.* sémaphore *m.*

semicolon, *s.* point (et) virgule *m.*

senate, *s.* sénat *m.*

senator, *s.* sénateur *m.*

send, *v.a.* envoyer; *(money)* remettre; ~ *back* renvoyer; ~ *for* envoyer chercher; ~ *forth* exha er; ~ *off* expédier; ~ *on* faire suivre; ~ *out* lancer.

sender, *s.* expéditeur, -trice *m. f.*

sense, *s.* sens *m.*

senseless, *adj.* insensé; sans connaissance.

sensibility, *s.* sensibilité *f.*

sensible, *adj.* sensible; sensé, raisonnable.

sensitive, *adj.* sensible.

sensual, *adj.* sensuel.

sentence, *s.* jugement *m.*; sentence *f.*; phrase *f.*; — *v. a.* condamner.

sentiment, *s.* sentiment *m.*

sentry, *s.* sentinelle *f.*

separate, *adj.* séparé; à part; — *v.a.* séparer; *v.n.* se séparer.

separation, *s.* séparation *f.*

September, *s.* septembre *m.*

serenade, *s.* sérénade *f.*

sergeant, *s.* sergent *m.*

series, *s.* série *f.*

serious, *adj.* sérieux.

sermon, *s.* sermon *m.*

servant, *s.* serviteur, -vante *m. f.*; domestique *m. f.*

serve, *v. a. & n.* servir.

service, *s.* service *m.*; utilité *f.*

service-station, *s.* station-service *f.*

session, *s.* séance *f.*, session *f.*

set, *v.a.* mettre, placer; *(limb)* remettre; *(fashion)* donner; *(jewels)* monter; *(watch)* régler; *(problem)* donner; *(appoint)* fixer; *(trap)* tendre; — *v.n.* *(sun)* se coucher; — ~ *about* se mettre à: ~ *aside* mettre de côté; ~ *down* déposer; noter; ~ *forth* exposer; ~ *in* commencer; ~ *off, out* partir; ~ *on* pousser (à); ~ *up* dresser; établir; ~ *up for* se donner pour. — *s* ensemble *m.*, assortiment *m.*, collection *f.*; *(tea)* service *m.*; *(radio)* poste *m.*; *(ornaments)* garniture *f.*; *(tennis)* set *m.*; *(gang)* bande *f.*; ~ *of furniture* ameublement *m.*; ~ *of false teeth* dentier *m.*

setting, *s.* mise *f.*, pose *f.*; montage *m.*; installation *f.*; coucher *m.*

settle, *v. a.* fixer; arranger; régler, payer; décider, résoudre; *v.n.* s'établir; se poser (sur); se décider à; ~ *down* s'établir.

settlement, *s.* colonie *f.*

seven, *adj.* & *s.* sept.

seventeen, *adj.* dix-sept.

seventh, *adj.* septième.

seventy, *adj.* & *s.* soixante-dix.

several, *adj.* plusieurs; différent.

severe, *adj.* sévère.

sew, *v.a.* coudre.

sewing-machine, *s.* machine *f.* à coudre.

sex, *s.* sexe *m.*

sexual, *adj.* sexuel.

shabby, *adj.* usé, râpé.

shade, *s.* ombre *f.*; ombrage *m.*; — *v.a.* ombrager.

shadow, *s.* ombre *f.*

shady, *adj.* ombreux.

shaft, *s.* bois *m.*; trait *m.*; flèche *f.*; arbre *m.*

shake, *v.a.* secouer; ébranler; *(hands)* serrer; *v.n.* trembler; s'ébranler; — *s.* secousse *f.*

shaky, *adj.* tremblant, branlant; cassé; faible.

shall, *(future see Grammar)*; *(command)* vouloir; *(duty)* devoir.

shallow, *adj.* peu profond.

shame, *s.* honte *f.*

shameless, *adj.* éhonté; honteux.

shampoo, *s.* shampooing *m.*

shank, *s.* jambe *f.*

shape, *s.* forme *f.*; — *v. a.* façonner; former; diriger; *v.n.* se développer; promettre.

shapeless, *adj.* sans forme.

share, *s.* part *f.*; action *f.*; *have a* ~ *in* contribuer (à); *go* ~*s (in)* partager; — *v. a.* & *n.* partager.

shareholder, *s.* actionnaire *m. f.*

sharp, *adj.* tranchant; aigu; aigre; piquant; perçant; — *s. (music)* dièse *m.*; — *adv.* net; *9.0* ~ 9 heures précises.

sharpen, *v.a.* aiguiser; tailler.

shatter, *v.a.* fracasser; déranger.

shave, *v.a.* raser; *v.n.* se raser.

shawl, *s.* châle *m.*

she, *pron.* elle.

shear, *v.a.* tondre; cou-

per; — *s. (pair of)* ~s cisailles *f. pl.*
sheath, *s.* étui; fourreau *m.*
shed, *v.a.* verser; *(light)* répandre.
sheep, *s.* mouton *m.*
sheer, *adj.* pur; perpendiculaire.
sheet, *s.* drap *m.; (paper)* feuille *f.; ~ iron* tôle *f.*
shelf, *s.* rayon *m.*
shell, *s. (egg, nut)* coque *f.; (peas)* cosse *f.*
shelter, *s.* abri *m.; take ~* s'abriter; — *v.a.* abriter (de); *v. n.* se mettre à l'abri (de).
shepherd, *s.* berger.
shield, *s.* bouclier *m.;* écu *m.*
shift, *s.* changement *m.; (work)* équipe *f.; make ~ to* s'arranger (de); — *v. n. & a.* changer de place.
shine, *v. n.* briller; rayonner (de); *the sun is shining* il fait du soleil.
ship, *s.* vaisseau *m.,* navire *m.;* — *v. a.* embarquer.
shipping, *s.* embarquement *m.;* navires *m. pl.; ~ company* compagnie *f.* de navigation.
shipping-agent, *s.* agent maritime, *m.; (goods)* expéditeur *m.*
shipwreck, *s.* naufrage *m.;* — *v.a. be ~ed* faire naufrage.
shipyard, *s.* chantier *m.* de construction.
shirt, *s.* chemise *f.*
shiver, *v.n.* frissonner; *(cold)* grelotter;
shock, *s.* choc *m.;* coup *m.;* — *v.a.* choquer; frapper d'horreur.
shocking, *adj.* affreux; choquant.
shoe, *s.* soulier *m.*
shoeblack, *s.* décrotteur *m.,* cireur *m.*
shoe-lace, *s.* lacet *m.*
shoemaker, *s.* cordonnier *m.*
shoot, *v.a.* tirer, fusiller; lancer; décharger; *(game)* chasser; *(plant)* pousser; *(rays)* darder; *(film)* tourner; *v.n.* tirer; se précipiter, se lancer; *(plant)* pousser; *(pain)* élancer.
shooting, *s.* tir *m.,* fusillade *f.; (game)* chasse *f.;* — *adj. (pain)* lancinant.
shop, *s.* boutique *f.,* magasin *m.;* — *v.n. go ~ping* faire des achats *or* emplettes.
shop-assistant, *s.* commis *m.;* demoiselle *f.,* vendeur, -euse *m. f.*
shopkeeper, *s.* marchand, -e *m. f.;* commerçant, -e *m. f.*
shore, *s.* rivage *m.;* rive *f.*
short, *adj.* court; petit; bref, brève; *(lacking)* de manque; — *adv. be ~ of* manquer de.
shorten, *v. a. & n.* raccourcir; abréger.
shorthand, *s.* sténographie *f.*
shortly, *adv.* sous peu; bientôt; brièvement.
shot, *s.* coup *m.;* trait *m.; (bullet)* balle f., *(can-*

non) boulet *m.*
shoulder, *s.* épaule *f.*
shout, *s.* cri *m.*; — *v. a.* & *n.* crier.
shove, *v.a.* pousser.
shovel, *s.* pelle *f.*
show, *v.a.* montrer; indiquer; manifester; exposer; expliquer; *v.n.* se montrer; ~ *in* faire entrer; ~ *off* étaler; faire ressortir; se donner des airs; ~ *out* reconduire; ~ *up* ressortir; — *s.* blant *m.*; spectacle *m.*; parade *f.*; exposition *f.*
shower, *s.* averse *f.*; — *v.a.* faire pleuvoir.
shower-bath, *s.* douche *f.*
shrill, *adj.* aigre; aigu, -ë.
shrine, *s.* châsse *f.*; lieu saint *m.*
shrink, *v.a.* & *n.* rétrécir; reculer.
shroud, *s.* linceul *m.*
shrub, *s.* arbrisseau *m.*, arbuste *m.*
shrug, *s.* haussement *m.* d'épaules; — *v.a.* hausser.
shudder, *s.* frisson *m.*; — *v. n.* frissonner (de).
shut, *v.a.* fermer; *(also ~ in)* enfermer; ~ *off* couper; ~ *up* fermer; se taire.
shutter, *s.* volet *m.*
shy, *adj.* timide.
sick, *adj.* malade; *be* ~ vomir; *be* ~ *of* être dégoûté de; *fall* ~ tomber malade.
sickle, *s.* faucille *f.*
sickly, *adj.* maladif; malsain.
sickness, *s.* maladie *f.*
side, *s.* côte *m.*; bord *m.*; *(team)* équipe *f.*
siege, *s.* siège *m.*
sieve, *s.* crible *m.*
sift, *v.a.* cribler.
sigh, *s.* soupir *m.*; — *v. n.* soupirer.
sight, *s.* vue *f.*; spectacle *m.*; ~*s* curiosités *f. pl.*
sightseeing: *go* ~ visiter les curiosités.
sign, *s.* signe *m.*; enseigne *f.*; — *v. a.* & *n.* signer; ~ *on* engager.
signal, *s* signal *m.*; — *v.a.* signaler; *v.n.* faire des signaux.
signature, *s.* signature *f.*
significant, *adj.* significatif.
signify, *v.a.* signifier; *v.n.* importer.
signpost, *s.* poteau *m.* indicateur.
silence, *s.* silence *m.*
silent, *adj.* silencieux; muet.
silk, *s.* soie *f.*
silly, *adj.* sot.
silver, *s.* argent *m.*; — *adj.* d'argent; argenté.
similar, *adj.* semblable.
simple, *adj.* simple.
simultaneous, *adj.* simultané.
sin, *s.* péché *m.*; — *v.n.* pécher.
since, *adv.* & *prep.* depuis; — *conj.* depuis que; *(because)* puisque.
sincere, *adj.* sincère.
sinew, *s.* tendon *m.*
sinful, *adj.* pécheur.
sing, *v. a.* & *n.* chanter.

singer, *s.* chanteur, -euse *m. f.; cantatrice f.*
single, *adj.* simple; seul; célibataire; particulier; ~ *ticket* billet *m.* d'aller.
singular, *s.* singulier *m.*; — *adj.* remarquable; singulier.
sink, *v. n.* tomber au fond, sombrer; s'enfoncer; baisser; *v. a.* enfoncer; faire baisser; foncer; couler; — *s.* évier *m.*
sinner, *s.* pécheur, -eresse *m. f.*
sir, *s.* monsieur *m.*; Sir *m.*
sister, *s.* sœur *f.*; *(nurse)* infirmière *f.*
sister-in-law, *s.* belle-sœur *f.*
sit, *v.n.* s'asseoir; être assis; rester; ~ *down* s'asseoir; se mettre (à); ~ *for (exam)* se présenter à; ~ *up* se dresser; *(at night)* veiller.
site, *s.* emplacement *m.*; terrain *m.*; site *m.*
sitting-room, *s.* petit salon *m.*
situation, *s.* situation *f.*; *(employment)* position *f.*; emploi *m.*
six, *adj.* & *s.* six *(m.)*.
sixteen, *adj.* & *s.* seize *(m.)*.
sixth, *adj.* sixième; six.
sixty, *adj.* & *s.* soixante.
size, *s.* grandeur *f.*, mesure *f.*; *(shoes etc.)* pointure *f.*; numéro *m.*, taille *f.*; *(pers.)* taille *f.*
skate, *v.n.* patiner.
skating, *s.* patinage *m.*
sketch, *s.* croquis *m.*; esquisse *f.*; — *v.a.* esquisser.
ski, *s.* ski *m.*
skid, *v.n.* déraper.
skier, *s.* skieur *m.*
skiff, *s.* esquif *m.*
skilful, *adj.* adroit.
skill, *s.* adresse *f.*
skim, *v.a.* écrémer.
skin, *s.* peau *f.*; — *v.a.* écorcher; peler.
skip, *v. a.* & *n.* sauter.
skirt, *s.* jupe *f.*
skull, *s.* crâne *m.*
sky, *s.* ciel *m.* *(pl.* **cieux)**.
slack, *adj.* lâche; négligent.
slacken, *v.a.* ralentir; relâcher; *v.n.* se relâcher; diminuer.
slacks, *s. pl.* pantalon *m.*
slander, *s.* calomnie *f.*; — *v.a.* calomnier.
slant, *s.* biais *m.*; — *v. a.* faire pencher; *v. n.* être en pente.
slap, *s.* claque *f.*; soufflet *m.*; — *v. a.* claquer; souffleter.
slate, *s.* ardoise *f.*
slaughter, *s.* massacre *m.*
slave, *s.* esclave *m. f.*
sledge, *s.* traîneau.
sleep, *s.* sommeil *m.*; *go to* ~ s'endormir; — *v. a.* & *n.* dormir.
sleeping-car, *s.* wagon-lit *m.*
sleepy, *adj.* somnolent; *be* ~ avoir sommeil.
sleeve, *s.* manche *f.*
slender, *adj.* mince, faible.
slice, *s.* tranche *f.*
slide, *s.* glissade *f.*; *(photo)* diapositive *f.*
slight, *adj.* mince; léger.

slim, *adj*. mince, svelte.
sling, *s*. fronde *f*.
slip, *v.n.* glisser; se glisser (dans); *v.a.* filer; pousser, glisser; ~ *off* ôter; ~ *on* mettre; ~ *out* s'esquiver; — *s*. glissade *f*.; *(mistake)* faux pas *m*.; *(paper)* fiche *f*.; *(underwear)* combinaison *f*.
slipper, *s*. pantoufle *f*.
slope, *s*. biais *m*.; pente *f*.; — *v. n.* incliner.
slot, *s*. fente *f*.
slow, *adj*. lent; *(clock)* en retard; *(dull)* peu intelligent; ~ *to* lent à; — *v.n.* & *a*. ~ *down* ralentir.
slumber, *s*. sommeil *m*.; — *v.n.* sommeiller.
slump, *s*. débâcle *f*.; *(in trade)* mévente *f*.; dépression *f*.
sly, *adj*. rusé.
small, *adj*. petit; faible; peu important; menu.
smart, *adj*. *(clever)* habile, débrouillard; *(witty)* spirituel; *(dress, pers.)* élégant, chic; pimpant; *(society)* élégant.
smash, *v. a*. briser; *fig*. écraser; — *s*. fracas *m*.; collision *f*.
smear, *v.a.* enduire; — *s*. tache *f*.
smell, *s*. odorat *m*.; odeur *f*.; — *v. a*. & *n*. sentir; ~ *out* flairer.
smile, *s*. sourire *m*.; — *v.n.* sourire (at à).
smoke, *s*. fumée *f*.; — *v.a.* & *n*. fumer.
smooth, *adj*. lisse; uni; doux, -ce; *(sea)* calme; — *v.a.* aplanir; lisser.
smuggle, *v.a.* ~ *in* faire passer en contrebande; *v.n.* faire la contrebande.
smuggler, *s*. contrebandier *m*.
snack, *s*. morceau (sur le pouce) *m*.; *have a* ~ casser la croûte.
snail, *s*. colimaçon *m*.
snake, *s*. serpent *m*.
snap, *s*. fermoir *m*.; coup *m*. de dents; claquement *m*.; *(photo)* instantané *m*.; — *v. a*. faire claquer; fermer; ~ *at* happer; ~ *off* casser.
snapshot, *s*. instantané *m*.
snatch, *s*. action de saisir, *f*.; accès *m*.; fragment *m*.; — *v. a*. saisir; ~ *at* saisir au vol.
sneeze, *v. n.* éternuer; — *s*. éternuement *m*.
sniff, *v.a.&n.* renifler.
snore, *v. n*. ronfler.
snow, *s*. neige *f*.; — *v.n.* neiger.
snug, *adj*. commode.
so, *adv*. ainsi; si; donc; ~ *that* de sorte que; afin que.
soak, *v.n.* tremper.
soap, *s*. savon *m*.
soar, *v.n.* prendre son essor; *fig*. s'élancer.
sob, *v.n.* sangloter; — *s*. sanglot.
sober, *adj*. sobre; sensé;
social, *adj*. social.
socialism, *s*. socialisme *m*.
society, *s*. société *f*.
sock, *s*. chaussette *f*.

socket, *s.* cavité *f.*; *(electric)* prise *f.* de contact.
soda-water, *s.* eau *f.* de Seltz.
sofa, *s.* canapé *m.*
soft, *adj.* mou, mol molle; doux, -ce.
soil, *s.* terroir; *(stain)* tache; — *v. a.* souiller.
soldier, *s.* soldat *m.*
sole[1], *s.* plante *f.*; semelle *f.*; *(fish)* sole *f.*
sole[2], *adj.* seul.
solicit, *v. a.* solliciter.
solicitor, *s.* avoué *m.* solicitor *m.*
solidarity, *s.* solidarité *f.*
solitude, *s.* solitude *f.*
solution, *s.* solution *f.*
solve, *v.a.* résoudre.
some, *adj.* quelque; de; — *pron.* quelques-uns; les uns; en *(+ verb)* — *adv.* environ.
somebody, -one, *pron.* quelqu'un.
somehow, *adv.* d'une façon quelconque; ~ *or other* d'une façon ou d'une autre.
something, *s.* & *pron.* quelque chose *m.*
sometime, *adv.* quelque jour, autrefois.
sometimes, *adv.* quelquefois, parfois.
somewhere, *adv.* quelque part.
son, *s.* fils *m.*
song, *s.* chanson *f.*
son-in-law, *s.* gendre *m.*
soon, *adv.* bientôt.
sore, *adj.* douloureux; *have a* ~ ... avoir mal à ...; — *s.* plaie *f.*
sorrow, *s.* douleur *f.*
sorry, *adj.* *be* ~ *for* regretter; ~*!* pardon!
sort, *s.* sorte *f.*; genre *m.*; type *m.*; ~ *of* une espèce de.
soul, *s.* âme *f.*
sound[1], *s.* son *m.*; bruit *m.*; — *v. n.* sonner; — *v.a.* sonner; sonder; *(physician)* ausculter.
sound[2], *adj.* sain; solide; droit; profond; en bon état.
soup, *s.* potage *m.*; *(clear)* consommé *m.*; *(thick)* soupe *f.*
sour, *adj.* aigre; acide; *(milk)* tourné.
source, *s.* source *f.*
south, *s.* sud *m.*, midi *m.*; — *adj.* sud; du sud; — *adv.* vers le sud.
southeast, *adj.* & *s.* sud-est *(m.)*; — *adv.* vers le sud-est.
southern, *adj.* du sud.
southwest, *adj.* & *s.* sud-ouest *(m.)*; — *adv.* vers le sud-ouest.
sovereign, *s.* souverain, -e *m. f.*
sow[1], *v. a.* & *n.* semer (de).
sow[2], *s.* truie *f.*
space, *s.* espace *m.*
space-craft, -ship, -vehicle, *s.* astronef *m.*
space-flight, *s.* navigation *f.* astronautique.
spaceman, *s.* cosmonaute *m.*, astronaute *m.*
spade, *s.* bêche *f.*; *(cards)* pique *m.*
span, *s.* empan *m.*; ouverture; — *v.a.* traverser; couvrir.
Spaniard, *s.* Espagnol, -e.

Spanish, *adj.* & *s.* espagnol *(m.).*
spanner, *s.* clef *f.*
spare, *adj.* maigre; disponible; de réserve; ~ *parts* pièces de rechange *f. pl.;* ~ *time* loisir *m.;* — *v.a.* épargner; économiser; *(evade)* éviter.
spark, *s.* étincelle *f.*
sparrow, *s.* moineau *m.*
speak, *v.n.* parler; *v.a.* dire; ~ *out* parler hardiment; ~ *up* parler plus haut; ... ~*ing* ici ...
spear, *s.* lance *f.*
special, *adj.* spécial.
specialist, *s.* spécialiste *m. f.*
specific, *adj.* spécifique.
specify, *v.a.* spécifier.
speck, *s.* grain *m.;* tache *f.*
spectacles, *s. pl.* lunettes *f.*
spectacular, *adj.* impressionnant.
spectator, *s.* spectateur, -trice *m. f.*
speech, *s.* parole *f.;* langage *m.;* *(address)* discours *m.*
speed, *s.* vitesse *f.*
speedy, *adj.* rapide; prompt.
spell[1], *v.a.* & *n.* épeler; orthographier, écrire; *how is it spelt?* comment cela s'écrit-il?
spell[2], *s.* période *f.;* tour *m.*
spelling, *s.* ortographe *f.*
spend, *v.a.* dépenser; *(time)* passer; *v.n.* dépenser.
sphere, *s.* sphère *f.*
spice, *s.* épice *f.*
spider, *s.* araignée *f.*
spill, *v.a.* répandre; renverser.
spin, *v.a.* & *n.* filer; faire tourner.
spinach, *s.* épinards *m. pl.*
spine, *s.* épine (dorsale) *f.*
spinster, *s.* vieille fille *f.;* célibataire *f.*
spiral, *adj.* en spirale.
spire, *s.* flèche *f.*
spirit, *s.* esprit *m.;* âme *f.;* spectre *m.;* caractère *m.,* cœur *m.;* ~*s* spiritueux *m. pl.*
spiritual, *adj.* spirituel.
spit, *s.* crachat *m.;* — *v. a.* & *n.* cracher.
spite, *s.* dépit *m.;* *in* ~ *of* malgré.
splash, *s.* éclaboussement *m.;* — *v. a.* & *n.* éclabousser (de).
spleen, *s.* rate *f.*
splendid, *adj.* splendide.
splinter, *s.* éclat *m.;* *(bone)* esquille *f.*
split, *v. a.* fendre; (also ~ *up)* partager; *v.n.* se fendre; se diviser.
spoil, *v.a.* gâter; dépouiller (de); endommager; *v.n.* se gâter.
sponge, *s.* éponge *f.*
spontaneous, *adj.* spontané.
spoon, *s.* cuiller *f.*
spoonful, *s.* cuillerée *f.*
sport, *s.* sport *m.;* amusements *m. pl.*
sportsman, *s.* sportsman *m.*
spot, *s.* tache *f.;* *(place)* endroit *m.;* — *v.a.* tacher; reconnaître.
spout, *s.* gouttière *f.;* bec

m.; — *v.a.* lancer.
sprain, *v.a.* donner une entorse (à).
spray, *s.* embrun *m.*, vaporisateur *m.*; atomiseur *m.*; — *v.a.* vaporiser, atomiser; arroser.
spread, *v.a.* étendre; répandre; *(cloth)* mettre; *(cover)* couvrir; *(news)* faire circuler; *v.n.* s'étendre; — *s.* propagation *f.*; étendue *f.*
spring[1], *s.* printemps *m.*
spring[2], *v.n.* sauter; pousser; jaillir; provenir (de), descendre (de), naître (de); ~ *up* se lever vite; jaillir; — *s.* saut *m.*; *(watch etc.)* ressort *m.*
sprinkle, *v.a.* répandre; asperger (de), arroser.
sprout, *v. a. & n.* germer; pousser; — *s.* pousse *f.*; *Brussels* ~*s* choux *m. pl.* de Bruxelles
spur, *s.* éperon *m.*, aiguillon *m.*; — *v. a.* éperonner; ~ *on* pousser à.
spy, *s.* espion, -onne *m. f.*; — *v.n.* espionner.
squander, *v. a.* gaspiller.
square, *s.* carré *m.*; *(town)* place *f.*; — *adj.* carré; honnête.
squeeze, *v.a.* serrer; presser.
squint, *v.n.* loucher; — *s.* strabisme *m.*
squire, *s.* écuyer *m.*; châtelain *m.*
squirrel, *s.* écureuil *m.*
stability, *s.* stabilité *f.*
stable, *s.* écurie *f.*; — *adj.* stable.
stack, *s.* pile *f.*; meule *f.*
stadium, *s.* stade *m.*
staff, *s.* état-major *m.*; bâton *m.*; hampe *f.*; *(institution)* personnel *m.*; ~ *officer* officier d'état-major *m.*
stag, *s.* cerf *m.*
stage, *s.* scène *f.*; *(drama)* théâtre *m.*; *(period)* période *f.*; *(platform)* estrade *f.*; — *v.a.* mettre en scène.
stagger, *v.n.* chanceler; *v.a.* bouleverser.
stain, *s.* tache *f.*; — *v.a.* tacher; salir.
stair, *s.* marche; ~*s* escalier *m.*
staircase, *s.* escalier *m.*
stake, *s.* pieu *m.*; *at* ~ en jeu; — *v.a.* garnir de pieux; mettre au jeu; jouer.
stale, *adj.* rassis.
stall, *s.* stalle *f.*; fauteuil *m.*; *(books)* kiosque *m.* à journaux.
stammer, *v. n.* bégayer.
stamp, *s.* timbre-poste *m.*; estampe *f.*; contrôle *m.*; empreinte *f.*; — *v.a.* timbrer; estamper; contrôler.
stand, *v.n.* être debout, se tenir debout, se soutenir; *(be situated)* se trouver; *(remain)* rester; ~ *out* ressortir; ~ *up* se lever; — *s.* position *f.*; *(vehicles)* station *f.*; *(stall)* étalage *m.*; stand *m.*
standard, *s.* étendard *m.*; étalon *m.*; niveau *m.*;

— *adj.* régulateur; au titre; *(authors)* classique.
star, *s.* étoile *f.*
stare, *v.n.* (also ~ *at)* regarder fixement.
start, *v.n.* partir; commencer; *v. a.* faire partir; faire lever; commencer; lancer; — *s.* commencement *m.*; départ *m.*
starve, *v.n.* mourir de faim; *v. a.* faire mourir de faim.
state, *s.* état *m.*; — *v. a.* affirmer; porter; déclarer.
statement, *s.* déclaration *f.*
statesman, *s.* homme *m.* d'état.
station, *s.* poste *m.*; endroit *m.*; *(railway)* gare *f.*; *(police)* poste *m.* de police.
stationer, *s.* papetier *m.*; *~'s shop* papeterie *f.*
statistic(al), *adj.* statistique.
statistics, *s.* statistique *f.*
statue, *s.* statue *f.*
statute, *s.* statut *m.*; ordonnance *f.*
stay, *v.n.* rester; être installé; ~ *away* rester absent; ~ *up* veiller.
steady, *adj.* ferme; soutenu; *(pers.)* rangé; — *int.* attention!
steak, *s.* tranche *f.*; bifteck *m.*
steal, *v.a.* voler.
steam, *s.* vapeur *f.*
steamboat, *s.* bateau *m.* à vapeur.
steam-engine, *s.* locomotive *f.*
steel, *s.* acier *m.*
steep, *adj.* raide, escarpé.
steeple, *s.* clocher *m.*
steer, *v.a.* gouverner; diriger.
steering-gear, *s.* appareil *m.* de direction.
steering-wheel, *s.* volant *m.*
stem, *s.* tige *f.*; queue *f.*
step, *s.* pas *m.*; *(stair)* marche *f.*; *(ladder)* échelon *m.*; *take ~s* faire des démarches; — *v.n.* faire un pas; marcher; aller, venir; ~ *in* entrer.
stepmother, *s.* belle-mère *f.*
stereotype, *s.* cliché *m.*
sterile, *adj.* stérile.
stern, *s.* arrière *m.* — *adj.* sévère.
stew, *s.* ragoût *m.*; *(fruit)* compote *f.*; — *v.a.* *(meat)* faire un ragout de; *(fruit)* faire une compote de.
steward, *s.* régisseur *m.*; steward *m.*
stewardess, *s.* hôtesse *f.* de l'air.
stick, *s.* bâton *m.*, canne *f.*, petite branche *f.*; — *v.a.* coller; *v.n.* se coller; ~ *on* attacher; ~ *to* rester fidèle à.
sticky, *adj.* gluant.
stiff, *adj.* raide; dur.
still, *adj.* calme — *adv.* toujours; encore; ce-

pendant.
sting, *s.* aiguillon *m.;* — *v.a.* & *n.* piquer.
stink, *v.n.* puer; — *s.* puanteur *f.*
stipulate, *v.a.* stipuler.
stir, *v.a.* remuer; exciter; *v. n.* remuer; bouger; — *s.* remuement *m.*
stirrup, *s.* étrier *m.*
stitch, *s.* point *m.;* — *v.a.* & *n.* coudre.
stock, *s.* marchandises *f. pl.;* provision *f.; (tree)* tronc *m.; (cattle)* bestiaux *m. pl.; (finance)* valeurs *f. pl.; Stock Exchange* Bourse *f.*
stockholder, *s.* actionnaire *m. f.*
stocking, *s.* bas *m.*
stomach, *s.* estomac *m.*
stone, *s.* pierre; *(fruit)* noyau *m.;* — *v.a.* lapider.
stony, *adj.* pierreux.
stool, *s.* tabouret *m.,* escabeau *m.*
stop, *v.a.* arrêter; empêcher (de); *(teeth)* plomber; retenir suspendre, *v.n.* s'arrêter; cesser; — *s.* halte *f.;* arrêt *m.; (organ)* jeu *m.; (sign)* signe de ponctuation, *m.*
store, *s.* provision *f.;* *~s* grand magasin *m.;* — *v.a.* emmagasiner.
stork, *s.* cigogne *f.*
storm, *s.* orage *m.*
story[1], *s.* histoire *f.*
story[2], *s.* étage *m.*
stout, *adj.* fort; intrépide.
stove, *s.* poêle *m.;* fourneau *m.*
straight, *adj.* droit; honnête; d'aplomb; — *adv.* juste; droit.
straighten, *v.a.* (re)dresser; *v.n.* se redresser.
strain, *s.* effort *m.;* tension *f.;* — *v. a.* tendre; *(filter)* passer; *(muscle)* forcer.
strange, *adj.* étrange(r).
stranger, *s.* étranger -ère *m. f.*
strap, *s.* courroie *f.*
straw, *s.* paille *f.*
strawberry, *s.* fraise *f.*
stray, *adj.* égaré; — *v. n.* errer.
streak, *s.* raie *f.;* bande *f.*
stream, *s.* courant *m.;* — *v.n.* couler, ruisseler.
street, *s.* rue *f.*
strength, *s.* force *f.*
strengthen, *v.a.* fortifier.
stress, *s.* force *f.; (grammar)* accent *m.*
stretch, *s.* effort *m.;* étendue *f.;* — *v.a.* étendre; élargir.
stretcher, *s.* brancard *m.*
strew, *v.a.* semer.
strict, *adj.* strict.
stride, *s.* enjambée *f.;* grand pas *m.;* — *v. n.* enjamber.
strike, *v.a.* frapper; *(blow)* asséner; *(work)* cesser; *v.n.* frapper; *(clock)* sonner; *(workers)* se mettre en grève — *s.* grève *f.;* *be on ~* être en grève.
striking, *adj.* frappant.
string, *s.* ficelle *f.;* corde *f.*
strip, *s.* bande *f.;* bout

m.; — *v. a.* déshabiller; *v.n.* se déshabiller.
stripe, *s.* bande *f.*
strip-lighting, *s.* éclairage *m.* par luminescent.
strive, *v. n.* s'efforcer (de).
stroke, *s.* coup *m.*; *(swimming)* brasse *f.*; *(pen)* trait *m.*
strong, *adj.* fort; vigoureux; puissant; solide.
structure, *s.* structure *f.*
struggle, *v.n.* lutter (avec); faire de grands efforts (pour); — *s.* lutte *f.*; mêlée *f.*
stub, *s.* souche *f.*; bout *m.*
stubborn, *adj.* obstiné.
stud, *s.* bouton *m.*
student, *s.* étudiant, -e *m. f.*
studio, *s.* atelier *m.*
study, *s.* étude *f.*; cabinet *m.* de travail — *v. a.* & *n.* étudier.
stuff, *s.* étoffe *f.*; materiaux *m.pl.*; — *v.a.* remplir; fourrer.
stumble, *v. n.* trébucher; ~ *(up)on* tomber sur; — *s.* faux pas *m.*
stump, *s.* souche *f.*; — *v.a.* estomper.
stupid, *adj.* stupide.
style, *s.* style *m.*
subject, *s.* sujet, -te *m. f.*; — *adj.* ~ *to* sujet à; — *v.a.* assujettir (à).
submarine, *s.* sous-marin *m.*
submission, *s.* soumission *f.*
submit, *v.a.* soumettre.
subordinate, *adj.* & *s.* subordonné; — *v.a.* subordonner.
subscribe, *v.a.* & *n.* (~ *to)* souscrire (à); s'abonner (à).
subscriber, *s.* souscripteur *m.*; abonné; -e souscripteur *m.*; abonné, -e *m. f.*
subscription, *s.* souscription *f.*; abonnement *m.*
subsequent, *adj.* subséquent.
subsequently, *adv.* par la suite.
subsidy, *s.* subside *m.*
subsist, *v. n.* exister; subsister (de).
subsistence, *s.* subsistance *f.*
substance, *s.* substance *f.*
substantial, *adj.* substantiel.
substantive, *s.* substantif *m.*
substitute, *v.a.* substituer *(for* à).
substitution, *s.* substitution *f.*
subtle, *adj.* subtil.
subtract, *v.a.* soustraire.
subtraction, *s.* soustraction *f.*
suburb, *s.* faubourg *m.*; ~*s* banlieue *f.*
subway, *s.* souterrain *m.*; métro *m.*
succeed, *v.a.* succéder (à); *v.n.* *(be successful)* réussir (à); faire ses affaires; ~ *to* succéder à.
success, *s.* succès *m.*
successful, *adj.* heureux, *(exam)* reçu.
succession, *s.* succession *f.*

successive, *adj.* successif.
such, *adj.* tel, -le; *~ and ~* tel(le) ou tel(le); — *pron. ~ as* ceux, celles.
suck, *v.a. & n.* sucer; — *s. give ~ to* allaiter.
sudden, *adj.* soudain.
suddenly, *adv.* soudain.
suet, *s.* graisse *f.* de rognon.
suffer, *v. a. & n.* souffrir.
sufficient, *adj.* suffisant.
sufficiently, *adv.* suffisamment.
sugar, *s.* sucre *m.*
suggest, *v.a.* suggérer; proposer.
suggestion, *s.* suggestion *f.*
suicide, *s.* suicide *m.*
suit, *s. (clothes)* complet *m.; (cards)* couleur *f.; (law)* procès *m.; (request)* requête *f.;* — *v.a.* convenir (à); adapter (à); *v.n.* convenir (à); aller (avec).
suitable, *adj.* convenable; *~ for* adapté à.
suitcase, *s.* mallette *f.*, valise *f.*
sum, *s.* somme *f.; ~ total* somme totale, *f.;* — *v.a. ~ up* résumer
summary, *s.* résumé *m.*
summer, *s.* été *m.*
summon, *v.a.* convoquer; appeler.
sun, *s.* soleil *m.*
Sunday, *s.* dimanche *m.*
sunny, *adj.* ensoleillé; exposé au soleil.
sunrise, *s.* lever *m.* du soleil.
sunset, *s.* coucher *m.* du soleil.
sunshine, *s.* soleil *m.*
sunstroke, *s.* coup *m.* de soleil.
superannuate, *v. a.* mettre à la retraite.
superficial, *adj.* superficiel.
superfluous, *adj.* superflu.
superior, *s. & adj.* supérieur *(m.).*
supermarket, *s.* supermarché *m.*
supersonic, *adj.* supersonique.
superstition, *s.* superstition *f.*
superstitious, *adj.* superstitieux.
supervise, *v.a.* surveiller.
supervision, *s.* surveillance *f.*
supper, *s.* souper *m.*
supplement, *s.* supplément *m.;* — *v.a.* suppléer (à).
supplementary, *adj.* supplémentaire
supply, *s.* provision *f.;* approvisionnement *m.; ~ and demand* l'offre et la demande; — *v.a.* fourner (de); suppléer.
support, *s.* appui *m.;* support *m.;* — *v.a.* supporter; soutenir; appuyer.
suppose, *v.a.* supposer.
supposition, *s.* supposition *f.*
suppress, *v.a.* supprimer.
suppression, *s.* suppression *f.;* répression *f.*
supreme, *adj.* suprême.

sure, *adj.* sûr; *be* ~ *to* ne pas manquer de; *make* ~ *that* s'assurer que.
surely, *adv.* sûrement.
surface, *s.* surface *f.*
surgeon, *s.* chirurgien *m.*
surgery, *s.* chirurgie *f.*
surname, *s.* nom *m.* de famille.
surpass, *v.a.* surpasser.
surprise, *s.* surprise *f.*; — *v.a.* surprendre.
surprising, *adj.* surprenant.
surrender, *s.* abandon *m.*; reddition *f.*; — *v.a.* rendre; renoncer; *v.n.* se rendre.
surround, *v.a.* entourer (de).
surroundings, *s. pl.* environs *m. pl.*; entourage *m.*
survey, *s.* vue *f.*; examen *m.*; — *v.a.* contempler, regarder; examiner; expertiser.
survive, *v. n.* & a. survivre (à).
suspect, *adj.* & *s.* suspect, -e *(m. f.)*; — *v. a.* & *n.* soupçonner.
suspenders, *s. pl.* jarretelles *f. pl.*
suspicion, *s.* soupçon *m.*
suspicious, *adj.* soupçonneux; suspect.
swallow[1], *s.* hirondelle *f.*
swallow[2], *v. a.* avaler; gober.
swan, *s.* cygne *m.*
swarm, *s.* essaim *m.*; foule *f.*; — *v.n.* essaimer; s'assembler en foule.
swear, *v.a.* jurer; prêter; *v.n.* jurer.
sweat, *s.* sueur *f.*; — *v.a.* exploiter; *v.n.* suer.
Swede, *s.* Suédois, -e *m. f.*
Swedish, *adj.* & *s.* suédois *(m.)*.
sweep, *v.a.* balayer; *(chimney)* ramoner; — *s.* coup *m.* de balai; courbe *f.*; grand geste *m.*; *(pers.)* ramoneur *m.*
sweet, *adj.* doux; *(pers.)* gentil; — *s.* bonbon *m.*; entremets *m.*
sweetheart, *s.* bien-aimé, -ée *m. f.*; ~*!* mon amour!, ma chérie!
swell, *v.n.* (s')enfler; se gonfler; grossir; *v.a.* gonfler; bouffir; — *s.* houle *f.*; élévation *f.*
swim, *v. n.* nager; aller à la nage; flotter; *v.a* nager; — *s. have a* ~ aller nager.
swimmer, *s.* nageur, -euse *m. f.*
swimming-pool, *s.* piscine *f.*
swine, *s.* cochon *m.*
swing, *s.* va-et-vient *m.*; rythme *m.*; *(for children)* escarpolette *f.* balançoire *f.*; — *v.a.* balancer; *v. n.* osciller; se balancer.
Swiss, *adj.* suisse; — *s.* Suisse *m. f.*
switch, *s.* badine *f.*; aiguille *f.*; interrupteur *m.*, commutateur *m.*; — *v.a.* cingler; aiguiller; couper; ~ *off* couper (le courant);

~ *on* donner (le courant), tourner (le bouton).
sword, *s.* épée *f.;* sabre *m.*
syllable, *s.* syllabe *f.*
symbol, *s.* symbole *m.*
symmetrical, *adj* symétrique.
symmetry, *s.* symétrie *f.*
sympathy, *s.* sympathie *f.*
symphony, *s.* symphonie *f.*
synagogue, *s.* synagogue *f.*
synthetic, *adj.* synthétique.
syringe, *s.* seringue *f.*
syrup, *s.* sirop *m.*
system, *s.* système *m.*
systematic(al), *adj.* systématique.

T

table, *s.* table *f.; clear the* ~ desservir; *lay the* ~ mettre le couvert.
table-cloth, *s.* nappe *f.*
table-spoon, *s.* cuiller *f.* à soupe.
tablet, *s.* tablette *f.*
tack, *s.* broquette *f.*, petit clou *m.*
tackle, *s.* attirail *m.;* apparaux *m. pl.;* — *v.a.* saisir à bras le corps; *(problem)* essayer de résoudre.
tact, *s.* tact *m.*
tag, *s.* ferret *m.;* étiquette (volante) *f.;* bout *m.*
tail, *s.* queue *f.*
tailor, *s.* tailleur *m.*
take, *v.a.* prendre; *(carry)* porter; *(walk)* faire; ~ *after* ressembler à; ~ *away* enlever; ~ *down* descendre, *(write)* prendre (par écrit); ~ *in (paper)* s'abonner à; ~ *off* ôter; *(v.n.)* prendre son élan; ~ *on* se charger de; ~ *to* se mettre à; ~ *up* ramasser, relever.
tale, *s.* conte *m.*, histoire *f*
talent, *s.* talent *m.*
talk, *v.a. & n.* parler *(about, of* de); *~ing of* à propos de; — *s.* conversation *f.;* causerie *f.*
tall, *adj.* grand; *how* ~ *is he?* quelle est sa **taille?**
tame, *adj.* apprivoisé.
tan, *s.* tan *m.*
tank, *s.* réservoir *m.;* char *m.* d'assaut.
tankard, *s.* chope *f.*
tap, *s.* robinet *m.; (blow)* tape *f.;* petit coup *m.;* — *v.a.* mettre en perce; *(strike)* frapper légèrement, taper.
tape, *s.* ruban *m.* (de coton).
tape-recorder, *s.* magnétophone *m.*
tapestry, *s.* tapisserie *f.*
target, *s.* cible *f.*
tariff, *s.* tarif *m.*
tart, *s.* tart *f.*
task, *s.* tâche *f.; (school)* devoir *m.*
taste, *s.* goût *m.*
tasteless, *adj.* sans saveur.
tasty, *adj.* savoureux,

de bon goût.
tatter, *s.* lambeau *m.*
tavern, *s.* taverne *f.*
tax, *s.* impôt *m.*; ~ *free* exempt d'impôts.
taxi, *s.* taxi *m.*
tea, *s.* thé *m.*
teach, *v.a.* enseigner, instruire; *(how to)* apprendre (à).
teacher, *s.* instituteur, -trice *m. f.*; professeur *m. f.*
teaching, *s.* enseignement *m.*
team, *s.* équipe *f.*
tea-pot, *s.* théière *f.*
tear[1], *s.* *(eye)* larme *f.*
tear[2], *v.a.* déchirer; ~ *away, down, out* arracher; ~ *up* déchirer; — *s.* déchirure *f.*
tease, *v.a.* taquiner.
tea-spoon, *s.* cuiller *f.* à thé.
technical, *adj.* technique.
technique, *s.* technique *f.*
technology, *s.* technologie *f.*
tedious, *adj.* ennuyeux.
teenager, *s.* adolescent, -e *m. f.*
telecast, *v.a.* téléviser.
telegram, *s.* télégramme *m.*
telegraph, *s.* télégraphe *m.*
telephone, *s.* téléphone *m.*; — *v.a. & n.* téléphoner (*to* à).
telescope, *s.* téléscope *m.*; réfracteur *m.*; — *v.a.* télescoper.
televise, *v.a.* téléviser.
television, *s.* télévision *f.*
television-set, *s.* appareil *m.* de TV, téléviseur *m.*
telex, *s.* télex *m.*
tell, *v.a.* dire; raconter; distinguer; ~ *s.o. to do sth.* enjoindre, dire à qn de faire qch.
temper, *s.* colère *f.*; tempérament *m.*
temperature, *s.* température *f.*
temporary, *adj.* temporaire.
tempt, *v.a.* tenter.
ten, *adj. & s.* dix *(m.)*.
tenant, *s.* locataire *m. f.*
tend, *v.n.* tendre (à).
tendency, *s.* tendence *f.*
tender[1], *v.a.* offrir; ~ *for* soumissionner; — *s.* soumission *f.*
tender[2], *adj.* tendre.
tennis, *s.* tennis *m.*
tension, *s.* tension *f.*
tent, *s.* tente *f.*
tenth, *adj.* dixième; dix.
term, *s.* terme *m.*; *(school)* trimestre *m.*; *be on good ~s* être bien (avec); — *v.a.* appeler.
terminate, *v.a.* terminer; *vn.* se terminer.
terminus, *s.* (gare *f.*) terminus *m.*
terrace, *s.* terrasse *f.*
terrible, *adj.* terrible.
territory, *s.* territoire *m.*
test, *s.* épreuve *f.*; examen *m.*; *(school)* composition *f.*, *(oral)* épreuve *f.*; orale — *v.a.* mettre à l'épreuve.
testify, *v.a.* affirmer.
testimony, *s.* témoignage *m.*

text, *s.* texte *m.*
text-book, *s.* manuel *m.*
textile, *s.* textile *m.*
than, *conj.* que; *(with numbers)* de.
thank, *v.a.* remercier; ~ *you* merci; — *s.* ~*s* remerciements *m. pl.;* merci.
thankful, *adj.* reconnaissant.
that[1], *adj.* ce, cet, cette, ces; — *pron.* celui, celle, ceux; cela; ~*'s it* c'est cela.
that[2], *conj.* que.
the, *art.* le, la, les; ce, cet, cette; ces.
theatre, *s.* théâtre *m.*
their, *pron.* leur, leurs.
theirs, *pron.* le leur, la leur, les leurs; à eux, à elles.
them, *pron.* les; leur; eux, elles.
theme, *s.* thème *m.;* sujet *m.*
themselves, *pron.* se; eux-mêmes, elles-mêmes.
then, *adv.* alors; *(after that)* puis; *(consequently)* donc.
theology, *s.* théologie *f.*
theoretical, *adj.* théorique.
theory, *s.* théorie *f.*
there, *adv.* là; *(with verb)* y; ~ *is, are* il y a.
therefore *adv.* donc.
thermometer, *s.* thermomètre *m.*
thermos, *s.* thermos *f.*
they, *pron.* ils, elles; ~ *say* on dit
thick, *adj.* épais.
thief, *s.* voleur, -euse *m. f.*
thigh, *s.* cuisse *f.*
thimble, *s.* dé *m.*
thin, *adj.* mince; maigre; *fig.* pauvre.
thing, *s.* chose *f.;* ~*s* effets *m. pl.*
think, *v.a.* croire; concevoir; *v.n.* croire; penser *(about, of* à); ~ *out* élaborer; ~ *over* réfléchir à, penser.
third, *adj.* troisième; trois; — *s.* tiers *m.*
thirsty, *adj.* altéré; *be* ~ avoir soif.
thirteen, *adj.* & *s.* treize *(m.).*
thirty, *adj.* & *s.* trente *(m.).*
this, *pl.* **these,** *pron.* cela, — *adj.* ceci; ce, cet, cette; ces.
thorn, *s.* épine *f.*
thorough, *adj.* profond, complet; consommé.
thoroughfare, *s.* artère *f.* principal, grande rue *f.; no* ~ rue barrée, passage interdit.
thoroughly, *adv.* tout à fait, à fond.
though, *conj.* quoique, bien que; — *adv.* tout de même.
thought, *s.* pensée *f.;* idée *f.; (care)* souci *m.*
thoughtful, *adj.* pensif; attentif.
thoughtless, *adj.* étourdi; insouciant.
thousand, *s.* & *adj.* mille *(m.)*
thrash, *v.a.* battre.
thread, *s.* fil *m.;* — *v. a.*

enfiler.
threat, *s.* menace *f.*
threaten, *v. a. & n.* menacer (de).
three, *adj. & s.* trois *(m.)*.
threshold, *s.* seuil *m.*
thrifty, *adj.* économe.
thrill, *s.* tressaillement *m.*; — *v. a.be ~ed with* frissonner de.
thrive, *v. n.* prospérer.
throat, *s.* gorge *f.*
throne, *s.* tône *m.*
through, *prep.* à travers; au travers de; par; par suite de; pendant; — *adv.* d'un bout à l'autre; *be ~ with* avoir fini qch.; — *adj.* direct.
throughout, *prep. & adv.* d'un bout à l'autre.
throw, *v.a.* jeter; *~ away* jeter, dissiper; *~ down* renverser; jeter à terre; *~ off* se débarrasser de; ôter; *~ out* rejecter; *~ over* abandonner; — *s.* jet *m.*
thrust, *v.a.* fourrer, pousser; enforcer; — *s.* poussée *f.*; botte *f.*
thumb, *s.* pouce *m.*
thunder, *s.* tonnerre *m.*; — *v.n.* tonner.
Thursday, *s.* jeudi *m.*
thus, *adv.* ainsi.
ticket, *s.* billet *m.*; étiquette *f.*
ticket-collector, *s.* contrôleur *m.*
tide, *s.* marée *f.*; courant *m.*
tidy, *adj.* propre; bien rangé; *(pers.)* ordonné; — *v.a.* *(also ~ up)* mettre en ordre.
tie, *v.a.* attacher; lier; nouer; *~ down* lier; *~ up* attacher; — *s.* lien *m.*; cravate *f.*; *(sport)* partie *f.* égale.
tiger, *s.* tigre, -esse *m. f.*
tight, *adj.* serré; tendu.
tighten, *v.a.* serrer.
tile, *s.* tuile *f.*
till, *prep.* jusqu'à; — *conj.* jusqu'à ce que.
tilt, *s.* inclinaison *f.*; — *v. n.* s'incliner, pencher; *v.a.* pencher.
time, *s.* temps *m.*; moment *m.*; *(clock)* heure *f.*; *(occasions)* fois; *at ~s* de temps en temps; *by the ~ that* avant que; *for the ~ being* actuellement; *what ~ is it?* quelle heure est-il?; *have a good ~* s'amuser bien; *keep good ~* marcher bien.
timely, *adj.* opportun.
timetable, *s.* horaire *m.*; indicateur *m.*; *(school)* emploi *m.* du temps.
tin, *s.* étain *m.*; *(conserve)* boîte *f.* (en fer blanc).
tinned, *adj.* en boîte; conservé.
tint, *s.* teinte *f.*
tiny. *adj.* tout petit.
tip[1], *s.* bout *m.*; — *v.a.* renverser; *v.n.* *(also ~ over)* se renverser.
tip[2], *s.* *(money)* pourboire *m.*; — *v.a.* donner un pourboire (à).
tire[1], **tyre,** *s.* pneu(matique) *m.*

tire², *v.a.* fatiguer; *v.n.* se fatiguer.
tired, *adj.* *be ~ of* être las de.
tissue, *s.* tissu *m.*
tissue-paper, *s.* papier *m.* de soie.
title, *s.* titre *m.*
to, *prep.* à; vers; en,
toast, *s.* rôtie *f.*; *(bread, drink)* toast *m.*; — *v.a.* rôtir.
tobacco, *s.* tabac *m.*
tobacconist, *s.* marchand *m.* de tabac; *~'s* débit *m.* de tabac.
today, *adv.* aujourd'hui.
toe, *s.* orteil *m.*, doigt *m.* du pied.
together, *adv.* ensemble; en même temps.
toil, *s.* travail *m.*; — *v.n.* travailler.
toilet, *s.* toilette *f.*
toilet-paper, *s.* papier *m.* hygiénique.
tomato, *s.* tomate *f.*
tomb, *s.* tombeau *m.*
tomorrow, *adv.* demain.
ton, *s.* tonne *f.*
tone, *s.* ton *m.*
tongs, *s. pl.* pincettes *f. pl.*; pince *f.*
tongue, *s.* langue *f.*
tonight, *adv.* cette nuit; ce soir.
tonsil, *s.* amygdale *f.*
too, *adv.* trop; *(also)* aussi.
tool, *s.* outil *m.*; instrument *m.*
tooth, *s.* dent *f.*
toothache, *s.* mal *m.* de dents.
toothbrush, *s.* brosse *f.* à dents.
toothpaste, *s.* pâte *f.* dentrifrice.
top, *s.* sommet *m.*, faîte *m.*; dessus *m.*; couvercle *m.*; tête *f.*; premier, -ère *m. f.*; — *v.a.* couronner; dépasser.
topic, *s.* sujet *m.*; *~s of the day* actualités *f. pl.*
torch, *s.* torche *f.*
tortoise, *s.* tortue *f.*
toss, *s.* mouvement *m.*; — *v.a.* jeter; lancer en l'air; ballotter; *~ up* lancer en l'air.
total, *adj.* & *s.* total *(m.)*.
totter, *v.n.* chanceler.
touch, *s.* toucher *m.*; attouchement *m.*; touche *f.*; légère *f.* attaque,; — *v.a.* toucher.
tough, *adj.* dur; robuste; rude.
tour, *s.* voyage *m.*; tour *m.*; tournée *f.*; — *v.n.* voyager.
tourism, *s.* tourisme *m.*
tourist, *s.* touriste *m.*
tournament, *s.* tournoi *m.*
tow, *s.* étoupe *f.*; remorque *f.*; — *v.a.* remorquer.
toward(s), *prep.* vers; envers; pour.
towel, *s.* essuie-main(s) *m.*, serviette *f.*
tower, *s.* tour *f*
town, *s.* ville *f.*
town-hall, *s.* hôtel *m.* de ville.
toy, *s.* jouet *m.*; — *v.n.* jouer (avec).
trace, *s.* trace *f.*; trait *m.*; — *v.a.* tracer; *~ back* remonter à.

ack, *s.* traces *f. pl.*; sentier *m.*; *(railw.)* voie *f.*; *(running)* piste *f.*
actor, *s.* tracteur *m.*
ade, *s.* commerce *m.*; *(occupation)* métier *m.*; *v.n.* commercer; ~ *in* faire le commerce de.
ade-mark, *s.* marque *f.* de fabrique.
adesman, *s.* commerçant *m.*
ade(s)-union, *s.* syndicat *m.*
adition, *s.* tradition *f.*
aditional, *adj.* traditionnel.
affic, *s.* trafic *m.*; circulation *f.*; ~ *lights* feux *m.pl.* de signalisation.
agedy, *s.* tragédie
agic(al), *adj.* tragique.
ail, *s.* trace *f.*; — *v.a.* & *n.* trainer.
ain, *s.* train *m.*; *(series)* suite *f.*; — *v.a.* entraîner; iormer.
iner, *s.* entraîneur *m.*
itor, *s.* traître *m.*
am, *s.* tramway *m.*
mp, *v.n.* aller à pied; — *s.* bruit *m.* de pas; *(pers.)* chemineau *m.*
nsaction, *s.* transaction *f.*
nsfer, *s.* transport *m.*; — *v.a.* transférer.
nsform, *v.a.* transformer (en).
nsfusion, *s.* transfusion *f.*
nsgress, *v.a.* transgresser; *v.n.* pécher.
transistor, *s.* transistor *m.*
transit, *s.* transit *m*; *in* ~ en cours de route.
translate, *v.a.* traduire.
translation, *s.* traduction *f.*
translator, *s.* traducteur, -trice *m. f.*
transmission, *s.* transmission *f.*
transmit, *v.a.* transmettre, émettre.
transmitter, *s.* (poste) émetteur *m.*
transparency, *s.* diapositive *f.*
transport, *s.* transport *m.*; — *v.a.* transporter.
trap, *s.* piège *m.*
trash, *s.* rebut *m.*; niaiseries *f. pl.*
travel, *v.n.* voyager; — *s.* voyage *m.*
traveller, *s.* voyageur, -euse *m. f.*
tray, *s.* plateau *m.*
treachery, *s.* trahison *f.*
tread, *s.* pas *m.*; — *v.n.* & *a.* marcher (sur).
treasure, *s.* trésor *m.*
treasury, *s.* trésor *m.*; trésorerie *f.*
treat, *v.a.* traiter.
treatment, *s.* traitement *m.*
treaty, *s.* traité *m.*
tree, *s.* arbre *m.*
tremble, *v.n.* trembler.
tremendous, *adj.* terrible; immense.
trench, *s.* tranchée *f.*
trend, *s.* tendance *f.*
trespass, *v.n.* envahir sans autorisation; ~

against offenser; ~ *on* abuser de; — *s.* offense *f.*
trial, *s.* essai *m.; épreuve f.; (law)* procès *m.*
tribe, *s.* tribu *f.*
tribute, *s.* tribut *m.*
trick, *s.* ruse *f.;* tour *m.;* truc *m.;* — *v.a.* duper.
trifle, *s.* bagatelle *f.; a* ~ un peu; — *v.n.* ~ *with* traiter légèrement.
trim, *s.* état *m.;* tenue *f.;* — *adj.* bien tenu; — *v.a.* arranger; garnir, orner; dresser.
trip, *s.* excursion *f.;* voyage *m.;* — *v.a.* ~ *up* faire trébucher.
triumph, *s.* triomphe *m.;* — *v.n.* triompher.
triumphant, *adj.* triomphant.
trolley, *s.* fardier *m.,* diable *m.;* trolley *m.*
trolley-bus, *s.* trolleybus *m.*
troop, *s.* troupe *f.*
trophy, *s.* trophée *m.*
tropic(al), *adj.* tropique.
tropics, *s. pl.* tropiques *m. pl.*
trot, *s.* trot *m.;* — *v.n.* trotter.
trouble, *s.* affliction *f.;* malheur *m.;* dérangement *m.;* difficulté *f.;* — *v.a.* inquiéter; déranger; affliger.
troublesome, *adj.* ennuyeux.
trousers, *s. pl.* pantalon *m.*
trout, *s* truite *f.*
truck, *s.* wagon *m.*
true, *adj.* vrai; exact; fidèle; *come* ~ se réaliser.
truly, *adv.* vraiment.
trumpet, *s.* trompette *f.;* — *v. a.* proclamer.
trunk, *s.* malle *f. (tree)* tronc *m.*
trunk-call, *s.* appel *m.* interurbain.
trust, *s.* confiance *f.;* espoir *m.;* dépôt *m.;* trust *m.;* — *v.a.* se confier (à); faire crédit (à); *v.n.* espérer; compter sur.
truth, *s.* vérité *f.*
try, *v.a.* essayer, éprouver; *(law)* mettre en jugement; ~ *on* essayer; — *s.* essai *m.*
tub, *s.* bac *m.; (bath)* tub *m.*
tube, *s.* tube *m.;* tuyau *m.;* métro *m.*
Tuesday, *s.* mardi *m.*
tug, *s.* effort *m.;* — *v.a.* tirer; remorquer.
tug-boat, *s.* (bateau) remorqueur *m.*
tuition, *s.* enseignement *m.*
tumble, *v. n.* tomber
tumour, *s.* tumeur *f.*
tune, *s.* air *m.;* accord *m.* harmonie *f.; in* ~ d'accord; *out of* ~ faux; — *v.a.&n.* accorder; ~ *in to* mettre sur; ~ *up* régler; s'accorder.
tunnel, *s.* tunnel *m.*
turbine, *s.* turbine *f.*
turbo-jet: ~ *engine* turboréacteur *m.*
turbo-prop, *s.* turbopropulseur *m.*

turkey, *s.* dindon, dinde *m. f.*
Turkish, *adj.* turc, -que: — *s.* Turc, -que *m. f.*; *(lang.)* turc *m.*
turn, *v.a.* tourner, détourner; diriger; *v.n.* tourner; se diriger; devenir; avoir recours (à); ~ *about* (se) tourner; ~ *back* retourner; ~ *down* plier, baisser; repousser; ~ *upside down* renverser; ~ *in* se coucher; ~ *off* fermer, serrer; éteindre; ~ *on* ouvrir; allumer; ~ *over* (se) renverser; ~ *up* arriver, apparaitre — *s.* tour *m.*; détour *m.*; *(mind, style)* tournure *f.*; *(tide)* changement *m.*
urning, *s.* tournant *m.*
urnip, *s.* navet *m.*
urnover, *s.* chiffre *m.* d'affaires.
urret, *s.* tourelle f.
urtle, *s.* tortue *f.*
utor, *s.* précepteur *m.*; — *v.a.* instruire.
welfth, *adj.* douzième; douze.
welve, *adj.* & *s.* douze *(m.).*
ventieth, *adj.* vingtième.
venty, *adj.* & *s.* vingt *(m.).*
vice, *adv.* deux fois.
vig, *s.* brindille *f.*
vin, *adj.* & *s.* jumeau *(m.)*, jumelle *(f.).*
vist, *s.* *(road)* coude *f.*; torsion *f.*: — *v. a.* tordre; dénaturer; *v. n.* s'entortiller.
twitter, *v.n.* gazouiller.
two, *adj.* & *s.* deux *(m.).*
type, *s.* type *m.*; caractère *m.*; — *v.a.* taper (à la machine).
type-script, *s.* manuscrit *m.* dactylographié.
typewriter, *s.* machine à écrire, *f.*
typical, *adj.* typique.
typist, *s.* dactilo(graphe) *m. f.*
tyre *see* **tire.**

U

udder, *s.* mamelle *f.*
ugly, *adj.* laid.
ulcer, *s.* ulcère *m.*
ultimate, *adj.* final, dernier.
umbrella, *s.* parapluie *m.*
umpire, *s.* arbitre *m. f.*
unable, *adj.* incapable; ~ *to* impuissant à faire qch.; dans l'impossibilité de.
unaccustomed, *adj.* inaccoutumé, peu habitué (à).
unaided, *adj.* sans aide.
unanimous, *adj.* unanime.
unassisted, *adj.* sans aide.
unaware: *be ~ of* ignorer.
unbearable, *adj.* insupportable.
uncertain, *adj.* incertain,
uncertainty, *s.* incertitude *f.*
unchangeable, *adj.* immuable.
uncle, *s.* oncle *m.*
uncomfortable, *adj.* peu confortable.

uncommon, *adj.* rare; extraordinaire.
unconditional, *adj.* sans conditions.
unconscious, *adj.* sans connaissance; ~ *of* sans conscience de.
uncover, *v. a.* découvrir.
undamaged, *adj.* non endommagé.
undefined, *adj.* non défini.
undeniable, *adj.* incontestable.
under, *prep* sous; au-dessous de; dans.
undercarriage, *s.* châssis *m.*, train (d'atterrissage) *m.*
underclothes, *s. pl.* vêtements *m. pl.* de dessous.
underdeveloped, *adj.* sous-développe.
underdone, *adj.* pas assez cuit, saignant.
undergo, *v.a.* subir.
undergraduate, *s.* étudiant, -e (non diplomé) *m. f.*
underground, *s.* métro(politain) *m.*
underline, *v.a.* souligner.
undermine, *v.a.* miner.
underneath, *prep.* & *adv.* au-dessous (de).
undersigned, *adj.* & *s.* soussigné, -e *(m. f.)*.
understand, *v.a.&n.* comprendre; *it is understood that* il est convenu que.
understanding, *s.* entendement *m.*; intelligence *f.*
undertake, *v.a.* entreprenare; ~ *to* se char[ger] de, s'engager à.
undertaking, *s.* entrepris[e] *f.*
underwear, *s.* vêtemen[ts] *m.pl.* de dessous.
undesirable, *adj.* peu d[é]sirable.
undo, *v.a.* défaire.
undress, *v. n.* se déshabi[l]ler.
undue, *adj.* indu.
uneasy, *adj.* inquiet; m[al] à l'aise; incomm[o]de.
uneducated, *adj.* sans in[s]truction.
unemployed, *adj.* & sans travail; *the* les chômeurs *m.*
unemployment, *s.* chôm[a]ge *m.*
unequal, *adj.* inégal.
uneven, *adj.* inégal; i[m]pair.
unexpected, *adj.* inatte[n]du; soudain.
unfair, *adj.* injuste; dé[loy]al.
unfavorable, *adj.* défa[vo]rable.
unfortunate, *adj.* m[al]heureux.
unfortunately, *adv.* m[al]heureusement.
unhappy, *adj.* malh[eu]reux.
unhealthy, *adj.* mala[de]; *(place)* insalubre.
uninhabited, *adj.* inh[abi]té.
uninteresting, *adj.* [peu] intéressant, sans int[érêt].
union, *s.* union *f.*
unique, *adj.* unique.
unit, *s.* unité *f.*; *(m*

bloc *m.*
unite, *v.a.* unir; *v.n.* s'unir.
unity, *s.* unité *f.;* harmonie *f.*
universal, *adj.* universel.
university, *s.* université *f.*
unjust, *adj.* injuste.
unkind, *adj.* dur; peu aimable.
unknown, *adj.* inconnu.
unless, *conj.* à moins que... ne; à moins de.
unlike, *adj.* dissemblable.
unload, *v.a.* décharger.
unlock, *v.a.* ouvrir.
unmarried, *adj.* célibataire.
unnatural, *adj.* non naturel, dénaturé.
unnecessary, *adj.* inutile.
unnoticed, *adj.* inaperçu.
unoccupied, *adj.* inoccupé; libre; non occupé.
unpack, *v.a.* déballer.
unpaid, *adj.* impayé.
unparalleled, *adj.* incomparable.
unpleasant, *adj.* désagréable.
unprecedented, *adj.* sans exemple. *or.* précédent.
unprejudiced, *adj.* sans préjugés, impartial.
unprepared, *adj.* non préparé; *be* ~ *for* ne pas s'attendre à qch.
unprofitable, *adj.* peu profitable.
unpromising, *adj.* qui s'annonce mal; peu prometteur.
unqualified, *adj.* non qualifié; sans restriction.
unreal, *adj.* irréel.
unreasonable, *adj.* déraisonnable.
unsatisfactory, *adj.* peu satisfaisant.
unseen, *adj.* invisible; inaperçu.
unsettled, *adj.* non réglé; *(in mind)* indécis; incertain.
unskilled, *adj.* non spécialisé.
unsolved, *adj.* non résolu.
unspeakable, *adj.* inexprimable.
unsteady, *adj.* tremblant; peu fixe; chancelant; inconstant.
unsuccessful, *adj.* malheureux; infructueux.
unsuitable, *adj.* inconvenant; peu propre (à).
untidy, *adj.* sans ordre, malpropre; en désordre.
until, *prep.* jusqu'à; — *conj.* jusqu'à ce que; avant que.
unto, *prep.* jusqu'à.
unusual, *adj.* rare, peu commun.
unwell, *adj.* indisposé; souffrant.
unwilling, *adj.* peu disposé (à).
unworthy, *adj.* indigne.
unyielding, *adj.* inflexible.
up, *adv.* en montant, vers le haut; (en) haut; *go* ~ monter; *be* ~ *in* être fort en; *what's* ~*?* qu'est-ce qu'il y a?; — *prep.* vers le haut de; en haut; — *adj.* montant.
uphill, *adj.* montant; — *adv. go* ~ monter.

uphold, *v.a.* soutenir; appuyer.
upholsterer, *s.* tapissier *m.*
upon, *prep* sur.
upper, *adj.* supérieur; *(deck)* deuxième; *the ~ classes* les hautes classes.
upright, *adj.* droit; honnête.
upset, *v.a.* renverser; *fig.* troubler, bouleverser; — *adj.* renversé; *fig.* dérangé; *be ~* être indisposé.
upside do\`n, *adv.* sens dessus dessous.
upstairs, *adv.* en haut; *go ~* monter (l'escalier).
up-to-date, *adj* moderne, à la mode.
upwards, *adv.* en haut, vers le haut, en montant.
urge, *v.a.* prier instamment (de); recommander instamment; pousser en avant.
urgent, *adj.* urgent; pressant.
us, *pron.* nous.
usage, *s.* usage *m.*
use, *v.a.* se servir de; traiter; faire usage (de); consommer; *~ up* user; consommer; *~d to* habitué à; *get ~d to* s'habituer à; — *s.* usage *m.*; emploi *m.*; utilité *f.*; *be of ~* être utile (à); *(of) no ~* inutile; *out of ~* hors d'usage *or* de service.
useful, *adj.* utile (à).
useless, *adj.* inutile.
usher, *s.* *(court)* (huissier) audiencier *m.*
usherette, *s.* *(theatre)* ouvreuse *f.*
usual, *adj.* usuel.
usually, *adv.* ordinairement.
utensil, *s.* ustensile *m.*
utility, *s.* utilité *f.*
utilize, *v.a.* utiliser.
utmost, *adj.* extrême; le plus grand; — *s.* le plus; tout son possible.
utter[1], *adj.* le plus grand; absolu.
utter[2], *v.a.* dire, prononcer; pousser.
utterance, *s.* prononciation. *f.*; expression *f.*; parole *f.*

V

vacancy, *s.* vacance *f.*
vacant, *adj.* vacant; vide; sans expression.
vacation, *s.* vacances *f. pl.*
vaccinate, *v.a.* vacciner.
vaccination, *s.* vaccination.
vacuum-cleaner, *s.* aspirateur *m.*
vague, *adj.* vague.
vain, *adj.* vain; vaniteux; *in ~* en vain.
valid, *adj.* valide.
validity, *s.* validité *f.*
valley, *s.* vallée *f.*
valuable, *adj.* de valeur.
value, *s.* valeur *f.*; — *v.a.* évaluer; priser.
valve, *s.* soupape *f.*;

lampe *f.*, tube *m.*
van, *s.* fourgon *m.*; camion *m.* de livraison; wagon *m.*
vanish, *v.n.* disparaître; *(also* ~ *away)* s'évanouir.
vanity, *s.* vanité *f.*
variety, *s.* variété *f.*
various, *adj.* divers.
varnish, *s.* vernis *m.*
vary, *v.a.* & *n.* varier.
vase, *s.* vase *m.*
vast, *adj.* vaste.
vault, *s.* voûte *f.*; cave *f.*, caveau *m.*
veal, *s.* veau *m.*
vegetable, *s.* légume *m.*
vehicle, *s.* véhicule *m.*
veil, *s.* voile *m.*
vein, *s.* veine *f.*
velvet, *s.* velours *m.*
venison, *s.* venaison *f.*
vent, *s.* ouverture *f.*; *give* ~ *to* donner libre cours à.
ventilation, *s.* ventilation *f.*
ventilator, *s.* ventilateur *m.*
venture, *s.* risque *m.*; hasard *m.*; — *v.a.* risquer; hasarder; *v.n.* ~ *(up-) on* se hasarder à, se risquer à.
verb, *s.* verbe *m.*
verdict, *s.* décision *f.*, verdict *m.*
verge, *s.* bord *m.*
verify, *v.a.* vérifier.
verse, *s.* vers *m.*; strophe *f.*
version, *s.* version *f.*
vertical, *adj.* vertical.
very, *adv.* très; ~ *good* très bien; — *adj.* vrai; même.
vessel, *s.* vaisseau *m.*
vest, *s.* gilet *m.*; chemise *f.* américaine.
vestry, *s.* sacristie *f.*; assemblée *f.*
veterinary, *adj.* ~ *surgeon* vétérinaire *m.*
veto, *s.* véto *m.*; — *v.a.* mettre son véto (à).
vex, *v.a.* vexer.
vibrate, *v.n.* vibrer, osciller.
vibration, *s.* vibration *f.*
vicar, *s.* curé *m.*
vice-, *prefix* vice-.
vicinity, *s.* voisinage *m.*
victim, *s.* victime *f.*
victorious, *adj.* victorieux.
victory, *s.* victoire *f.*
victuals, *s. pl.* victuailles *f. pl.*
view, *s.* vue *f.*; avis *m.*; *on* ~ exposé; *have in* ~ se proposer (de); *with a* ~ *to* en vue de; *point of* ~ point *m.* de vue; — *v.a.* voir; regarder; envisager.
viewer, *s.* spectateur, -trice *m. f.*
vigorous, *adj.* vigoureux.
vigour, *s.* vigueur *f.*
village, *s.* village *m.*
villain, *s.* scélérat *m.*
vine, *s.* vigne *f.*
vinegar, *s.* vinaigre *m.*
vineyard, *s.* vignoble *m.*
vintage, *s.* vendange *f.*
violate, *v.a.* violer.
violation, *s.* violation *f.*
violence, *s.* violence *f.*
violent, *adj.* violent.
violet, *s.* violette *f.*; *(colour)* violet *m.*; —

adj. violet.
violin, *s.* violon *m.*
violinist, *s.* violoniste *m. f.*
violoncellist, *s.* violoncelliste *m.*
violoncello, *s.* violoncelle *m.*
virgin, *s.* vierge *f.*
virtue, *s.* vertu *f.*
visa, visé, *s.* visa *m.*
visibility, *s.* visibilité *f.*
visible, *adj.* visible.
vision, *s.* vision *f.*, vue *f.*
visit, *s.* visite *f.*; séjour *m.*; *be on a ~ to* être en visite chez; — *v.a.* visiter.
visitor, *s.* visiteur, -euse *m. f.*
vital, *adj.* vital.
vitamin, *s.* vitamine *f.*
vocabulary, *s.* vocabulaire *m.*
vocation, *s.* vocation *f.*
voice, *s.* voix *f.*; — *v.a.* exprimer.
voltage, *s.* voltage *m.*
volume, *s.* volume *m.*
voluntary, *adj.* volontaire.
volunteer, *s.* volontaire *m.*; — *v.n.* s'engager (pour).
vomit, *v.a.* & *n.* vomir.
vote, *s.* voix; — *v.a.* & *n.* voter (sur).
voucher, *s.* pièce *f.* de dépense ; pièce *f.* de recette; bon *m.*
vow, *s.* vœu *m.*; — *v. a.* vouer; jurer; *v. n.* faire un vœu; jurer.
vowel, *s.* voyelle *f.*
voyage, *s.* voyage *m.*; — *v. n.* voyager (par mer).
vulgar, *adj.* vulgaire.

W

wade, *v.a.* passer à gué.
wafer, *s.* gaufrette *f.*, hostie *f.*
wag, *v.a.* hocher; *(tail)* agiter; *v.n.* s'agiter.
wage(s), *s.* *(pl.)* salaire *m.*, gages *m. pl.*, — *v.a.* *~ war* faire la guerre.
wag(g)on, *s.* wagon *m.*
waist, *s.* taille *f.*
waistcoat, *s.* gilet *m*
wait, *v. a.* & *n.* attendre *(for* qn, qch).
waiter, *s.* garçon *m* (de restaurant); *head~* premier garçon *m.* maître *m.* d'hôtel.
waiting-room, *s.* salle *f* d'attente.
wake, *v.a.* (also *~ up)* réveiller; *v.n.* (also *~ up)* s'éveiller.
waken, *v.a.* éveiller *v.n.* s'éveiller .
walk, *s.* marche *f.*; promenade *f.*; *(path)* allée *f.*; *go for a ~* faire une promenade; — *v.n.* aller à pied; marcher; *(pleasure)* se promener; *~ off* s'en aller; *~ out* sortir.
wall, *s.* mur *m.*
wallet, *s.* portefeuill[e] *m.*
walnut, *s.* noyer *m.* *(fruit)* noix *f.*
waltz, *s.* valse *f.*
wander, *v.n.* errer; s'égarer (de); divaguer.

want, *s.* besoin *m.; man*que *m.; for* ~ *of* faute de; — *v.a.* avoir besoin (de); manquer (de); vouloir; demander; *v. n.* faire défaut; *be* ~*ing in* manquer de.

war, *s.* guerre *f.*

ward, *s.* pupille *m. f.; (hospital)* salle *f.*

warden, *s.* gouverneur *m.;* directeur *m.*

warder, *s.* gardien, -enne *m. f.*

wardrobe, *s.* armoire *f.*

ware, *s.* marchandise(s) *f. (pl.)*; article *m.*

warehouse, *s.* magasin *m.*; dépôt *m.*

warm, *adj.* chaud; *be* ~ avoir chaud; — *v.a.* chauffer; ~ *up* réchauffer; *v.n.* se chauffer.

warmth, *s.* chaleur *f.*

warn, *v.a.* avertir; prévenir; mettre sur ses gardes (contre).

warning, *s.* avertissement *m.;* avis *m.*

warrant, *s.* autorisation *f.;* mandat *m.;* — *v. a.* garantir; justifier.

wash, *v.a.* laver; *v.n.* se laver; ~ *away* effacer; ~ *up the dishes* faire la vaisselle; — *s.* lavage *m.;* lotion *f.*; toilette *f.*; lessive *f.*

wash-basin, *s.* cuvette *f.* (de lavabo).

washing-machine, *s.* machine *f.* à laver.

wasp, *s.* guêpe *f.*

waste, *s.* désert *m.*, *(money)* gaspillage *m.; (energy)* déperdition *f.; (loss)* perte *f.;* déchets *m. pl.;* ~ *of time* perte de temps *f.;* — *adj.* inculte; de rebut; ~ *paper* papier *m.* de rebut; — *v.a.* gaspiller; perdre; ravager.

watch, *s.* garde *f.;* gardien *m.*, garde *m.; (to indicate time)* montre *f.;* — *v. a.* veiller, garder; observer; regarder; *v.n.* veiller; ~ *out!* ouvrez l'œil!

watch-maker, *s.* horloger *m.*

water, *s.* eau *f.*

water-closet , *s.* cabinet *m.*

waterfall, *s.* chute *f.* d'eau

watering-place, *s.* station *f.* balnéaire; ville *f.* d'eaux.

waterproof, *adj.* imperméable; — *s.* caoutchouc *m.*

wave, *s.* vague *f.;* onde *f.;* — *v.a.* agiter; *(hair)* onduler; *v. n.* flotter; onduler.

wave-length, *s.* longueur *f.* d'onde.

waver, *v.n.* vaciller.

wax, *s.* cire *f.*

way, *s.* chemin *m.*, route *f.;* distance *f.;* côte *m.; (means)* moyen *m.;* façon *f.*, manière *f.; which* ~*?* de quel côté?; *it's a long* ~ *to* il y a loin pour aller (à); *on the* ~ chemin faisant; ~ *in* entrée *f.;* ~ *out* sortie *f.*; *out of the* ~ retiré; extraordinaire; *this* ~ de ce côté-ci, par ici; *by* ~ *of* par; *by the* ~ à propos; *in a* ~ à certains égards; *give* ~ *to* céder à.

we, *pron.* nous.

weak, *adj.* faible.

weakness, *s.* faiblesse *f.*

wealth, *s.* richesse *f.*; profusion *f.*

wealthy, *adj.* riche.

weapon, *s.* arme *f.*

wear, *v.a.* porter; ~ *away, down, out* (s')user; ~ *off* (s')effacer; — *s.* usage *m.*; usure *f.*

weary, *adj.* las, fatigué.

weather, *s.* temps *m.*

weather-forecast, *s.* prévisions *f. pl.* du temps; bulletin *m.* météorologique.

weave, *v. a.* tisser.

web, *s.* tissu *m.*; *(spider)* toile *f.*

wedding, *s.* mariage *m.*

wedding-ring, *s.* alliance *f.*, anneau *m.* de mariage.

wedge, *s.* coin *m.*; — *v.a.* coincer; caler.

Wednesday, *s.* mercredi *m.*

weed, *s.* mauvaise herbe *f.*; — *v.a.* sarcler.

week, *s.* semaine *f.*

week-day, *s.* jour *m.* de semaine; *on* ~*s* en semaine.

week-end, *s.* fin *f.* de semaine, week-end *m.*

weekly, *adj.* de la semaine; hebdomadaire; — *s.* (journal) hebdomadaire *m.*

weep, *v.n.* pleurer.

weigh, *v.a. & n.* peser; ~ *down* faire pencher, surcharger, accabler.

weight, *s.* poids *m.*; *put on* ~ prendre du corps.

welcome, *adj.* bienvenu; ~*!* soyez le bienvenu!; — *s.* accueil *m.*: — *v.a.* souhaiter la bienvenue (à); accueillir (avec plaisir).

well[1], *adv.* bien; ~, ~*!* allons, allons!; — *adj.* bien (portant).

well[2], *s.* puits *m.*

well-being, bien-être *m.*

well-informed, *adj.* bien informé, renseigné.

well-to-do, *adj.* aisé; *be* ~ être dans l'aisance

west, *s.* ouest *m.*

western, *adj.* de l'ouest.

westward, *adv.* vers l'ouest.

wet, *adj.* mouillé, humide; pluvieux; ~ *through* trempé jusqu'aux os; — *v.a.* mouiller; tremper.

whale, *s.* baleine *f.*

what, *rel. pron.* ce qui, ce que; — *interrog. pron.* qu'est-ce qui, que; — *int.* quoi!

wheat, *s.* blé *m.*, froment *m.*

wheel, *s.* roue *f.*; *(steering)* volant *m.*

when, *adv. & conj.* quand.

whenever, *adv.* toutes les fois que.

where, *adv.* où.

whereas, *conj.* tandis que;

vu que.
wherever, *adv.* partout où.
whether, *conj.* soit que; *(if)* si; ~ *or not*... qu'il en soit ainsi ou non...
which, *(interrogative) adj.* quel, quelle; *pron.* lequel; *(relative) adj.* lequel, laquelle; *pron.* qui, que, lequel.
while, *conj.* pendant que; *(whereas)* tandis que; *(as long as)* tant que; — *s.* temps *m.*; *be worth* ~ *to* cela vaut la peine de; — *v.a.* ~ *away* faire passer.
whip, *s.* fouet.
whisk, *v.a.* fouetter; — *s.* époussette *f.*; *(eggs)* fouet à œufs, *m.*
whisper, *s.* chuchotement *m.*; murmure *m.*; *v.a.* dire à l'oreille; *v.n.* chuchoter; murmurer.
whistle, *s.* sifflet *m.*; — *v.a.* & *n.* siffler.
white, *adj.* blanc, blanche; pâle.
Whit Sunday, dimanche *m.* de la Pentecôte.
who, *pron.* qui.
whole, *s.* tout *m.*; totalité *f.*; *on the* ~ à tout prendre; — *adj.* tout le, toute la; entier, -ère.
wholesale, *adj.* & *adv.* en gros.
wholesome, *adj.* sain.
wholly, *adv.* entièrement.
whom, *pron.* que; lequel; *interrog.* qui?, qui est-ce que?
whose, *pron.* dont; *interrog.* de qui?
why, *adv.* pourquoi.
wicked, *adj.* méchant.
wide, *adj.* large; étendue; *6 feet* ~ 6 pieds de largeur.
widow, *s.* veuve *f.*
widower, *s.* veuf *m.*
width, *s.* largeur *f.*
wife, *s.* femme *f.*
wild, *adj.* sauvage; déréglé; impétueux; frénétique.
wilful, *adj.* volontaire.
will, *s.* volonté *f.*; intention *f.*; testament *m.*; *at* ~ à volonté; *of one's own free* ~ de plein gré; — *v.n.* & *aux.* vouloir; *(future tense unexpressed, see grammar).*
willing *adj.* bien disposé; *be* ~ vouloir bien.
willingly, *adv.* volontiers.
win, *v. a.* & *n.* gagner.
winch, *s.* manivelle *f.*
wind[1], *s.* vent *m.*; souffle *m.*
wind[2], *v. a.* enrouler; dévider; ~ *up (clock)* remonter; *fig.* liquider; *v.n.* tourner, serpenter; s'enrouler.
window, *s.* fenêtre *f.*; *(car)* glace *f.*
windscreen, *s.* pare-brise *m.*
windy, *adj.* venteux.
wine, *s.* vin *m.*
wing, *s.* aile *f.*; vol *m.*; *take* ~ s'envoler.
wink, *s.* clin d'œil, *m.*; — *v.a.* clignoter.
winner, *s.* gagnant *m.*

winter, *s.* hiver *m.*
wipe, *v.a.* essuyer; *~ out* effacer; — *s.* coup *m.* de torchon.
wire, *s.* fil *m.* (de fer); télégramme *m.; live ~* fil *m.* en charge; — *v.a.* & *n.* télégraphier.
wireless, *s.* T.S.F.; télégraphie sans fil; *~ set* poste *m.* (de T.S.F.).
wise, *adj.* sage; prudent.
wish, *s.* désir *m.; ~es* vœux *m. pl.;* — *v.a.* désirer (de); souhaiter; *(should like)* vouloir *(in conditional).*
wit, *s.* esprit *m.; (pers.)* bel esprit *m.*
witch, *s.* sorcière *f.*
with, *prep.* avec; *(at)* chez.
withdraw, *v.n.* se retirer; *v.a.* retirer.
within, *adv.* dedans; — *prep. (time)* en; *(place)* dans; à.
without, *prep.* sans; *(place)* en dehors de.
witness, *s.* témoignage *m.; (pers.)* témoin *m.;* — *v.a.* être témoin de; *(attest)* témoigner; *(document)* signer (à).
witty, *adj.* spirituel.
wizard, *s.* sorcier *m.*
wolf, *s.* loup, louve *m. f.*
woman, *s.* femme *f.*
womb, *s.* matrice *f.; fig.* sein *m.*
wonder, *s.* étonnement *m.; (a thing)* merveille *f.;* — *v.n. ~ at* être étonné de; *(curious)* se demander; *I ~* je me le demande.
wonderful, *adj.* étonnant.
wood, *s.* bois *m.*
wooden, *adj.* de bois.
woodman, *s.* bûcheron *m.*
wool, *s.* laine *f.*
woollen, *adj.* de laine.
word, *s.* mot *m.; (utterance)* parole *f.; (term)* terme *m.; (information* avis *m.; upon my ~!* ma parole! ; *have a ~ with* avoir deux mots avec.
work, *s.* travail *m.; (achievement)* ouvrage *m.; ~ (of art)* œuvre *f.* d'art; *~s (of s.o.)* œuvres *f.pl., (factory)* usine *f.; set to ~* se mettre à l'œuvre; — *v.a.* faire travailler; *(wood)* ouvrager; *v.n.* travailler; *(operate)* fonctionner, marcher.
worker, *s.* travailleur, -euse *m. f.*, ouvrier, -ère *m. f.*
workman, *s.* ouvrier *m.*
workshop, *s.* atelier *m.*
world, *s.* monde *m.*
world-war, *s.* guerre *f.* mondiale.
world-wide, *adj.* universel; mondial.
worm, *s.* ver *m.*
worry, *s.* ennui *m.*, tracas *m.;* — *v.a.* tracasser; importuner; *v. n.* se tracasser (de), se tourmenter; *don't ~!* soyez tranquille!

worse, *adj.* pire, plus mauvais; *grow* ~ empirer; — *adv.* pis.
worship, *s.* culte *m.;* — *v.a.* & *n.* adorer.
worst, *adj.* le, la pire; le, la plus malade; — *adv.* le plus mal; — *s.* pis *m.*
worth, *s.* valeur *f.;* — *adj.* *be* ~ valoir; *is it* ~ *while?* cela (en) vaut-il la peine?; *it is not* ~ *the trouble* cela ne vaut pas la peine.
worthless, *adj.* sans valeur, indigne.
worthy, *adj.* digne.
wound, *s.* blessure *f.*
wounded, *adj.* blessé; *the* ~ les blessés.
wrap, *s.* *(garment)* peignoir *m.; v.a.* ~ *up* envelopper; *fig.* être absorbé *(in* dans).
wrapper, *s.* toile d'emballage *f.; (book)* bande *f.*
wreck, *s.* naufrage *m.;* navire *m.* naufragé; *fig.* ruine *f.; v.a.* ruiner: *be* ~*ed* faire naufrage; être naufragé.
wrench, *s.* torsion *f.; (tool)* clef (à écrous) *f.;* — *v.a.* tordre; *(ankle)* fouler.
wrestle, *v.n.* lutter (avec).
wrestler, *s.* lutteur *m.*
wrestling, *s.* lutte *f.*
wring, *v.a.* tordre.
wrinkle, *s.* ride *f.; (crease)* faux pli *m.;* — *v.a.* rider.
wrist, *s.* poignet *m.*
writ, *s.* exploit *m.*
write, *v.a.* & *n.* écrire; ~ *down* noter; ~ *off* amortir; ~ *out* transcrire.
writer, *s.* écrivain *m.*
writing, *s.* écriture *f.;* écrit *m.; in* ~ par écrit.
writing-desk, *s.* bureau *m.*
wrong, *adj.* incorrect, faux; *be* ~ avoir tort; se tromper (de); *take the* ~ *train* se tromper de train; *it is the* ~ *book* ce n'est pas le livre qu'il faut.

X

Xmas, *s.* Noël *m.*
x-ray, *adj.* ~ *treatment* radiothérapie *f.;* ~ *photograph* radiograph e *f.*

Y

yacht, *s.* yacht *m.*
yard, *s.* yard *m.;* cour *f.*
yarn, *s.* fil *m;* histoire *f.*
yawn, *s.* bâillement *m.;* — *v. n.* bâiller.
year, *s.* an *m.;* année *f.*
yearly, *adv.* annuellement.
yearn, *v.n.* ~ *for* soupirer après.
yeast, *s.* levure *f.*
yell, *v. n.* hurler.
yellow, *adj.* jaune.
yes, *adv.* oui; *(after negation)* si.
yesterday, *adv.* hier.

yet, *adv.* encore; *not* ~ pas encore; *as* ~ jusqu'à présent; — *conj.* néanmoins.
yield, *v.a.* produire; accorder; rendre; *v.n.* céder (à); fléchir.
yoke, *s.* joug *m.*
yolk, *s.* jaune *m.*
you, *pron.* tu; vous.
young, *adj.* jeune; *(animal)* petit; *~er* plus jeune. cadet.
your, *adj.* votre, *(pl.)* vos.
yours, *pron.* à vous; le, la vôtre, les vôtres.
yourself, *pron.* vous-même, *-s.*
youth, *s.* jeunesse *f.*; *(pers.)* jeune homme *m.*
youth-hostel, *s.* auberge *f.* de la jeunesse.

Z

zeal, *s.* zèle *m.*
zealous, *adj.* zélé.
zero, *s.* zéro *m.*
zest, *s.* enthousiasme *m.*; goût *m.*
zigzag, *s.* zigzag *m.*; — *adv.* en zigzag.
zinc, *s.* zinc *m.*
zipper, *s.* fermeture éclair. *f.*
zone, *s.* zone *f.*
zoo, *s.* zoo *m.*
zoology, *s.* zoologie *f.*

FRENCH - ENGLISH DICTIONARY

I. Consonnes. La plupart des consonnes se prononcent à peu près comme en français. Il faut cependant faire attention:

1. Au **th**, qui se produit en appliquant la langue contre les alvéoles des dents d'en haut en expirant fortement, tantôt sans vibration des cordes vocales (comme dans **thin.** mince); tantôt avec vibration (comme dans **this,** ce, ceci);

2. **à l'r.** Au commencement d'un mot, ce son est roulé; au milieu, il est plutôt grasseyé; tandis qu'à la fin il est muet, à moins d'être suivi d'un mot commençant par une voyelle. Dans ce cas il se rattache à cette voyelle, et reprend la valeur roulée;

3. **au g**, qui au début d'un mot est tantôt dur (comme dans **get**, obtenir), tantôt doux (comme dans **general,** général), où il a la valeur du **g** français précédé d'un **d.**

II. Voyelles. Les sons de la plupart des voyelles se retrouvent également en français, mais ce ne sont pas toujours les mêmes lettres qui les représentent.

Le **a** de **pas** se retrouve dans **ask,** demander, etc.

Le **a** de **patte** est le premier son de la diphtongue **ai**, qui s'entend dans **mine,** le mien; de la diphtongue **aou** qui s'entend dans **down,** en bas.

La voyelle de **man,** homme, a la valeur de l'**a** faubourien de **Clamart.**

La voyelle de **cut**, couper, est entre l'**a** et l'**é** français.

La voyelle **i** a deux sons: tantôt long, comme dans **machine,** machine (même valeur qu'en français); tantôt bref, comme dans **it,** il, où il est plus bref que l'**i** d'**ami.**

Le son bref de l'**e** anglais e celui de l'**e de livret.** Il s'en tend dans **get,** obtenir; e dans la diphtongue de **day** jour (où il est suivi de l'**i** bref Le son long est celui de l'è français, mais il est toujou suivi d'un **e** muet, comm dans **where,** où (qui peut s figurer par les lettres *wèe*).

Le son de l'**e** muet est trè fréquent en anglais, surtou dans les syllabes non accent uées (comme dans **ago**, il y où l'**a** se prononce ainsi) et à l fin d'un mot (comme dans **fa ther**, père). Ce même son prolongé (comme dans **heu** heu français), s'entend dan **bird,** oiseau. L'**e** muet fa partie, on l'a vu, de la diph tongue de **where,** où; et aus de la diphtongue de **beer** bière (qui peut se figurer pa *bie*), et de **poor,** pauvre (qu peut se figurer par *poue*).

L'**o** anglais a trois valeur Il est tantôt bref, comme dan **box,** boîte (comme l'**o** d **note**); tantôt long, comm dans le son de l'**a** de **all** (où a presque la valeur de l'**ô** d **dôme**); et tantôt il fait parti de la diphtongue qui s'enten dans **no,** non, où il a presqu la valeur de l'**e** muet suiv d'un son qui peut se figure par *ou*. Le son bref s'enten aussi dans la diphtongue d **boy,** garçon.

L'**u** anglais a deux valeur Il est tantôt bref (exactemen comme l'**ou** de **bout**) et s'en tend dans **put,** mettre; tant long (comme l'**ou** de **cours** et s'entend dans **shoe,** soulie (L'on a vu déjà qu'il fait pa tie de la diphtongue de **poo** pauvre).

NOMS

Abyssinie, *s. f.* Abyssinia.
Adriatique, *s. f.* Adriatic.
Afrique, *s. f.* Africa.
Albanie, *s. f.* Albania.
Alexandre, *s. m.* Alexander.
Alexandrie, *s. f.* Alexandria.
Alger, *s. m.* Algiers.
Algérie, *s.f.* Algeria, Algiers.
Allemagne, *s. f.* Germany.
(les) Alpes, *s. f. pl.* The Alps.
Amérique, *s. f.* America; *l'~ du Nord, du Sud* North America, South America.
Angleterre, *s. f.* England.
(les) Antilles, *s. f. pl.* The Antilles, the West Indies.
Antoine, *s. m.* Anthony.
Anvers, *s. m.* Antwerp.
Apennins, *s. m. pl.* Apennines.
Arabie, *s. f.* Arabia.
Argentine, *s. f.* Argentina, the Argentine.
Asie, *s. f.* Asia.
Assyrie, *s. f.* Assyria.
Athènes, *s. f.* Athens.
Atlantique, *s. m.* The Atlantic.
Auguste, *s.m.* Augustus.
Australie, *s. f.* Australia.
Autriche, *s. f.* Austria.
Azincourt, *s. m.* Agincourt.

Bâle, *s. f.* Basle.
Baltique, *s. f.* Baltic.
Barcelone, *s. f.* Barcelona.
Belgique, *s. f.* Belgium.
(les) Bermudes, *s. f. pl.* The Bermudas.
Bethléem, *s.m.* Bethlehem.
Beyrouth, *s.f.* Beirut, Beirout.
Birmanie, *s. f.* Burmah.
Bohême, *s. f.* Bohemia.
Bolivie, *s. f.* Bolivia.
Bosphore, *s. m.* The Bosphorus.
Bourgogne, *s.f.* Burgundy.
Brême, *s. f.* Bremen.
Brésil, *s. m.* Brazil.
Bretagne, *s. f.* Brittany.
Britanniques (Îles), *adj.* The British Isles.
Bruxelles, *s. f.* Brussels.
Bucarest, *s. m.* Bucharest.
Bulgarie, *s. f.* Bulgaria.

Cachemire, *s. m.* Kashmir.
(le) Caire, *s. m.* Cairo.
Calais, *s. m.* Calais.
Californie, *s. f.* California.
(le) Calvaire, *s. m.* (Mount) Calvary.
Cambodge, *s. m.* Cambodia.
(le) Cap, *s. m.* Capetown.
(les) Carpathes, *s. m. pl.* The Carpathian Mountains.
Carrache, *s. m.* Carracci.
Caspienne (la Mer), *s. f.* The Caspian Sea.
(le) Caucase, *s. m.* The

Caucasus.
César, *s. m.* Caesar.
Ceylan, *s. f.* Ceylon.
Chaldée, *s. f.* Chaldea.
Chili, *s. m.* Chile.
Chine, *s. f.* China.
Chypre, *s. f.* Cyprus.
Cléopâtre. *s. f.* Cleopatra.
Colombie, *s. f.* Columbia, Colombia.
Copenhague, *s. f.* Copenhagen.
Cordoue, *s. f.* Cordova, Cordoba.
Corée, *s. f.* Korea, Corea.
Cornouailles, *s.f. pl.* Cornwall.
Corse, *s. f.* Corsica.
Cracovie, *s. f.* Cracow.
Crimée, *s. f.* Crimea.
Croatie, *s. f.* Croatia.

Dalmatie, *s. f.* Dalmatia.
Danemark, *s. m.* Denmark.
Denis, *s. m.* Denis.
Dominique, *s. f.* Dominique.
Douvres, *s. m.* Dover.
Dresde, *s. f.* Dresden.
Dunkerque, *s. m.* Dunkirk.

Écosse, *s. f.* Scotland.
Édimbourg, *s. m.* Edinburgh.
Égypte, *s. f.* Egypt.
Élisabeth, *s. f.* Elizabeth.
Équateur, *s.m.* Ecuador.
Espagne, *s. f.* Spain.
Esthonie, *s. f.* Esthonia.
(les) États-Unis, *s. m. pl.* The United States.
Europe, *s. f.* Europe.

(les) Fidji, Viti, *s. f. pl.* The Fiji Islands.
Finlande, *s. f.* Finland.
Flandre, *s. f.* Flanders.
Florence, *s. f.* Florence.
Floride, *s. f.* Florida.
France, *s. f.* France.
Francfort, *s. m.* Frankfurt, Frankfort.
Fribourg, *s. m.* **1.** *(Switzerland)* Fribourg; 2. *(Germany)* Freiburg.

Galilée, **1.** *s. m.* Galileo; **2.** *s. f.* Galilee.
Galles (Pays de), *s. m.* Wales.
Gambie, *s. f.* Gambia.
Gand, *f. m.* Ghent.
Gange, *f. m.* Ganges.
Gascogne, *s. f.* Gascony.
Gaule, *s. f.* Gaul.

Gédéon, *s. m.* Gideon.
Gênes, *s. f.* Genoa.
Genève, *s. f.* Geneva.
Georges, *s. m.* George.
Géorgie, *s. f.* Georgia.
Grande-Bretagne, *s. f.* Great Britain.
Grèce, *s. f.* Greece.
Groenland, *s. m.* Greenland.
Guinée, *s. f.* Guinea.

Hambourg, *s. m.* Hamburg.
Hanovre, *s. m.* Hanover.
(le) Havre, *s. m.* **Havre.**
Hawaï, *s. m.* **Hawaii.**
(la) Haye, *s. f.* **the Hague.**
Hongrie, *s. f.* **Hungary.**

Iéna, *s. f.* Jena.
Inde, *s. f.* India; ***les* ~s** *Occidentales* West In-

dies; *les ~s Orientales* East Indies.
Indonésie, *s. f.* Indonesia.
Irlande, *s. f.* Ireland.
Islande, *s. f.* Iceland.
Israël *s. m.* Israel.
Italie, *s. f.* Italy.

Jacques, *s. m.* James.
(la) Jamaïque, *s. f.* Jamaica.
Japon, *s. m.* Japan.
Jean, *s. m.* John.
Jeanne, *s. f.* Joan; Jean, Jane.
Jourdain *s. m.* Jordan.
Jupiter, *s.m.* Jupiter, Jove.

Laponie, *s. f.* Lapland.
Léon, *s. m.* Leo.
Lia, *s. f.* Leah.
Lisbonne, *s. f.* Lisbon.
Lithuanie, *s.f.* Lithuania.
Livourne, *s. f.* Leghorn.
Londres, *s. m.* London.
St. Luc, *s. m.* St Luke.
Luxembourg, *s. m.*Luxemburg.
Lyon, *s. m.* Lyons.

Mahomet, *s. m.* Mohammed, Mahomet.
(la) Manche, *s. f.* The English Channel.
Mantoue, *s. f.* Mantua.
St. Marc, *s. m.* Mark, St. Mark.
Marie, *s. f.* Mary.
Marseille, *s. m.* Marseilles.
Marthe, *s. f.* Martha.
(St) Matthieu, *s.m.* St. Matthew.
Maurice, (l'Île) *s. f.* Mauritius.
Moscou, *s. f.* Moscow.

Nicée, *s. f.* Nicaea.
Nil, *s. m.* The Nile.
Normandie, *s.f.* Normandy.
Norvège, *s. f.* Norway.
Nouvelle-Zélande, *s.f.* New Zealand.

Ostende, *s. f.* Ostend.
Oural, *s. m.* Ural.

Padoue, *s. f.* Padua.
Palerme, *s. f.* Palermo.
Parnasse, *s. m.* (Mount) Parnassus.
(les) Pays-Bas, *s. m. pl.* The Netherlands.
Pékin, *s. m.* Peking, Pekin.
Pensylvanie, *s. f.* Pennsylvania.
Pérou, *s. m.* Peru.
Perse, *s. f.* Persia.
Philadelphie, *s. f.* Philadelphia.
Philippes, *s. f.* Philippi.
Pierre, *s. m.* Peter.
Pise, *s. f.* Pisa.
Pologne, *s. f.* Poland.
(le) Pont-Euxin, *s. m.* The Black Sea.
Portugal, *s. m.* Portugal.
Pyrénées, *s. f. pl.* Pyrenees.

Raguse, *s. f.* Ragusa.
Reims, *s. m.* Rheims.
(le) Rhin, *s.m.* The Rhine.
Roumanie, *s. f.* Rumania.
Russie, *s. f.* Russia.
Salzbourg, *s. m.* Salzburg.
Sardaigne, *s. f.* Sardinia.
Scandinavie, *s. f.* Scandi-

..avia.
Serbie, *s. f.* Serbia.
Sicile, *s. f.* Sicily.
Singapour, *s. m.* Singapore.
Sophie, *s. f.* Sophia.
Spitzberg, *s.m.* Spitzbergen.
Suède, *s. f.* Sweden.
Suisse, *s. f.* Switzerland.
Syrie, *s. f.* Syria.

Tchécoslovaquie, *s. f.* Czechoslovakia.
Thuringe, *s. f.* Thuringia.
Tunisie, *s. f.* Tunis.
Turquie, *s. f.* Turkey.

Upsal, *s. f.* Uppsala.

Vienne, *s. f.* Vienna.

Yougoslavie, *s. f.* Yugoslavia.

PHRASES

Bonjour. Bonsoir. Au revoir.	Good morning. Good evening. Good-bye.
Je vous demande pardon. Pardon.	I beg your pardon. Excuse me.
Comment allez-vous? Très bien — et vous?	How are you? Very well — and you?
Enchanté (de faire votre connaissance) monsieur (madame, mademoiselle).	How do you do (delighted to meet you).
Permettez-moi! Vous êtes très gentil.	Allow me! You are very kind.
Cela m'est égal.	It's all the same to me
A votre santé.	Your good health.
Permettez-moi de vous présenter à . . .	Allow me to introduce you to . . .
Il fait beau (mauvais) temps.	It is fine (bad) weather.
Vous avez raison. Vous avez tort.	You are right. You are wrong.
Ce n'est pas ma faute.	It is not my fault.
Faire son possible.	To do one's best.
C'est très ennuyeux.	It is very annoying.
Vous vous moquez de moi.	You're pulling my leg.
Tant mieux (pis).	So much the better (worse).
C'est un chic type.	He's a jolly nice fellow.
Mettre les pieds dans le plat.	To put one's foot in it.
Rien ne va bien. Tout va mal.	Things are going badly.

Je suis anglais (anglaise).	I am an Englishmen (Englishwoman).
Je ne parle pas français.	I cannot speak French.
Je cherche . . .	I am looking for . . .
Je ne vous comprends pas.	I don't understand you.
Parlez lentement, s'il vous plaît!	Please speak slowly!
Y-a-t-il quelque'un qui parle anglais?	Is there anyone here who speaks English?
Où est le consulat britannique?	Where is the British Consulate?
C'est épatant, formidable!	It is wonderful, splendid!
Défense de . . . sous peine d'amende.	No . . . Trespassers will be prosecuted.
Entrée interdite.	No entry.
Les toilettes, les lavabos, les cabinets.	Lavatory.
Quelle heure est-il?	What time is it?
Il est une heure cinq.	It is five past one.
Nous sommes pressés.	We are in a hurry.
Combien de temps faut-il pour . . .?	How long does it take to . . . ?
Ce soir. Hier soir.	This evening, tonight. Last night.
Depuis quand êtes-vous ici?	How long have you been here?
Je suis ici depuis un mois.	I have been here a month.
Est-ce qu'on peut déjeuner (dîner) ici?	Can we lunch (dine) here?
Nous sommes quatre.	There are four of us.
Nous voudrions seulement un casse-croûte.	We only want a snack.
Voulez-vous nous donner le menu, s'il vous plaît.	Please give us the menu.
Apportez-nous la carte des vins, s'il vous plaît.	Bring us the wine list, please.
Nous voudrions du café noir (café au lait).	We would like black coffee (white coffee).
L'addition, s'il vous plaît.	The bill, please.
Je voudrais de l'essence (de l'huile, de l'eau).	I want some petrol (oil, water).
Je suis en panne.	I have had a breakdown.
Mon auto est sur la route à deux kilomètres d'ici.	My car is on the road two kilometres from here.
Connaissez-vous la route de . . .?	Do you know the road to . . .?

Is the post office (bank) near here?	Y a-t-il un bureau de poste (bureau de change) près d'ici?
Are there any letters for me?	Y a-t-il des lettres pour moi?
Do you sell . . .?	Est-ce que vous vendez...?
You have given me the wrong change.	Vous vous êtes trompé en me rendant la monnaie
Have you anything to declare?	Avez-vous quelque chose à déclarer?
I cannot find my ticket.	Je ne peux pas trouver mon billet.
J'ai laissé quelque chose dans le train.	I have left something in the train.
J'ai un train à prendre.	I have a train to catch.
A quelle heure est le premier (dernier) train pour . . .?	What time is the first (last) train for . . .?
Sur quel quai?	From which platform?
Où est-ce que je change pour . . .?	Where do I change for . . .?
Est-ce qu'il y a un hôtel où je peux passer la nuit?	Is there a hotel where I can stay the night?
Le dernier train est parti.	The last train has gone
Je ne me sens pas bien.	I do not feel well.
Je veux descendre à . . .	I want to get off at . . .
Allez-vous près de . . .?	Do you go near . . .?
Puis-je avoir une chambre pour la nuit?	Can I have a room for the night?
Je reste deux ou trois jours seulement.	I am only staying for two or three days.
Je désire une chambre avec un grand lit.	I want a room with a double bed.
Pouvez-vous me donnez une chambre pour la nuit?	Can you put me up for the night?
Je serai de retour à trois heures.	I shall be back at three.
Avez-vous des journaux anglais?	Have you any English newspapers?
Combien met-on sur une lettre pour . . .?	What does it cost to send a letter to . . .?
Où puis-je acheter . . .?	Where can I buy . . .?
Voulez-vous me reserver cette place?	Will you reserve this place for me?

Acceptez-vous un cheque de voyage?	Will you take a traveller's cheque?
Voulez-vous faire suivre mon courrier à cette adresse?	Will you have letters sent on to this address?
J'ai besoin d'un guide qui parle anglais.	I need a guide who speaks English.
Est-ce bien la route pour . . .?	Is this the right road for . . .?
Combien de kilomètres d'ici à . . .?	How far is it from here to . . . ?
Avez-vous des cartes postales?	Have you any post-cards?
Avez-vous une carte (un plan)?	Have you a map (plan)?
Savez-vous ce qu'on donne au cinéma (Théatre)?	Do you know what is on at the cinema (theatre)?
Ce chemin, ou mène-t-il?	Where does this road lead?
Pouvez-vous recommander un restaurant pas trop cher?	Can you recommend a cheap restaurant?
C'est trop cher. Avez-vous quelque chose de meilleur marché?	It is too dear. Have you anything cheaper?
Nous sommes perdus.	We are lost.
Avez-vous une pièce d'identite?	Have you any identification papers?
Avez-vous un sac en papier?	Have you a carrier bag?
Voici mon adresse.	Here is my address.
Je vous en prie.	That's all right.
Il n'y a pas de quoi.	Don't mention it.
Prenez ma place, madame.	Take my seat, madame.
Puis-je vous aider?	Can I help you?
Est-ce que je vous dérange?	Am I disturbing you?
Je suis navré (désolé).	I am terribly sorry.
Je vous remercie de votre hospitalité.	Thank you for your hospitality.
Nous nous sommes bien amusés.	We had a very good time.
C'est trop. C'est trop cher.	It's too much. It's too dear.

Attention !	Look out !
Vous avez raison. Vous avez tort.	You are right. You are wrong.
Ecoutez. Regardez.	Listen. Look.
Qu'est-ce qu-il y a?	What is the matter?
Parlez lentement, s'il vous plait.	Please speak slowly.
Attendez, je cherche la phrase dans ce livre.	Wait, I am looking for the phrase in this book.
Je vous ai déjà payé.	I have already paid you.
C'est tordant, c'est rigolo.	It's terribly funny.
Sans blague !	You don't say !
Vous plaisantez. Blague à part.	You are joking. Joking apart.
Entendu. D'accord.	Agreed. O.K.
Quel dommage !	What a pity !
Ne pas toucher.	Do not touch.
Prenez garde à la peinture.	Wet paint.
Vous avez tout le temps.	You have plenty of time.
Je n'ai pas le temps.	I have no time.
Avant-hier.	The day before yesterday.
Après-demain.	The day after tomorrow.
Garçon apportez-nous du pain, s'il vous plaît.	Waiter, bring us some bread, please.
Encore un peu de . . .	A little more . . .
Que désirez-vous boire (comme boisson)?	What would you like to drink?
Le service (le couvert), est-il compris?	Is the service (the cover charge) included?
Vous pouvez garder la monnaie.	Keep the change.
Il y a une erreur dans l'addition.	There is a mistake in the bill.
Je vous en prie.	Please don't mention it.
Est-ce que le garage est ouvert la nuit?	Is the garage open all night?
Je veux partir demain de bonne heure.	I want to leave early tomorrow.
Combien de temps faut-il attendre?	How long shall I have to wait?
Pouvez-vous me prêter . . .?	Can you lend me . . . ?
Combien est-ce que je vous dois?	How much do I owe you?

J'ai deux places réservées en première (en seconde).	I have two first class (second class) seats reserved.
Pardon monsieur, cette place est à moi.	Excuse me, sir, that seat is mine.
Porteur, je veux mettre ces bagages à la consigne.	Porter I want to put this luggage in the cloakroom (left-luggage office).
Je vous suis.	I am coming with you.
Est-ce qu'il y a un porter de l'hôtel . . . ici?	Is there a porter from the . . . Hotel here?
Où est le bureau de renseignements?	Where is the enquiry office?
A quelle heure arrive-t-on à . . .?	When do we get to . . . ?
Combien de temps le train s'arrête-t-il ici?	How long does the train stop here?
L'avion pour . . . a déjà vingt minutes de retard.	The plane for . . . is twentv minutes late already.
L'avion de . . . est signalé.	The . . . plane is announced.
Où est le bureau de la compagnie aérienne?	Where is the Airline Office?
Je voudrais réserver une place dans l'avion qui part demain pour . .	I want to reserve a seat on the plane leaving tomorrow for . .
Est-ce qu'il y a un avion pour . . . audjourd'hui?	Is there a plane for . . . today?
Je ne me sens pas bien.	I do not feel well.
Apportez-moi du café (cognac, un verre d'eau), s'il vous plait.	Bring me some coffee (brandy, a glass of water), please.
Eteignez vos cigarettes et attachez vos ceintures, s'il vous plait.	Put out your cigarettes and fasten your seat-belts, please.
Appelez-moi un taxi.	Call me a taxi.
Dépêchez-vous, je suis très pressé.	Go quickly, I am in a great hurry.
Attendez-moi ici quelques minutes, s'il vous plait.	Please wait here for a few minutes.
Où est le bureau?	Where is the office?
Avez-vous une chambre avec salle de bains?	Have you a room with a private bathroom?
Quel est le prix d'une chambre par nuit?	What is the price of a room per night?

J'attends un monsieur (une dame, une demoiselle).	I am expecting a gentleman (a lady, a young lady).
Donnez-moi deux timbres de vingt-cinq centimes et deux de quinze.	Give me two 25 centime stamps and two at 15 centimes.
Je voudrais envoyer une dépêche.	I want to send a telegram.
Avez-vous l'horaire des trains pour . . . ?	Have you the time-table of trains for . . . ?
Peut-on avoir un petit déjeuner anglais?	Can we have an English breakfast?
Commandez un taxi pour neuf heures et demie, s'il vous plaît.	Order a taxi for 9.30, please.
Préparez la note, s'il vous plait.	Please have my bill made out.
Nous voudrions être ensemble.	We want to be together.
Quelle distance d'ici à . . . ?	How far it to . . . ?
Quel est le nom de cette ville (ce village)?	What is the name of this town (village)?
Où est le marché?	Where is the market place?
Si le temps le permet, nous comptons partir à l'aube.	Weather permitting, we hope to leave at dawn.
Voulez-vous me demander Molitor quarante-quatre, quatre-vingt quatorze, s'il vous plait.	Get me Molitor 44—94, please.
Combien vous dois-je pour la communication?	How much do I owe you for the call?
Puis-je prendre un rendezvous?	Can I make an appointment?
Puis-je avoir de la lecture?	Can I have something to read?
Pouvez-vous faire cette ordonnance, s'il vous plait?	Can you make up this prescription, please?
Pouvez-vous me donner quelque chose pour les piqûres d'insects (de fourmis, de moustiques)?	Can you give me something for insect (ant, mosquito) bites?

La peau me cuit; avez-vous quelque-chose de calmant?
My skin is smarting; have you anything to soothe it?

Pour l'usage externe.
For external use.

Je voudrais un film en couleur inversible (negatif).
I want a reversal (negative) colour film.

Est-ce que vous vendez ...?
Do you sell ...?

Avez-vous quelque chose de moins cher (de meilleure qualité)?
Have you anything cheaper (better)?

Je voudrais quelque chose comme ceci (cela).
I want something like this (that).

Pouvez-vous le (la) commander?
Can you order it for me?

Voulez-vous l'envoyer à cette adresse?
Will you send it to this address?

Voilà ce qu'il me faut.
That's exactly what I want.

Vous vous êtes trompé en me rendant la monnaie.
You have given me the wrong change.

Pouvez-vous le changer?
Can you change it?

Est-ce que vous vendez des cigarettes anglaises (du tabac anglais)?
Do you sell English cigarettes (tobacco)?

Il y a eu un accident.
There has been an accident.

Y a-t-il un médecin près d'ici?
Is there a doctor near here?

Je vous souhaite la bienvenue en Angleterre (France).
Welcome to England (France).

Avez-vous fait un bon voyage?
Did you have a good journey?

A quelle heure est le petit déjeuner (le déjeuner, le goûter, le dîner)?
What time is breakfast (lunch, tea, dinner)?

Y a-t-il une banque (un bureau de change) près d'ici?
sithere a bank (money, exchange bureau) near here?

A

à, au, *prep.* to; at.
abaisser, *v. a.* lower, let down; **s'~** stoop.
abandonner, *v. a.* forsake, abandon.
abat-jour, *s. m.* lampshade.
abbaye, *s. m.* abbey.
abbé, *s. m.* abbot.
abdication, *s. f.* abdication.
abdiquer, *v. n.* abdicate; *v. a.* renounce.
abeille, *s. f.* bee.
abject, *adj.* abject, low.
abjurer, *v.a.* abjure; give up.
abolir, *v. a.* abolish.
abondance, *s. f.* plenty, abundance.
abondant, *adj.* abundant.
abonder, *v. n.* abound.
abonner: s'~ subscribe to, take in.
abord, *adv. d'~* (at) first.
aboutir, *v. n.* end in, come to.
aboyer, *v. n.* bark.
abricot, *s. m.* apricot.
abrupt, *adj.* steep.
absence, *s. f.* absence; *~ d'esprit* absence of mind.
absent, *adj.* absent.
absenter: s'~ leave, depart.
absolu, *adj.* absolute.
absorber, *v. a.* absorb;
absoudre*, *v. a.* absolve.
abstraction, *s. f.* abstraction.
abstrait, *adj.* abstract.
absurde, *adj.* absurd.
abus, *s. m.* abuse.
académie, *s. f.* academy.
accélérer, *v. a.* accelerate, hasten.
accent, *s.m.* accent, stress.
accentuer, *v.a.* accent.
accepter, *v. a.* accept; admit.
accès, *s. m.* access; fit.
accessible, *adj.* accessible.
accident, *s. m.* accident; *par ~* accidentally.
accidentel, -elle, *adj.* accidental.
acclamer, *v.a.* acclaim.
acclimater, *v.a.* acclimatize; **s'~** become acclimatized.
accommoder, *v. a.* accommodate; fit up; **s'~** put up with, come to terms.
accompagner, *v. a.* accompany.
accomplir, *v. a.* accomplish, carry out.
accord, *s. m.* agreement, accord, harmony.
accorder, *v.a.* grant, confer; agree.
accoutumer, *v. a.* accustom; **s'~** get accustomed (to).
accréditer, *v. a.* accredit.
accrocher, *v. a.* hang up, hook; run against.
accroître, *v. a.* increase; **s'~** increase.
accueil, *s. m.* reception.
accueillir, *v. a.* receive, welcome.
accumuler, *v. a.* accumulate, heap up.
accusation, *s. f.* accusation, charge.

accuser, *v.a.* accuse.
achat, *s. m.* purchase; *faire des* ~s go shopping.
acheter, *v.a.* purchase, buy.
achèvement, *s. m.* completion.
achever, *v.a.* complete finish; achieve.
acide, *adj.* acid, sour; — *s. m.* acid.
acier, *s. m.* steel.
acoustique, *s. f.* acoustics.
acquérir*, *v.a.* acquire, purchase; get.
âcre, *adj.* acrid, sour.
acte, *s. m.* action, deed, act; transaction, document, certificate; *(theatre)* act.
acteur, *s. m.* actor.
actif, -ive, *adj.* active; — *s.m.* assets *(pl.)*;
action, *s. f.* action; act, deed; effect; lawsuit; plot; story.
activité, *s. f.* activity.
actrice, *s. f.* actress.
actualité, *s. f.* topic of the hour; ~s current events; news-reel.
actuel, -elle, present, of present interest; actual.
adapter, *v.a.* adapt; s'~ adapt oneself.
addition, *s. f.* addition; bill.
additionner, *v. a.* add up.
adhérer, *v. a.* adhere, stick.
adieu, *s. m. (pl.* -x) goodbye; *faire ses* ~x take one's leave.
adjoint, *adj.* & *s. m.* assistant; deputy.
adjuger, *v. a.* adjuge.
administrateur, -trice, *s. m. f.* manager, director.
administratif, -ive- *adj.* administrative.
administration, *s. f.* management, direction; administration.
administrer, *v.a.* administer; manage.
admirable, *adj.* admirable.
admiration, *s. f.* admiration.
admirer, *v. a.* admire, wonder at.
admission, *s. f.* admission, admittance.
adolescent, *s. m.* adolescent, youth.
adopter, *v.a.* adopt, pass.
adoption, *s. f.* adoption.
adorer, *v.a.* adore.
adresse, *s. f.* address; skill, dexterity.
adresser, *v. a.* address, direct; s'~ apply (to).
adroit, *adj.* clever, skilful.
adulte, *adj.* & *s.* adult.
adversaire, *s. m.* adversary.
aérien, -enne, *adj.* aerial.
aérodrome, *s. m.* airport.
aéroport, *s. m.* airport.
affaiblir, *v. a.* weaken.
affaire, *s. f.* business, affair, matter; lawsuit.
affamé, *adj.* hungry.
affecter, *v. a.* affect, feign; move; assume.
affection, *s. f.* affection; disease.
affectueux, -euse, *adj.* affectionate.
affermir, *v. a.* strengthen; s'~ become stronger.
affiche, *s. f.* poster, bill.
afficher, *v. a.* post up, stick up, placard.

affiler, *v.a.* sharpen.
affirmatif, -ive, *adj.* affirmative.
affirmer, *v. a.* affirm.
affliger, *v. a.* afflict.
affluer, *v. n.* flow into.
affranchir, *v. a.* (set) free; stamp.
affreux, -euse, *adj.* dreadful, terrible.
affronter, *v.a.* face.
afin, *conj.* ~ *de* in order to; ~ *que* in order that, so that.
africain (A.), *adj.* & *s. m. f.* African.
âge, *s. m.* age; period; *quel* ~ *avez-vous?* how old are you?
agence, *s. f.* agency.
agent, *s. m.* agent; policeman.
aggraver, *v. a.* aggravate.
agile, *adj.* agile, active.
agilité, *s. f.* agility.
agir, *v. n.* act; take effect; behave; s'~ be in question.
agitation, *s. f.* agitation.
agiter, *v. a.* agitate.
agneau, *s. m.* lamb.
agonie, *s. f.* agony.
agréable, *adj.* agreeable.
agréer, *v. a.* accept, receive favourably.
agrément, *s. m.* consent, approval; pleasure.
agressif, -ive, *adj.* aggressive.
agression, *s. f.* aggression, attack.
agriculture, *s. f.* agriculture.
aide, *s. f.* help.
aider, *v. a.* help.
aïeux, *s. m. pl.* ancestors.
aigle, *s. m.* eagle.
aigre, *adj.* sour, acid.
aigrir: s'~ turn sour.
aigu, *adj.* pointed, sharp; keen; *accent* ~ acute accent.
aiguille, *s. f.* needle; hand, index; point, switch; *grande* ~ minute hand.
aiguiser, *v. a.* sharpen.
ail, *s. m.* garlic.
aile, *s. f.* wing; flank; aisle; mudguard.
ailleurs, *adv.* somewhere else, elsewhere; *d'*~ in addition, besides.
aimable, *adj.* amiable, pleasant, kindly.
aimer, *v. a.* & *n.* like, love, be fond of, care to.
aîné, *adj.* & *s. m. f.* elder, eldest; senior.
ainsi, *adv.* & *conj.* so, thus; likewise; ~ *de suite* and so on; ~ *que* as well as.
air, *s. m.* air; look(s), appearance, manner; *(music)* air.
aisance, *s. f.* ease; comfort; facility; *être dans l'*~ be well off.
aise, *s. f.* ease, comfort.
aisé, *adj.* easy; well-off.
ajourner, *v.a.* adjourn.
alcool, *s. m.* alcohol.
alcoolique, *adj.* alcoholic.
algèbre, *s. f.* algebra.
aliment, *s. m.* aliment, food.
alimentation, *s. f.* alimentation; feeding.
alimenter, *v. a.* feed.
aliter, *v. a.* *être alité* be confined to bed, be laid up.
allaiter, *v. a.* give suck to; nurse.
allée, *s. f.* (garden) path, lane, walk, alley.

alléger, *v.a.* lighten; alleviate, soothe.
allégresse, *s. f.* gaiety, delight.
allemand (A.), *adj.* & *s. m. f.* German.
aller*, *v. n.* go, proceed; get on; grow, get; ~ *à pied* walk; ~ *en auto* drive; ~ *en avion* fly; ~ *bien* be well; *comment allez-vous?* how are you?; *allons!* come on!; *allez!* indeed; **s'en** ~ go away, be off.
alliance, *s. f.* alliance, union; wedding-ring.
allié, -e, *s. m. f.* ally; — *adj.* allied.
allier, *v.a.* alloy; match; unite; **s'**~ join with, unite.
allonger, *v.a.* lengthen, stretch out, prolong; ~ *le pas* step out; **s'**~ get longer.
allumer, *v. a.* light (up), set on fire; excite.
allumette, *s. f.* match.
allure, *s. f.* gait, pace; manner, behaviour; direction.
allusion, *s. f.* allusion, hint; reference.
alors, *adv.* then.
alpinisme, *s. m.* mountaineering.
altérer, *v. a.* alter, change; **s'**~ alter, degenerate.
alternance, *s. f.* alternation.
alternatif, -ive, *adj.* alternate, alternative.
alterner, *v. n.* & *a.* alternate.
altitude, *s. f.* altitude.
aluminium, *s. f.* aluminium.
amaigrir, *v.a.* make thin; **s'**~ grow thin.
amant, -e, *s. m. f.* lover.
amas, *s.m.* heap, mass, pile.
amateur, *s. m.* amateur, lover, fancier.
ambassade, *s. f.* embassy.
ambassadeur, *s. m.* ambassador.
ambassadrice, *s. f.* ambassadress.
ambitieux, -euse, *adj.* ambitious.
ambition, *s. f.* ambition.
ambulance, *s. f.* ambulance; ~ *(automobile)* ambulance(-car).
âme, *s. f.* soul; mind.
améliorer, *v. a.* ameliorate, improve; **s'**~ improve.
aménager, *v.a.* fit up, out.
amender, *v.a.* amend, improve.
amener, *v. a.* bring, draw; bring before, in, out; introduce; induce.
amer, -ère, *adj.* bitter.
américain, -e (A.), *adj.* & *s. m. f.* American.
ami, -e, *s. m. f.* friend; sweetheart; *bon* ~, *bonne* ~*e* sweetheart.
amical, *adj.* friendly, kind.
amiral, *s. m.* admiral.
amitié, *s. f.* friendship; affection; *meilleures* ~*s* kindest regards.
amortir, *v.a.* lessen, soften; pay (off), write off.
amortisseur, *s. m.* shock-absorber.
amour, *s. m.* love; *faire l'*~ court, make love to; *mon* ~ my darling.
amoureux, -euse, *adj.* in

love *(de* with), enamoured *(de* of).
amplificateur, *s.m.* amplifier.
amplifier, *v. a.* amplify.
ampoule, *s. f.* blister; bulb.
amulette, *s. f.* amulet.
amusant, *adj.* amusing.
amusement, *s. m.* amusement, pastime, fun.
amuser, *v.a.* amuse, entertain; **s'~** enjoy oneself.
an, *s. m.* year; *il y a un ~* . a year ago.
analogie, *s. f.* analogy.
analogue, *adj.* analogous.
analyse, *s. f.* analysis.
analyser, *v. a.* analyse.
ananas, *s. m.* pineapple.
anatomie, *s. f.* anatomy.
ancêtre, *s. m. f.* ancestor.
ancien, -enne, *adj.* ancient, old, antique.
ancre, *s. f.* anchor; *lever l'~* weigh anchor.
âne, *s. m.* ass.
anéantir, *v. a.* annihilate.
anecdote, *s. f.* anecdote.
ange, *s. m.* angel.
anglais, -e (A.), *adj.* English; — *s. m. f.* Englishman, Englishwoman.
angle, *s. m.* angle, corner; bend.
angoisse, *s.f.* anguish.
animal, *s.m.* animal; **beast.**
anneau, *s. m.* circle, ring.
année, *s. f.* year; *~ scolaire* school-year; *bonne ~* a happy New Year!
annexer, *v. a.* annex.
anniversaire, *s. m.* anniversary, b rthday.
annonce, *s. f.* announcement, advertisement.
annoncer, *v. a.* announce, give notice of; advertise.
annuaire, *s. m.* year-book, annual, directory.
annuel, -elle, *adj.* annual.
annuler, *v. a.* annul.
anonyme, *adj.* anonymous; *société ~* joint-stock company.
anormal, *adj.* abnormal.
anse, *s. f.* handle; creek.
antécédent, -e, *adj. & s. m.* antecedent.
antenne, *s. f.* aerial.
antérieur, *adj.* anterior, previous.
antibiotique, *s. m.* **antibiotic.**
antichambre, *s. f.* **entrance hall.**
anticiper, *v. a. & n.* **anticipate**; encroach.
antipathie, *s. f.* antipathy.
antiquaire, *s. m.* antiquarian.
antique, *adj.* antique, **ancient.**
antiquité, *s. f.* **antiquity.**
antiseptique, *adj. & s. m.* antiseptic.
anxiété, *s. f.* anxiety.
anxieux, -euse, *adj.* **anxious.**
août, *s.m.* August.
apaiser, *v. a.* **appease,** pacify, quiet.
apercevoir, *v. a.* **perceive,** catch sight of; **remark,** notice.
aplanir, *v. a.* smooth, **level,** even off; **s'~ become** level.
aplatir, *v.a.* **fl atten.**
apologie, *s. m.* **apology,** defence.
apoplexie, *s. f.* **apoplexy.**
apostolique, *adj.* **apostolic(al).**

apostrophe, *s. f.* apostrophe.
apôtre, *s. m.* apostle.
apparaître, *v. n.* appear.
appareil, *s. m.* apparatus, device, appliance, gear; camera; *~ de TV* TV-set; *~ de direction* steering-gear.
apparence, *s. f.* appearance, look(s); likelihood; *en ~* apparenty.
apparent, *adj.* apparent.
apparition, *s. f.* appearance; apparition.
appartement, *s.m.* flat; apartment.
appartenir, *v.n.* belong, appertain *(à* to*)*.
appel, *s. m.* call; appeal; *faire l'~* call the roll.
appeler, *v. a.* call in, out, up, down; ring up; name, term; *en ~* appeal; *faire ~* send for; **s'~** be called, call oneself.
appendice, *s. m.* appendix.
appendicite, *s.f.* appedicitis.
appesantir, *v.a.* make heavy, weigh down.
appétit, *s. m.* appetite.
applaudir, *v. n.* applaud, clap.
application, *s. f.* application; diligence.
appliquer, *v. a.* apply; lay on.
apporter, *v.a.* bring.
appréciation, *s.f.* appreciation; estimation.
apprécier, *v. a.* value.
appréhension, *s. f.* apprehension, fear.
apprendre, *v. a.* learn, acquire; hear of; teach.
apprentissage, *s. m.* apprenticeship.
apprêter, *v. a.* prepare; season; dress; **s'~** prepare oneself, get ready.
approbation, *s. f.* approbation, approval.
approche, *s. f.* approach advance.
approcher, *v.a.* bring toward, forward.
approprié, *adj.* appropriate.
approprier: s'~ appropriate, take; accommodate, adapt oneself.
approuver, *v. a.* sanction; approve.
approximatif, -ive, *adj.* approximate.
approximation, *s.f.* approximation.
appui, *s. m.* support.
appuyer, *v. a.* support; lean; *v. n.* *~ sur* lay stress (up)on; **s'~** lean, rest, rely (upon).
après, *adv.* after; behind; next (to); *~ coup* too late; *~ tout* after all; *d'~* after, according to; by.
après-demain, *adv.* & *s. m.* (the) day after tomorrow.
après-midi, *s. m.* afternoon.
à-propos, *adv.* in good time; — *s. m.* timely word; fitness.
apte, *adj.* apt, suitable.
aptitude, *s. f.* aptitude, ability, talent.
aquarelle, *s.f.* water-color.
arabe (A.), *adj.* & *s, m. f.* Arab, Arabian; Arabic.
araignée, *s. f.* spider.
arbitre, *s. f.* arbiter, judge;

umpire, referee.
arbre, *s. m.* tree; shaft; ~ *fruitier* fruit-tree; ~ *coudé* crank shaft.
arc, *s. m.* bow; arc(h).
arcade, *s. f.* arcade.
arche, *s. f.* arch, vault.
archet, *s.m.* bow.
archevêque, *s.m.* archbishop.
architecture, *s. f.* architecture.
archives *s. f. pl.* archives.
ardemment, *adv.* ardently.
ardent, *adj.* burning, fiery, ardent, eager.
ardeur, *s. f.* keenness; ardour, zeal.
arête, *s. f.* fish-bone; edge; ridge.
argent, *s. m.* silver; money; ~ *en caisse* cash in hand ~ *comptant* ready money; ~ *de la poche* pocket-money; *à-court d'*~ pressed for money.
argenterie, *s. f.* plate.
argentin[1], *adj.* silvery.
argentin[2], **-e (A.),** *adj. & s. m. f.* Argentine.
argile, *s.f.* clay.
argot, *s. m.* slang.
argument, *s.m.* argument, proof, evidence.
aristocratie, *s.f.* aristocracy.
aristocratique, *adj.* aristocratic.
arme, *s.f.* arm, weapon; ~*s à feu* fire-arms; *faire des* ~*s* fence.
armée, *s. f.* army.
armer, *v.a.* arm; fortify; s'~ arm oneself.
armoire, *s. f.* cupboard; wardrobe.
armure, *s. f.* armour; armature.
arracher, *v.a.* pull (out), tear up; extract, draw; remove from.
arrangement, *s. m.* arrangement; agreement, settlement; ~*s* terms.
arranger, *v. a.* arrange, settle, fix (up); s'~ come to an agreement, make arrangements (for); make shift (to).
arrestation, *s. f.* arrest.
arrêt, *s. m.* stop (of bus, tram etc.); pause; standstill; sentence; arrest; ~ *facultatif* request stop; *sans* ~ non-stop.
arrêter, *v.a.* check, stop; arrest; engage, book; decide, decree; settle; s'~ stop; draw up; leave off.
arrière, *adv.* behind, backward; *en* ~ back(ward); ~ *s. m.* back part, rear.
arriéré, *adj.* overdue; backward; under-developed; — *s.m.* arrears *(pl.)*.
arrivée, *s. f.* arrival; *à l'*~ on arrival.
arriver, *v. n.* arrive, come; turn up; happen; occur; ~ *à* attain, arrive at, reach; *le train arrive à* the train is due at.
arrogance, *s. f.* arrogance.
arroser, *v. a.* water, sprinkle; baste.
art, *s. m.* art; *les beaux* ~*s* the fine arts.
artère, *s.f.* artery; thoroughfare.
article, *s. m.* article; ~*s de grande consommation* consumer(s') goods.
articulation, *s. f.* joint.
articuler, *v.a.* articulate.

artificiel, -elle, *adj.* artificial.
artillerie, *s. f.* artillery.
artisan, *s. m.* craftsman.
artiste, *s. m. & f.* artist; player
ascenseur, *s. m.* lift.
asile, *s. m.* refuge, asylum.
aspect, *s.m.* aspect.
asperge, *s. f.* asparagus.
aspirateur, *s.m.* vacuum-cleaner.
aspiration, *s. f.* aspiration.
aspirer, *v.a.* inspire; *v. n.* aspire *(à to)*.
assaillir*, *v. a.* assault.
assaisonner, *v.a.* season; dress.
assassin, *s. m.* assassin.
assassiner, *v. a.* assassinate, murder.
assaut, *s.m.* assault.
assemblage, *s. m.* assemblage, gathering, collection.
assemblée, *s.f.* assembly, meeting.
assembler, *v. a.* assemble; put together; gather; s'~ assemble.
asseoir*, *v. a.* seat; place; s'~ take a seat.
assez, *adv.* enough; pretty, fairly.
assiduité, *s.f.* assiduity.
assiéger, *v.a.* attack, besiege.
assiette, *s. f.* posture; seat; position; plate.
assimiler, *v. a.* assimilate *(à* to).
assistance, *s.f.* presence, attendance; audience; assistance, help.
assister, *v. n.* attend, be present *(à* at); *v. a.* assist, help.
association, *s. f.* association; partnership, company.
associer, *v.a.* **associate, link up; share interests with; s'~ associate oneself** *(avec* with).
assommant, *adj.* **boring,** dull.
assortir, *v.a.* **match,** assort; **s'~ be suitable, go** well together.
assoupir, *v. a.* **make drowsy,** sleepy; **s'~ grow** sleepy.
assujettir, *v.a.* **subject,** subjugate.
assumer, *v. a.* assume.
assurance, *s. f.* assurance; insurance; *~ sur la vie* life-insurance.
assuré, *adj.* assured, confident, sure; insured.
assurer, *v. a.* **assure,** secure; insure; **s'~** make sure (of).
astre, *s. m.* star.
astronaute, *s. m.* astronaut, spaceman.
astronautique, *s. f.* astronautics, space travel.
astronef, *s. m.* spacecraft, space-ship.
atelier, *s.m.* workshop; studio.
athée, *s.m.f.* atheist.
athlète, *s.m.* athlete.
athlétique, *adj.* athletic.
atome, *s.m.* atom.
atomique, *adj.* atomic; *bombe ~* atom(ic) bomb *énergie ~* atomic energy.
attache, *s. f.* tie, fastener; bond, strap; *fig.* attachment.
attaché, *s. m.* attaché.
attacher, *v.a.* fasten, tie (up), attach; associate; engage; **s'~** attach (to),

become **attached** (to).
attaque, *s. f.* attack.
attaquer, *v.a.* attack.
attarder, *v.a.* delay; *être attardé* be delayed.
atteindre*, *v. a.* attain, reach; hit, stirke.
atteinte, *s. f.* blow, stroke; fit; injury; *hors d'*~ out of reach.
attendre, *v. a. & n.* await, wait for, expect; s'~ hope for, expect.
attendrir, *v. a.* soften; *fig.* move, touch; s'~ be moved.
attendrissement, *s.m.* compassino; tenderness.
attente, *s. f.* waiting; hope
attentif, -ive, *adj.* attentive, considerate.
attention, *s.f.* attention, notice, heed, care; *(pl.)* attentions; *faire* ~ be careful, mind, take notice of, take heed (to); ~*!* look out!
atténuer, *v. a.* extenuate, attenuate.
atterrir, *v. n.* land.
atterrissage, *s. m.* landing; *piste d'*~ landing-strip.
attester, *v.a.* attest.
attirail, *s. m.* implements *(pl.)*, utensils *(pl.)*, gear; tackle.
attirer, *v.a.* attract.
attitude, *s. f.* attitude.
attraction, *s. f.* attraction.
attrape, *s. f.* trap; catch.
attribuer, *v. a.* assign, allot; attribute, ascribe.
attribut, *s. m.* attribute.
au *(pl.* **aux**), to the, at the.
auberge, *s. f.* inn, tavern; ~ *de la jeunesse* youth hostel.
aucun, *adj. & pron.* no, none, no one, not any.
au-dessous, *adv.* below; ~ *de* under.
au-dessus, *adv.* *(~ de)* above, over.
audience, *s. f.* **audience**; public; sitting, session.
audiovisuel, -elle, *adj.* audio-visual.
auditeur, -trice, *s. m. f.* listener; auditor.
auditoire, *s. m.* audience; congregation.
auge, *s.m.* trough; bucket.
augmentation, *s.f.* augmentation, increase; rise.
augmenter, *v. a.* augment, increase; s'~ increase.
aujourd'hui, *adv.* today.
auparavant, *adv.* previously, earlier; before.
auprès, *adv.* near, by, close by; ~ *de* **near.**
auquel, *rel.pron.* to **whom,** to which.
aurore, *s.f.* dawn.
aussi, *adv.* also, too; ~ ... *que* as ... as; — *conj.* and so, therefore; ~ *bien que* as well as; ~ *bien* in fact.
austère, *adj.* austere, severe.
autant, *adv. & conj.* as much, as many, as far; ~ *que* as far as, as much as.
autel, *s. m.* altar.
auteur, *s. m.* author.
authentique, *adj.* authentic, genuine.
auto, *s. f.* car.
autobus, *s.m.* (motor-)bus.
autocar, *s. m.* (motor-) coach.

automatique, *adj.* automatic; — *s.m.* dial-telephone.
automne, *s. m. f.* autumn.
automobile, *s. m. f.* motorcar.
autonomie, *s.f.* autonomy.
autorisation, *s. f.* authorization, permission; licence.
autoriser, *v.a.* authorize.
autorité, *s. f.* authority; rule.
autoroute, *s. f.* motorway.
auto-stop, *s. m.* hitch-hiking.
auto-stoppeur, -euse, *s. m. f.* hitch-hiker.
autour, *adv. & prep.* *~ de* about, (a)round; *tout ~* all round.
autre, *adj.* different, other, another, else; *un ~* another; *d'~ part* on the other hand; *~ part* elsewhere; *de temps ~* now and then, at times; *l'~ jour* the other day; *l'un et l'~* both; *l'un l'~* each other.
autrefois, *adv.* formerly, long ago.
autrichien, -enne (A.), *adj. & s.m.f.* Austrian.
autrui, *pron.* others, other people.
avalanche, *s.f.* avalanche.
avaler, *v.a.* swallow; *fig.* endure, pocket.
avance, *s.f.* advance.
avancé, *adj.* advanced.
avancement, *s.m.* advance, progress; promotion.
avancer, *v.a.* advance, bring, put forward; pay in advance; — *v. n.* advance, proceed, move on; *s'~* come, move ,go forward.
avant, *prep. & adv.* before, in front (of), in advance; *~ tout* above all, before everything; *en ~* forward, to the front; *mettre en ~* bring forward; *en ~ de* in front of; — *s.m.* front (part); bow (of ship); forward.
avantage, *s. m.* advantage, benefit, profit; *(tennis)* vantage.
avantageux, -euse, *adj.* advantageous.
avant-hier, *adv.* day before yesterday.
avant-propos, *s. m.* foreword, preface.
avare, *s. m. f.* miser; — *adj.* avaricious, miserly.
avarice, *s.f.* avarice.
avec, *prep.* with.
avenir, *s. m.* future; *à l'~* in the future.
aventure, *s. f.* adventure; chance, luck.
aventurer, *v.a.* risk; **(s'~)** venture.
aventurier, -ère, *s. m. f.* adventurer.
avenue, *s. f.* boulevard; avenue.
averse, *s.f.* shower (of rain).
aversion, *v. f.* aversion, dislike.
avertir, *v.a.* inform, let know; warn; *faire ~ de* give notice of.
avertissement, *s. m.* information, notification; advice; warning.
aveu, *s. m.* admission, confession; consent.

aveugle, *adj.* blind.
aveuglement, *s. m.* blindness.
avide, *adj.* greedy, eager.
avidité, *s.f.* avidity.
avilir, *v.a.* debase, disgrace, degrade.
avion, *s.m.* (aero)plane; ~ *de ligne* air-liner; ~ *à réaction* jet plane; *par* ~ by air-mail.
avis, *s. m.* opinion; advice, counsel; information, notice; hint; mind; *changer d'*~ change one's mind.
aviser, *v.a.* perceive; inform; let know; advise; *s'*~ *de* think, find.
avocat, *s. m.* barrister, advocate, counsel.
avoine, *s.f.* oat(s).
avoir*, *v. a.* have, possess; have on, wear; feel; ~ *raison* be right; ~ *faim* be hungry; ~ *de* take after; ~ *à* have to; *il y a* there is, there are; ago.
avorter, *v. n.* miscarry, have a miscarriage.
avorton, *s. m.* abortion.
avoué, *s. m.* attorney, solicitor; lawyer.
avouer, *v. a. & n.* admit, confess; acknowledge; approve.
avril, *s.m.* April.
axe, *s.m.* axis; axle.
azote, *s.m.* nitrogen.

B

baccalauréat, *s. m.* baccalaureate, bachelor's degree.
bachelier, *s. m.* bachelor (of arts etc.).
bacille, *s.m.* bacillus.
bagage, *s. m.* luggage; *plier* ~ pack up one's kit.
bague, *s.f.* ring.
bai, *adj.* bay.
baie[1], *s. f.* bay.
baie[2], *s. f.* berry.
baigner: se ~ bathe.
baignoire, *s.m.* bath, bathtub; pit-box.
bâiller, *v. n.* yawn, gape.
bain, *s. m.* bath; *salle de* ~ bath-room.
baïonette, *s.f.* bayonet.
baiser, *v.a.* kiss.
baisse, *s.f.* fall; decline.
baisser, *v.a.* lower, let down; bring down; turn down; cast down; *v.n.* decline, fall; sink; **se** ~ stoop.
bal, *s. m.* ball; ~ *costumé* fancy-dress ball.
balai, *s.m.* broom, mop; (house-)brush; *donner un coup de* ~ sweep.
balance, *s. f.* balance, scales *(pl.)*.
balancer, *v.a.&n.* balance; weigh; swing, rock; give the sack; **se** ~ swing, wave; balance.
balayer, *v.a.* sweep (out), clear away.
balcon, *s. m.* balcony; dress-circle.
baleine, *s.f.* whale.
ballade, *s.f.* ballad.
balle, *s.f.* ball; bullet; bale.
ballon, *s.m.* balloon; (foot-)ball.
balnéaire, *adj.* pertaining to baths; *station* ~ watering place.

bambou, *s.m.* bamboo.
ban, *s. m.* ban; *~s de mariage* banns.
banal *adj.* banal, common, ordinary.
banane, *s. f.* banana.
banc, *s. m.* bench, form; bank; pew; stand.
bande, *s.f.* band, strip; bandage; troop, gang, set; *~ de papier* slip of paper; *~ transporteuse* conveyer belt.
bander, *v. a.* bind up.
bandit, *s. m.* bandit.
banlieu, *s. f.* outskirts, suburbs *(pl.)*.
bannir, *v. a.* banish, exile.
banque, *s. f.* bank; *billet de ~* banknote; *compte en ~* bank-account.
banquet, *s. m.* banquet, feast.
banquier, -ère, *s.m.f.* banker.
baptême, *s. m.* baptism.
baptiser, *v.a.* baptize.
barbare, *adj.* & *s.m.* barbarian.
barbarie, *s. f.* barbarousness, cruelty.
barbe, *s. f.* beard; *faire la ~ à* shave.
barbet, *s. m.* poodle.
barbier, *s. m.* barber.
baron, *s. m.* baron.
baronne, *s.f.* baroness.
barque, *s.f.* boat, barge.
barrage, *s.m.* barrier, barrage, dam.
barre, *s.f.* bar.
barreau, *s. m.* (small) bar; the Bar.
barrer, *v.a.* fasten, bar; cut off, shut out; steer.
barrière, *s.f.* barrier, town-gate, gate; bar; obstacle.
barrique, *s.f.* barrel, cask.
bas[1], *adj.* low; *à ~ prix* cheap; *terre ~se* lowland; *en ~* (down) below, down(-wards), — *s. m.* bottom, lower part
bas[2], *s. m.* stocking; *~ nylons* nylon stockings.
base, *s. f.* base; basis.
basique, *adj.* basic.
basse, *s.f.* bass; bass-viol.
bassesse, *s.f.* lowness, meanness.
basset, *s. m.* basset (dog).
bassin, *s. m.* basin, pool.
bataille, *s.f.* battle.
bataillon, *s. m.* battalion.
bateau, *s. m.* boat.
batelier, *s.m.* boatman.
bâtiment, *s. m.* building; building trade; ship.
bâtir, *v.a.* build, erect.
bâtisseur, -euse *s. m. f.* builder.
bâton, *s. m.* stick, staff.
batte, *s.f.* bat; beater.
battement, *s.m.* clap(ping); flapping.
batterie, *s.f.* battery; fight, row; percussive instruments *(pl.)*; *~ de cuisine* kitchen utensils *(pl.)*.
battre*, *v. a.* & *n.* beat, strike, thrash; *se ~* fight.
battu, *adj.* beaten.
bavard, -e *s.m.f.* gossip.
bavarder, *v.n.* chat(ter), gossip.
bazar, *s.m.* bazaar.
beau, bel; belle; **beaux, belles,** *adj.* beautiful, handsome, good-look-

ing, fair; considerable; *il y a ~ temps que* it seems an age since; *un ~ jour* one fine day; — *s.m.* beauty.
beaucoup, *adv.* (*~ de*) a good deal, many, much; plenty (of); *à ~ près, de ~* by far.
beau-frère, *s. m.* brother-in-law.
beau-père, *s. m.* father-in-law.
beauté, *s. f.* beauty
beaux-arts, *s. m. pl.* (the) fine arts.
bébé, *s. m.* baby.
bec, *s. m.* beak, bill nib; mouth-piece; jet; *~ de gaz* gas-burner, gas-jet.
bêche, *s. f.* spade.
bégayer, *v. n. &a.* stammer, stutter.
belge (B.), *adj. & s. m. f.* Belgian.
belle-fille, *s. f.* daughter-in-law; step-daughter.
belle-mère, *s. f.* mother-in-law; stepmother.
belle-sœur, *s. f.* sister-in-law.
bémol, *s. m. & adj.* flat *(music).*
bénédiction, *s.f.* benediction, blessing.
bénéfice, *s. m.* benefit, advantage, profit.
bénir, *v. a.* bless; praise.
berceau, *s. m.* cradle; *fig.* origin.
bercer, *v. a.* rock, lull (to sleep); *fig.* lull (with promises).
béret, *s.m.* beret.
berger, *s. m.* shepherd.
bergère, *s. f.* shepherdess; deep easy chair.
bésicles, *s. f. pl.* spectacles; goggles.
besogne, *s. f.* (piece of) work, job, task.
besoin, *s. m.* need, want; requirement; *avoir ~ de* want, need; *être dans le ~* be poor.
bétail, *s. m.* cattle.
bête, *s. f.* beast; animal; — *adj.* foolish, silly, stupid, dull.
bêtise, *s. f.* foolishness, stupidity; nonsense; trifle.
beurre, *s. m.* butter.
biais, *s. m.* bias, slant, slope.
biaiser, *v. n.* slant, slope.
bibelot, *s. m.* trinket, gew-gaw.
biberon, *s. m.* feeding-bottle.
bible, *s. f.* Bible.
bibliothécaire, *s. m. f.* librarian.
bibliothèque, *s. f.* library; bookcase; book-stall.
bicyclette, *s. f.* bicycle, bike.
bicycliste, *s. m. f.* cyclist.
bien, *adv.* well, right, properly, fully; *assez ~* fairly; *faire du ~* benefit; *ou ~* or else; *très ~* very well, all right; *~ avant* long before; very bad indeed; *~ que* (al)though; — *s. m.* good, welfare, benefit; property, goods; *aller à ~* prosper, be successful.
bien-être, *s. m.* welfare, well-being.

bienfaisance, *s. f.* beneficence.

bienfaisant, *adj.* charitable, kind; humane.

bienfait, *s.m.* kindness; benefaction.

bientôt, *adv.* soon, shortly; *à ~!* so long!

bienveillance, *s.f.* benevolence, kindness.

bienveillant, *adj.* kind(ly), benevolent, charitable.

bienvenu, *adj.* welcome; *soyez le ~* welcome!

bière, *s.f.* beer.

bifteck, *s. m.* beef-steak.

bijou, *s. m.* *(pl.* -x) jewel.

bijouterie, *s.f.* jewellery; jeweller's shop.

bijoutier, -ière *s. m. f.* jeweller.

bile, *s. f.* bile; *se faire de la ~* worry, fret.

bille, *s. f.* billiard-ball.

billet, *s. m.* note; ticket; certificate; *~ d'aller et retour* return ticket; *~ d'entrée* admission ticket; *~ de banque* banknote.

billot, *s. m.* block; yoke.

biographe, *s. m. f.* biographer.

biographie, *s. f.* biography.

biologie, *s. f.* biology.

biologiste, biologue, *s. m. f.* biologist.

bis, *int.* encore!

biscuit, *s. m.* biscuit.

bison, *s. m.* bison.

bistro, *s. m.* pub; wine-shop.

bizarre, *adj.* strange, odd.

blague, *s.f.* pouch.

blaireau, *s. m.* badger; shaving-brush.

blâme, *s. m.* blame, reprimand.

blâmer, *v. a.* blame; find fault with.

blanc, blanche, *adj.* white; hoary; blank.

blanchir, *v.a.* whiten, bleach; whitewash; *v.n.* turn white, whiten.

blasphème, *s. m.* blasphemy.

blasphémer, *v.a. & n.* blaspheme.

blé, *s. m.* wheat.

blême, *adj.* pale.

blesser, *v. a.* wound, injure, hurt; offend; *se ~* wound oneself; be offended.

blessure, *s. f.* wound, injury; offence.

bleu, *adj. & s. m.* blue; *~ marine* navy blue.

bloc, *s. m.* block; *en ~* in the lump.

blond, *adj.* fair, blond.

bloquer, *v.a.* blockade; block (up); tighten.

blouse, *s.f.* blouse, smock.

bobine, *s. f.* bobbin, spool.

bœuf, *s. m.* ox, beef.

bohème, *adj.* bohemian.

boire*, *v. a. & n.* drink; swallow; *~ à la santé de X* drink X's health; — *s. m.* drink(ing).

bois, *s. m.* wood; timber; *de, en ~* wood(en).

boisson, *s. f.* drink, beverage.

boîte, *s. f.* box, case; can, tin; *~ aux lettres* letter-box; *~ de vitesse* gear-box; *en ~* tinned.

boiteux, -euse *adj.* lame.

bombardement, *s. m.* bombardment.

bombarder, *v. a.* bombard, shell.

bombe, *s. f.* bomb, shell; ~ *H* H-bomb.

bon, bonne, *adj.* good; kind, nice; right; valid; *c'est ~!* (all) right!; ~ *à rien* good for nothing; *~ne année!* happy new year!; *de ~ne heure* early; — *s. m.* good(ness); bond, order.

bonbon, *s. m.* bonbon, sweet.

bond, *s. m.* bound, leap.

bondé, *adj.* crowded.

bonder, *v. a.* load, cram.

bondir, *v. n.* bound, leap, spring.

bonheur, *s. m.* happiness; good fortune; success.

bonhomme, *s. m.* good-natured man; simple man; fellow.

bonjour, *s. m.* good morning; salutation.

bonne, *s. f.* maid-servant; ~ *(d'enfants)* nursery-maid.

bonnet, *s. m.* cap, hood.

bonsoir, *s. m.* good evening.

bonté, *s. f.* goodness, kindness, benevolence.

bord, *s. m.* edge, border, brink, (b)rim, verge; side, board, bank; *à ~* on board; *monter à ~* go on board.

border, *v. a.* border, adjoin.

bordure, *s. f.* border, edging; verge; kerb.

borne, *s. f.* milestone; (boundary), limit.

borner, *v. a.* bound, limit, restrict.

bosse, *s. f.* bump, protuberance; knob.

botanique, *adj.* botanical; — *s. f.* botany.

botte[1], *s. f.* (high) boot.

botte[2], *s. f.* bottle; truss.

bottine, *s. f.* boot.

bouche, *s. f.* mouth; orifice, muzzle.

boucher, *s. m.* butcher.

boucherie, *s. f.* butcher's (shop).

bouchon, *s. m.* plug, cork, stopper.

boue, *s. f.* mud, dirt.

bouger, *v. n.* stir, budge.

bougie, *s. f.* candle. (sparking-)plug.

bouillir*, *v. n. & a.* (also *faire ~*) boil.

bouillon, *s. m.* bubble; stock; *~ de bœuf* beef-tea.

bouillotte, *s. f.* kettle.

boulanger, -ère, *s. m. f.* baker; baker's wife.

boulangerie, *s. f.* bakery, baker's (shop).

boule, *s. f.* ball, bowl.

boulevard, *s. m.* boulevard.

bouleverser, *v. a.* overthrow, upset; turn upside down; distract.

boulon, *s. m.* bolt, pin.

bouquet, *s. m.* cluster, bunch; bouquet.

bourdonnement, *s.m.* buzz(ing), humming.

bourdonner, *v.n.* buzz, hum, drone.

bourg, *s. m.* (small) town; village.

bourgeois, e, *s. m. f.* citizen; townsman.

bourgeoisie, *s. f.* citizens *(pl.)*; middle class.

bourse, *s. f.* purse; ex-

change; Stock Exchange; scholarship, bursary.
bousculade, *s. f.* hustling.
bousculer, *v. a.* upset, hustle, jostle; **se** ~ hustle each other.
bout, *s. m.* end, extremity, tip, top, button; *un* ~ *de chemin* a short distance.
bouteille, *s. f.* bottle.
boutique, *s.f.* shop; booth, stall.
bouton, *s. m.* button; stud; bud; nipple; knob; *~s de manchette* cuff-links.
boutonnière, *s. f.* button-hole.
boxer, *v. n.* box, fight.
boxeur, *s.m.* boxer.
bracelet, *s. m.* bracelet.
braconner, *v. n.* poach.
braconnier, *s. m.* poacher.
brancard, *s. m.* stretcher; shaft.
branche, *s.f.* branch.
branler, *v. a.* shake, totter, waver.
bras, *s. m.* arm; hand; branch.
braser, *v.a.* braze, solder
brasserie, *s. f.* brewery; beershop.
brave, *adj.* brave; honest. worthy, good.
braver, *v. a.* face, brave.
bravoure, *s. f.* bravery, courage.
brebis, *s. f.* ewe, sheep.
brèche, *s. f.* breach, gap.
bref, brève, *adj.* brief, short.
bretelles, *s. f. pl.* braces.
brevet, *s. m.* patent; certificate.
bride, *s. f.* bridle, reins.
brièveté, *s. f.* brevity.
brigade, *s. f.* brigade.
brigadier, *s. m.* corporal, overseer.
brigand, *s. m.* brigand, armed robber.
brillant, *adj.* brilliant, shiny, glittering.
briller, *v.n.* shine, glitter, sparkle.
brin, *s. m.* shoot, sprig, blade (of grass).
brioche, *s. f.* brioche.
brique, *s. f.* brick; bar (of soap).
briquet *s. m.* lighter.
briquette, *s. f.* briquette.
brise, *s. f.* breeze.
briser, *v. a.* break (to pieces), smash; *v. n.* break; **se** ~ break to pieces.
britannique, *adj.* British.
broche, *s. f.* brooch; knitting-needle; spindle spit.
brochure, *s. f.* pamphlet.
broder, *v. a.* embroider.
broderie, *s. f.* embroidery, braid.
bronchite, *s. f.* bronchitis.
bronze, *s. m.* bronze.
brosse, *s. f.* brush; ~ *à barbe* shaving-brush; ~ *à dents* tooth-brush; ~ *à cheveux* hairbrush; *donner un coup de* ~ a brush up.
brosser, *v.a.* brush; se ~ brush oneself.
brouillard, *s. m.* mist, fog.
brouille, *s. f.* quarrel.
brouiller, *v.a.* mingle, mix; confuse, embroil;

shuffle (cards).

broyer, *v. a.* crush, pound.

bruire, *v.n.* rustle.

bruit, *s. m.* noise, din; fuss; rumour.

brûlant, *adj.* burning, hot, scorching; fiery.

brûler, *v. a. & n.* burn, schorch, roast; ~ *de* long for.

brume, *s. f.* mist, fog.

brumeux,-euse *adj.* foggy.

brun, *adj.* brown.

brusque, *adj.* sudden, curt, gruff.

brutal, *adj.* brutal, rude savage.

brute, *s. f.* brute.

bruyant, *adj.* noisy, loud.

budget, *s. m.* budget.

buffet, *s. m.* sideboard; buffet; refreshment room.

buisson, *s. m.* bush, shrub.

bulbe, *s. m.* bulb.

bulle, *s. f.* bubble; bull.

bulletin, *s.m.* bulletin.

bureau, *s. m.* (writing-) desk; bureau, office; department; board, committee; ~ *de location* box-office; ~ *de poste* post-office; ~ *de tabac* tobacconist's (shop); ~ *central* exchange.

burlesque, *adj.* burlesque, ridiculous; — *s.m.* burlesque.

but, *s. m.* butt, target; goal; aim, object, purpose; scope.

buter, *v.n.* stumble (*contre* against); se ~ grow obstinate.

butin, *s. m.* booty.

butte, *s. f.* hill, mound, knoll.

C

ça, *pron.* that; *comme* ~ in that way; — *adv.* here; — *int.* now then!

cabaret, *s. m.* tavern; wine-shop; night-club, music-hall.

cabine, *s. f.* cabin, berth; cage, car; ~ *téléphonique* call-box.

cabinet, *s. m.* small room; study; water-closet; office; business; cabinet (council); cabinet; ~ *de consultation* consulting room; surgery.

câble, *s. m.* rope, cable.

cabriolet, *s. m.* cabriolet,

cacao, *s. m.* cocoa.

cacher, *v.a.* hide, conceal; se ~ hide oneself.

cadeau, *s. m.* present, gift.

cadet, *adj. & s.m.* younger, junior; cadet.

café, *s. m.* coffee; café, coffee-house; ~ *au lait* white coffee; ~ *concert* music-hall.

cafetière, *s. f.* coffee-pot.

cage, *s.f.* cage; coop; case, crate.

cahier, *s. m.* exercise book.

caillou, *s.m.* pebble, stone.

caisse, *s.f.* box, case; cash(-box), till; cashier's office; drum; *en* ~ in hand.

caissier, -ère, *s.m.f.* cashier.

calcul, *s. m.* calculation, reckoning; arithmetic.
calculateur, *s. m.* calculator, computer.
calculer, *v.a. & n.* calculate, reckon, compute.
caleçon, *s. m.* pants *(pl.)*; ~ *de bain* bathing-drawers *(pl.)*.
calendrier, *s. m.* calendar.
calme, *adj.* quiet, calm; *fig.* cool; — *s. m.* calm.
calmer, *v. a.* quiet, calm.
calomnier, *v. a.* calumniate, slander.
calorie, *s. f.* calorie.
calorifère, *s. m.* heating apparatus.
calvaire, *s. m.* Calvary.
camarade, *s. m.* comrade, fellow; ~ *d'école* school-friend.
cambrioler, *v. a.* burgle, break into.
cambrioleur, *s.m.* burglar.
caméra, *s. f.* (cine-)camera.
camion, *s. m.* lorry.
camp, *s. m.* camp; side.
campagnard, *s. m.* countryman, peasant.
campagne, *s. f.* country(side), fields *(pl.)*; campaign, expedition.
camper, *v. n.* camp.
camping, *s. m.* camping; *(terrain de)* ~ camping site; *matériel de* ~ camping equipment; *faire du* ~ camp.
canal, *s. m.* canal; channel.
canapé, *s. m.* sofa, couch.
canard, *s. m.* duck, drake.
candidature, *s. f.* candidature, candidacy.
canif, *s. m.* penknife.
canne, *s. f.* stick, cane; ~ *à pêche* fishing-rod.
canon, *s. m.* gun, cannon
canot, *s. m.* boat.
cantine, *s. f.* canteen.
canton, *s.m.* canton, district.
cantonade, *s.f.* wings *(pl.)*; *à la* ~ behind the scenes.
caoutchouc, *s.m.* rubber; waterproof, mackintosh.
capable, *adj.* capable, able; efficient; fit.
capacité, *s. f.* capacity, (cap)ability.
capitaine, *s. m.* captain, leader.
capital, *adj.* capital, chief; —*s.m.* main point; capital, fund.
capitale, *s.f.* capital; capital letter.
capitalisme, *s. m.* capitalism.
capituler, *v. n.* capitulate.
caprice, *s. m.* caprice.
capricieux, *adj.* capricious, fickle.
capsule, *s. f.* capsule.
captif, -ive, *adj. & s. m. f.* captive.
captiver, *v. a.* captivate.
capturer, *v. a.* capture.
car, *conj.* for, because.
caractère, *s. m.* character, temper; nature; type, print, letter.
caractériser, *v.a.* characterize, distinguish.
caractéristique, *adj. & s.f.* characteristic.

cardinal, *s.m.* cardinal; — *adj.* chief, cardinal; *points cardinaux* cardinal points.
caresser, *v.a.* caress, fondle; foster.
caricature, *s. f.* caricature.
carnaval, *s. m.* carnival.
carnet, *s. m.* note-book, pocket-book; book of tickets; *~ de chèques* cheque-book.
carotte, *s. f.* carrot.
carreau, *s. m.* square; (paving-)tile; tile flooring; pane; diamond.
carrière, *s.f.* career; race-course; race; quarry.
carrosserie, *s.f.* body.
carte, *s.f.* card; map; ticket; bill (of fare); *partie de ~s* game of cards; *~ postale* post-card; *~ routière* road-map; *~ de visite* visiting-card; *~ marine* chart; *~ d'entrée* admission ticket; *~ grise* driving licence; *à la ~* à la carte.
carton, *s. m.* pasteboard, cardboard; (paper) box.
cas, *s.m.* case, event; instance, fact; *dans le ~ où, en ~ de* in case; *en tout ~* in any case.
caserne, *s.f.* barracks *(pl.)*.
casquette, *s. f.* cap.
casser, *v. a. & n.* break; crack, snap; annul; dismiss; *se ~* break, get broken.
casserole, *s. v.* saucepan.
casuel, -elle, *adj.* casual, accidental.
catalogue, *s. m.* catalogue.
catastrophe, *s. f.* catastrophe, disaster.
catégorie, *s. f.* category, class.
cathédrale, *s. f.* cathedral.
catholicisme, *s. m.* catholicism.
catholique, *adj.* catholic.
cause, *s. f.* cause, reason, ground; case; *à ~ de* on account of, owing to.
causer[1], *v. a.* cause.
causer[2], *v.n.* talk, converse, chat.
cavalerie, *s. f.* cavalry.
cavalier, *s. m.* horseman, cavalier.
cave, *s. f.* cave; cellar
caverne, *s. f.* cave(rn)
ce[1], **c',** *pron.* this, it.
ce[2], **cet; cette;** *dem. adj.* *(pl.* **ces)** this *(pl.* these); that *(pl.* those).
ceci, *pron.* this.
céder, *v. a.* give up, yield, cede, make over; *v. n.* yield, give in, up.
ceinture, *s. f.* belt, girdle.
cela, *pron.* that, it; *c'est ~* that's right.
célébration, *s. f.* celebration.
célèbre, *adj.* celebrated.
célébrer, *v. a.* celebrate.
célibataire, *adj.* unmarried, single.
cellule, *s. f.* cell.
celtique, *adj.* Celtic.
celui, celle, *dem. pron.* *(pl.* **ceux, celles)** he, she, they, those.
celui-ci, celui-là, celle-ci, celle-là, *dem. pron.*

(*pl.* ceux-ci, -là, celles-ci, -là) this one, this person, the latter, these ones.
ciment, *s. m* cement.
cendre, *s. f.* ash(es).
cendrier, *s. m.* ash-tray.
cent, *adj.* & *s. m.* hundred; *pour* ~ per cent.
centime, *s. m.* centime.
centimètre, *s. m.* centimetre.
central, *adj.* central.
centrale, *s. f.* ~ *électrique* power-plant, -station.
centre, *s. m.* centre.
cependant, *conj.* however, yet, still, nevertheless; in the meantime; ~ *que* while.
céramique, *s. f.* ceramics; — *adj.* ceramic.
cercle, *s. m.* circle, ring; party, club.
cercueil, *s. m.* coffin.
cérémonie, *s. f.* ceremony.
cerf. *s. m.* stag, hart,
cerise, *s. f.* cherry.
certain, *adj.* certain, sure.
certainement, *adv.* certainly, surely.
certificat, *s. m.* certificate, testimonial.
certifier, *v. a.* certify.
certitude, *s. f.* certainty.
cerveau, *s. m.* brain(s).
ces *see* **ce²**
cesse, *s. f.* ceasing, pause; *sans* ~ unceasingly.
cesser, *v. a.* & *n.* cease, stop; give up; *faire* ~ put an end to.
c'est-à-dire, *conj.* that is to say, viz., i.e.
cet *see* **ce²**.
ceux *see* **celui.**
chacun, *pron.* each, each one, every one; everybody.
chagrin, *s. m.* grief, sorrow, vexation; — *adj.* sad, sorrowful; sorry; gloomy.
chaîne, *s. f.* chain; range (of mountains); ~ *de montage* assembly line.
chair, *s. f.* flesh; pulp (of fruit).
chaire, *s. f.* chair; pulpit; seat, see.
chaise, *s. f.* chair.
châle, *s. m.* shawl.
chaleur, *s. f.* heat; fire.
chambre, *s. f.* room; bedroom; chamber; apartment; hall; ~ *à coucher* bedroom; ~ Haute Upper House; ~ *de commerce* chamber of commerce.
chameau, *s. m.* camel.
champ, *s. m.* field, country; *fig.* space, opportunity, theme.
champagne, *s. m.* champagne.
champignon, *s. m.* mushroom.
champion, -onne, *s. m. f.* champion.
championnat, *s. m.* championship.
chance, *s. f.* chance, fortune, risk; luck.
chancelier, *s. m.* chancellor.
chancellerie, *s. f.* chancery.
chandail, *s. m.* sweater,

pullover.
chandelle, *s. f.* candle.
change, *s. m.* change, changing; succession; (foreign) exchange, barter; *agent de* ~ stock-broker; *bureau de* ~ exchange office; *lettre de* ~ bill of exchange.
changer, *v. a.* change, alter; exchange; **se** ~ betransformed; change one's clothes.
chanson, *s. f.* song.
chant, *s. m.* singing; song, tune; chant(ing).
chanter, *v. a. & n.* warble; chant; praise.
chanteur, -euse, *s.m.f.* singer
chantier, *s.m.* yard, timber-yard, work-yard.
chapeau. *s.m.* hat; bonnet; cap.
chapelain, *s. m.* chaplain.
chapelle, *s. f.* chapel.
chapitre, *s.m.* chapter; subject, head.
chaque, *adj.* each, every.
charbon, *s. m.* coal; embers *(pl.)*; ~ *de bois* charcoal.
charcuterie, *s. f.* pork-butchery.
charcutier, -ière, *s. m. f.* pork-butcher.
charge, *s. f.* load, burden; post, function, charge office; attack; accusation.
charger, *v. a. & n.* load; burden; charge; entrust.
charité, *s. f.* charity.
charmant, *adj.* charming.
charme, *s. m.* charm.
charpente, *s. f.* timber-work.
charpentier, *s.m.* carpenter.
charrette, *s.f.* cart, wagon.
charrue, *s. f.* plough.
charte, *s. f.* charter.
chasse, *s. f.* chase, hunt(ing), shooting.
chasser, *v. a. & n.* chase, pursue, hunt, shoot, go shooting; drive out.
chasseur, *s.m.* hunter; page-boy.
chaste, *adj.* chaste, pure.
chat, *s. m.* (he-)cat.
châtaigne, *s. f.* chestnut.
château, *s.m.* castle; palace.
chatte, *s. f.* (she-)cat.
chaud, *adj. & adv.* hot, warm; ardent.
chauffage, *s. m.* heating, warming; ~ *central* central heating.
chauffe-bain, *s.m.* geyser.
chauffer, *v. a. & n.* heat, warm; urge on; coach.
chauffeur, *s. m.* driver.
chausse, *s.f.* hose
chausser, *v. a. & n.* put on (shoes etc.), wear; **se** ~ put on one's stockings etc.
chaussette, *s. f.* sock.
chaussure, *s. f.* footwear, shoes *(pl.)*.
chauve, *adj.* bald.
chef, *s. f.* chief; ~ *de train* guard; ~ *d'orchestre* conductor.
chemin, *s. m.* road, way; lane; *se mettre en* ~ start; ~ *de fer* railway.
cheminée, *s. f.* chimney.

fireplace, funnel.
chemise, *s. f.* shirt.
chêne, *s. m.* oak(-tree).
chèque, *s. m.* cheque; ~ *en blanc* blank cheque; ~ *de voyage* traveller's cheque.
cher, chère, *adj.* dear.
chercher, *v. a.* seek, look for, search for.
chéri, -e, *adj.* dear; — *s. m. f.* darling.
cheval, *s. m.* horse; *à* ~ on horseback; *monter à* ~ ride.
chevalerie, *s. f.* chivalry.
chevalier, *s. m.* knight.
chevelure, *s. f.* hair.
cheveu, *s. m.* hair; *en* ~ bareheaded.
cheville, *s.f.* wooden pin, peg; ankle.
chèvre, *s.f.* (she-)goat.
chevreau, *s.m.* kid-(leather).
chez, *prep.* at, in, at the house of; ~ *X* at X's.
chic, *adj.* smart, spruce, fashionable; — *s. m.* chic; trick; elegance.
chien, -enne, *s. m. f.* dog.
chiffon, *s. m.* rag, scrap; chiffon.
chiffre, *s. m.* figure, digit; number.
chignon, *s.m.* knot (of hair), bun.
chimie, *s.f.* chemistry.
chimique, *adj.* chemical.
chimiste, *s. m. f.* chemist.
chinois, -e (Ch.), *adj & s.m.f.* Chinese.
chirurgie, *s. f.* surgery.
chirurgien, -enne, *s.m.f.* surgeon.
choc, *s.m.* shock, clash, collision.
chocolat, *s. m.* chocolate.
chœur, *s. m.* chorus; choir.
choisir, *v.a.* choose, pick out, select.
choix, *s. m.* choice.
chômage, *s. m.* stoppage, cessation of work; unemployment.
choquer, *v. a.* run into, strike against, collide with; shock, offend; *se* ~ come into collision; be shocked.
chose, *s. f.* thing, object, matter; goods; event; *quelque* ~ something, anything.
chou, *s. m.* cabbage, cole.
chou-fleur, *s. m.* cauliflower.
chrétien, -enne, *adj. & s. m. f.* Christian.
christianisme, *s.m.* Christianity.
chronique, *adj.* chronic; — *s. f.* chronicle.
chuchoter, *v.n.&a.* whisper.
chute, *s. f.* fall, downfall, descent; slope.
ci, *adv.* here.
ci-dessous, *adv.* below, underneath.
ci-dessus, *adv.* above; aforesaid.
cidre, *s. m.* cider.
ciel, *s. m.* (*pl.* cieux) heaven; sky; weather; climate.
cierge, *s. m.* wax candle.
cigare, *s. m.* cigar.
cigarette, *s. f.* cigarette.
cigogne, *s. f.* stork.
cil, *s. m.* eyelash.
cime, *s. f.* top, summit.

ciment, *s. m.* cement.
cimetière, *s. m.* cemetery; churchyard.
cinéma, *s. m.* cinema.
cinérama, *s. m.* cinerama.
cinq, *adj.* & *s. m.* five; fifth.
cinquante, *adj.* & *s. m.* fifty; fiftieth.
circonstance, *s.f.* circumstance; occurrence, occasion, event.
circuit, *s. m.* circuit.
circulation, *s. f.* circulation; currency; traffic.
circuler, *v. n.* circulate; *circulez!* move on!
cire, *s. f.* wax.
cirer, *v. a.* wax; polish.
ciseau, *s.m.* chisel.
ciseaux, *s. m. pl.* scissors.
citation, *s.f.* citation.
cité, *s. f.* city, town.
citer, *v.a.* cite; quote.
citoyen, -enne, *s.m.f.* citizen.
citron, *s. m.* lemon.
citronnade, *s.f.* lemon squash.
civil, *adj.* civil; —, *s. m.* civilian.
civilisation, *s. f.* civilization, culture.
clair, *adj.* light, clear.
clapet, *s. m.* valve.
claquement, *s. m.* clap(ping); snap.
claquer, *v. n. a.* crack, clap; chatter; bang,
clarté, *s. f.* light, brightness; clearness.
classe, *s. f.* class; order, rank; form, class-room.
classer, *v.a.* class, rank.
classifier, *v.a.* classify.
classique, *adj.* classic(al).
clause, *s. f.* clause.
clé, clef, *s. f.* key; spanner, wrench; *fig.* clue; *~ de contact* ignition key.
clerc, *s. m.* clerk; scholar.
clergé, *s. m.* clergy.
clérical, *adj.* clerical.
client, *s. m.* client, customer, patron.
clientèle, *s. f.* clients *(pl.)*.
cligner, *v. a.* & *n.* wink.
clignotant, *s. m.* indicator.
clignoter, *v.a.&n.* blink, wink.
climat, *s. m.* climate.
clinique, *adj.* & *s.f.* clinic, clinical.
cloche, *s. f.* bell.
cloître, *s. m.* cloister.
clore*, *v. a.* shut, close.
clos, *adj.* closed.
clôture, *s. f.* enclosure, fence; close.
clou, *s. m.* nail, stud; boil, furuncle.
clouer, *v. a.* nail (down).
club, *s. m.* club.
cocher, *s. m.* coachman, driver.
cochon, *s. m.* pig, swine.
code, *s. m.* code; law, rule.
cœur, *s. m.* heart; *fig.* mind, soul, courage; *par ~* by heart.
coffre, *s. m.* chest.
coffre-fort, *s. m.* safe.
cognac, *s. m.* cognac.
cogner, *v. n.* & *a.* beat, knock, strike; *se ~* knock against.
coiffer, *v. a.* put on (hat); dress, do s.o.'s hair.
coiffeur, -euse, *s.m.f.* hairdresser.

coiffure, *s. f.* head-dress, cap; hair-do; *salon de* ~ hairdresser.
coin, *s. m.* corner; angle.
coïncider, *v.n.* coincide.
coke, *s.m.* coke.
col, *s.m.* collar; neck.
colère, *s.f.* anger.
colis, *s.m.* parcel; item (of luggage).
collaborateur, -trice, *s. m. f.* fellow worker; collaborator.
collaborer, *v.n.* work jointly, collaborate.
collectif, -ive, *adj.* collective.
collection, *s. f.* collection.
collège, *s.m.* college; grammar school.
collègue, *s.m.f.* colleague, fellow worker.
coller, *v.a.* stick, paste.
collet, *s.m.* collar; neck.
collier, *s.m.* necklace; collar.
colline, *s.f.* hill.
collision, *s.f.* collision; *entrer en* ~ collide.
colombe, *s. f.* dove.
colonel, *s.m.* colonel.
colonie, *s. f.* colony; dominion.
colonne, *s.f.* column.
coloré, *adj.* coloured; colourful.
colossal, *adj.* colossal.
combat, *s.m.* fight, combat.
combattre, *v.a.&n.* fight (against), combat (with).
combien, *adv.* (~ *de*) how much, how many, how far; ~ *de temps?* how long?
combinaison, *s.f.* combination.
combiner, *v.a.* combine, unite; contrive, devise.
comédie, *s.f.* comedy.
comédien, *s.m.* comedian, actor.
comestible, *adj.* edible.
comique, *adj.* comic; — *s. m.* comic actor.
comité, *s. m.* committee.
commandant, *s. m.* commander.
commande, *s.f.* order.
commandement, *s. m.* command, order; commandment.
commander, *v. a.* command, order; control.
comme, *adv. & conj.* as, like; as . . . as; while; ~ *il faut* decent, proper; *tout* ~ just like; ~ *si* as if, as though.
commémorer, *v.a.* commemorate.
commencant, -e, *s. m. f.* beginner; — *adj.* beginning.
commencement, *s.m.* beginning.
commencer, *v. a. & n.* begin, commence.
comment, *adv.* how, in what manner; why; ~ *allez-vous?* how are you?; ~ *(dites-vous)?* (I beg your) pardon?
commentaire, *s. m.* comment; commentary.
commenter, *v. a.* comment (on); criticize.
commercant, -e, *s. m. f.* merchant, dealer.
commerce, *s. m.* commerce, trade; *voyageur*

de ~ commercial traveller; ~ *de gros* wholesale trade; *faire le* ~ trade.
commercer, *v. n.* trade, deal with, in.
commercial, *adj.* commercial.
commettre, *v. a.* commit; *se* ~ commit oneself.
commis, *s.m.* clerk, employee.
commissaire, *s.m.* commisary; commissioner.
commissariat, *s.m.* police-station.
commission, *s. f.* commission; charge; committee; errand.
commode, *adj.* convenient, handy, comfortable; — *s. f.* chest of drawers.
commun, *adj.* common; joint; usual; vulgar; *peu* ~ unusual; — *s.m.* common people.
communauté, *s. f.* community.
commune, *s. f.* district.
communication, *s. f.* communication, message; call.
communier, *v. n.* communicate.
communion, *s.f.* communion.
communiqué, *s. m.* communiquè.
communiquer, *v. a. & n.* communicate.
compact, *adj.* compact.
compagnie, *s.f.* company.
compagnon, *s. m.* companion, fellow.
comparaison, *s. f.* comparison.
comparer, *v. a.* compare.
compartiment, *s. m.* compartment; ~ *de fumeurs* smoking compartment; ~ *pour non-fumeurs* non-smoker.
compas, *s.m.* compass(es).
compatriote, *s. m. f.* compartiot, (fellow) countryman.
compensation, *s. f.* compensation.
compenser, *v.a.&n.* compensate.
compétent, *adj.* competent.
compétiteur, -trice, *s. m. f.* competitor.
compétition, *s. f.* competition.
compilation, *s. f.* compilation.
compiler, *v. a.* compile.
complainte, *s.f.* complaint.
complaisance, *s. f.* complaisance, kindness.
complaisant, *adj.* complaisant, obliging, kind.
complément, *s. m.* complement; object.
complémentaire, *adj.* complementary.
complet, -ète, *adj.* complete, full.
compléter, *v.a.* complete.
complexe, *adj.* complex, compound.
complication, *s. f.* complication.
compliment, *s. m.* compliment; congratulation.
compliquer, *v.a.* com-

plicate.
comploter, *v.a.* plot.
composant, -e, *adj.* & *s. f.* component.
composer, *v. a.* compose, **se** ~ *de* be composed of, consist of.
compositeur, -trice ,*s. m. f.* composer.
composition, *s. f.* composition; paper.
comprendre, *v. a.* comprehend; unterstand.
comprimé, -e, *adj.* pressed; — *s. m.* tablet.
compromettre, *v. a.* compromise, commit; **se** ~ commit oneself.
compromis, *s. m.* compromise.
comptabilité, *s. f.* bookkeeping, accounts *(pl.)*
compte, *s.m.* account; amount, sum; ~ *courant* current account; *faire le* ~ *de* count; *régler un* ~ settle an account; ~ *rendu* report, account, statement; review; *tenir* ~ *de* take into account.
compter, *v. a.* & *n.* count, reckon, calculate.
comptoir, *s. m.* counter.
computer, *v. a.* compute.
comte, *s. m.* count.
comtesse, *s. f.* countess.
concéder, *v. a.* grant.
concentration, *s. f.* concentration; reduction.
concentrer, *v. a.* condense, concentrate.
concept, -tion, *s. m. f.* concept(ion), idea.
concernant, *prep.* concerning.
concerner, *v. a.* concern, relate to.
concert, *s. m.* concert.
concevoir*, *v. a.* & *n.* conceive; think; imagine; apprehend.
concierge, *s. f. m.* porter.
concile, *s. m.* council.
concis, *adj.* concise.
conclure*, *v.a.&n.* conclude, end.
conclusion, *s.f.* conclusion, end.
concombre, *s. m.* cucumber.
concorder, *v.n.* agree.
concourir, *v. n.* contribute, concur; compte.
concours, *s. m.* concourse; help; assistance; competition.
concret, -ète, *adj.* concrete.
concurrence, *s. f.* competition: rivalry.
concurrent, *s. m.* competitor; rival.
condamnation, *s. f.* condemnation; sentence.
condamner, *v.a.* condemn, sentence.
condenser, *v. a.* condense.
condition, *s. f.* condition, state; service; stipulation, condition; *à* ~ *que* on condition that, provided that.
conditionnel, *adj.* conditional.
conditionnement, *s.m.* ~ *de l'air* air-conditioning.
conducteur, -trice, *s. m. f.* conductor; driver.
conduire*, *v. a.* & *n.* conduct, lead; drive; show (to), take (to); manage; *permis de* ~ driving licence.

conduit, *s. m.* pipe, tube.
conduite, *s. f.* conducting, leading; driving; behaviour, conduct.
cône, *s. m.* cone.
confection, *s. f.* ready-made clothes *(pl.)*.
confédération, *s. f.* confederation, confederacy.
conférence, *s. f.* comparison; conference; lecture; *maître de ~s* lecturer; *faire une ~* deliver a lecture.
conférencier, -ère, *s. m. f.* lecturer.
conférer, *v.a.* grant, confer, bestow; compare.
confesser, *v.a.* confess.
confession, *s. f.* confession.
confiance, *s. f.* confidence, trust, reliance; *avoir ~* count on, trust.
confiant, *adj.* confident.
confidence, *s. f.* confidence.
confidentiel, -elle *adj.* confidential.
confier, *v.a.* trust; entrust, give in charge.
confinement, *s. m.* imprisonment.
confiner, *v. n. & a.* confine.
confirmation, *s.f.* confirmation.
confirmer, *v.a.* confirm.
confiserie, *s.f.* confectionery, sweet-shop.
confiture, *s.f.* jam, preserve.
conflit, *s. m.* conflict.
confondre, *v. a.* confound.
conformer, *v. a.* conform, adapt; **se** *~ à* conform oneself (to).
confort, *s.m.* comfort, ease.
confortable, *adj.* comfortable.
confrère, *s.m.* fellow-worker, colleague.
confronter, *v. a.* confront, compare.
confus, *adj.* confused.
confusion, *s. f.* confusion.
congé, *s. m.* leave, holiday; permission; discharge; warning, notice; *donner ~* give notice (to); dismiss; *prendre ~ de* take leave of; *être en ~* be on holiday.
congédier, *v. a.* dismiss.
congratulation, *s. f.* congratulation.
congrès, *s.m.* congress, assembly.
conjecture, *s.f.* conjecture.
conjecturer, *v.a.&n.* conjecture, guess.
conjonction, *s.f.* conjunction, union.
connaissance, *s. f.* knowledge; acquaintance; *faire ~ avec* get acquainted with.
connaître*, *v.a.* know, understand; be acquainted with.
connexion, *s.f.* connection.
conquérir*, *v. a. & n.* conquer; win (over).
conscience, *s.f.* consciousness; conscience; *avoir la ~ de* be con-

scious of, be aware of.
conscient, *adj.* conscious.
conscrit, *s. m.* conscript.
conseil, *s. m.* counsel, advice; adviser; council, board, staff.
conseiller[1], -ère, *s. m. f.* counsellor, councillor.
conseiller[2], *v. a.&n.* advise, counsel.
consentir, *v. n.* consent, agree *(à* to).
conséquence, *s. f.* consequence, result.
conséquent, *adj.* consistent; *par* ~ consequently.
conservatoire, *s. m.* conservatory.
conserver, *v.a.* keep, preserve; tin.
considérable, *adj.* considerable.
considération, *s. f.* consideration; esteem.
considérer, *v. a.* consider; esteem.
consigne, *s. f.* cloak-room, left-luggage office.
consigner, *v.a.* deposit.
consister, *v.n.* consist (of), be made (of).
consoler, *v.a.* console.
consommateur, -trice, *s. m. f.* consumer, customer.
consommer, *v.a.* consummate; consume.
consomption, *s.f.* consumption.
consonne, *s. f.* consonant.
conspiration, *s.f.* conspiracy.
conspirer, *v. a. & n.* conspire, plot.
constant, *adj.* constant, firm.
constipation, *s.f.* constipation.
constituer, *v. a.* constitute, compose.
constitution, *s. f.* constitution.
constitutionnel, -elle, *adj.* constitutional.
constructeur, *s. m.* builder.
construction, *s.f.* construction, building.
construire*, *v.a.* build, construct.
consul, *s. m.* consul.
consulat, *s. m.* consulate.
consulter, *v.a.* consult.
consumer, *v. a.* consume.
contact, *s.m.* contact, touch, switch.
contaminer, *v. a.* contaminate.
conte, *s.m.* story, tale.
contemplation, *s.f.* contemplation.
contempler, *v.a. & n.* contemplate.
contemporain, -e, *adj. & s. m. f.* contemporary.
contenance, *s. f.* capacity, contents *(pl.).*
contenir, *v.a.* contain, hold; restrain; **se** ~ restrain oneself.
content, *adj.* content.
contentement, *s. m.* content, satisfaction.
contenter, *v.a.* content, satisfy; se ~ be contented, do with.
contenu, *s.m.* contents *(pl.).*
conter, *v.a. & n.* tell, relate.
continent, *s. m.* continent.
continental, *adj.* conti-

nental:
continuation, *s.f.* continuation, continuance.
continuel, -elle, *adj.* continual.
continuer, *v.a.* & *n.* go on (with), keep on; **se ~** be continued.
contour, *s.m.* contour, outline.
contracter, *v. a.* contract, bargain for.
contradiction, *s. f.* contradiction.
contraindre*, *v. a.* compel, force; **se ~** restrain oneself.
contrainte, *s.f.* constraint.
contraire, *adj.* & *s. m.* contrary; *au* ~ on the contrary.
contrairement, *adv.* ~ *à* contrary to.
contraste, *s. m.* contrast.
contraster, *v. n.* contrast (*avec* with).
contrat, *s.m.* contract.
contre, *prep.* against.
contrée, *s.f.* country.
contrefaçon, *s. f.* counterfeit(ing); forgery.
contrefaire, *v. a.* counterfeit; pirate; forge.
contre-partie, *s. f.* counterpart.
contresigner, *v. a.* countersign.
contribuant, *s. m.* contributor.
contribuer, *v. n.* contribute (*à* to).
contribution, *s.f.* contribution, tax.
contrôle, *s.m.* control, check; hall-mark.
contrôler, *v.a.* control, check.
contrôleur, *s. m.* ticket-collector.
contusion, *s. f.* bruise.
convaincre, *v.a.* convince.
convenable, *adj.* suitable, appropriate.
convenance, *s.f.* suitability, convenience.
convenir, *v.n.* suit, be convenient (to), fit.
conventionnel, -elle, *adj.* conventional.
conversation, *s.f.* conversation, talk.
converser, *v. n.* converse.
convertir, *v.a.* convert.
conviction, *s. f.* conviction.
convier, *v.a.* invite.
convive, *s.m.* guest.
convoi, *s.m.* convoy; funeral procession.
convoquer *v.a.* convoke.
coopération, *s. f.* co-operation.
coopérer, *v. n.* co-operate.
copie, *s. f.* (fair) copy.
copier, *v.a.* copy.
coq, *s. m.* cock.
coquille, *s. f.* shell.
coquin, *s.m.* rogue.
corail, *s.m.* coral.
corbeau, *s. m.* raven.
corbeille, *s. f.* basket.
corde, *s.f.* cord, rope.
cordial, *adj.* cordial.
cordonnier, *s.m.* shoemaker.
corne, *s. f.* horn; hooter.
corneille, *s. f.* crow, rook.
cornet, *s. m.* horn; cornet.
cornichon, *s. m.* gherkin.
corporation, *s. f.* corporation.

corps, *s. m.* body, corpse; corporation, corps.
correct, *adj.* correct.
correction, *s. f.* correction.
correspondance, *s. f.* correspondence; relation; communication; connection.
correspondant, *adj.* corresponding.
correspondre, *v. n.* correspond; communicate.
corriger, *v.a.* correct.
corrompre, *v.a.* corrupt, spoil; se ~ become corrupted.
corruption, *s. f.* corruption.
corset, *s. m.* stays *(pl.)*.
cortège, *s. m.* escort.
cosmétique, *adj.* cosmetic; — *s. m.* ~s cosmetics.
cosmonaute, *s. m.* cosmonaut, spacemen.
costume, *s. m.* dress, costume; ~ *de bain(s)* bathing-costume.
côte, *s. f.* rib; slope; shore.
côté, *s. m.* side, part; *à* ~ by the side; *de* ~ on one side; *d'un* ~ on the one hand; *de l'autre* ~ on the other hand; *passer à* ~ pass by; *à* ~ *de* next (door) to; beside.
côtelette, *s. f.* chop.
coton, *s. m.* cotton.
cottage, *s. m.* cottage.
cou, *s. m.* neck.
couche, *s. f.* bed; napkin, diaper; coat; layer; *(pl.)* confinement.
coucher, *v. a.* put to bed; lay; *v.n.* lie down; sleep; *être couché* lie; se ~ go to bed, lie down; — *s. m.* bedtime; setting.
couchette, *s.f.* berth, bunk; napkin.
coude, *s. m.* elbow; angle, bend.
coudre*, *v. a. & n.* sew.
couler, *v.n.* flow, run, stream; leak; sink.
couleur, *s. f.* colour.
coulisse, *s. f.* groove; slip, wings *(pl.)*; *dans les* ~s behind the scenes.
couloir, *s.m.* passage; corridor; lobby.
coup, *s. m.* blow, stroke, knock; smack; pull; kick; shot; draught; cast, move; *d'un seul* ~ at once; ~ *de feu* rush hours *(pl.)*; *de froid* chill; ~ *de main* sudden attack; ~ *d'œil* glance, look; ~ *de soleil* sunstroke.
coupe, *s.f.* wine-cup.
couper, *v.a.* cut; cut down, off, up; divide; cross; mix; se ~ cut oneself, cut one's (finger etc.).
couple, *s. f.* pair, brace; *m.* couple.
cour, *s. f.* (court)yard; court; courting, courtship; *faire la* ~ *à* court, make love to.
courage, *s. m.* courage.
courageux, -euse, *adj.* courageous, brave.
courant, *adj.* current; running; — *s.m.* current; stream; course

run; ~ *d'air* draught.
courbe, *s. f.* curve, bend.
courbé, *adj.* curved; bent.
courber, *v. a. & n.* bend, bow; **se** ~ bend, be bent; bow.
courir*, *v. n.* run; hurry; flow; be curent.
couronne, *s.f.* crown.
couronner, *v.a.* crown.
courrier, *s. m.* messenger, courier, post, mail.
cours, *s. m.* course; current, flow; currency.
course, *s. f.* race, run; course; drive.
court, *adj.* short, brief; — *adv.* short; suddenly; — *s. m.* tennis-court.
courtiser, *v. a.* pay court to, court.
courtois, *adj.* courteous, polite.
courtoisie, *s. f.* courtesy.
cousin, -e *s. m. f.* cousin.
coussin, *s.m.* cushion.
coût, *s.m.* cost, price.
couteau, *s.m.* knife.
coûter, *v. n. & a.* cost.
coûteux, -euse, *adj.* costly, expensive, dear; *peu* ~ inexpensive.
coutume, *s.f.* custom, habit; *de* ~ customary.
couture, *s.f.* sewing, seam; needlework; scar.
couturière, *s.m.* dressmaker.
couvent, *s.m.* convent.
couver, *v.a.* brood (on), sit; hatch, breed.
couvercle, *s. m.* cover, lid, cap.
couvert, *adj.* covered; covert, sheltered; cloudy; secret; — *s.m.* set (of fork and spoon); cover; protection; *mettre le* ~ lay the table.
couverture, *s. f.* cover(ing); blanket; ~*s* bedclothes.
couvrir*, *v.a.* cover; load; protect; be sufficent for.
crabe, *s. m.* crab.
cracher, *v.n. & a.* spit.
craie, *s. f.* chalk.
craindre, *v.a.* fear, be afraid of.
crainte, *s. f.* fear; *de* ~ *de* for fear of; *de* ~ *que* lest.
crampe, *s.f.* cramp.
crampon, *s.m.* cramp.
crâne, *s. m.* skull; — *adj.* bold.
craquer, *v.n.* crack.
cravate, *s. f.* (neck)tie.
crayon, *s. m.* pencil; crayon.
créance, *s. f.* credence, belief, trust.
créancier, -ère, *s. m. f.* creditor.
création, *s. f.* creation.
créature, *s. f.* creature.
crèche, *s. f.* crèche.
crédit, *s. m.* credit; *à* ~ on credit.
créditer, *v.a.* credit.
crediteur, *s.m.* creditor.
créer, *v.a.* create, make.
crème, *s. f.* cream, custard; ~ *à raser* shaving cream.
crémerie, *s. f.* dairy.
crêpe, *s. m.* crape, crêpe.
creuser, *v. a.* dig; deepen.
creux, -euse, *adj.* hollow, empty; — *s. m.* hollow.

crevaison, *s. f.* puncture.
crever, *v. a. & n.* burst; puncture; die.
cri, *s. m.* cry, scream; call, shout.
crible, *s.m.* sieve, screen.
cric, *s. m.* jack.
crier, *v.a. & n.* cry (out).
crime, *s. m.* crime, guilt.
criminel, -elle, *adj. & s. m. f.* criminal.
crise, *s. f.* crisis.
crisper, *v.a.* contract, shrivel.
cristal, *s. m.* crystal.
critique, *adj.* critical; — *s.f.* criticism, critique; *s.m.f.* critic, reviewer.
crochet, *s. m.* hook; crochet(-work); hanger.
croire*, *v. a. & n.* believe, credit, trust; think.
croiser, *v.a.* cross; *v.n.* cruise.
croître*, *v.n.* grow, increase; grow up; *v.a.* increase.
croix, *s. f.* cross.
croquis, *s.m.* sketch.
crouler, *v. n.* fall (to pieces), fall in.
croûte, *s. f.* crust; *casser la ~* have a snack.
croyance, *s.f.* belief, faith; creed.
croyant, -e, *s. m. f.* believer; — *adj.* faithful.
cru, *adj.* raw; crude.
cruauté, *s. f.* cruelty.
crue, *s. f.* rise, growth.
cruel, -elle, *adj.* cruel.
crypte, *s. f.* crypte.
cube, *s. m.* cube.
cueillir*, *v.a.* gather, pick, glean.
cuiller, -ère, *s. f.* spoon; *~ à pot* ladle; *~ à café* teaspoon.
cuir, *s. m.* skin; leather.
cuire*, *v. a. & n.* cook; boil; roast; burn; *faire trop ~* overdo.
cuisine, *s. f.* kitchen; cooking, cookery; *batterie de ~* kitchen utensils; *de ~* culinary; *livre de ~* cookery-book.
cuisinière, *s.f.* cook; kitchen range, cooker.
cuisse, *s. f.* thigh; leg.
cuit, *adj.* cooked, baked.
cuivre, *s. m.* copper.
cul, *s. m.* bottom.
culinaire, *adj.* culinary.
culotte, *s. f.* panties; breeches *(pl.)*.
culte, *s. m.* cult, worship.
cultivateur, -trice, *s. m. f.* farmer.
cultiver, *v.a.* cultivate, till; *fig.* improve.
culture, *s.f.* culture.
culturel, -elle, *adj.* cultural.
cure, *s. f.* care; cure.
curé, *s. m.* priest; vicar.
cure-dent, *s.m.* toothpick.
curieux, -euse, *adj.* curious, strange, inquisitive.
curiosité, *s. f.* curiosity; *~s* sights.
cuve, *s. f.* tub, vat.
cuvette, *s. f.* *~ (de lavabo)* wash-basin.
cycle, *s. m.* cycle.
cygne, *s. m.* swan.
cylindre, *s. m.* cylinder.

D

dactylo(graphe), *s. m. f.* typist.
dame, *s.f.* lady; queen.
danger, *s. m.* danger.
dangereux, -euse, *adj.* dangerous.
danois, -e (D.), *adj. & s. m. f.* Dane, Danish.
dans, *prep.* in, into; inside; during; ~ *le temps* formerly.
danse, *s. f.* dance.
danser, *v. n.* dance.
danseur, *s. m.* dancer.
danseuse: *s. f.* ballet-girl, dancer.
date, *s. f.* date; *prendre* ~ fix a day.
dater, *v. a. & n.* date.
datte, *s. f.* date.
davantage, *adv.* more, further; *bien* ~ much more; *pas* ~ no more; *en* ~ some more.
de, *prep.* of, from, out of, on account of.
dé, *s. m.* thimble.
déballer, *v. a.* unpack.
débarquer, *v. a. & n.* land, disembark, arrive.
débarrasser, *v. a.* clear (up), rid, free; se ~ get rid (of).
débat, *s. m.* debate.
débattre, *v. a. & n.* debate.
débit, *s. m.* sale; debit; output; utterance; ~ *de tabac* tobbaconist's shop.
déborder, *v. n. & a.* overflow, run over.
débouché, *s. m.* outlet, issue.
déboucher, *v. a.* uncork, open; *v. n.* run into.
débourser, *v. a.* disburse.
debout, *adv.* upright, standing; *être* ~ stand.
début, *s.m.* start, outset; first appearance.
débuter, *v. n.* begin, start; make one's first appearance.
décadence, *s.f.* decadence.
décagramme, *s.m.* decagramme.
décéder, *v.n.* die, decease.
décembre, *s. m.* December.
déception, *s. f.* deception, deceit; disappointment.
décharge, *s. f.* discharge; outlet.
décharger, *v.a.* unload, unburden; release; discharge; se ~ unburden oneself.
déchausser, *v.a.* take off (shoes).
déchéance, *s.f.* decadence, decay; decline.
déchiffrer, *v.a.* decipher; make out.
déchirer, *v.a.* tear, rend.
dechoir*, *v.n.* fall off, decay.
décider, *v. a. & n.* decide, settle; se ~ make up one's mind; be settled.
décilitre, *s. m.* decilitre.
décimal, -e, *adj. & s. f.* decimal.
décimètre, *s.m.* decimetre.
décisif, -ive, *adj.* decisive, final.
décision, *s.f.* decision.

déclaration, *s.f.* declaration, statement.

déclarer, *v.a.* declare, state; se ~ declare itself.

décliner, *v.n.* decline.

décolletage, *s.m.* low neck.

décolleter, *v.a.* cut low turn; *tour à* ~ turning lathe.

décomposer, *v. a.* decompose; spoil; se ~ decompose.

décomposition, *s. f.* decomposition.

décompte, *s. m.* discount; particulars *(pl.)*.

décor, *s. m.* decoration; scene, environment; scenery.

décoratif, -ive, *adj.* decorative.

décorer, *v.a.* decorate; trim.

découper, *v.a.* cut out, carve.

décourager, *v.a.* discourage

découverte, *s. f.* discovery.

découvrir*, *v. a.* discover, find out; uncover; se ~ uncover oneself, disclose oneself.

décret, *s. m.* decree, order.

décrier, *v.a.* cry down.

décrire, *v.a.* describe.

décrocher, *v.a.* unhook, take down.

décroissance, *s. m.* decrease.

décroître, *v. n.* decrease.

déçu, *adj.* disappointed.

dédain, *s.m.* disdain, scorn.

dedans, *adv.* within, inside; indoors, at home.

dédicace, *s. f.* dedication.

dédier, *v.a.* dedicate.

déduire*, *v.a.* deduct.

défaire, *v. a.* undo; break; unfasten; take off; defeat; se ~ come undone.

défaite, *s. f.* defeat.

défaut, *s. m.* defect, deficiency, want; fault; flaw; *à* ~ *de* for want of; *sans* ~ faultless.

défavorable, *adj.* unfavourable.

défendre, *v.a.* defend; forbid; se ~ defend oneself.

défense, *s.f.* defence, protection; prohibition; tusk; *se mettre en* ~ stand on one's guard.

défiance, *s.f.* distrust, mistrust.

défier, *v. a.* defy.

défigurer, *v. a.* disfigure, deface, spoil.

défiler, *v. n.* defile.

défini, *adj.* definite.

définir, *v. a.* define.

définitif, -ive, *adj.* definitive, final.

définition, *s. f.* definition.

défunt, -e, *adj. & s. m. f.* deceased, defunct.

dégager, *v. a.* redeem, release, disengage; emit.

dégorger, *v.a.* disgorge, discharge; *v.n.* discharge, overflow.

dégoût, *s. m.* disgust.

dégoûtant, *adj.* disgusting.

dégoûter, *v.a.* disgust; **se ~** get tired of.
dégradation, *s. f.* degradation.
dégrader, *v.a.* degrade; damage.
degré, *s. m.* degree.
déguisement, *s.m.* disguise.
déguiser, *v.a.* disguise, hide.
dehors, *adv.* out, outside, out of doors; *au* ~ outside, abroad; *en* ~ *de* outside of, apart from.
déjà, *adv.* already; previously.
déjeuner, *s. m.* lunch(eon); *petit* ~ breakfast; — *v.n.* have breakfast; take lunch.
delà, *prep.* beyond; *au* ~ *de* beyond.
délai, *s. m.* delay; *à bref* ~ at short notice.
délégation, *s. f.* delegation.
déléguer, *v. a.* delegate.
délibération, *s. f.* deliberation, resolution; *en* ~ under consideration.
délibérer, *v. n.* deliberate, ponder; *v.a.* bring under discussion.
délicat, *adj.* delicate; feeble; fastidious, dainty.
délicatesse, *s. f.* delicacy; delicateness; daintiness.
délice, *s. m.* delight.
délicieux, -euse, *adj.* delicious, delightful.
délier, *v. a.* untie; loosen.
délivrance, *s. f.* deliverance.
délivrer, *v.a.* deliver, (set) free.
déloyal, *adj.* disloyal, unfair.
demain, *adv.* tomorrow.
demande, *s.f.* request, application, inquiry, call, request, demand.
demander, *v.a.* ask, inquire (after); beg, demand; request, require; **se ~** wonder.
démanger, *v.n.* itch.
démarche, *s. f.* walk, gait; proceeding.
démasquer, *v. a.* unmask.
déménagement, *s. m.* removal, moving.
déménager, *v.n.&a.* move (house); remove.
démesuré, *adj.* immoderate, excessive.
demeure, *s.f.* delay; home, dwelling.
demeurer, *v.n.* live; stay.
demi, -e, *adj.* half; *à* ~ by half; *une heure et ~e* half past one; an hour and a half; — *s. f.* half-hour.
demi-cercle, *s. m.* semicircle.
demi-heure, *s. f.* half an hour.
demi-jour, *s. m.* twilight.
démobiliser, *v.a.* demobilize.
démocratie, *s. f.* democracy.
démocratique, *adj.* democratic.
démodé, *adj.* old-fashioned.
demoiselle, *s.f.* young lady, miss.
démolir, *v. a.* demolish,

pull down.
démon, *s. m.* demon.
démonstratif, -ive, *adj.* demonstrative.
démonstration, *s.f.* demonstration.
démontrer, *v. a.* demonstrate.
dénaturé, *adj.* unnatural.
dénombrer, *v. a.* number.
dénomination, *s. f.* denomination.
dénoncer, *v. a.* denounce.
dénoter, *v. a.* denote; indicate.
dense, *adj.* dense, compact.
densité, *s. f.* density.
dent, *s. f.* tooth; *mal de ~s* toothache.
dental, *adj.* dental.
dentelle, *s. f.* lace.
dentier, *s. m.* set of (false) teeth, denture.
dentifrice, *s. m. pâte ~* tooth-paste.
dentiste, *s. m. f.* dentist.
dénué, *adj.* destitute.
dénuement, *s. m.* destitution.
départ, *s. m.* departure.
département, *s. m.* department; territory.
départir, *v. a.* grant, allot; se ~ give up
dépasser, *v. a. & n.* pass, exceed, go beyond.
dépêche, *s. f.* despatch, wire, telegram.
dépêcher, *v. a.* dispatch; *v. n.* & se ~ hurry.
dépendance, *s. f.* dependance.
dépendant, -e, *adj.* dependent; — *s. m. f.* dependant.
dépendre, *v. n.* depend.
dépense, *s. f.* expense; larder.
dépenser, *v. a. & n.* spend; waste.
dépit, *s. m.* spite; *en ~ de* in spite of.
déplacement, *s. m.* displacement; shift.
déplacer, *v.a.* displace, move, shift; se ~ move.
déplaire, *v.n.* displease.
déplier, *v.a.* unfold, lay out.
déplorer, *v. a.* deplore.
déportation, *s. f.* transportation, deportation.
déposer, *v. a.* put down, set down; deposit; — se ~ settle.
dépôt, *s.m.* deposit; store-room, warehouse; lock-up.
dépourvu, *adj.* needy.
dépraver, *v. a.* deprave.
déprécier, *v. a.* depreciate.
dépression, *s. f.* depression.
déprimer, *v. a.* depress.
depuis, *prep.* since, from; ~ *longtemps* long since.
députation, *s. f.* deputation.
député, *s.m.* deputy; member of the French parliament.
dérangé, *adj.* deranged; upset.
déranger, *v. a.* upset, put out of order.
déraper, *v. n.* skid.
dérèglement, *s. m.* irregularity; disorder.
dérivation, *s. f.* derivation.
dériver, *v.n.* drift; be

derived.
dernier, -ère, *adj.* & *s. m. f.* latter, last, latest; *le* ~ the latter.
dernièrement, *adv.* lately.
dérober, *v. a.* rob, steal. **se** ~ steal away.
déroger, *v.n.* derogate (from).
dérouler, *v.a.* unroll, unfold.
déroute, *s.f.* defeat.
derrière, *adv.* & *prep.* behind, back; — *s. m.* back (part); bottom.
dès, *prep.* from, as early as, since; ~ *que* as soon as.
désagréable, *adj.* disagreeable, unpleasant.
désarmer, *v.a.* disarm.
désastre, *s.m.* disaster.
désavantage, *s. m.* disadvantage.
descendance, *s.f.* descent.
descendant, *adj.* descending; *en* ~ downward, downhill.
descendre, *v. n.* descend, come down, go down; alight; ~ *terre* land; — *v.a.* take down.
descente, *s.f.* descent; landing.
description, *s. f.* description.
désert[1], *s. m.* desert.
désert[2], *adj.* deserted, desolate.
déserter, *v. n.* & *a.* leave, desert.
désespérer, *v.n.* despair, give up.
désespoir, *s. m.* despair.
déshabiller, *v. a.* undress; take off clothes.
déshonneur, *s.m.* dishonour, disgrace.
déshonorer, *v.a.* dishonour, disgrace.
désigner, *v. a.* designate; denote; appoint.
desinfecter, *v. a.* disinfect.
désir, *s. m.* desire.
désirable: *adj.* desirable.
désirer, *v. a.* & *n.* desire, long for.
désireux, -euse, *adj.* desirous, anxious.
désobéir, *v.n.* disobey.
désobéissance, *s.f.* disobedience.
désobéissant, *adj.* disobedient.
désœuvré, *adj.* idle, unoccupied.
désolation, *s. f.* devastation; desolation.
désoler, *v.a.* desolate; afflict, distress; **se** ~ grieve, be sorry.
désordre, *s.m.* disorder.
dessert, *s. m.* dessert.
dessin, *s.m.* drawing, sketch; design; ~ *animé* cartoon.
dessiner, *v.a.* draw; sketch; design.
dessous, *adv.* & *prep.* under, underneath, below, beneath; — *s. m.* under-part; undies *pl.*
dessus, *adv.* & *prep.* on, upon, over, above, on top; — *s. m.* upper part, top.
destin, *s. m.* destiny, fate.
destinataire, *s. m. f.* re-

ceiver, addressee.
destination, *s. f.* destination.
destinée, *s.f.* destiny.
destiner, *v.a.* destine; mean (for); **se** ~ be destined (*à* for).
détachement, *s. m.* disengagement; detachment.
détacher, *v.a.* loose(n), unfasten; detach; **se** ~ get loose, come undone.
détail, *s.m.* detail, particular; retail; *en* ~ in detail.
détention, *s. f.* detention.
détermination, *s.f.* determination.
déterminé, *adj.* definite, determinate; resolute; limited.
déterminer, *v.a.* determine, fix; limit; settle.
détestable, *adj.* hateful.
détester, *v.a.* detest.
détonation, *s.f.* detonation.
détour, *s.m.* turning, winding, turn; roundabout way; evasion.
détourner, *v.a.* turn aside; lead astray.
détroit, *s. m.* strait, pass.
détruire*, *v.a.* destroy, ruin; do away with.
dette, *s. f.* debt.
deuil, *s.m.* mourning.
deux, *adj.* & *s. m.* two; both.
deuxième, *adj.* second.
devancer, *v. a.* precede; anticipate.
devant, *prep. adv.* before; in front of; opposite to; ~ *que* before; *au-*~ *de* ~ in front of; — *s. m.* front; foreground.
dévaster, *v. a* devastate, destroy.
développement, *s. m.* development, growth.
développer, *v.a.* (*also* **se** ~) develop.
devenir, *v.n.* become, get, turn, grow.
dévier, *v. a.* & *n.* deviate, turn away.
devise, *s. f.* device.
dévoiler, *v. a.* unveil, reveal.
devoir*, *v.a.* owe, be in debt for; have to, must, be bound to, ought to; — *s. m.* duty; task; work., prep.
dévorer, *v. a.* devour, eat up.
dévouement, *s. m.* devotion.
dévouer, *v. a.* devote, dedicate; **se** ~ devote oneself.
diable, *s. m.* devil; trolley, truck.
diacre, *s. m.* deacon.
diadème, *s. m.* diadem.
diagnostic, *s. m.* diagnosis.
dialecte, *s. m.* dialect.
dialogue, *s. m.* dialogue.
diamant, *s. m.* diamond.
diapositive, *s. f.* transparency, slide.
diarrhée, *s. f.* diarrhoea.
dictée, *s. f.* dictation.
dicter, *v. a.* dictate.
dictionnaire, *s. m.* dictionary.
diesel, *s. m.* diesel engine.
dieu, *s. m.* (*pl.* -x) God.
différence, *s. f.* difference.
différent, *adj.* different.
différer, *v.a.* defer, put

off; *v.n.* differ, be different, vary.
difficile, *adj.* difficult, hard.
difficulté, *s. f.* difficulty, trouble.
diffusion, *s. f.* diffusion.
digne, *adj.* worthy; ~ *de* . . . worthy of . . .
dignité, *s.f.* dignity.
diligence, *s.f.* diligence.
diligent, *adj.* diligent.
dimanche, *s. m.* Sunday.
dimension, *s.f.* dimension.
diminuer, *v.a.* &. *n.* diminish, lessen, reduce.
dindon, *s.m.* turkey.
dîner,* *s. m.* dinner; — *v. n.* dine.
diplomate, *s. m.* diplomat.
diplomatie, *s. f.* diplomacy.
diplomatique, *adj.* diplomatic.
diplôme, *s.m.* diploma.
dire*, *v.a.* say, tell; speak; ~ *à qn de faire qch.* tell s.o. to do sth.; *c'est à* ~ that is to say; *pour ainsi* ~ as it were; *vouloir* ~ mean; *dites donc!* look here!
direct, *adj.* direct.
directeur, *s.m.* director, manager; head master.
direction, *s.f.* direction; management; guidance; streering-gear.
directrice, *s. f.* directress; ~ head mistress.
diriger, *v.a.* direct; lead, guide; manage; turn; steer.
disciple, *s.m.* disciple, follower.
discipline, *s. f.* discipline.
discorde, *s.f.* discord.
discours, *s.m.* discourse, speech.
discrédit, *s.m.* discredit.
discréditer, *v. a.* discredit.
discret, -ète *adj.* discreet; discrete.
discrètement, *adv.* discreetly.
discrétion, *s. f.* discretion.
discussion, *s. f.* discussion.
discuter, *v.a.* discuss, debate.
disparaître, *v.n.* disappear.
dispenser, *v. a.* dispense; se ~ *de* dispense with.
disposer, *v. a.* & *n.* dispose, lay out; **se** ~ prepare (to), be about (to); *bien disposé* willing.
disposition, *s. f.* disposition, arrangement; *la* ~ *de qn.* at s.o.'s disposal.
dispute, *s. f.* dispute.
disputer, *v. a.* & *n.* dispute, contest, argue; se ~ quarrel, dispute.
disqualifier, *v.a.* disqualify.
disque, *s. m.* disc, record; discus; ~ *microsillon* or *longue durée* long playing record.
dissimulation, *s. f.* dissimulation, dissembling.
dissimuler, *v.a.* & *n.* dissemble, conceal; **se** ~ conceal oneself.
dissolution, *s. f.* dissolution; undoing, break-

ing up.
dissoudre*, *v. a.* dissolve, disperse.
distance, *s. f.* distance; *a quelle ~ est-ce?* how far is it?
distant, *adj.* distant, far.
distiller, *v.a. & n.* distil.
distinct, *adj.* distinct, clear.
distinction, *s.f.* distinction.
distinguer, *v.a.* distinguish, discriminate; make out, tell.
distraction, *s. f.* abstraction; recreation; entertainment; distraction.
distraire, *v.a.* subtract; divert, distract; amuse, entertain.
distrait, *adj.* inattentive, absent-minded.
distribuer, *v. a.* distribute; deal out.
district, *s.m.* district.
divan, *s.m.* sofa, divan.
divergence, *s.f.* divergence; difference.
divers, *adj.* diverse, different, miscellaneous.
diversion, *s. f.* diversion.
divertir, *v. a.* divert, entertain; **se ~** enjoy oneself.
divertissement, *s. m.* diversion; entertainment.
divin, *adj.* divine.
diviser, *v.a.* divide, separate.
division, *s.f.* division, department.
divorce, *s. m.* divorce.
divorcer, *v n. & n.* divorce, be divorced.
dix, *adj. s. m.* ten.
dix-huit, *adj. & s.m.* eighteen.
dixième, *adj. & s.f.* tenth.
dix-neuf, *adj. & s.m.* nineteen.
dix-sept, *adj. & s.m.* seventeen.
dizaine, *s. f.* ten.
docteur, *s. m.* doctor.
document, *s.m.* document.
documentaire, *s. m.* documentary (film).
dogme, *s. m.* dogma.
doigt, *s.m.* finger; toe.
dollar, *s.m.* dollar.
domaine, *s.m.* domain; landed property.
dôme, *s. m.* dome.
domestique, *adj. & s. m. f.* domestic, servant.
domicile, *s. m.* domicile, dwelling.
domination, *s. f.* domination, rule.
dominer, *v. a. & n.* dominate, rule.
dommage, *s. m.* damage; pity.
dompter, *v. a.* subdue, master, tame.
don, *s. m.* present, gift.
donateur, *s.m.* giver.
donc, *conj.* therefore, then, so; of course.
donne, *s. f.* deal.
donner, *v. a.* give, grant, present with, afford, hand over; *~ congé* give notice to; **se ~** *pour* claim to be.
dont, *pron.* whose, of whom; of which.
dormir*, *v.n.* sleep.

dortoir, *s. m.* dormitory.
dos, *s. m.* back.
dose, *s. f.* dose.
dossier, *s. m.* back-piece; record, file.
dot, *s. f.* dowry.
doter, *v. a.* endow.
douane, *s.f.* customs; custom-house; duty; *déclaration de* ~ customs declaration; *droits de* ~ customs duties; *la visite de la* ~ customs formalities.
douanier, *s.m.* custom-house officer.
double, *s.m.* double; *en* ~ duplicate; — *adj.* double, dual.
doubler, *v. a.* double (up); line; dub.
doublure, *s.f.* lining; understudy.
douce *see* **doux.**
douceur, *s. f.* sweetness; gentleness.
douche, *s. f.* shower-bath.
douer, *v. a.* endow, gift.
douleur, *s. f.* pain, ache.
douloureux, -euse, *adj.* painful.
doute, *s. m.* doubt; *sans* ~ no doubt, undoubtedly.
douter, *v. n.* doubt; **se** ~ suspect.
douteux, -euse, *adj.* doubtful, dubious.
doux, douce, *adj.* sweet; mild, soft.
douzaine, *s.f.* dozen.
douze, *adj. & s. m.* twelve; twelfth.
douzième, *adj.* twelfth.
dramatique, *adj.* dramatic; *l'art* ~ drama.
drame, *s.m.* drama.
drap, *s.m.* cloth, sheet.
drapeau, *s.m.* flag.
dresser, *v. a.* set up, erect; prepare; **se** ~ stand up, get up.
drogue, *s. f.* drug.
droguerie, *s. f.* drugs *pl.*
droit, *s. m.* right; law; duty, due; *avoir* ~ *à* be entitled to; ~ *de cité* citizenship; ~ *d'auteur,* copyright; *exempt de* ~*s* duty-free; ~*(s) de sortie,* export duty; — *adj.* right, direct, straight.
droite, *s. f.* right hand.
drôle, *adj.* droll, funny, strange; — *s. m.* rouge.
du, *art.* of the, some, any.
dû, *adj. & s. m.* due.
duc, *s. m.* duke.
duchesse, *s.f.* duchess.
duel, *s. m.* duel.
duplicata, *s. m.* duplicate, copy.
dur, *adj.* hard, tough.
durable, *adj.* lasting.
durant, *prep.* during, for.
durcir, *v. a. & n.* harden.
durée, *s.f.* duration, term.
durer, *v.n. & a.* last, endure, hold out.
dureté, *s. f.* hardness.
dynastie, *s.f.* dynasty.

E

eau, *s. f. (pl. -x)* water; ~ *de mer* salt water; ~ *de Seltz* soda-water.
ébaucher, *v.a.* sketch;

outline.
ébouriffer, *v.a.* ruffle.
ébullition, *s.f.* boiling.
écaille, *s.f.* scale.
écailler, *v.a.* scale.
écart, *s.m.* deviation; *à l'*~ aside, apart.
écarter, *v.a.* set aside; dispel, take away; **s'**~ turn aside.
ecclésiastique, *adj. & s. m.* ecclesiastic.
échafaud, *s. m.* scaffold(ing).
échange, *s. m.* exchange.
échanger, *v. a.* exchange.
échapper, *v. n.* escape, get away.
échauder, *v.a.* scald.
échauffer, *v. a.* heat; **s'**~ get hot.
échéance, *s. f.* expiration.
échéant, *adj.* due.
échec, *s. m.* check.
échecs, *s. m. pl.* chess.
échelle, *s.f.* ladder; scale.
échine, *s.f.* backbone.
écho, *s.m.* echo.
échoir*, *v.n.* expire, fall due; happen.
éclabousser, *v. a.* splash, spatter with mud.
éclair, *s.m.* lightning; flash.
éclairage, *s. m.* lighting; ~ *au néon* strip-lighting.
éclaircir, *v. a.* make clear, clear up; clarify; throw light on; **s'**~ become clear, clear up.
éclairer, *v. a.* light, illuminate; enlighten.
éclaireur, *s. m.* boy scout.
éclat, *s.m.* splinter; burst; brightness.
éclatant, *adj.* bright.
éclater, *v. n.* split; burst; break out; flash.
éclipser, *v. a.* eclipse; **s'**~ be eclipsed; take French leave.
école, *s.f.* school; *maître d'*~ schoolmaster; ~ *normale* teachers' training college; ~ *secondaire* grammar-school.
écolier, *s. m.* schoolboy.
écolière, *s. f.* schoolgirl.
économe, *adj.* economical; — *s. m.* bursar.
économie, *s. f.* economy; thrift; ~ *politique* political economy; ~**s** savings; *faire des* ~**s** save up.
économique, *adj.* economic; economical.
économiser, *v. a. & n.* economize, save, spare.
écorce, *s. f.* bark; rind.
écossais, *adj.* Scottish, Scotch.
Écossais, *s. m.* Scotsman.
écouler, *v.a.* sell.
écouter, *v.a.* listen to; hear.
écouteur, *s.m.* headphone; receiver.
écran, *s.m.* screen; *le petit* ~ television.
écrier: **s'**~ cry out.
écrire*, *v. a.* write (down); *machine à* ~ typewriter.
écrit, *adj.* written; — *s. m.* writing; *par* ~ in writing.
écriture, *s.f.* writing, handwriting; style.
écrivain, *s.m.* writer,

author.
écuelle, *s. f.* bowl, basin, dish.
écume, *s.f.* foam.
écureuil, *s.m.* squirrel.
écurie, *s.f.* stable.
édifice, *s.m.* building.
édifier, *v.a.* build, erect; edify.
édit, *s.m.* edict, decree.
éditer, *v. a.* publish; edit.
éditeur, *s. m.* publisher.
édition, *s. f.* publication; edition.
éducation, *s. f.* education; training.
effacer, *v. a.* efface, rub out; wipe out.
effectif, -ive *adj.* actual, real.
effectuer, *v.a.* effect, carry out.
effet, *s. m.* effect, result; impression; bill (of exchange); *(pl.)* clothes, belongings.
efficacité, *s. f.* efficacy.
effondrer: s'~ fall in, collapse.
effort, *s. m.* effort, exertion, endeavour.
effrayant, *adj.* frightful.
effrayé, *adj.* afraid.
effrayer, *v.a.* frighten; s'~ be frightened.
effroi, *s.m.* fright.
effroyable, *adj.* frightful.
effusion, *s.f.* effusion, gush.
égal, *adj.* equal, like, alike; (all the) same; even.
également, *adv.* equally.
égaler, *v.a.* equal.
égalité, *s.f.* equality.
égard, *s. m.* regard; *à cet ~* on that account; *à l'~ de* with regard to; *en ~ à* considering.
égarer, *v. a.* mislead, misguide; s'~ lose one's way.
égayer, *v. a.* cheer (up); s'~ cheer up.
église (É), *s. f.* church.
égoïste, *adj.* egoistic, selfish.
egyptien, -enne (E.), *adj. & s.m.f.* Egyptian.
eh, *int.* ah!;~ *bien!* well!
élaborer, *v. a.* work out, think out, elaborate.
élan, *s.m.* dash; run; élan, zest.
élancé, *adj.* slim.
élancer, *v. n.* shoot; s'~ bound, dash, rush; soar.
élargir, *v. a.* make wider, enlarge; set at liberty.
élastique, *adj. & s. m.* elastic.
électeur, -trice, *s. m. f.* voter.
élection, *s.f.* election.
électricien, -enne, *s. m. f.* electrician.
électricité, *s.f.* electricity; *usine d'~* power-plant, -station.
électrique, *adj.* electric(al).
électron, *s.m.* electron.
électronique, *adj.* electronic.
élégance, *s.f.* elegance.
élégant, *adj.* elegant.
élément, *s. m.* element.
élémentaire, *adj.* elementary.
éléphant, *s. m.* elephant.
élévation, *s.f.* eleva-

tion.

élève, *s.m.f.* pupil.

élevé, *adj.* educated.

élever, *v. a.* raise, lift up; increase; bring up, educate; rear; s'~ rise; exalt oneself.

éliminer, *v. a.* eliminate.

élire, *v. a.* choose; elect.

elle, *pron.* (*pl.* elles) she, it, her; they.

elle-même, *pron.* herself.

éloigné, *adj.* far, distant.

éloigner, *v.a.* remove; take away; set aside.

émail, *s. m.* enamel.

émaner, *v.n.* emanate.

emballer, *v.a.* pack up; pack off.

embarquement, *s. m.* embarking; shipment.

embarquer, *v.a.* ship, embark; *v.n.* go on board.

embarrasser, *v. a.* embarrass.

embellir, *v. a.* embellish.

embêter, *v.a.* bore; annoy.

emblème, *s. m.* emblem.

embouchure, *s. f.* mouthpiece; mouth (of river).

embranchement, *s.m.* branchline; junction.

embrasser, *v. a.* embrace; kiss; s'~ kiss.

embrayage, *s. m.* clutch, coupling.

embrouillement, *s.m.* tangle; muddle.

embrouiller, *v. a.* embroil, entangle; muddle; s'~ become confused.

émetteur, *s. m.* transmitter.

émettre *v. a.* emit; transmit, broadcast.

émigration, *s. f.* emigration.

émigré, -e, *s.m.f.* emigrant.

émigrer, *v.n.* emigrate.

éminent, *adj.* eminent.

emmener, *v.a.* take away.

émotion, *s.f.* emotion; feeling.

émouvoir, *v.a.* move, touch; s'~ be moved.

emparer: s'~ *de* get hold of, seize.

empêchement, *s. m.* hindrance.

empêcher, *v.a.* keep from; prevent; hinder.

empire, *s.m.* empire.

emplette, *s. f.* purchase.

emplir, *v.a.* fill (up).

emploi, *s.m.* employment, job; use.

employé, -e, *s.m.f.* employee; clerk; attendant.

employer, *v.a.* employ; use.

empoigner, *v.a.* grasp, grip; lay hands on.

empoisonner, *v. a.* poison.

emporter, *v.a.* carry, take away, carry off, remove; s'~ get angry, lose one's temper.

empreinte, *s. f.* stamp, print, impression.

empresser: s'~ hurry, hasten.

emprisonnement, *s.m.* imprisonment.

emprisonner, *v.a.* imprison.

emprunter, *v. a.* borrow.

en, *prep.* in; to; into; at; like, as; by, through;

— *pron.* of him, of her, of it, of them, their; any, some.
encan, *s.m.* auction.
enceinte, *adj.* pregnant.
enchaîner, *v.a.* chain; link up; detain.
enchantement, *s. m.* spell; delight.
enchanter, *v.a.* charm, delight.
enclore, *v.a.* enclose.
enclose, *s. m.* enclosure; close.
enclume, *s.f.* anvil.
encombrement, *s. m.* stoppage; (traffic) jam.
encombrer, *v. a.* block up, jam.
encore, *adv.* yet, still; again; *pas* ~ not yet; ~ *une fois* once again; ~ *que* although; ~ *du* some more; ~ *quelque chose, Madame?* anything else, madam?
encouragement, *s. m.* encouragement.
encourager, *v. a.* encourage; cheer.
encre, *s.f.* ink.
encyclopédie, *s. f.* encyclopaedia.
endommager, *v.a.* damage; injure.
endormir, *v.a.* put to sleep; s'~ go to sleep, fall asleep.
endosser, *v.a.* endorse.
énergie, *s. f.* energy; ~ *atomique* atomic energy.
énergique, *adj.* energetic.
enfance, *s.f.* infancy, childhood.
enfant, *s. m. f.* infant, child; *chambre d'~s* nursery; *d'~s* juvenile.
enfermer, *v.a.* shut in, up, lock up.
enfin, *adv.* at last; finally; in short.
enflammer, *v. a.* set on fire; s'~ take fire.
enfler, *v. a.* swell (up); s'~ swell.
enflure, *s. f.* swelling.
engagement, *s. m.* obligation; commitment; engagement.
engager, *v. a. & n.* pledge; pawn; engage, sign on.
engloutir, *v. a.* swallow up, devour.
engraisser, *v.a.* fatten; *v.n.* grow fat.
enlèvement, *s.m.* removal.
enlever, *v.a.* remove, clear away, take away.
ennemi, *s.m.* enemy.
ennui, *s. m.* bore(dom); vexation; nuisance.
ennuyer, *v. a.* bore, weary; s'~ be bored.
ennuyeux, -euse, *adj.* boring, tedious.
énoncer, *v.a.* state.
énorme, *adj.* enormous.
enquérir: s'~ *de* inquire about.
enrager, *v. n.* be enraged.
enregistrer, *v. a.* register, enter, record.
enrhumer, *v.a.* *être enrhumé* have a cold; s'~ catch a cold.
enrôler, *v. a.* enrol, draft.
enroué, *adj.* hoarse.
enrouler, *v. a.* roll (up).
enseignement, *s. m.* instruction, tuition.
enseigner. *v.a. & n.*

teach, instruct (in).
ensemble, *adv.* together; — *s. m.* whole, mass; unity; two-piece suit; set of furniture, suite.
ensuite, *adv.* then; next.
ensuivre: s'~ follow, ensue.
entasser, *v.a.* heap up.
entendement, *s. m.* understanding.
entendre, *v. a. & n.* hear; understand; ~ *parler de* hear of; *ne pas* ~ miss; *qu'entendez-vous par là?* what do you mean by that?; *bien entendu* of course; *c'est entendu!* that's settled!; agreed!
entente, *s.f.* meaning; understanding; agreement.
enterrement, *s. m.* burial.
enterrer, *v.a.* bury.
enthousiasme, *s. m.* enthusiasm.
enthousiaste, *adj.* enthusiastic; keen.
entier, -ère, *adj.* entire.
entièrement, *adv.* entirely, wholly.
entorse, *s.f.* sprain; *donner une ~ à* sprain one's (foot, ankle).
entourage, *s. m.* circle of friends; surroundings *(pl.)*; attendants *(pl.)*.
entourer, *v.a.* surround; encircle.
entracte, *s. m.* interval.
entrailles, *s. f. pl.* entrails.
entraîner, *v.a.* draw along; carry away; involve, entail; coach.
entraîneur, *s. m.* trainer, coach.
entre, *prep.* between, among; into, in.
entrée, *s. f.* entry, entrance, beginning; free access; duty.
entremets, *s. m.* second course.
entreprendre, *v.a.* attempt, undertake, contract for; worry.
entrepreneur, *s.m.* contractor.
entreprise, *s. f.* undertaking, enterprise.
entrer, *v. n.* enter; come in, go in; get in; get into; *faire* ~ show in.
enveloppe, *s. f.* envelope; wrapper, cover.
envelopper, *v. a.* wrap up, do up; envelop.
envers, *prep.* towards, to.
enviable, *adj.* enviable.
envie, *s. f.* envy; desire.
envier, *v. a.* envy; desire.
environ, *adv. & prep.* about.
environner, *v.a.* surround.
environs, *s. m. pl.* surroundings.
envoi, *s. m.* sending; consignment, shipment.
envoler: s'~ fly away, take wing.
envoyer*, *v.a.* send, dispatch, forward.
envoyeur, *s.m.* sender.
épais, -aisse, *adj.* thick.
épaisseur, *s. f.* thickness.
épargne, *s.f.* savings *(pl.)*.
épargner, *v. a.* save (up).
épaule, *s.f.* shoulder.
épée, *s.f.* sword.
éperon, *s.m.* spur.
épice, *s. f.* spice.

épicerie, *s.f.* grocery, grocer's (shop).
épicier, -ère, *s. m. f.* grocer.
épidémie, *s. f.* epidemic.
épinard, *s.m.* spinach.
épine, *s. f.* thorn; spine, backbone; obstacle.
épingle, *s. f.* pin; ~ *de sûreté* safety-pin.
épisode, *s.m.* episode.
éplucher, *v. a.* peel; pick; sift, preen, thin out.
éponge, *s.f.* sponge.
éponger, *v. a.* sponge; mop (up).
époque, *s. f.* period, age, epoch, time.
épouse, *s.f.* wife.
épouser, *v.a.* marry.
épouvante, *s.f.* fright.
époux, *s. m.* husband.
épreuve, *s. f.* test, trial; proof; print.
éprouver, *v. a.* test, prove; feel; experience.
épuisé, *adj.* exhausted; out of print.
épuiser, *v. a.* exhaust; use up; wear out.
équation, *s.f.* equation.
équilibre, *s.m.* balance, equilibrium.
équipage, *s. m.* suite, retinue; carriage; crew.
équipe, *s. f.* gang, shift; crew, team, side; train.
équipement, *s. m.* equipment.
équiper, *v.a.* equip.
équivalent, *adj.* equivalent.
ère, *s.f.* era.
errant, *adj.* wandering.
errer, *v. n.* stray; err.
erreur, *s. f.* error, mistake.
érudit, *adj.* learned.
érudition, *s.f.* learning.
escalateur, *s. m.* escalator.
escale, *s.f.* port; landing; *sans* ~ non-stop.
escalier, *s. m.* stairs *(pl.)*, staircase; ~ *de sauvetage* fire-escape; ~ *de service* backstairs *(pl.)*; ~ *roulant* escalator.
escargot, *s.m.* snail.
escarpins, *s. m. pl.* pumps.
esclavage, *s.m.* slavery.
esclave, *s. m. f.* slave; — *adj.* slavish.
escrime, *s.f.* fencing; *faire de l'*~ fence.
escrimer, *v.n.* fence.
espace, *s. m.* space; room.
espagnol, -e (E.), *adj.* Spanish; — *s. m. f.* Spaniard; Spanish.
espèce, *s. f.* species, kind.
espérance, *s. f.* hope, expectation.
espérer, *v. a.* hope (for).
espion, -onne, *s.m.f.* spy.
espionnage, *s. m.* espionage, spying.
espoir, *s.m.* hope.
esprit, *s. m.* spirit; mind; character; wit; sense.
esquille, *s.f.* splinter.
esquiver, *v.a.* evade.
essai, *s.m.* trial, test; essay; attempt.
essayer, *v. a.* try, attempt; essay; assay.
essence, *s.f.* essence; petrol.
essentiel, -elle, *adj.* essential.
essieu, *s.m.* axle.
essor, *s.m.* flight.
essoreuse, *s. f.* spin-drier.
essuie-glace, *s. m.* wind-

screen wiper.
essuie-main(s), *s. m. (pl.)* towel; ~ *à rouleau* roller-towel.
essuyer, *v.a.* dust; wipe; dry; mop up.
est, *s.m.* east.
esthétique, *adj.* aesthetic.
estime, *s.f.* esteem.
estimer, *v.a. & n.* estimate, value; esteem, regard; consider.
estomac, *s.m.* stomach.
estrade, *s.f.* platform.
estuaire, *s.m.* estuary.
et, *conj.* and; ~ ...~ both ... and.
étable, *s.f.* cow-shed; ~ *à porcs* pigsty.
établi, *s.m.* (joiner's) bench.
établir, *v.a.* establish, found, settle, set up; build; prove; **s'~** settle (down).
établissement, *s. m.* establishment.
étage, *s. m.* floor, stor(e)y.
étagère, *s. f.* shelf.
étaler, *v.a.* display; spread (out); show off; **s'~** stretch oneself out.
étang, *s.m.* pond.
étape, *s.f.* stage.
état, *s.m.* state; condition; profession, station office; statement; ***homme d'~*** statesman; ***coup d'~*** revolt.
été, *s.m.* summer.
éteindre*, *v. a.* put out, extinguish; turn off; **s'~** be extinguished.
étendre, *v. a.* spread out; stretch out; extend; **s'~** lie down; stretch one-self out.
étendu, *adj.* wide, vast, extensive.
étendue, *s.f.* expanse, reach, range; extent.
éternel, -elle, *adj.* eternal.
éternuement, *s. m.* sneeze.
éternuer, *v.n.* sneeze.
étincelle, *s.f.* spark.
étiquette, *s.f.* ticket, label; etiquette.
étoffe, *s.f.* cloth, material.
étoile, *s.f.* star.
étonnant, *adj.* astonishing, amazing.
étonnement, *s. m.* astonishment, wonder.
étonner, *v.a.* astonish, amaze; **s'~** be astonished.
étouffer, *v.a.* choke.
étrange, *adj.* strange.
étranger, -ère, *adj.* foreign, strange; — *-s.m.f.* foreigner; *à l'~* abroad.
être*, *v.n.* be, exist; *il est...* it is...; ~ *bien* be good-looking; be well; *c'est que* the fact is; ~ *à* belong to; — *s.m.* being.
étreindre*, *v.a.* clasp; press; embrace.
étreinte, *s.f.* embrace.
étrier, *s. m.* stirrup.
étroit, *adj.* narrow, strait; close.
étude, *s. f.* study; chambers *(pl.)*.
étudiant, -e, *s.m.f.* student, undergraduate.
étudier, *v. a.* study, read; practise.
étui, *s.m.* case, box.

étuver, *v.a.* stew, steam.
eucharistie, *s.f.* eucharist.
européen, -enne, *adj.* European.
eux, *pron. m.* they, them.
évader: **s'~** escape; get away.
évaluer, *v. a.* value, estimate.
évangélique, *adj.* evangelical.
évangile, *s.m.* gospel.
évaporer, *v. a.* evaporate; **s'~** evaporate.
éveil, *s. m. en* **~** on the lookout.
éveiller, *v. a.* awaken; **s'~** wake up.
événement, *s.m.* event.
éventail, *s.m.* fan.
éventuel, -elle, *adj.* eventual.
évêque, *s.m.* bishop.
évidemment, *adv.* evidently, obviously.
évidence, *s.f.* evidence.
évident, *adj.* evident, obvious.
éviter, *v. a.* avoid, evade.
évoluer, *v.n.* evolve.
évolution, *s. f.* evolution.
exact, *adj.* exact, accurate.
exactement, *adv.* exactly.
exactitude, *s.f.* exactitude, precision.
exagérer, *v. a.* exaggerate.
examen, *s. m.* exam(ination); test.
examiner, *v. a.* examine; investigate, look into.
excédent, *s.m.* surplus; *~s de bagages* excess luggage.
excéder, *v. a.* exceed, surpass; tire out.
excellence, *s. f.* excellence; excellency.
excellent, *adj.* excellent.
excepté, *adj.* excepted; — *prep.* except(ing), but.
excepter, *v.a.* except.
exception, *s. f.* exception.
exceptionnel, -elle, *adj.* exceptional.
excès, *s. m.* excess.
excessif, -ive, *adj.* excessive.
excitation, *s.f.* excitement.
exciter, *v.a.* excite, stir up; urge on.
exclamation, *s.f.* exclamation.
exclure*, *v.a.* exclude.
exclusif, -ive, *adj.* exclusive.
excursion, *s. f.* excursion.
excursionniste, *s.m.f.* holiday-maker, tourist.
excuse, *s. f.* excuse; apology; *faire des ~s* apologize.
excuser, *v.a.* excuse; pardon; apologize for; **s'~** apologize; ask to be excused; *excusez-moi* I beg your pardon; excuse me.
exécuter, *v.a.* execute, carry out, perform.
exécutif, -ive, *adj.* executive.
exécution, *s. f.* execution.
exemplaire, *s.m.* copy.
exemple, *s. m.* example; *par* **~** for example; *sans* **~** unprecedented.
exempt, *adj.* exempt, free *(de* from).
exemption, *s.f.* exemp-

tion.
exercer, *v.a.* exercise; practise; carry on; **s'~** practise.
exercice, *s.m.* exercise.
exhibition, *s.f.* exhibition; display.
exigence, *s.f.* demand; exigency.
exil, *s.m.* exile.
existence, *s. f.* existence.
exister, *v. n.* exist.
expansif, -ive, *adj.* expansive.
expansion, *s.f.* expansion.
expédient, *s.m.* expedient, device.
expédier, *v.a.* forward, send off.
expéditeur, -trice, *s. m. f.* sender, shipping-agent.
expédition, *s. f.* consignment; expedition, forwarding, dispatch.
expérience, *s. f.* experience; experiment; *faire des ~s* to experiment.
expérimental, *adj.* experimental.
expert, *adj.* expert.
expirer, *v.n.* expire; die.
explication, *s. f.* explanation.
expliquer, *v.n.* explain, account for, show.
exploration, *s. f.* exploration.
explorer, *v.a.* explore.
explosion, *s. f.* explosion.
exportateur, *s.m.* exporter.
exportation, *s. f.* export, exportation.
exporter, *v. a.* export.
exposé, *s.m.* statement.
exposer, *v.a.* expose, show; state; set forth.
exposition, *s. f.* exhibition, display; statement, exposure; exposition.
exprès, *adv.* on purpose.
express, *adj.* express; — *s.m.* express (train).
expression, *s.f.* expression
exprimer, *v.a.* express.
expulser, *v.a.* expel.
expulsion, *s.f.* expulsion.
extension, *s. f.* extension; extent.
exténuer, *v.a.* tire out, exhaust.
extérieur, *s. m.* exterior; outside; *à l'~* outwards — *adj.* outward.
extinction, *s.f.* extinction; quenching.
extraire, *v. a.* extract; draw, pull out.
extraordinaire, *adj.* extraordinary, unusual.
extravagant, *adj.* extravagant.
extrême, *adj.* extreme.
extrêmement, *adv.* extremely, very.
extrémité *s. f.* extremity; last moment.

F

fabricant, *s.m.* manufacturer, maker.
fabrication, *s.f.* manufacture; fabrication.
fabrique, *s.f.* factory, works.
fabriquer, *v.a.* manufacture, make.
façade, *s.f.* front.
face, *s.f.* face; look;

en ~ *de* opposite, in front of.
facétieux, -euse, *adj.* facetious; humorous.
fâché, *adj.* offended.
fâcher, *v. a.* offend; make angry; **se ~** get angry.
facile, *adj.* easy; fluent.
facilité, *s.f.* ease; facility; convenience.
faciliter, *v.a.* facilitate; make easy.
façon, *s. f.* making; fashion, shape; way, manner; *de ~ à* so as to; *de ~ que* so that; *en aucune ~* by no means; *d'une ~ quelconque* somehow.
facteur, *s.m.* factor; postman; porter, carrier; *fig.* circumstance.
faction, *s.f.* faction; sentry, watch.
facture, *s.f.* bill, invoice.
facultatif, -ive, *adj.* optional.
faculté, *s.f.* faculty.
fade, *adj.* flat, insipid.
faible, *adj.* weak; feeble.
faiblesse, *s. f.* weakness.
faiblir, *v. n.* become weak.
faillir, *v. n.* fail, fall short; err; *~ + inf.* nearly; *j'ai failli manquer le train* I nearly missed the train.
faim, *s. f.* hunger; *avoir ~* be hungry.
faire*, *v.a.* make; do; build; cause; *~ allusion* refer to; *~ attention (à)* pay attention (to); *~ une chambre* do a room; *~ le commerce* trade; *~ la cuisine* do the cooking; *~ ses études* study; be at school; *~ la guerre* make war; *~ un lit* make a bed; *~ mal à* hurt; *~ part à* let know; *~ des progrès* make progress; *~ une promenade* take a walk; *~ queue* queue; *~ savoir* let know, inform (of); *~ usage (de)* make use (of); *~ voir* show; *que ~?* what's to be done?; *qu'est-ce que cela fait?* what does it matter?; *n'avoir rien à ~* have nothing to do; *deux et deux font quatre* two and two make four; *~ 70 km. à l'heure* do 70 km. an hour; *il fait du vent* it is windy; *il fait chaud* it is warm; *il fait jour* it is daylight; — **se ~** be made, be done; get used (to).
faisan, *s. m.* pheasant.
fait, *s. m.* fact; *en ~* in fact, after all, as a matter of fact.
falloir*, *v. impers.* be necessary, be required; must, have to, should, ought to; *comme il faut* proper, decent; **s'en ~** be wanting.
fameux, -euse, *adj.* famous.
familier, -ière, *adj.* familiar.
famille, *s. f.* family.
faner, *v.n.* fade.
fantaisie, *s.f.* fancy.

fantastique, *adj.* fantastic.
fardeau, *s.m.* burden.
farine, *s.f.* flour, meal.
fatal, *adj.* mortal, fatal.
fatigant, *adj.* fatiguing.
fatigue, *s.f.* fatigue.
fatigué, *adj.* tired, weary.
fatiguer, *v. a.* tire, weary, fatigue.
faubourg, *s.m.* suburb.
faucher, *v.a.* mow, cut.
faucheuse, *s.f.* ~ *(à moteur)* (lawn-)mower.
faucille, *s. f.* sickle.
faucon, *s.m.* falcon.
faute, *s. f.* mistake, error, fault; lapse; want; *faire* ~ fail.
fauteuil, *s. m.* arm-chair, easy chair; stall, dress-circle seat.
fauve, *s.m.* wild beast.
faux[1], **fausse,** *adj.* false.
faux[2], *s. f.* scythe.
faveur, *s. f.* favour; *en ~ de* in favour of, on behalf of.
favorable, *adj.* favourable.
favori, -ite, *adj.* favorite.
fécond, *adj.* fertile.
féconder, *v.a.* fertilize.
fédéral, *adj.* federal.
fédération, *s.f.* federation.
fédéré, -e, *adj. & s. m. f.* federate.
feindre*, *v. a. & n.* feign.
félicitation, *s.f.* congratulation.
félicité, *s.f.* happiness.
féliciter, *v.a.* congratulate.
féminin, *adj.* feminine.
femme, *s.f.* woman; wife.
fendre, *v. a.* split; rend.
fenêtre, *s. f.* window.
fente, *s. f.* crack, split.
fer, *s. m.* iron; ~ *à cheval* horseshoe.
férié, *adj. jour* ~ holiday.
ferme[1], *adj.* firm; — *adv.* fast; firmly.
ferme[2], *s. f.* farm.
fermé, *adj.* closed.
fermer, *v. a.* close, shut; **se** ~ close, be shut.
fermeté, *s. f.* firmness.
fermeture, *s. f.* shutting; shutter; ~ *éclair* zip fastener, zipper.
fermier, *s. m.* farmer.
féroce, *adj.* wild, cruel.
férocité, *s. f.* ferocity.
ferronnerie, *s.f.* iron-works.
fertile, *adj.* fertile.
fervent, *adj.* fervent.
ferveur, *s. f.* fervour.
fesse, *s.f.* buttock.
festin, *s.m.* feast.
fête, *s. f.* feast, holiday; birthday.
fêter, *v. a.* observe; celebrate.
fêteur, -euse, *s. m. f.* holiday-maker.
feu, *s. m.* fire, flame; light; *mettre le ~ à* set on fire; *prendre ~* take fire; ~ *d'artifice* fire-works *(pl.)*; ~*x de circulation* traffic lights; ~*x d'arrière* tail lights.
feuillage, *s.m.* foliage.
feuille, *s.f.* leaf; sheet.
février, *s.m.* February.
fiancé, -e, *s. m. f.* fiancé, -e.
fiancer, *v.a.* engage; **se**

~ be engaged.
fibre, *s. f.* fibre.
ficelle, *s. f.* string.
fiche, *s. f.* pin, peg; slip (of paper).
ficher, *v. a.* drive in, fix; do, work; deal (a blow).
fidèle, *adj.* faithful.
fidélité, *s. f.* fidelity.
fier: se ~ trust, count on.
fierté, *s. f.* pride.
fièvre, *s. f.* fever.
figue, *s. f.* fig.
figure, *s. f.* form, shape; face; figure.
figurer, *v.a.* figure, represent; se ~ imagine.
fil, *s.m.* thread, yarn; edge; clue; ~ *(de fer)* wire.
file, *s. f.* row, file, line.
filer, *v.a.* & *n.* spin.
filet, *s.m.* net; fillet; rack.
fille, *s. f.* daughter; girl; maid; *jeune* ~ young lady.
fillette, *s.f.* little girl.
filleul, -e, *s. m. f.* godson, god-daughter.
film, *s. m.* film; *le grand* ~ feature film; ~ *avec* film featuring ... ; ~ *annonce* trailer.
fils, *s. m.* son.
fin[1], *s.f.* end; close; *à la* ~ in the end, finally; *mettre* ~ *à* put an end to; *tirer à sa* ~ come to an end; ~ *de semaine* week-end.
fin[2], *adj.* fine; nice.
final, *adj.* final.
finance, *s. f.* finance.
financier, *adj.* financial.
fini, *adj.* finished; ended; over.
finir, *v. a.* & *n.* end, finish, put an end to; eat up.
finlandais, -e (F.), *adj.* Finnish; — *s. m. f.* Finn; Finnish.
fixe, *adj.* fixed, firm.
fixer, *v.a.* fix, fasten; stare at; settle.
flacon, *s. m.* flagon, bottle.
flagrant, *adj.* flagrant.
flairer, *v. a.* smell, scent.
flambeau, *s. m.* torch.
flamboyer, *v.n.* flame, flare.
flamme, *s.f.* flame.
flanelle, *s. f* flannel.
flanquer, *v.a.* fling.
flatter, *v. a.* caress; flatter.
flatterie, *s.f.* flattery.
flèche. *s. f.* arrow.
fléchir, *v. a.* bend, bow; *fig.* move.
fleur, *s. f.* flower, blossom.
fleurir, *v.n.* flower, blossom.
fleuve, *s. m.* river.
flirter, *v. n.* flirt.
flocon, *s. m.* flake *(snow etc.).*
flot, *s. m.* wave; flood; *être à* ~ be floating.
flottant, *adj.* floating.
flotte, *s.f.* fleet; navy.
flotter, *v.n.* & *a.* float.
fluide, *s. m.* & *adj.* fluid.
flute, *s. f.* flute.
foi, *s.f.* faith, belief; credit.
foie, *s. m.* liver.
foin, *s.m.* hay; grass.
foire, *s.f.* fair, market.
fois, *s.f.* time; *une* ~ once; *encore une* ~ again; *deux* ~ twice; *à la* ~ at same time;

chaque ~ every time.
folie, *s. f.* folly, madness.
folle *see* **fou.**
foncer, *v. a.* sink; darken, deepen.
fonction, *s.f.* function, duty.
fonctionnaire, *s.m.f.* functionary, official.
fonctionner, *v.n.* function, operate, work.
fond, *s. m.* bottom, ground, foundation; *a* ~ thoroughly.
fondamental, *adj.* fundamental, basic.
forcer, *v. a.* force; break open; compel, impel.
forêt, *s. f.* forest.
forger, *v. a.* forge.
formalité, *s. f.* formality.
forme, *s. f.* form, shape.
formel, -elle, *adj.* formal, express; flat.
former, *v. a.* form, shape.
formidable, *adj.* formidable, terrible.
formule, *s.f.* formula.
formuler, *v. a.* formulate, draw up.
fort, *adj.* strong, robust; fat; stout, stiff; skilful; heavy; *être* ~ *en* be well up in; — *adv.* very (much), highly, hard; ~ *bien* very well; — *s. m.* strong man; stronghold.
forteresse, *s.f.* fortress.
fortification, *s. f.* fortification.
fortifier, *v. a.* strengthen, fortify.
fortune, *s.f.* fortune; chance; luck; wealth, property.
fou, fol, folle, *adj.* mad, foolish; crazy.
foudre, *s.f.* lightning, thunderbolt.
fouille, *s. f.* excavation.
fouiller, *v. a.* & *n.* dig, excavate.
fouillis, *s.m.* muddle, mess.
foule, *s. f.* crowd, mass.
four, *s. m.* oven, furnace.
fourchette, *s.f.* fork *(table)*.
fourgon, *s. m.* (delivery) van; wagon; ~ *(aux bagages)* luggage-van.
fourmi, *s.f.* ant.
fourneau, *s.m.* stove, range; ~ *à gaz* gas-ring, -stove; ~ *électrique* electric cooker.
fourniment, *s.m.* outfit, kit.
fournir, *v.a.* furnish (with), supply; provide (with).
fourreau, *s.m.* sheath, case, scabbard.
fourreur, *s.m.* furrier.
fourrure, *s.f.* fur.
foyer, *s.m.* fireside, home; foyer, lounge.
fracas, *s.m.* crash; uproar; fuss; noise.
fracasser, *v.a.* shatter, smash.
fraction, *s.f.* fraction; portion; instalment.
fracture, *s.f.* fracture.
fragile, *adj.* fragile.
frais[1]**, fraîche,** *adj.* fresh, cool; chilly.
frais[2]**,** *s. m. pl.* expenses, charges, fees.
fraise, *s.f.* strawberry.
framboise, *s. f.* raspberry.
franc, franche, *adj.* frank,

free, open.
français (F.), *adj.* French; — *s. m.* Frenchman; French (language).
Française, *s.f.* Frenchwoman.
franchir, *v.a.* clear, jump over, cross.
franchise, *s. f.* exemption; frankness.
frapper, *v.a.* strike, hit, knock; impress; surprise.
frein, *s. m.* bit (of bridle); brake; *fig.* check.
frêle, *adj.* weak, frail.
fréquent, *adj.* frequent.
frère, *s.m.* brother.
fricassée, *s.f.* fricassee.
friction, *s.f.* friction.
frigidaire, *s.m.* refrigerator.
frigo, *s.m.* fridge.
frileux, -euse, *adj.* chilly.
frire*, *v.n.* & *a.* fry.
friser, *v.a.* & *n.* curl.
frissonner, *v. n.* shiver, tremble.
frivole, *adj.* frivolous, flimsy.
froid, *s. m.* cold; *avoir* ~ feel cold; — *adj.* cold, cool; *il fait froid* it is cold.
froisser, *v.a.* rumple, crumple; bruise; *fig.* offend, hurt; **se** ~ take offence.
frôler, *v.a.* graze.
fromage, *s.m.* cheese.
front, *s.m.* forehead; face; front (part).
frontière, *s.f.* frontier, border.
frotter, *v. a.* rub.
fruit, *s.m.* fruit; produce.
fruitier, *s.m.* fruiterer, greengrocer.
fuir*, *v. n.* & *a.* run away, flee.
fuite, *s. f.* flight; leakage, leak.
fumée, *s.f.* smoke.
fumer, *v. a.* & *n.* smoke.
fumeur, -euse *s.m.f.* smoker.
fumier, *s.m.* dung.
funèbre, *adj.* funereal.
funérailles, *s.f.pl.* funeral.
funiculaire, *s.m.* rope railway.
fureur, *s.f.* fury, rage.
furie, *s. f.* fury.
furieux, -euse, *adj.* furious.
furoncle, *s.m.* boil, furuncle.
fusée, *s.f.* fuse; rocket.
fusil, *s.m.* gun.
fusillade, *s.f.* firing, shooting.
futur, *adj.* & *s. m.* future.
fuyant, *adj.* flying, fleeing; passing.

G

gâchis, *s.m.* mortar; mire; *fig.* muddle, mess.
gaffe, *s. f.* blunder.
gage, *s. m.* pledge; security; ~*s* wages.
gagner, *v. a.* gain; win.
gai, *adj.* gay, cheerful.
gaieté, *s.f.* gaiety.
gain, *s.m.* gain, profit.
galant, *adj.* courteous.
galerie, *s. f.* gallery.
galop, *s. m.* gallop.

gamin, *s.m.* urchin.
gamme, *s. f.* scale; range.
gant, *s. m.* glove.
garage, *s.m.* garage; siding.
garantie, *s. f.* guarantee.
garantir, *v. a.* guarantee.
garçon, *s. m.* boy; young man; fellow; bachelor; waiter.
garde[1], *s. f.* guard; watch; police; nurse.
garde[2], *s.m.* warden, guardian; watch.
garde-bébé, *s. m.* baby-sitter, sitter-in.
garde-boue, *s.f.* mud-guard.
garde-chasse, *s. m.* game-keeper.
garder, *v.a.* keep, take care of; attend (to).
garde-robe, *s.f.* wardrobe.
gardien, **-enne**, *s.m.f.* guardian, keeper; warden; watch(man); *~ de la paix* constable; *~ (de but)* goalkeeper.
gare, *s. f.* station; depot; *~ des marchandises* goods station; *aller recevoir qn à la ~* meet sy at the station.
garni, *s.m.* furnished lodgings *(pl.)*, digs.
garnir, *v. a.* furnish; fit up, trim.
garnison, *s. f.* garrison.
garniture, *s.f.* fittings *(pl.)*; set; garnishing.
gâteau, *s. m.* cake.
gâter, *v. a.* waste, impair; spoil.
gauche, *adj.* left.
gaz, *s. m.* gas; *usine à ~* gas-works.
gazon, *s. m.* grass; lawn.
géant, *s. m.* giant.
gelée, *s. f.* jelly.
gémir, *v. n.* groan.
gênant, *adj.* inconvenient, annoying.
gendre, *s. m.* son-in-law.
gêne, *s. f.* inconvenience; trouble; *être dans la ~* be hard-up.
gêné, *adj.* uneasy; stiff; embarrassed.
gêner, *v.n.* inconvenience; be in the way of; interfere with.
général, *adj. & s. m.* general; *en ~* in general, generally.
généraliser, *v.a. & n.* generalize.
générateur, *s.m.* generator.
génération, *s.f.* generation.
généreux, **-euse**, *adj.* generous.
générosité, *s.f.* generosity.
génie, *s. m.* genius; corps of engineers.
genou, *s.m.* *(pl.* **-x)** knee; *(pl.)* lap; *se mettre à ~s* kneel down.
genre, *s. m.* genus, kind.
gens, *s.m. f.* people; attendants.
gentil, **-ille**, *adj.* gentle.
géographie, *s.f.* geography.
géographique, *adj.* geographic(al).
géologie, *s. f.* geology.
géométrie, *s. f.* geometry.
géométrique, *adj.* geometric(al).

gérant, -e, *s. m. f.* manager; manageress.
gérer, *v. a.* manage.
germanique, *adj.* Germanic.
germe, *s.m.* germ.
gésir*, *v.n.* lie.
geste, *s.m.* gesture.
gesticuler, *v. n.* gesticulate.
gibier, *s. m.* game.
gifle, *s. f.* slap, box on the ear.
gifler, *v. a.* give s.o. a slap (in the face).
gilet, *s.m.* waistcoat, vest.
girafe, *s. f.* giraffe.
glace, *s. f.* ice; ice-cream; mirror; *mer de ~* glacier.
glacer, *v. a.* freeze, chill.
glacial, *adj.* icy, glacial.
glacier, *s. m.* glacier.
glissade, *s. f.* slide; slip.
glissant, *adj.* slippery.
glisser, *v.n.* slide; slip; glide over; **se ~** slip, creep (into).
globe, *s. m.* globe; earth.
gloire, *s. f.* glory, fame.
glorieux, -euse, *adj.* glorious; proud.
gober, *v.a.* swallow.
golfe, *s. m.* gulf.
gomme, *s. f.* gum; india-rubber.
gommer, *v. a.* gum.
gonfler, *v.a.* inflate.
gorge, *s.f.* throat, gullet.
gorgée, *s. f.* gulp.
gosse, *s.m.* kid, brat.
gothique, *adj.* Gothic.
goudron, *s. m.* tar.
gourmand, *adj.* greedy.
goût, *s. m.* taste; savour.
goûter, *v. a.* taste; relish, enjoy; — *s.m.* tea *(meal)*.
goutte, *s. f.* drop.
gouvernail, *s. m.* rudder, helm.
gouvernante *s. f.* governess.
gouvernement, *s.m.* government.
gouverner, *v. a.* govern, control, rule; manage; steer.
gouverneur, *s. m.* governor; tutor, preceptor.
grâce, *s. f.* grace; pardon; thanks *(pl.)*; favour.
gracieux, -euse, *adj.* graceful; gracious.
grade, *s. m.* rank, grade.
grain, *s. m.* grain, berry, corn; a touch (of).
graine, *s. f.* seed, berry.
graissage, *s. m.* lubrication.
graisse, *s. f.* fat, grease, lard.
graisser, *v.a.* grease, lubricate.
grammaire, *s. f.* grammar.
grammatical, *adj.* grammatical.
gramme, *s. m.* gramme.
gramophone, *s. m.* gramophone.
grand, *adj.* great; large; big; tall; grand.
grandeur, *s.f.* size; length; breadth; greatness.
grandir, *v.n.* grow (up); grow big, tall.
grand'mère, *s. f.* grandmother.
grand-père, *s. m.* grandfather.

granit, *s. m.* granite.
grappe, *s. f.* bunch; ~ *de raisin* bunch of grapes.
gras, grasse, *adj.* fat; thick.
gratitude, *s.f.* gratitude.
gratter, *v. a. & n.* scratch, overtake; brush.
gratuit, *adj.* free (of charge).
grave, *adj.* grave; heavy.
graver, *v.a.* engrave.
gravure, *s.f.* engraving.
grec, grecque (G.), *adj. & s. m. f.* Greek.
grêle, *adj.* slender, delicate, slim.
grelotter, *v.n.* shiver.
grenier, *s. m.* loft; granary.
grenouille, *s. f.* frog.
grève, *s. f.* strike; beach.
grief, *s. m.* grievance.
griffe, *s. f.* claw; clutch.
grill, *s. m.* grill, gridiron.
grille, *s. f.* iron railing, grating.
griller, *v.a.* grill, toast.
grimace, *s.f.* grimace.
grimacer, *v.n.* grimace.
grimper, *v. n. & n.* climb.
grincer, *v. n. & a.* grind, grate; creak.
grippe, *s.f.* influenza.
gris, *adj.* gray.
grogner, *v.n.* groan; grunt, grumble.
gronder, *v. n.* roar; rumble; *v.a.* scold.
gros, grosse, *adj.* large, big; stout; great; thick: — *s. m.* bulk; wholesale; *en* ~ roughly; wholesale.
grossier, *adj.* coarse, gross.
grossir, *v. a.* make bigger; increase; *v. n.* grow bigger.
grotesque, *adj.* grotesque.
groupe, *s.m.* group.
grouper, *v.a.* group.
grue, *s.f.* crane.
gué, *s. m.* ford (*across river*).
guêpe, *s. f.* wasp.
guérir, *v.a.* cure, heal; *v. n.* & **se** ~ be cured, get well again.
guerre, *s. f.* war.
gueule, *s. f.* mouth, jaws (*pl.*); opening.
guichet, *s.m.* ticket window; counter; booking-office.
guide, *s. m.* guide; conductor; guide-book.
guider, *v. a.* guide, lead.
guillemets, *s. m. pl.* inverted commas.
guise, *s. f.* way, manner; *à votre* ~ as you like.
guitare, *s. f.* guitar.
gymnastique, *s. f.* gymnastics.

H

habile, *adj.* able, clever.
habileté, *s. f.* skill, cleverness; ability.
habiller, *v. a.* clothe; dress (up); **s'**~ dress, put on one's clothes.
habit, *s. m.* (dress-)suit; coat; ~*s* clothes.
habitant, -e, *s.m.f.* inhabitant.
habitation, *s. f.* habitation, dwelling.

habiter, *v. a. & n.* inhabit, live in, dwell in.
habitude, *s. f.* habit, use.
habituel, -elle, *adj.* habitual, usual.
habituer, *v. a.* accustom; **s'~** *à* get accustomed to, get used to.
hache, *s. f.* axe.
hacher, *v.a.* chop, cut up, hack, mince.
hachis, *s. m.* hash.
haine, *s. f.* hate, hatred.
haïr*, *v.a.* hate.
haleine, *s. f.* breath.
hall, *s. m.* lounge; *~ de montage* erecting shop.
halle, *s.f.* market-hall.
hanche, *s.f.* haunch, hip.
hangar, *s. m.* shed, hangar.
happer, *v.a.* snap up.
harasser, *v.a.* harass.
hardi, *adj.* bold, daring.
hareng, *s.m.* herring.
haricot, *s.m.* bean; *~s verts* French-beans.
harmonie, *s. f.* harmony.
harmonieux, -euse, *adj.* harmonious.
harnais, *s.m.* harness.
harpe, *s.f.* harp.
hasard, *s. m.* hazard, risk; *par ~* by chance.
hasarder, *v.a.* hazard, risk, stake.
hasardeux, -euse, *adj.* risky; unsafe.
hâte, *s. f.* haste, hurry, rush; *à la ~* in a hurry.
hâter, *v. a.* hasten, urge on; **se ~** hurry (up).
hausse, *s. f.* rise.
hausser, *v. a. & n.* raise, lift; **se ~** rise.
haut, *adj.* high; elevated; upright; loud; upper; *terre ~e* highland; *à voix ~e* aloud. — *adv.* high, highly, up; aloud; *en ~* at the top; upstairs; — *s. m.* top, height, summit.
hauteur, *s.f.* height, altitude.
haut-parleur, *s. m.* loudspeaker.
havresac, *s.m.* haversack, knapsack.
hebdomadaire, *adj. & s. m.* weekly.
hébreu (H.), *adj. & s. m.* Hebrew.
hectare, *s.m.* hectare.
hélice, *s.f.* air-screw, propeller.
hélicoptère, *s.m.* helicopter.
herbe, *s.f.* herb, grass; pot-herb.
herbeux, -euse, *adj.* grassy.
hérédité, *s.f.* heredity.
hérisser, *v.a.* bristle; ruffle; se ~ bristle up, stand on end.
hérisson, *s. m.* hedgehog.
héritage, *s. m.* inheritance, heritage.
hériter, *v.a. & n.* inherit.
héritier, *s.m.* heir.
héritière, *s.f.* heiress.
heroïne, *s.f.* heroine.
héros, *s. m.* hero.
hésitation, *s.f.* hesitation.
hésiter, *v.n.* hesitate.
heure, *s. f.* hour, time; *quelle ~ est-il?* what time is it?; *il est dix ~s*

moins le quart it's a quarter to ten; *dix ~s* ten o'clock; *dix ~s et quart* a quarter past ten; *dix ~s et demie* half past ten; *de bonne ~* early; *~s de pointe* rush hours; *~s d'ouverture* business hours; *~s supplémentaires* overtime.

heureux, -euse, *adj.* happy, fortunate, successful.

heurter, *v. a. & n.* knock against, hit, run into, against; se ~ run, hit, dash against, collide.

hibou, *s. m. (pl.* **-x)** owl.

hideux, -euse, *adj.* hideous, terrible.

hier, *adv.* yesterday; *~ soir* last night.

hirondelle, *s. f.* swallow.

histoire, *s. f.* (hi)story,

historique, *adj.* historic.

hiver, *s.m.* winter.

hollandais, -e (H.), *adj. & s. m. f.* Dutch(man), Dutch-woman.

homard, *s.m.* lobster.

homme, *s.m.* man; *~ d'affaires* business man; *~ d'état* statesman.

hongrois, -e, (H.), *adj. & s.m.f.* Hungarian.

honnête, *adj.* honest.

honnêteté, *s. f.* honesty.

honneur, *s.m.* honour; credit.

honorable, *adj.* honourable.

honoraires, *s. m. pl.* fee(s).

honorer, *v.a.* honour.

honte, *s.f.* shame; *avoir ~ de* be ashamed of.

honteux, -euse, *adj.* shameful, disgraceful.

hôpital, *s. m. (pl.* **-aux)** hospital.

hoquet, *s.m.* hiccup.

horaire, *s.m.* time-table.

horizon, *s.m.* horizon.

horizontal, *adj.* horizontal.

horloge, *s.f.* clock.

horloger, *s.m.* watchmaker.

horreur, *s.f.* horror.

horrible, *adj.* horrible.

hors, *adv.* out, outside; — *prep.* out of, outside.

hospitalité, *s. f.* hospitality.

hostie, *s.f.* wafer *(Church).*

hostile, *adj.* hostile.

hostilité, *s.f.* hostility.

hôte, *s.m.* host; guest.

hôtel, *s.m.* hotel; large house; *~ de ville* town-hall.

hôtesse, *s. f.* hostess; *~ de l'air* air-hostess.

houe, *s. f.* hoe.

houillère, *s.f.* colliery.

hublot, *s.m.* window.

huile, *s. f.* oil.

huissier, *s. m.* usher.

huit, *adj. & s. m.* eight.

huitième, *adj.* eighth.

huître, *s. f.* oyster.

humain, *adj.* human.

humanité, *s. f.* humanity.

humble, *adj.* humble.

humecter, *v.a.* wet.

humer, *v. a.* inhale, suck in.

humide, *adj.* humid, wet.

humidité, *s. f.* humidity.

humiliation, *s. f.* humiliation.

humilier, *v. a.* humiliate.

humilité, *s. f.* humility.

humoristique, *adj.* humor-

ous.
humour, *s. m.* humour.
hurlement, *s. m.* howl(ing), roar(ing).
hurler, *v.n.* howl, roar.
hutte, *s.f.* hut, cabin.
hydrogène, *s. m.* hydrogen.
hygiène, *s. f.* hygiene.
hymne, *s. m.* hymn.
hypocrite, *s. m. f.* hypocrite; — *adj.* hypocritical.
hypothèse, *s. f.* supposition; hypothesis.
hystérique, *adj.* hysterical.

I

ici, *adv.* here; *d'~* from here; *par ~* this way.
idéal, -e, *adj.* ideal.
idéalisme, *s. m.* idealism.
idéaliste, *s. m. f.* idealist.
idée, *s. f.* idea, notion; *il m'est venu à l'~* it occurred to me.
identique, *adj.* identical.
identité, *s.f.* identity.
idiome, *s. m.* language, dialect.
idiot, *adj.* idiotic; — *s. m.* idiot.
idiotisme, *s. m.* idiom.
ignition, *s. f.* ignition.
ignorance, *s. f.* ignorance.
ignorant, *adj.* ignorant.
ignorer, *v.a.* not know, be ignorant of, be unaware of.
il, elle, *pron.* *(pl.* **ils, elles)** he, she, it; they; there.
île, *s. f.* island.
illégal, *adj.* illegal.
illicite, *adj.* illicit, unlawful.
illumination, *s. f.* illumination; *~ par projecteurs* flood-lighting.
illuminer, *v. a.* illuminate, light up; *~ par projecteurs* flood-light.
illusion, *s.f.* illusion, delusion.
illustration, *s. f.* illustration.
illustrer, *v.a.* illustrate, explain.
image, *s. f.* image, picture, likeness.
imagé, *adj.* vivid.
imaginaire, *adj.* imaginary, fantastic.
imaginatif, -ive, *adj.* imaginative.
imagination, *s. f.* imagination, fancy.
imaginer, *v.a.* **s'~** imagine.
imbécile, *s.m. f.* fool, idiot; — *adj.* foolish.
imitation, *s.f.* imitation, copy.
imiter, *v. a.* imitate, copy.
immédiat, *adj.* immediate.
immense, *adj.* immense.
immeuble, *s. m.* real estate, landed property.
immigrant, -e, *adj.* & *s. m. f.* immigrant.
immigration, *s.f.* immigration.
immigrer, *v. a.* immigrate.
immobile, *adj.* immobile.
immoral, *adj.* immoral.
immortel, -elle, *adj.* immortal.
imparfait, *adj.* & *s. m.* imperfect.
impartial, *adj.* impartial.

impatience, *s. f.* impatience.
impatient, *adj.* impatient.
impayé, *adj.* unpaid.
impératif, -ive, *adj.* & *s. m.* imperative.
impératrice, *s. f.* empress.
imperfection, *s.f.* imperfection.
impérial, *adj.* imperial.
impérialisme, *s.m.* imperialism.
imperméable, *adj.* impermeable; waterproof.
impertinent, *adj.* impertinent.
impétueux, -euse, *adj.* impetuous, headlong.
impliquer, *v. a.* implicate, involve, imply.
implorer, *v.a.* implore, beg.
impoli, *adj.* impolite.
impopulaire, *adj.* unpopular.
importance, *s.f.* importance.
important, *adj.* important.
importateur, -trice, *s. m. f.* importer.
importation, *s.f.* importation; ~s imports.
importer, *v.n.* matter, be of moment; *n'importe* it does not matter.
importun, *adj.* troublesome, importunate.
importuner, *v.a.* annoy, molest, worry.
imposer, *v.a.* impose, inflict, lay (on); levy.
impossible, *adj.* impossible.
impôt, *s. m.* tax, duty.
impression, *s. f.* impression; print, edition; *faute d'~* misprint.
impressionner, *v. a.* impress, affect.
imprimé, *s.m.* printed matter.
imprimer, *v. a.* (im)print, impress; publish.
imprimerie, *s. f.* printing; printing office.
impropre, *adj.* unfit, improper.
imprudent, *adj.* imprudent.
impuissant, *adj.* powerless, ineffectual, helpless.
impulsion, *s. f.* spur, impulse.
inaccoutumé, *adj.* unaccustomed.
inachevé, *adj.* unfinished.
inanimé, *adj.* inanimate.
inapplicable, *adj.* inapplicable, irrelevant.
inattendu, *adj.* unexpected.
inattentif, -ive, *adj.* inattentive, heedless.
incapable, *adj.* incapable, unable, inefficient.
incendie, *s. m.* fire.
incendier, *v. a.* set fire to.
incertain, *adj.* uncertain.
incessant, *adj.* incessant.
incident, *s. m.* incident; — *adj.* incidental.
inciter, *v.a.* incite, urge.
inclinaison, *s. f.* inclination, gradient.
inclination, *s. f.* inclination; bent; love.
incliner, *v. a.* & *n.* incline, bend; slope; slant; s'~ bow down bend.

inclusif, -ive *adj.* inclusive.
incommode, *adj.* inconvenient, uncomfortable.
incommoder, *v.a.* inconvenience, annoy.
incomparable, *adj.* incomparable.
incompatible, *adj.* incompatible.
incompétent, *adj.* incompetent.
incomplet, *adj.* incomplete, imperfect.
inconscient, *adj.* unconscious.
inconséquent, *adj.* inconsistent.
inconvenant, *adj.* improper, unsuitable.
inconvénient, *s.m.* inconvenience.
incorrect, *adj.* incorrect.
incroyable, *adj.* incredible.
incurable, *adj.* incurable.
indécis, *adj.* uncertain.
indécision, *s. f.* indecision.
indéfini, *adj.* indefinite, undefined.
indépendance, *s.f.* independence.
index, *s.m.* forefinger, index.
indicateur, *s. m.* indicator, gauge; time-table.
indication, *s. f.* indication; direction; sign.
indice, *s. m.* sign, token, mark; index.
indien, -enne (I.), *adj. & s.m.f.* Indian.
indifférent, *adj.* indifferent.
indigestion, *s. f.* indigestion.
indignation, *s. f.* indignation.
indiquer, *v.a.* indicate, point out, show.
indirect, *adj.* indirect.
indiscret, -ète, *adj.* indiscreet.
indiscrétion, *s. f.* indiscretion.
indispensable, *adj.* indispensable, essential.
indisposé, *adj.* unwell; upset.
individu, *s. m.* individual, person.
individuel, -elle, *adj.* individual.
indulgence, *s. f.* indulgence.
indulgent, *adj.* indulgent.
industrie, *s. f.* industry.
industriel, -elle, *adj.* industrial; — *s. m.* manufacturer.
inefficace, *adj.* inefficient.
inégal, *adj.* unequal.
inégalité, *s. f.* inequality.
inerte, *adj.* inert; dull.
inévitable, *adj.* inevitable.
inexpérimenté, *adj.* inexperienced.
inexplicable, *adj.* inexplicable.
infâme, *adj.* infamous.
infanterie, *s. f.* infantry.
infection, *s. f.* infection.
inférieur, *adj.* inferior.
infinitif, *s. m.* infinitive.
infirmerie, *s. f.* infirmary.
infirmier, -ère, *s. m. f.* nurse.
influence, *s. f.* influence.
influencer, *v. a.* influence.
information, *s. f.* information.

informer, *v. a.* inform, let know; s'~ *de* inquire about.
infructueux, -euse, *adj.* unsuccessful.
ingénieur, *s. m.* engineer.
ingénieux, -euse, *adj.* ingenious.
ingéniosité, *s. f.* ingenuity.
ingrat, *adj.* ungrateful.
ingrédient, *s. m.* ingredient.
inhabité, *adj.* uninhabited.
inintéressant, *adj.* uninteresting.
initial, -e, *adj.* & *s. f.* initial.
initiative, *s. f.* initiative; *syndicat d'*~ tourist office.
injection, *s. f.* injection.
injure, *s.f.* injury.
injurier, *v.a.* insult.
injurieux, -euse, *adj.* injurious.
injuste, *adj.* unjust.
injustice, *s. f.* injustice.
innocence, *s. f.* innocence.
innocent, *adj.* innocent.
innombrable, *adj.* innumerable, countless.
inoccupé, *adj.* unoccupied.
inoculer, *v.a.* inoculate.
inondation, *s. f.* flood.
inonder, *v. a.* flood.
inquiet, -ète, *adj.* anxious, restless, uneasy.
inquiéter, *v.a.* worry.
insecte, *s.m.* insect.
insensé, *adj.* insane, mad.
insensible, *adj.* insensible.
inséparable, *ad.j* inseparable.
insigne, *s. m.* badge.
insignifiant, *adj.* insignificant.
insipide, *adj.* dull, flat.
insister, *v. a.* insist, lay stress on.
insolence, *s. f.* insolence.
insolent, *adj.* insolent.
insouciant, *adj.* careless.
inspecter, *v.a.* inspect, survey.
inspiration, *s. f.* inspiration.
inspirer, *v.a.* inspire, suggest; inhale.
installation, *s. f.* installation; fitting up.
installer, *v.a.* install; fit up; *v.n.* s'~ to settle down.
instant, *adj.* instant, pressing; — *s.m.* instant, moment; *à l'*~ instantly, at once.
instantané, *s.m.* snap(shot).
instinct, *s. m.* instinct.
instituer, *v.a.* institute.
institut, *s.m.* institute.
institution, *s. f.* institution; boarding-school.
instruction, *s. f.* instruction, tuition; knowledge, learning; direction; inquiry.
instruire*, *v.a.* instruct, teach.
instrument, *s. m.* instrument, implement, tool.
instrumental, *adj.* instrumental.
insuffisance, *s. f.* insufficiency.
insuffisant, *adj.* insufficient, deficient.
insulte, *s. f.* insult.
insulter, *v. a.* & *n.* insult.

insupportable, *adj.* intolerable, unbearable.
intact, *adj.* intact, entire.
intégral, *adj.* integral.
intégrité, *s.f.* integrity.
intellectuel, -elle, *adj.* & *s.m.* intellectual.
intelligence, *s. f.* intelligence, understanding.
intelligent, *adj.* intelligent, clever.
intendant, *s. m.* manager.
intense, *adj.* intense.
intensité, *s. f.* intensity.
intention, *s. f.* intention, purpose; *avoir l'~* intend, mean.
interdire, *v. a.* forbid.
intéressant, *adj.* interesting; *peu* ~ uninteresting.
intéressé, *adj.* interested, concerned.
intéresser, *v. a.* & *n.* interest; concern; **s'~ take** an interest (*à* in); **be** concerned.
intérêt, *s.m.* interest; concern; share; *avoir ~ à* have an interest in.
intérieur, *s.m.* inside, interior; *à l'~* inside, indoors; *Ministre de l'Intérieur* Home Secretary.
intermédiaire, *adj.* intermediate; — *s. m. f.* intermediary.
international, *adj.* international.
interne, *adj.* internal, inward.
interpellation, *s. f.* interpellation.
interpeller, *v. a.* interpellate, question.
interposer, *v. a.* interpose.
interprétation, *s. f.* interpretation.
interprète, *s. m. f.* interpreter.
interpréter, *v.a.* interpret; render.
interrogation, *s. f.* interrogation; inquiry.
interrogatoire, *s.m.* (cross-)examination.
interroger, *v.a.* interrogate, cross-examine, question.
interrompre, *v.a.* interrupt.
interrupteur, *s. m.* interrupter; switch.
interruption, *s. f.* interruption.
intervalle, *s.m.* interval; *dans l'~* in the meantime.
intervenir, *v.n.* intervene, interfere, go between.
intervention, *s. f.* intervention.
interview, *s. f. m.* interview.
intime, *adj.* intimate.
intimité, *s.f.* intimacy.
intolérable, *adj.* intolerable.
intrigue, *s.f.* intrigue.
intriguer, *v.n.* & *n.* intrigue.
introduction, *s. f.* introduction.
introduire, *v.a.* introduce; show in.
inutile, *adj.* useless.
invalide, *adj.* invalid, dis-

abled.
invasion, *s. f.* invasion.
inventer, *v.a.* make up.
inventeur, *s. m.* inventor.
invention, *s. f.* invention.
investigation, *s. f.* investigation, inquiry.
invisible, *adj.* invisible.
invitation, *s.f.* invitation.
invité, -e, *s. m. f.* guest.
inviter, *v. a.* invite.
iris, *s. m.* iris.
irlandais (I.), *adj.* Irish; — *s. m.* Irishman.
ironie, *s. f.* irony.
ironique, *adj.* ironical.
irradier, *v. a.* (ir)radiate.
irréel, *adj.* unreal.
irrésistible, *adj.* irresistible.
irritation, *s. f.* irritation.
irriter, *v.a.* irritate.
isolement, *s. m.* isolation.
isoler, *v.a.* isolate.
isotope, *s.m.* isotope.
issue, *s. f.* issue, outlet, way out.
italien, -enne (I.), *adj. & s. m. f.* Italian.
itinéraire, *adj.* itinerary; — *s.m.* guide-book.
ivre, *adj.* drunk.

J

j' *see* **je.**
jadis, *adv.* once, long ago, formerly.
jalousie, *s.f.* jealousy; blind.
jaloux, -se, *adj.* jealous.
jamais, *adv.* never, ever.
jambe, *s. f.* leg, shank.
jambon, *s. m.* ham.
janvier, *s. m.* January.
japonais, -e (J.), *adj. & s. m. f.* Japanese.
jardin, *s. m.* garden.
jardinier, -ère, *s. m. f.* gardener.
jarre, *s. f.* jar.
jarretière, *s. f.* garter.
jauge, *s. f.* gauge.
jauger, *v. a.* gauge.
jaune, *adj.* yellow; — *s. m.* yolk.
je, j', *pron.* I.
jersey, *s. m.* jersey.
jet, *s.m.* throw(ing).
jeter, *v.a.* throw, throw away, down; cast, fling; shoot; discharge; **se ~** rush.
jeton, *s. m.* counter.
jeu, *s.m.* game, play, set.
jeudi, *s. m.* Thursday.
jeune, *adj.* young.
jeûne, *s.m.* fast(ing).
jeûner, *v.n.* fast.
jeunesse, *s. f.* youth.
joie, *s. f.* joy, delight
joindre*, *v. a. & n.* join, unite; **se ~** join.
joint, *s. m.* joint, articulation.
jointure, *s. f.* joint.
joli, *adj.* pretty, nice.
jonction, *s. f.* junction.
jongleur, *s. m.* juggler.
joue, *s. f.* cheek *(face)*.
jouer, *v. a. & n.* play; gambol; gamble.
jouet, *s. m.* toy.
joueur, -euse, *s. m. f.* player; gambler.
joug, *s. m.* yoke.

jouir, *v.n.* (~ *de*) enjoy.
jouissance, *s.f.* enjoyment, pleasure, joy.
jour, *s. m.* day; daylight, light; life; ~ *de fête* holiday; ~ *de semaine* week-day; *un* ~ some day; *tous les* ~*s* every day; *à* ~ up to date.
journal, *s. m.* (news)paper; journal; diary.
journalier, -ère, *adj.* daily; — *s.m.* day-labourer.
journaliste, *s. m. f.* journalist.
journée, *s. f.* day; day's wages *(pl.)*; day's work.
joyau, *s. m.* jewel.
joyeux, -euse, *adj.* joyful, merry.
judiciaire, *adj.* judicial, legal.
judicieux, -euse, *adj.* judicious, sensible, reasonable.
juge, *s. m.* judge.
jugement, *s. m.* judg(e)ment; sentence.
juger, *v. a. & n.* judge.
juif, -ive (J.), *adj.* Jewish; — *s. m. f.* Jew.
juillet, *s. m.* July.
juin, *s. m.* June.
jumeau, -elle *adj. s. m. f.* twin; *f. pl.* binoculars.
jungle, *s. f.* jungle.
jupe, *s. f.* skirt.
juré, *s. m.* juryman.
jurer, *v. a. & n.* swear.
jurisprudence, *s..f* jurisprudence.
juron, *s. m.* oath.
jury, *s. m.* jury.
jus, *s.m.* juice.
jusque, jusqu'à, *prep.* till; as far as.
juste, *adj.* just, right; fair.
justice, *s.f.* justice.
justification, *s.f.* justification.
justifier, *v.a.* justify.
juvénile, *adj.* juvenile.

K

kangourou, *s. m.* kangaroo.
kayak, *s. m.* kayak.
képi, *s. m.* cap.
kilogramme, *s.m.* kilogram(me).
kilomètre, *s.m.* kilometre.
kiosque, *s. n.* kiosk.

L

l' = **le** or **la.**
la, *art.* the; —*pron.* her, it.
là, *adv.* there; here.
labeur, *s.m.* labour, work.
laboratoire, *s.m.* labo-

ratory.

laborieux, -euse, *adj.* laborious, hard-working.

labourer, *v.a.* plough.

lac, *s. m.* lake.

lacer, *v. a.* lace.

lacet, *s. m.* lace; braid; bowstring; shoe-lace.

lâche, *adj.* loose; cowardly; — *s. m.* coward.

lâcher, *v.a.* loosen, slacken; let go.

lactation, *s. f.* lactation.

laid, *adj.* ugly; plain.

laideur, *s. f.* ugliness.

lainage, *s.m.* woollen goods *(pl.)*; wool.

laine, *s. f.* wool; *pure* ~ all wool.

laïque, *adj.* lay.

laisser, *v.a.* leave, quit; give up; let alone; leave behind, off; ~ *aller* let go, neglect.

lait, *s. m.* milk.

laiterie, *s. f.* dairy.

laitier, *s. m.* milkman, dairyman.

laitière, *s. f.* dairymaid.

laitue, *s. f.* lettuce.

lambeau, *s. m.* rag, strip.

lame, *s. f.* blade; plate, sheet; ~ *de rasoir* razor-blade.

lamentation, *s. f.* lamentation.

lampe, *s. f.* lamp.

lançement, *s. m.* throwing; launching.

lancer, *v. a.* throw, fling; se ~ dart, rush.

langage, *s. m.* language, tongue; speech, way of speaking.

lange *s. m.* baby's nappy.

langue, *s. f.* tongue; language; ~ *maternelle* mother-tongue.

laper, *v. a.* lap (up).

lapin, *s. m.* rabbit.

laps, *s. m.* lapse, space (of time).

lapsus, *s. m.* lapse, slip.

laque, *s. f.* lacquer.

lard, *s. m.* bacon.

large, *adj.* broad, wise; generous; liberal; — *s.m.* room, breadth.

largeur, *s. f.* width.

larme, *s. f.* tear.

las, lasse, *adj.* weary.

lasser, *v.a.* tire, wear out; se ~ *de* get tired of.

latéral, *adj.* lateral, side.

latin, -e, *adj.* & *s. m. f.* Latin.

latitude, *s.f.* latitude; scope, freedom.

lavable, *adj.* washable.

lavabo, *s. m.* wash-basin; lavatory.

lavage, *s.m.* washing; ~ *de vaisselle* washing-up.

lavande, *s. f.* lavender.

laver, *v. a.* wash; se ~ wash (oneself); *machine à* ~ washing-machine.

layette, *s. f.* baby-linen.

le, la, l', *art.* the; —*pron.* *(pl.* les) him, her, it; them.

lécher, *v. a.* lick, lap.

leçon, *s. f.* lesson; lecture.

lecteur, -trice. *s. m. f.* reader; lector.

lecture, *s. f.* reading.
légal, *adj.* legal, lawful.
légende, *s. f.* legend.
léger, -ère, *adj.* light, slight; loose.
légèreté, *s. f.* lightness; ease.
légion, *s. f.* legion.
législation, *s.f.* legislation.
législature, *s. f.* legislature.
légitime, *adj.* legitimate, lawful.
légume, *s.m.* vegetable.
lendemain, *s.m.* next day, day after.
lent, *adj.* slow; tardy.
lenteur, *s.f.* slowness.
lentille, *s.f.* lentil; lens.
léopard, *s.m.* leopard
lequel, laquelle, *rel. pron.* *(pl.* **lesquels, lesquelles***)* who, whom; which, that.
lettre, *s.f.* letter; type character; *~s* literature; arts; *à la ~* literally, word for word; *~ de change* bill of exchange; *~ de crédit* letter of credit; *~ recommandée* registered letter; *boîte aux ~s* letter-box.
lettré, *adj.* learned; literary.
leur, *poss. adj.* *(pl.* -s) their; — *pron.* to them, them; *le* or *la ~*, *les ~s* theirs, their own.
levée, *s. f.* raising; removal; levy.
lever, *v. a.* lift (up), raise; hoist; *v. n.* rise; **se ~** rise get up.
levier, *s. m.* lever; *~ des vitesses* gear-lever.
lèvre, *s. f.* lip.
lexique, *s.m.* lexicon.
liaison, *s.f.* joining, junction; union; connection; tie; liaison.
libéral, *adj.* liberal.
libérer, *v.a.* liberate.
liberté, *s.f.* liberty.
libraire, *s.m. f.* bookseller.
librairie, *s. f.* bookshop.
libre, *adj.* free; unoccupied.
licence, *s.f.* licence, degree.
licencié, -e, *s. m. f.* licenciate; licensee.
licencieux, -euse, *adj.* licentious.
lie, *s. f.* dregs, grounds *(pl.)*.
liège, *s.m.* cork.
lien, *s.m.* tie, **bond;** band, strap, cord; **link.**
lier, *v. a.* bind, **tie (up);** fasten; link up.
lieu, *s. m.* place; ***au ~ de*** instead of; ***avoir ~*** take place.
lieutenant, *s. m.* **lieutenant.**
lièvre, *s. m.* hare.
ligne, *s. f.* line; ***~ aérienne*** air-line.
lilas, *s. m.* lilac.
limace, *s. f.* slug.
limaçon, *s. m.* snail.
lime, *s. f.* file.
limer, *v. a.* file.
limite, *s.f.* bound(s), border, limit.
limiter, *v.a.* limit, restrict.
limon, *s.m.* mud, silt.

limonade, *s. f.* lemonade.
lin, *s. m.* flax.
linge, *s. m.* linen.
linger, -ère, *s.m.f.* linendraper.
lingerie, *s. f.* ladies' underclothing, lingerie.
lion, *s. m.* lion.
liqueur, *s. f.* liqueur.
liquide, *adj.* liquid.
liquider, *v.a.* liquidate.
lire*, *v.a.* read.
liste, *s. f.* list, roll; panel.
lit, *s. m.* bed.
litre, *s. m.* litre.
littéraire, *adj.* literary.
littérature, *s.f.* literature.
livraison, *s.f.* delivery; part (of book).
livre[1], *s. m.* book; work; *teneur de ~s* bookkeeper.
livre[2], *s. f.* pound.
livrer, *v.a.* deliver; give up.
local, *s.m.* spot, premises; — *adj.* local.
localité, *s. f.* place, spot.
locataire, *s. m. f.* tenant, lodger.
location, *s. f.* letting out; hiring, renting; *prendre en ~* hire; *bureau de ~* box-office; *~ des places* seat reservation.
locomotive, *s.f.* (railway) engine.
loge, *s. f.* hut. cabin; box.
logement, *s. m.* lodging.
loger, *v.a.* accommodate, lodge; house; *v. n.* reside, live (in).
logeur, *s. m.* landlord.
logeuse, *s. f.* landlady.
logique, *s. f.* logic; — *adj.* logical.
loi, *s.f.* law, statute; *projet de ~* bill, draft.
loin, *adv.* far, far off, away; *au ~* far off.
lointain, *adj.* far, remote.
loisir, *s. m.* spare time, leisure.
long, longue, *adj.* & *s. m. f.* long; *être ~ à* be long in.
longitude, *s. f.* longitude.
longtemps, *adv.* long, a long time; *depuis ~* for a long time, long since.
longueur, *s. f.* length.
loquet, *s. m.* latch.
lors, *adv.* then; *dès ~* from that time.
lorsque, *conj.* when.
lot, *s. m.* lot, fate; prize.
loterie, *s. f.* lottery.
lotion, *s. f.* lotion.
louage, *s.m.* hiring; hire.
louche, *s.f.* ladle.
louer[1], *v.a.* hire (out); let; *à ~* for hire; to let.
louer[2], *v. a.* praise.
loup, *s. m.* wolf.
lourd, *adj.* heavy; clumsy.
louve, *s. f.* she-wolf.
loyal, *adj.* loyal, true.
loyauté, *s.f.* honesty.
loyer, *s. m.* rent; hire.
lubrifier, *v.a.* lubricate.
lucratif, -ive, *adj.* lucrative.
luge, *s. f.* sledge.
lugubre, *adj.* dismal.
lui, *pron.* (to) him, (to) her, (to) it.
lui-même, *pron.* himself.

luire*, *v. n.* shine, gleam.
lumière, *s. f.* light, daylight.
lumineux, -euse, *adj.* luminous, bright.
lundi, *s. m.* Monday.
lune, *s. f.* moon; ~ *de miel* honeymoon.
lunette, *s. f* telescope; *(pl.)* spectacles, specs; ~*s de soleil* sun-glasses.
luthérien, -enne, *adj.* & *s. m. f.* Lutheran.
lutte, *s. f.* wrestling; fight, struggle.
lutter, *v.n.* wrestle, fight.
lutteur, *s. m.* wrestler.
luxe, *s. m.* luxury.
luxeux, -euse, *adj.* luxurious.
lycée, *s.m.* secondary school, grammar-school.

M

m' *see* **me.**
ma *see* **mon.**
mâcher, *v. a.* chew.
machine, *s. f.* machine, engine, apparatus; ~ *à coudre*, sewing-machine.
mâchoire, *s. f.* jaw.
maçon, *s m.* mason.
madame, *s. f.* *(pl.* **mesdames)** madam.
mademoiselle, *s. f.* *(pl.* **mesdemoiselles)** miss.
magasin, *s.m.* shop; store; warehouse; *grand* ~ department store.
magique, *adj.* magic.
magnétique, *adj.* magnetic.
magnétophone, *s.m.* tape-recorder.
magnifique, *adj.* magnificent.
mai, *s. m.* May.
maigre, *adj.* lean, thin.
maigrir, *v.n.* grow lean, get thin.
maille, *s. f.* stitch; knot.
maillot, *s.m.* tights *(pl.)*; ~ *(de bain)* bathing-costume.
main, *s. f.* hand; lead; *en* ~ in hand; *se donner la* ~ shake hands; *tenir la* ~ *à* see to, see that; *de seconde* ~ second-hand.
maintenant, *adv.* now, at present
maintenir, *v. a.* (up)hold, support, keep (up), maintain.
maintien, *s. m.* maintenance.
maire, *s. m.* mayor.
mais, *conj.* but.
maïs, *s. m.* maize.
maison, *s. f.* house, residence; home; firm; *à la* ~ at home, indoors; *tenir* ~ keep house.
maître, *s.m.* master; proprietor; teacher; ~ *d'école* schoolmaster; ~ *de maison* host.
maîtresse, *s. f.* mistress; (land)lady; sweetheart; ~ *d'école* schoolmistress.
maîtrise, *s.f.* mastery, control.
maîtriser, *v.a.* master.
majesté, *s. f.* majesty.
majeur, *adj.* major; main; chief; — *s. m.* major.
majorité, *s. f.* majority.

majuscule, *s. f.* capital letter.
mal, *s. m.* ill, evil, wrong; pain, harm; trouble, hardship; *avoir* ~ *à* have a pain in; — *adv.* wrong, badly, ill.
malade, *adj.* sick, ill; *tomber* ~ fall ill, be taken ill; — *s. m. f.* invalid, patient.
maladie, *s.f.* illness; sickness; disease.
maladroit, *adj.* awkward, clumsy.
malaise, *s. m.* uneasiness.
malchance, *s.f.* bad luck.
mâle, *s. m.* male.
malentendu, *s. m.* misunderstandig.
malgré, *prep.* in spite of; ~ *tout* for all that.
malheur, *s. m.* misfortune, ill luck; mischance; accident.
malheureux, -euse, *adj.* unfortunate, unlucky.
malice, *s. f.* malice.
malin, maligne, *adj.* malicious, malignant; evil.
malle, *s. f.* trunk; mail; *faire la* ~ pack.
mallette, *s.f.* suitcase.
malpropre, *adj.* dirty, filthy; untidy.
malsain, *adj.* unhealthy.
malveillant, *adj.* malevolent, evil-minded.
maman, *s.f.* mamma.
manche[1], *s.m,* handle. holder.
manche[2], *s. f.* sleeve.
Manche, *s.f.* English Channel.
manchette, *s. f.* cuff.
mandat, *s. m.* mandate; money-order.
manger, *v.a.* eat; *donner à* ~ feed; *salle à* ~ dining-room; — *s. m.* eating; food.
manicure, *s. m. f.* manicure.
manier, *v.a.* handle.
manière, *s. f.* manner, way, fashion; *(pl.)* manners.
manifestation, *s. f.* manifestation.
manifester, *v.a.* manifest, show; **se** ~ manifest oneself.
manipuler, *v. a.* manipulate, operate.
manœuvre, *s.f.* action; proceeding; manœuvre; *s. m.* labourer.
manœuvrer, *v. a. & n.* handle, manœuvre, work.
manoir, *s. m.* manor.
manque, *s.m.* want; deficiency.
manquer, *v. a.* miss; *v. n.* fail; be missing, be wanting.
mansarde, *s.f.* garret.
manteau, *s. m.* coat.
manuel, -elle, *adj.* manual; — *s. m.* manual, handbook.
manufacture, *s. f.* manufacture; factory.
manufacturer, *v. a.* manufacture.
manuscrit, *s. m.* manuscript.
maquillage, *s.m.* make-up.
marbre, *s. m.* marble.

marchand, -e, *s. m. f.* merchant, tradesman; shopkeeper.
marchandise, *s. f.* merchandise, goods *(pl.).*
marche, *s. f.* walk; march; progress; move.
marché, *s. m.* market; bargain; agreement; *bon* ~ cheap.
marcher, *v.n.* walk; travel; march; work; run; proceed.
mardi, *s. m.* Tuesday; ~ *gras* Shrove Tuesday.
mare, *s.f.* pool, pond.
maréchal, *s. m.* marshal.
marée, *s.f.* tide, flood.
margarine, *s. f.* margarine.
marge, *s. f.* margin.
mari, *s.m.* husband.
mariage, *s. m.* marriage.
marié, -e, *adj.* married; — *s. m. f.* bridegroom, married man; bride, married woman.
marier, *v. a.* marry; match; — se ~ marry, get married.
marin, *adj.* marine; — *s.m.* seaman, sailor, mariner.
marmelade, *s. f.* marmalade.
marque, *s. f.* mark, imprint; trade-mark.
marquer, *v.a.* mark; stamp; brand.
marron, *s. m.* chestnut.
mars, *s. m.* March.
marteau, *s. m.* hammer.
martyr, -e, *s.m.f.* martyr.
masque, *s. m.* mask.
masquer, *v.a.* mask.
massacre, *s. m.* massacre.
massage, *s. m.* massage.
masse, *s. f.* mass; heap.
massif, -ive, *adj.* massive, bulky, clumsy.
mât, *s. m.* mast.
match, *s. m.* match.
matelas, *s. m.* mattress.
matelot, *s.m.* sailor, seaman.
matérialisme, *s. m.* materialism.
matériaux, *s.m.pl.* material(s).
matériel, -elle, *adj.* material; — *s. m.* matter; material; implements *(pl.).*
maternel, -elle, *adj.* maternal; motherly; *école* ~*le* infant-school.
mathématicien, -enne, *s. m. f.* mathematician.
mathématique, *adj.* mathematical; — *s. f.* mathematics.
matière, *s.f.* matter; material; substance; ~ *première* raw material.
matin, *s.m.* morning; *le* ~ in the morning; *du* ~ a.m.
matinal, *adj.* morning.
matinée, *s.f.* morning; matinée.
matrice, *s. f.* womb.
maturité, *s. f.* maturity.
maudire*, *v.a.* curse.
mauvais, *adj.* bad, ill, evil; — *s. m.* bad.
me, m' *pron.* (to) me; (to) myself.
mécanicien, *s. m.* mechanic; engine-driver.
mécanique, *adj.* mechan-

ic(al); — *s.m.* mechanics; machine; mechanism.
mécaniser, *v. a.* mechanize.
mécanisme, *s. m.* mechanism; machinery.
méchant, *adj.* evil, bad.
mécontent, *adj.* displeased, dissatisfied, unhappy.
mécontenter, *v. a.* dissatisfy.
médaille, *s. f.* medal.
médecin, *s.m.* doctor, physician.
médecine, *s. f.* medicine.
médical, *adj.* medical.
médicament, *s. m.* medicament; medicine.
médiéval, *adj.* medieval.
méditation, *s. m.* meditation.
méditer, *v. a. & n.* meditate.
méfiance, *s. f.* mistrust.
méfier: se ~ be suspicious *(de* of); mistrust.
meilleur, -e, *adj.* better; — *s. m. f.* the best.
mélancolie, *s. f.* melancholy, gloom.
mélancolique, *adj.* melancholy, sad.
mélange, *s.m.* mixture, blend.
mélanger, *v.a.* mix, blend.
mêler, *v.a.* mix (up), mingle; **se** ~ mingle, be mixed; interfere with.
mélodie, *s. f.* melody.
melon, *s.m.* melon.
membre, *s.m.* member, limb.
même, *adj.* same; self; — *adv.* even, also, likewise; *de* ~ in the same way; *de* ~ *que* as well as; *quand* ~ even if.
mémoire, *s.f.* memory; *s.m.* memorandum; bill; *(pl.)* memoirs.
menace, *s.f.* menace.
menacer, *v.a.* threaten.
ménage, *s. m.* housekeeping; household.
ménager, *v. a.* be sparing of; take care of; manage.
ménagère, *s.f.* housewife, housekeeper.
mendiant, -e, *s.m.f.* beggar.
mendier, *v. a. & n.* beg.
mener, *v.a.* guide, conduct, lead.
mensonge, *s.m.* lie.
mensuel, *adj.* monthly.
mental, *adj.* mental.
mention, *s.f.* mention.
mentionner, *v. a.* mention.
mentir*, *v.n.* lie, tell a lie.
menton, *s.m.* chin.
menu, *adj.* slim; small; minute; — *s. m.* bill of fare, menu.
menuisier, *s. m.* joiner, carpenter.
méprendre: se ~ make a mistake, be mistaken.
mépris, *s.m.* contempt.
mer, *s.f.* sea; *par* ~ by sea; *bord de la* ~ seaside.
mercerie, *s. f.* haberdashery.
merci, *s. f.* mercy; — *int.* thanks!, (no) thank you!

mercredi, *s. m.* Wednesday.
mercure, *s.m.* mercury.
mère, *s.f.* mother.
mérite, *s. m.* merit, worth.
mériter, *v.a.* merit, deserve.
merveille, *s.f.* wonder.
merveilleux, **-euse**, *adj.* wonderful.
message, *s.m.* message.
messe, *s.f.* mass.
mesure, *s.f.* measure, gauge, measurement; size; metre.
mesurer, *v.a.* measure.
métal, *s.m.* metal.
métallique, *adj.* metallic.
météorologie, *s. f.* meteorology.
méthode, *s.f.* method.
méthodique, *adj.* methodical, systematic.
métier, *s. m.* trade; business; employment, occupation.
mètre, *s. m.* metre.
métro, *s. m.* tube, underground.
métropolitain, *adj.* metropolitan; underground.
mets, *s.m.* dish, food.
mettre*, *v.a.* put, set, place; put in, on; bring; *~ de c té* set aside, save; *~ en ordre* set in order, tidy up; **se ~** sit down; *se ~ à* set about, take to.
meuble, *s. m.* (piece of) furniture; — *adj.* movable; *biens ~s* personal property.
meubler, *v.a.* furnish, fit up.
meunier, *s.m.* miller.
meurtre, *s.m.* murder.
meurtrier, *s. m.* murderer.
meurtrir, *v.a.* bruise, injure.
mi-, half, mid.
microbe, *s. m.* microbe.
microphone, *s. m.* microphone.
microscope, *s. m.* microscope.
midi, *s. m.* noon, midday; south.
miel, *s. m.* honey.
mien, *pron.* mine, my own.
miette, *s. f.* crumb.
mieux, *adv.* better.
mignon, **-onne**, *adj.* tiny; — *s.m.f.* darling.
migraine, *s. f.* headache.
milieu, *s.m.* middle, centre; environment.
militaire, *adj.* military; — *s. m.* soldier.
mille[1], *adj.* & *s.m.* thousand.
mille[2], *s. m.* mile (= 1609 metres).
millier, *s.m.* thousand.
million, *s.m.* million.
millionaire, *s. m. f.* millionaire.
mince, *adj.* thin, slim.
mine[1], *s.f.* mine.
mine[2], *s.f.* look(s); *de bonne ~* good-looking.
miner, *v. a.* (under)mine.
minerai, *s.m.* ore.
minéral, *adj.* mineral.
mineur[1], *s.m.* miner.
mineur[2], **-e**, *adj.* & *s. m. f.* minor.
ministère, *s. m.* ministry.
ministre, *s. m.* minister; *premier ~* prime minister, premier.

minorité, *s. f.* minority.
minuit, *s.m.* midnight.
minuscule, *s.f.* small letter.
minute, *s.f.* minute; instant.
miracle, *s.m.* miracle.
miraculeux, **-euse**, *adj.* miraculous, wonderful.
miroir, *s.m.* mirror.
misérable, *adj.* miserable.
misère, *s. f.* misery.
miséricorde, *s. f.* mercy.
mission, *s.f.* mission.
missionnaire, *adj.* & *s. m. f.* missionary.
mite, *s. f.* moth.
mobile, *adj.* movable, mobile.
mobilier, *s. m.* furniture, suite.
mobilisation, *s. f.* mobilization.
mobiliser, *v.a.&n.* mobilize.
mode[1], *s.f.* fashion, vogue; *à la* ~ in vogue, in fashion.
mode[2], *s. m.* mode, way; mood.
modèle, *s.m.* model.
modération, *s. f.* moderation.
modérer, *v.a.* moderate.
moderne, *adj.* modern.
modeste, *adj.* modest.
modestie, *s.f.* modesty.
modification, *s. f.* modification, change.
modifier, *v.a.* modify.
modiste, *s.f.* milliner.
moelleux, **-euse**, *adj.* soft, mellow.
mœurs, *s. f. pl.* manners, customs, ways.
moi, *pron.* me, to me.
moi-même, *pron.* myself.
moindre, *adj.* less, lesser, smaller; *le* ~ the least.
moineau, *s. m.* sparrow.
moins, *adv.* & *s. m.* less *(que, de* than); fewer *(de* than); minus; *le* ~ the least; *à* ~ *que* unless; *au* ~ at least.
mois, *s. m.* month; *par* ~ monthly; a month.
moisson, *s.f.* harvest, crop.
moissonner, *v. a.* harvest, reap.
moitié, *s.f.* half.
molécule, *s. f.* molecule.
mollet, *s. m.* calf *(of leg)*.
moment, *s. m.* moment, instant.
mon, **ma**, *pron.* *(pl.* **mes**) my.
monarchie, *s. f.* monarchy
monastère, *s. m.* monastery, convent.
mondain, *adj.* worldly.
monde, *s.m.* world; people, company; *mettre au* ~ give birth to; *tout le* ~ everybody.
monnaie, *s.f.* money, coin, change; currency; ~ *légale* legal tender; ~ *étrangère* foreign currency.
monopole, *s.m.* monopoly.
monotone, *adj.* monotonous.
monseigneur, *s.m.* my lord, your lordship.
monsieur, *s. m.* gentleman; *M.* Mr.
monstrueux, **-euse**, *adj.* monstrous.
mont, *s. m.* mountain.
montage, *s. m.* carrying

up; mounting, setting; wiring.
montagne, *s. f.* mountain.
montagneux, -euse, *adj.* mountainous.
montant, *adj.* ascending, uphill; *en* ~ upwards.
monte-charge, *s. m.* goods lift.
montée, *s. f.* rise, slope.
monter, *v.n.* go up, come up, ascend, climb; mount; ride; amount *(à* to); equip, fit up; ~ *à cheval* ride; *faire* ~ *qn. (dans sa voiture)* give s.o. a lift.
montre[1], *s.f.* watch.
montre[2], *s.f.* display, show; show-window.
montrer, *v.a.* show, display, point out; **se** ~ show oneself.
montueux, -euse, *adj.* hilly, steep.
monument, *s. m.* monument.
monumental, *adj.* monumental.
moquerie, *s. f.* mockery.
moral, *adj.* moral.
morale, *s. f.* ethics; morality.
moralité, *s. f.* morality, morals *(pl.)*.
morceau, *s. m.* piece, morsel, bit; snack.
mordre, *v. a.* bite; gnaw.
mors, *s. m.* bit; *fig.* check.
mort, *s. f.* death; — *adj.* dead, lifeless.
mortel, -elle, *adj.* mortal; boring, tedious.
mot, *s. m.* word; short note; ~*s croisés* crossword (puzzle).
motel, *s. m.* motel.
moteur, *s. m.* motor, engine.
motif, *s. m.* motive; cause.
motion, *s.f.* motion, movement.
motocyclette, *s. f.* motor-(bi)cycle, motor-bike.
mou, mol, molle, *adj.* soft; loose.
mouche, *s. f.* fly.
moucher: **se** ~ blow one's nose.
mouchoir, *s. m.* handkerchief.
moudre*, *v.a.* grind.
mouette, *s.f.* gull.
mouiller, *v.a.* & *n.* soak, wet.
moule, *s. m.* mould, cast.
moulin, *s. m.* mill; ~ *à vent* windmill; ~ *à café* coffee-mill.
mourant, *adj.* dying, expiring.
mourir*, *v. n.* die, expire.
mousse, *s. f.* foam, froth, lather; moss.
moustache, *s. f.* moustache.
moustique, *s.m.* mosquito.
moutarde, *sf.* mustard.
mouton, *s.m.* sheep; mutton.
mouvement, *s. m.* movement, motion, move.
mouvoir*, *v.a.* move; start; **se** ~ move, stir.
moyen, -enne, *adj.* mean, middle, average; *le* ~ *âge* the Middle Ages; — *s. m.* means, way, manner; *au* ~ *de* by means of; *avoir les* ~*s de* can afford.

moyenne, *s. f.* average, mean; *en* ~ on the average.
muet, -ette, *adj*. dumb, mute; speechless.
multiplication, *s. f.* multiplication.
multiplier, *v.a.&n.* multiply.
multitude, *s. f.* multitude, crowd.
municipal, *adj*. municipal, city.
munir, *v.a.* provide *(de* with).
munition, *s. f.* (am)munition.
mur, *s. m.* wall.
mûr, *adj*. ripe; mature.
mûrir, *v. a. & n.* ripen.
murmure, *s.m.* murmur.
murmurer, *v.n.* murmur.
muscle, *s.m.* muscle.
muse, *s. f.* muse.
museau, *s. m.* muzzle.
musician; — *adj.* musical.
musical, *adj.* musical.
musicien, -enne, *s. m. f.*
musique, *s.f.* music; *instrument de* ~ musical instrument.
mutuel, -elle, *adj*. mutual.
myope, *adj*. short-sighted.
mystère, *s.m.* mystery.
mystérieux, -euse, *adj.* mysterious.
mystification, *s. f.* mystification.
mystique, *adj.* mystic.

N

nacre, *s.f.* mother-of-pearl.
nage, *s.f.* swimming; rowing, paddling.
nager, *v.n.* swim; float; row.
nageur, -euse, *s. m. f.* swimmer.
naïf, -ïve, *adj.* naïve.
nain, -e, *s. m. f.* dwarf
naissance, *s. f.* birth; *lieu de* ~ birth-place.
naître*, *v. n.* be born; arise (from).
nappe, *s.f.* table-cloth.
narine, *s.f.* nostril.
nasal, *adj.* nasal.
natal, *adj.* natal, native, birth.
natif, -ive, *adj. & s. m. f.* native.
nation, *s.f.* nation.
national, *adj.* national.
nationalité, *s.f.* nationality.
naturaliser, *v.a.* naturalize.
nature, *s.f.* nature.
naturel, -elle, *adj.* natural, native.
naturellement, *adv.* naturally, of course.
naufrage, *s. m.* shipwreck; *faire* ~ be shipwrecked.
nausée, *s.f.* nausea.
nautique, *adj.* nautical.
naval, *adj.* naval.
navigateur, *s.m.* navigator.
navigation, *s.f.* navigation; sailing; *compagnie de* ~ shipping

company; ~ *spatiale* space-flight.
naviguer, *v. a. & n.* navigate.
navire, *s.m.* ship; *~s* shipping.
ne, n', *adv.* not; *~... pas* not; *~ ... que* only.
né, -e, *adj.* born; née.
nécessaire, *adj.* necessary.
nécessité, *s. f.* necessity.
nécessiter, *v.a.* necessitate, make necessary.
nef, *s. f.* ship, vessel; nave; *~ latérale* aisle.
négatif, -ive, *adj. & s. m.* negative.
négative, *s. f.* negative.
négligence, *s. f.* neglect, negligence.
négligent, *adj.* negligent.
négliger, *v.a.* neglect.
négociant, -e, *s. m. f.* merchant, trader.
négociation, *s. f.* negotiation, transaction.
nègre, *s.m.* negro.
neige, *s.f.* snow.
neiger, *v.n.* snow.
neigeux, -euse, *adj.* snowy
néon, *s. m.* neon.
nerf, *s. m.* nerve; sinew.
nerveux, -euse, *adj.* nervous.
net, nette, *adj.* clean, neat, clear, tidy; net; — *adv.* flatly, point-blank.
nettoyage, *s. m.* cleaning, cleansing.
nettoyer, *v.a.* clean, cleanse, clear.
neuf[1], *adj. & s. m.* nine.
neuf[2], neuve, *adj.* new.
neutre, *adj.* neutral.
neuvième, *adj.* ninth.
neveu, *s.m.* nephew.
nez, *s.m.* nose.
ni, *conj.* *~ ... ~* (n)either ... (n)or; *~ l'un ~ l'autre* neither (one).
nid, *s.m.* nest; berth.
nièce, *s.f.* niece.
nier, *v.a.* deny.
niveau, *s. m.* level.
noble, *adj.* noble.
noblesse, *s.f.* nobility.
noce, *s. f. (often pl.)* wedding; *(sing.)* revelry.
Noël, *s. m.* Christmas; *veillée de ~* Christmas eve.
nœud, *s. m.* knot, bow, tie.
noir, *adj.* black.
noix, *s. f.* (wal)nut; *~ de coco* coconut.
nom, *s. m.* name, surname; fame; noun; *~ de famille* surname.
nombre, *s.m.* number.
nombreux, -euse, *adj.* numerous.
nomination, *s. f.* nomination, appointment.
nommer, *v. a.* name, give name to; appoint, nominate.
non, *adv.* no, not.
nonne, *s. f.* nun.
nord, *s. m.* north; *du ~, au ~* northern.
nord-est, *s. m.* northeast.
nord-ouest, *s. m.* northwest.
normal, *adj.* normal.
norvégien, -enne (N.), *adj. & s. m. f.* Norwegian.
nos, *poss. adj.* our.
notable, *adj.* notable, re-

markable.
notaire, *s. m.* notary (-public).
note, *s. f.* note, mark; bill, account; note *(music)*; ~ *(au bas de la page)* foot-note.
noter, *v.a.* note, jot down; notice.
notice, *s. f.* notice.
notion, *s. f.* notion, idea.
notre, *poss. adj.* our.
nôtre, *pron. poss.* ours, our own.
nourrir, *v.a.* nourish, feed.
nourriture, *s. f.* nourishment food.
nous, *pron.* we; us.
nous-mêmes, *pron.* ourselves.
nouveau, -el, -elle, *adj.* new; further; *de* ~ again.
nouvelle, *s.f.* news; short story.
novembre, *s. m.* November.
noyau *s.m.* stone, kernel; nucleus, core.
noyer[1], *v. a.* drown; **se** ~ be drowning; drown oneself.
noyer[2], *s. m.* walnut-tree.
nu, *adj.* naked, bare.
nuage, *s. m.* cloud.
nuageux, -euse, *adj.* cloudy, clouded.
nuance, *s. f.* shade, tint, nuance.
nucléaire. *adj.* nuclear.
nuire*, *v. n.* hurt, harm, be harmful.
nuit, *s. f.* night; *il (se) fait* ~ it is night, it is getting dark; *de* ~ by night; *la* ~ at night, *bonne* ~*!* good night!
nul, nulle, *adj.* not one, not any; null, nil; — *pron.* no one, nobody.
numéro, *s. m.* number, size; ticket; copy, issue.
nu-pied, *adv.* barefoot.
nylon, *s. m.* nylon.

O

obéir, *v.n.* obey.
obéissance, *s. f.* obedience.
objectif, -ive, *adj.* objective; — *s. m.* object, purpose; lens.
objection, *s. f.* objection.
objet, *s. m.* object, thing, article; purpose; ~ *d'art* work of art.
obligation, *s. f.* obligation.
obligatoire, *adj.* compulsory, obligatory.
obliger, *v.a.* oblige, compel.
obscur, *adj.* dark, dim.
obscurité, *s. f.* darkness, dimness; *dans l'*~ in the dark.
observation, *s. f.* observation; remark.
observer, *v. a. & n.* observe, watch; keep.
obstacle, *s. m.* obstacle; hindrance; bar.
obstine, *adj.* obstinate.
obtenir, *v. a.* obtain, get.
occasion, *s. f.* occasion, chance, event; *a l'*~ if need be, eventually; *d'*~ second-hand.

occidental, *adj.* western, occidental.
occupant, -e, *s. m. f.* occupier, occupant.
occupation, *s. f.* occupation; pursuit.
occupé, *adj.* occupied, busy, engaged; *non* ~ unoccupied.
occuper, *v.a.* occupy, employ; s'~ occupy oneself *(de* with), be engaged; think *(de* of).
occurrence, *s.f.* occurrence; *en l'~* in this case.
océan, *s.m.* ocean.
octobre, *s.m.* October.
odieux, -euse, *adj.* odious.
œil, *s. m. (pl.* yeux) eye, sight; *coup d'~* glance; *au premier coup d'~* at first sight, at a glance; *ouvrez l'~!* look out!
œillet, *s.m.* carnation; eyelet.
œuf, *s.m.* egg; *~ à la coque* boiled egg; *~s brouillés* scrambled eggs; *~s durs* hard-boiled eggs; *blanc d'~* white of egg; *jaune d'~* egg-yolk.
œuvre, *s. f.* work; composition; *~ d'art* work of art.
offense, *s. f.* offence, insult; trespass.
offenser, *v.a.* offend, shock, injure; s'~ take offence, be offended *(de* with), be angry.
office, *s.m.* office; service; post; agency; *exercer un ~* hold an office.
officiel, -elle, *adj.* official.
officier, *s.m.* officer.
offre, *s. f.* offer, tender.
offrir*, *v. a.* offer, present, hold out; s'~ offer, propose oneself.
oh!, *int.* oh!, O!, indeed!
oie, *s.f.* goose.
oignon, *s. m.* onion; bulb.
oiseau, *s. m.* bird.
olympique, *adj.* Olympic; *les jeux ~* the Olympic games.
ombre, *s.m.* shade; ghost; obscurity, darkness.
ombreux, -euse, *adj.* shady, shaded.
omelette, *s.f.* omelet.
omettre, *v. a.* omit.
omission, *s. f.* omission, oversight.
omnibus, *s. m.* bus; — *adj.* slow; *train ~* slow train.
on, *pron.* one, we, people *(pl.)*; you; they; somebody; some one; *~ dit* they say, it is said, people say; *~ ferme!* closing time!
oncle, *s.m.* uncle.
onde, *s. f.* wave; undulation;
ondulation, *s. f.* undulation; waving.
onduler, *v. a. & n.* undulate, wave; ripple.
ongle, *s.m.* nail *(finger)*.
onze, *adj. & s. m.* eleven; eleventh.
opéra, *s. m.* opera; opera-house; *~ comique* comic opera.

opérateur, *s. m.* operator; cameraman.
opération, *s. f.* operation; *salle d'*~ operating-theatre.
opérer, *v. a. & n.* operate (on); *se faire* ~ undergo an operation.
opérette, *s.f.* operetta.
opinion, *s.f.* opinion.
opportun, *adj.* opportune, timely.
opposer, *v.a.* oppose.
opposition, *s. f.* opposition.
oppression, *s. f.* oppression.
opprimer, *v. a.* oppress.
optimiste, *adj.* optimistic; — *s. m. f.* optimist.
optique, *adj.* optic(al); — *s. f.* optics.
or, *s. m.* gold; *d'*~, *en* ~ golden.
orage, *s.m.* storm.
orange, *s.f.* orange.
orateur, *s.m.* speaker.
orbite, *s. f.* orbit.
orchestre, *s. m.* orchestra.
ordinaire, *adj.* ordinary, usual, common.
ordinairement, *adv.* usually, generally.
ordonnance, *s. f.* order; statute; prescription.
ordonner, *v.a.* order, command.
ordre, *s. m.* order, command; *mettre en* ~ arrange, clear up.
ordure, *s. f.* refuse, rubbish.
oreille, *s. f.* ear; hearing; *prêter l'*~ *à* listen to, lend an ear to.
oreiller, *s.m.* pillow.
organe, *s.m.* organ.
organique, *adj.* organic.
organisation, *s. f.* organization, arrangement.
organiser, *v. a.* organize.
organisme, *s. m.* organism, system.
orgue, *s.m.* organ.
orgueil, *s.m.* pride.
orient, *s. m.* the East; *de l'*~ eastern.
oriental, *adj.* oriental, eastern.
original, *adj.* original.
origine, *s. f.* origin, source; *avoir* ~ come from.
ornement, *s. m.* ornament, adornment.
orner, *v. a.* adorn, ornament, trim, decorate.
orphelin, -e, *s. m. f.* orphan.
orthographie, *s. f.* spelling.
os, *s. m.* bone.
osciller, *v.n.* oscillate.
oser, *v. a. & n.* dare, venture.
ôter, *v.a.* take away, take off, remove, pull off; s'~ remove oneself.
ou, *conj.* or, either, else.
où, *adv.* where; whence; at which, in which; *n'importe* ~ anywhere.
ouate, *s.f.* cotton-vool
oublier, *v. a. & n.* forget; overlook.
ouest, *s. m.* west; *à l'*~ to, in the west, westward; *de l'*~ western.
oui, *adv.* yes.
ouragan, *s. m.* hurricane.
ours, *s.m.* bear.
ourse, *s.f.* she-bear.
outil, *s.m.* tool.

outré, *adj.* exaggerated.
ouvert, *adj.* open; free; open-hearted; *à bras* ~*s* with open arms.
ouverture, *s. f.* opening; overtures *(pl.)*, proposal; overture.
ouvrage, *s. m.* (piece of) work.
ouvre-boîte, *s. m.* tin-opener.
ouvreuse, *s. f.* box-opener, attendant.
ouvrier, **-ère**, *s. m. f.* workman, worker; workwoman; hand; *premier* ~ foreman.
ouvrir*, *v. a. & n.* open (up); break open; **s'**~ be opened, open.
oxygène, *s. m.* oxygen.

P

pacifique, *adj.* pacific, peaceful; *l'Océan* ~ the Pacific Ocean.
pacte, *s. m.* pact.
page[1], *s. f.* page; *être à la* ~ be up to date.
page[2], *s. m.* page *(boy)*.
paiement *see* **payement**.
paille, *s. f.* straw, chaff.
pain, *s.m.* bread, loaf; cake, tablet.
pair[1], *adj.* equal, even; *au* ~ at par; "au pair".
pair[2], *s. m.* peer.
paire, *s. f.* pair; couple.
paisible, *adj.* peaceful.
paître*, *v. a. & n.* graze, feed.
paix, *s. f.* peace; calm.
palais[1], *s. m.* palace.
palais[2], *s. m.* palate.
pâle, *adj.* pale.
paletot, *s. m.* overcoat.
pâleur, *s. f.* pallor.
pâlir, *v. n. & a.* (grow) pale.
palmier, *s.m.* palm-tree.
palpiter, *v.n.* palpitate.
pamphlet, *s.m.* pamphlet.
pamplemousse, *s. m.* grapefruit.
pan, *s. m.* flap; coat-tail.
panache, *s.m.* plume.
panier, *s. m.* basket.
panique, *s. f.* panic.
panne, *s. f.* break-down; power-cut.
panneau, *s. m.* panel.
panorama, *s. m.* panorama.
pansement, *s. m.* dressing, bandage.
pantalon, *s. m.* trousers *(pl.)*.
pantoufle(s), *s. f. (pl.)* slipper(s).
papa, *s. m.* dad, daddy.
papauté, *s. f.* papacy.
pape, *s. m.* pope.
papeterie, *s. f.* paper-mill; stationery.
papetier, *s. m.* stationer.
papier, *s. m.* paper; ~ *hygiénique* toilet-paper; ~ *peint* wallpaper.
papillon, *s. m.* butterfly.
pâques, *s. m. pl.* Easter.
paquet, *s.m.* packet, parcel.
par, *prep.* by, by way of, by means of; across; through; per; for.
parade, *s. f.* parade, show.
paragraphe, *s. m.* paragraph.
paraître*, *v.n.* appear,

come in sight; come out; *faire* ~ publish.

parallèle, *adj. & s. f.* parallel.

paralysie, *s. f.* paralysis.

paralytique, *s. m. f.* paralytic.

parapluie, *s. m.* unbrella.

paratonnerre, *s. m.* lightning-conductor.

parbleu, *int.* indeed!

parc, *s. m.* park; fold.

parce que, *conj.* because, on account of.

parcourir, *v.n.* travel through, go over; cover; run over, look over.

parcours, *s.m.* course, run; distance; mileage.

pardessus, *s. m.* overcoat.

par-dessus, *prep.* above.

pardon, *s. m.* pardon; *je vous demande ~!* I beg your pardon!; pardon me!; excuse me!; ~? (I beg your) pardon?

pardonner, *v.a.* pardon.

pare-boue, *s.m.* mudguard.

pare-brise, *s.m.* windscreen.

pare-choc, *s. m.* bumper.

pareil, -eille, *adj.* like, similar; such; same.

parent, *s. m. f.* relative, relation; ~*s* parents; relatives.

parer, *v. a.* adorn, trim; parry, ward off.

paresseux, -euse, *adj.* lazy, idle.

parfait, *adj. & s. m.* perfect.

parfaitement, *adv.* perfectly; ~*!* quite so!

parfois, *adv.* sometimes.

parfum, *s. m.* perfume.

parfumer, *v. a.* perfume.

parfumerie, *s. f.* perfumery.

parier, *v. a.* bet, stake.

parisien, -enne, *adj. & s. m. f.* Parisian.

parlement, *s. m.* parliament.

parlementaire, *adj.* parliamentary.

parler, *v. n. & a.* speak, talk; — *s. m.* speech, utterance; parlance.

parmi, *prep.* among.

paroi, *s. f.* wall, partition.

paroisse, *s. f.* parish.

parole, *s. f.* speech, utterance; language; word.

parquet, *s. m.* parquet.

part, *s. f.* part, share; side; *prendre ~ à* take part in, participate; *faire ~ à* inform (of), let know; *à ~* apart; *d'une ~ . . . d'autre ~* on the one hand . . . on the other (hand).

partager, *v.a.* divide, share out; share.

partenaire, *s. m. f.* partner.

parterre, *s. m.* flower-bed; pit.

parti, *s. m.* party; side.

participant, -e, *s. m. f. & adj.* participant.

participation, *s. f.* participation, share.

participe, *s. m.* participle; ~ *passé* past participle.

participer, *v.n.* participate, take part (*à* in).

particulier, -ère, *adj.* particular, special, specific; peculiar; private;

— *s. m. f.* private person; *en* ~ in particular.
partie, *s. f.* part; match, game; party; *en* ~ partly, in part.
partir*, *v. n.* start, leave, go (away), set out.
partisan, *s. m.* partisan, follower.
partition, *s. f.* score.
partout, *adv.* everywhere.
parure, *s. f.* ornament; set.
parvenir, *v. n.* attain (*à* to), reach.
pas[1], *s. m.* step, pace.
pas[2], *adv.* no, not, not any; ~ *du tout* not at all; ~ *nécessaire* unnecessary.
passage, *s. m.* passing passage; corridor crossing; thoroughfare ~ *clouté* pedestrian crossing; ~ *à niveau* level-crossing; ~ *interdit* no thoroughfare.
passager, -ère, *adj.* passing, transient, fugitive; — *s. m. f.* passenger.
passant, -e, *adj. en* ~ by the way, cursorily; — *s. m. f.* passer-by.
passe, *s. f.* pass, passage; channel; permit.
passé, *adj.* past; — *prep.* after, beyond.
passeport, *s. m.* passport.
passer, *v. n. & a.* pass; pass along, by; cross; go on, pass on; hand; pass away; omit; forgive; strain; *en* ~ *par là* submit to it; ~ *un examen* take an examination; ~ *la nuit* spend the night; **se** ~ happen; disappear; do without.
passif, -ive, *adj.* passive — *s. m.* liabilities (*pl.*).
passion, *s. f.* passion.
passionné *adj.* passionate.
pastel, *s. m.* pastel.
pastille, *s. f.* pastille.
pâte, *s. f.* paste; dough.
pâté, *s. m.* pie, pasty; block (of buildings); blot.
patente, *s. f.* patent, licence.
patience, *s. f.* patience.
patient, -e, *adj. & s. m. f.* patient.
patin, *s. m.* skate.
patinage, *s. m.* skating.
patiner, *v. n.* skate.
patinoire, *s. f.* skating-rink.
pâtisserie, *s. f.* pastry; pastry-shop, cake-shop.
pâtissier, -ère, *s. m. f.* pastry-cook.
pâtre, *s. m.* shepherd.
patrie, *s. f.* country.
patriote, *adj.* patriotic; — *s. m. f.* patriot.
patron[1], **-onne,** *s. m. f.* patron; employer, boss.
patron[2], *s. m.* model, pattern.
patronage, *s. m.* patronage, support.
patronner, *v. a.* patronize, protect.
patrouille, *s. f.* patrol.
patte, *s. f.* paw, foot.
pâture, *s. f.* fodder, pasture.
paume, *s. f.* palm.
paupière, *s. f.* eyelid.
pause, *s. f.* pause, stop,

break; rest.
pauvre, *adj.* poor.
pauvreté, *s. f.* poverty.
pavé, *s. m.* paving-stone; pavement; street.
paver, *v. a.* pave.
pavillon, *s. m.* pavilion, summer-house; flag.
payable, *adj.* payable, due.
paye, *s.f.* pay, wages *pl.*
payement, paiement, *s. m.* payment.
payer, *v.a.* pay; pay down, for, off; repay.
pays, *s. m.* country, land; home; nation; district, region.
paysage, *s. m.* landscape; scenery.
paysan, -anne, *s. m. f.* peasant, countryman; countrywoman.
peau, *s. f.* skin; hide; leather.
pêche[1], *s. f.* peach.
pêche[2], *s. f.* fishing; angling; ~ *à la ligne* angling.
péché, *s. m.* sin, trespass.
pécher, *v. n.* sin, trespass.
pêcher, *v. a. & n.* fish, angle.
pécheur, -eresse, *s. m. f.* sinner.
pêcheur, *s.m.* angler, fisher.
pécuniaire, *adj.* pecuniary.
pédagogie, *s. f.* pedagogy.
pédale, *s. f.* pedal.
pédant, *adj.* pedant.
pédicure, *s. m.* pedicure.
peigne, *s. m.* comb.
peigner, *v. a.* comb.
peignoir, *s.m.* wrapper, dressing-gown.
peindre*, *v.a.* paint.
peine, *s. f.* punishment, pain, grief; trouble.
peintre, *s. m.* painter.
peinture, *s. f.* painting.
pêle-mêle, *adv.* pell-mell, in a muddle.
pelle, *s. f.* shovel, spade.
pellicule, *s. f.* film.
pelote, *s. f.* ball.
pelouse, *s. f.* lawn.
pelure, *s. f.* rind, peel.
pénalité, *s. f.* penalty.
penchant, *s. m.* slope, slant; bent, liking.
pencher, *v. a. & n.* incline, bend; stoop; lean (towards).
pendant[1], *adj.* hanging, pendent; — *s. m.* pendant; match.
pendant[2], *prep.* during; ~ *que* while.
pendre, *v. a. & n.* hang (up), suspend; hang down; be hanging.
pendule, *s. f.* clock.
pénétrer, *v. a. & n.* penetrate, go through; search; see through.
pénitence, *s. f.* penitence.
pensée, *s.f.* thought, thinking; mind; pansy.
penser, *v. n. & a.* think.
pension, *s.f.* pension; board (and lodging); boarding-house; boarding-school; life annuity; ~ *et chambre(s)* board and lodging; ~ *pour étudiants* hostel.
pensionnaire, *s.m.f.* boarder; paying guest.
pensionnat, *s. m.* boarding-school.

pente, *s. f.* slope, descent; *en* ~ downhill.
Pentecôte, *s. f.* Whitsuntide; *dimanche de la* ~ Whit Sunday.
pépier, *v.n.* chirp.
pépin, *s. m.* pip, stone.
perçant, *adj.* piercing.
perception, *s.f.* perception.
percer, *v. a. & n.* pierce, bore; punch; tap.
percevoir, *v. a.* perceive, understand.
perdre, *v. a. & n.* lose; waste; be the ruin of; **se** ~ get lost, disappear; be ruined.
perdrix, *s. f.* partridge.
père, *s. m.* father.
perfection, *s.f.* perfection.
perforation, *s. f.* perforation.
perforer, *v.a.* perforate.
peril, *s.m.* peril, danger.
période, *s. f.* period, term.
périodique, *adj.* periodic, periodical.
périr, *v. n.* perish.
perle, *s. f.* pearl, bead.
permanent, *adj.* permanent.
permanente, *s. f.* perm.
permettre, *v.a.* allow, permit, let; *permettez-moi de* allow me to; *vous permettez?* may I?
permis, *s.m.* permit, licence.
permission *s. f.* permission, leave (of absence).
perron, *s. m.* stair, steps *(pl.)*.
perroquet, *s. m.* parrot.
persan, -e (P.), *adj. & s. m. f.* Persian.
persécuter, *v. a.* persecute.
persécution, *s. f.* persecution.
persil, *s. m.* parsley.
persister, *v.n.* persist.
personnage, *s. m.* personage, person.
personnalité, *s. f.* personality.
personne, *s.f.* person; *grande* ~ grown-up; — *pron.* any one; anybody; no one.
personnel, -elle, *adj.* personal; — *s. m.* personnel, staff.
perspective, *s. f.* perspective, prospect, outlook.
persuader, *v. a.* persuade, convince.
persuasion, *s. f.* persuasion, conviction.
perte, *s. f.* loss; ruin.
pertinent, *adj.* pertinent.
peser, *v. a.* weigh; ponder.
pessimiste, *s. m. f.* pessimist; — *adj.* pessimistic.
petit, *adj.* small, little.
petite-fille, *s.f.* granddaughter.
petit-fils, *s. m.* grandson.
pétition, *s.f.* petition, request.
petits-enfants, *pl.* grandchildren.
pétrole, *s.m.* petroleum.
peu, *adv. & s. m.* little, bit, few; ~ *a* ~ little by little, bit by bit; *un (petit)* ~ a (little) bit; *quelque* ~ somewhat; ~ *abondant* scanty; ~ *commun* unusual; ~ *confortable* uncomfor-

table; ~ *nécessaire* unnecessary.
peuple, *s. m.* people.
peur, *s. f.* fear; fright; *avoir* ~ *(de)* be afraid (of); *de* ~ *que* for fear that.
peut-être, *adv.* perhaps.
phare, *s. m.* lighthouse; headlight.
pharmacie, *s. f.* pharmacy, chemist's (shop).
pharmacien, -enne, *s. m. f.* chemist.
phase, *s. f.* phase.
phénomène, *s. m.* phenomenon.
philologie, *s. f.* philology.
philosophe, *s. m.* philosopher.
philosophie, *s. f.* philosophy.
philosophique, *adj.* philosophical.
phono(graphe), *s.m.* gramophone.
photo, *s. f.* photo, snap.
photographe, *s.m.* photographer.
photographie, *s. f.* photograph; photography.
photographier, *v. a.* photograph.
photographique, *adj.* photographic; *appareil* ~ camera.
phrase, *s. f.* phrase; sentence.
phtisie, *s. f.* consumption.
physicien, -enne, *s. m. f.* physicist.
physique, *adj.* physical; — *s. f.* physics; ~ *nucléaire* nuclear physics; — *s. m.* physique, constitution.
pianiste, *s. m. f.* pianist.
piano(forte), *s. m.* piano.
pièce, *s. f.* piece, part, bit, coin; play; room; joint.
pied, *s. m.* foot, leg; *à* ~ on foot; *aller à* ~ walk.
pierre, *s. f.* stone; rock.
piéton, *s. m.* pedestrian.
pieu, *s. m.* stake, post.
pieux, -euse, *adj.* pious.
pigeon, -onne, *s. m. f.* dove, pigeon.
pile, *s. f.* pile, heap; battery.
pilier, *s. m.* pillar, post, column.
piller, *v. a. & n.* pillage.
pilot, *s. m.* pile.
pilote, *s. m.* pilot.
piloter, *v.a.* pilot, guide.
pilule, *s. f.* pill.
pin, *s. m.* pine(-tree).
pince, *s. f.* pinch; pincers, pliers, tongs *(pl.)*.
pincer, *v. a.* pinch.
pipe, *s. f.* pipe.
piquant, *adj.* pungent, sharp; piquant.
pique, *s. f.* pike; *s. m.* *(cards)* spade.
pique-nique, *s. m.* picnic.
piquer, *v. a. & n.* prick, sting; lard; goad, spur.
piqûre, *s. f.* prick, sting; puncture; injection.
pirate, *s. m.* pirate.
pire, *adj.* worse.
pis, *adv.* worse.
piscine, *s. f.* swimming-pool.
piste, *s. f.* track; trace; runway.
pistolet, *s. m.* pistol.
pitié, *s. f.* pity.
placard, *s. m.* placard, poster; cupboard.

place, *s. f.* place; room; seat; square.
placement, *s. m.* placing; investment; *bureau de* ~ labour-exchange.
placer, *v. a.* place, put, set; invest; sell.
plafond, *s. m.* ceiling.
plage, *s. f.* beach.
plaider, *v. a. & n.* plead.
plaindre, *v. a.* pity, feel compassion for; **se** ~ complain.
plaine, *s. f.* plain.
plainte, *s. f.* complaint.
plaire*, *v. n.* please; *vous plaît-il de?* would you like to?; *s'il vous plaît* (if you) please; **se** ~ take pleasure, enjoy.
plaisant, *adj.* pleasant, pleasing.
plaisanterie, *s.f.* joke, jest; *par* ~ as a joke.
plaisir, *s. m.* pleasure.
plan, *s. m.* plan; design; plane.
planche, *s.f.* board, plank.
plancher, *s. m.* floor.
planer, *v. a.* plane.
plante, *s. f.* plant; sole.
planter, *v. a.* plant; set.
planteur, *s. m.* planter.
plaque, *s. f.* plate; slab; plaque; ~ *de police* number-plate.
plaquer, *v. a.* plate; lay on.
plastique, *adj.* plastic, — *s. f.* plastic art; figure; — *s. m.* plastics *pl.*
plastron, *s. m.* (shirt-) front; plastron; stiff shirt.
plat, *adj.* flat; plain; dull; — *s. m.* flat (part); blade.
plateau, *s.m.* tray; scale (of balance); plateau.
plate-bande, *s. f.* flower-bed.
plate-forme, *s.f.* platform.
plâtre, *s. m.* plaster.
plein, *adj.* full; filled; *en* ~ fully, entirely.
pleurer, *v. n.* cry, weep.
pleuvoir: *il pleut* it rains.
pli, *s. m.* fold, crease.
pliant, *adj.* flexible, pliant; folding.
plier, *v. a. & n.* fold (up), bend; **se** ~ submit *(à* to).
plisser, *v. a. & n.* plait, fold, tuck; wrinkle.
plomb, *s.m.* lead.
plombage, *s. m.* filling.
plombier, *s. m.* plumber.
plonger, *v. a. & n.* plunge, immerse, dip, dive.
pluie, *s. f.* rain.
plume, *s. f.* feather, plume, pen.
plupart, *s. f.* most, the greatest part, majority.
pluriel, *s. m.* plural.
plus, *adv.* more, most; further, longer; any more; *de* ~ *en* ~ more and more; *en* ~ *de* in addition to; *ne . . .* ~ no more, no longer.
plusieurs, *adj.* several, many, some, a few; — *pron.* several people.
plutôt, *adv.* rather, preferably.
pluvieux, -euse, *adj.* rainy, wet.
pneu(matique), *s. m.* tyre.
pneumonie, *s. f.* pneu-

monia.
poche, *s. f.* pocket; pouch.
poêle[1], *s. m.* stove.
poêle[2], *s. f.* frying pan.
poème, *s. m.* poem.
poésie, *s. f.* poetry; poesy.
poète, *s. m.* poet.
poétique, *adj.* poetic(al).
poids, *s. m.* weight.
poignant, *adj.* poignant.
poigne, *s. f.* grip, grasp.
poignée, *s. f.* handle; hilt; handful.
poignet, *s. m.* wrist; cuff.
poil, *s. m.* hair; bristle; coat.
poinçon, *s.m.* punch, bodkin.
poinçonner, *v. a.* punch, clip; stamp.
poing, *s.m.* fist.
point, *s. m.* point, dot; full stop; *deux* ~*s* colon; ~ *et virgule* semicolon; *à* ~ just in time; *être sur le* ~ *de* be about to; ~ *de vue* point of view.
pointe, *s. f.* point, head, tip.
pointer, *v. a. & n.* point.
pointu, *adj.* sharp, pointed.
poire, *s. f.* pear.
pois, *s. m.* pea.
poison, *s. m.* poison.
poisson, *s. m.* fish.
poissonnier, **-ère**, *s. m. f.* fishmonger.
poitrine, *s. f.* chest, breast.
poivre, *s. m.* pepper.
pôle, *s. m.* pole.
poli, *adj.* polished; polite.
police, *s. f.* police; policy; *agent de* ~ policeman.
policier, *s. m.* policeman.
policlinique, *s.f.* out-patients' department.
polir, *v. a.* polish, refine.
politesse, *s. f.* politeness.
politicien, **-enne**, *s. m. f.* politician.
politique, *s. f.* politics.
polonais, **-e (P.)**, *adj.* Polish; — *s. m.* Pole; *s. f.* Polish woman; polonaise.
pomme, *s. f.* apple; ~ *de terre* potato.
pommier, *s. m.* apple tree.
pompe[1], *s. f.* pomp, ceremony.
pompe[2], *s. f.* pump; ~ *à incendie* fire-engine; ~ *à essence* petrol pump.
pompier, *s. m.* fireman; *les* ~*s* fire-brigade.
ponctuel, **-elle**, *adj.* punctual.
pont, *s. m.* bridge; deck; ~ *suspendu* suspension-bridge; ~ *inférieur* lower deck.
populaire, *adj.* popular; vulgar, common.
popularité, *s. f.* popularity.
population, *s. f.* population.
populeux, **-euse**, *adj.* populous.
porc, *s. m.* pig, hog; pork.
porcelaine, *s. f.* porcelain, china(ware).
pore, *s. m.* pore.
poreux, **-euse**, *adj.* porous.
port[1], *s.m.* harbour (sea-)port; *arriver à bon* ~ arrive safely.
port[2], *s. m.* bearing, gait; carriage; postage; ~ *payé* postage paid.

portable, *adj.* portable.
porte, *s. f.* door(way), entrance; ~ *d'entrée* front-door.
porte-cigarettes, *s. m. pl.* cigarette-case.
portée, *s. f.* litter; range, scope; *à* ~ within reach.
portemanteau, *s.m.* coat-stand; suit-case.
porter, *v. a. & n.* bear; carry; convey; wear, have on; hold; ~ *intérêt* yield interest; show interest; ~ *la santé de B* drink B's health; **se** ~ be worn, be carried; *comment vous portez-vous?* how are you?
porteur, *s. m.* porter, carrier; bearer.
portier, -ère, *s. m. f.* porter, door-keeper.
portière, *s. f.* door (on vehicle); (door-)curtain.
portion, *s. f.* portion, part, share; helping.
portrait, *s. m.* portrait.
portugais, -e (P.), *adj. & s. m. f.* Portuguese.
posemètre, *s. m.* light-meter.
poser, *v. a. & n.* place, lay down, put; state.
positif, -ive, *adj. & s. m. f.* positive.
position, *s.f.* position, situation; attitude.
posséder, *v.a.* possess.
possession, *s.f.* possession; property.
possibilité, *s.f.* possibility.
possible, *adj.* possible; *faire tout son* ~ do one's best.
postal, *adj.* postal; post; *carte* ~*e* post-card.
poste[1], *s. f.* post(-office), mail; *mettre à la* ~ post (a letter); *bureau de* ~ post-office; *timbre* ~ stamp; ~ *aérienne* air-mail.
poste[2], *s. m.* post, station, office; police-station; receiver, set; ~ *de T. S. F.* wireless-set.
postulant, -e, *s. m. f.* applicant, candidate.
pot, *s. m.* pot, can, jug, vessel, pitcher.
potager, *s.m.* kitchen garden.
poteau, *s. m.* post.
poterie, *s. f.* pottery.
potin, *s. m.* noise; (piece of) gossip.
poubelle, *s. f.* dustbin.
pouce, *s.m.* thumb.
pouding, *s. m.* pudding.
poudre, *s. f.* powder, dust.
poudrier, *s. m.* compact.
poule, *s.f.* hen; fowl.
poulet, *s.m.* chicken, fowl.
pouls, *s. m.* pulse.
poumon, *s. m.* lung(s).
poupée, *s. f.* doll.
pour, *prep.* for; ~ *cent* per cent; ~ *que* in order that.
pourboire, *s. m.* tip.
pourquoi, *conj. & adv.* why; what for; for what reason.
poursuite, *s. f.* pursuit, chase; ~*s* suit, action.
poursuivre, *v. a.* pursue, chase, prosecute.
pourtant, *adv.* however, still.

pourvoir, *v. n. & a.* provide (*à* for), supply, cater (*à* for).
pousser, *v. a. & n.* push; shove; urge; impel; grow; utter.
poussière, *s. f.* dust
poussiéreux, -euse *adj.* dusty.
pouvoir*, *v. a. & n.* be able, may; **se ~** be possible; *cela se peut* that may be; — *s. m.* power.
pratique, *s. f.* practice, execution; experience; customers *(pl.)*; — *adj.* practical, convenient.
pratiquer, *v. a.* practise, carry out; exercise.
préalable, *adj.* previous, *au* ~ first of all.
précédent, *adj.* precedent, previous; — *s. m.* precedent.
précéder, *v. a. & n.* precede; come before.
prêcher, *v. a. & n.* preach.
prêcheur, *s. m.* preacher.
précieux, -euse, *adj.* precious, valuable, costly.
précipice, *s. m.* precipice.
précipitation, *s. f.* precipitation, haste, hurry.
précipité, *adj.* hasty.
précipiter, *v. a.* precipitate; hasten, hurry.
précis, *adj.* exact, precise; — *s. m.* summary.
préciser, *v. a.* specify.
prédécesseur, *s. m.* predecessor.
prédire, *v. a.* foretell.
préfabriqué, *adj.* prefabricated.
préface, *s. f.* preface.
préférable, *adj.* preferable, better.
préférer, *v. a.* prefer; like better.
préfet, *s. m.* prefect.
préjugé, *s. m.* prejudice, presumtion.
prélat, *s. m.* prelate.
préliminaire, *adj.* preliminary.
premier, -ère, *adj.* first, former; ~ *plan* foreground; close-up; *de ~ ordre* first-rate; ~ — *s. m.* first floor.
première, *s. f.* first night; first class (in a carriage).
prendre*, *v. a.* take, take up, seize; receive, accept; put on, wear; charge; catch; ~ *place* take a seat; *à tout* ~ on the whole; ~ *pour* mistake for; ~ *du corps* put on weight; ~ *l'air* take a walk; se ~ be taken, be caught.
prénom, *s. m.* Christian name.
préoccuper, *v. a.* preoccupy, engross; worry; se ~ trouble oneself.
préparatifs, *s. m. pl.* preparations.
préparation, *s. f.* preparation.
préparer, *v. a.* prepare, make ready; read for; se ~ prepare oneself, get ready.
préposition, *s. f.* preposition.
prérogative, *s. f.* prerogative, privilege.

près, *adv.* & *prep.* near, close by, close to; nearly; *à peu* ~ nearly (so); *de* ~ closely.
prescription, *s. f.* prescription.
prescrire*, *v. t.* prescribe.
présence, *s. f.* presence, attendance; *en* ~ *de* in the presence of.
présent[1], *s. m.* present, gift; *faire* ~ *de* give as a present.
présent[2], *s. m.* present (time); present tense; — *adj.* present, current *à* ~ at present; *jusqu'à* ~ till now, as yet; *pour le* ~ for the time being.
présentation, *s. f.* presentation, introduction.
présenter, *v. a.* present, offer; introduce; **se** ~ appear.
préserver, *v. a.* preserve.
président, *s. m.* president.
présomption, *s. f.* presumption; conceit.
presque, *adv.* almost.
pressant, *adj.* pressing.
presse, *s. f.* press; printing-press; haste; crowd.
pressé, *adj.* pressing; *être* ~ be in a hurry.
pressentiment, *s. m.* presentiment; misgiving.
pressentir, *v.a.* have a presentiment of.
presser, *v. a.* press, crush; hurry; *pressez-vous!* hurry up!; **se** ~ hurry (up).
pression, *s.f.* pressure.
pressurer, *v.a.* press, squeeze; oppress.
prestige, *s.m.* marvel; influence, prestige.
présumer, *v. a.* suppose, expect; presume.
prétendre, *v. a.* & *n.* pretend, claim; intend.
prétention, *s. f.* pretension, claim.
prêter, *v.a.* lend, attribute; **se** ~ lend oneself (*à* to).
prétexte, *s. m.* pretext.
prêtre, *s. m.* priest.
preuve, *s. f.* proof; *faire* ~ *de* show.
prévaloir, *v.n.* prevail.
prévenir, *v. a.* anticipate, inform, let know.
préventif, -ive, *adj.* preventive.
prévention, *s.f.* bias, prejudice.
prévision, *s. f.* prevision, anticipation; forecast.
prévoir, *v.a.* foresee, anticipate, forecast.
prévoyance, *s. f.* foresight.
prier, *v. a.* pray, beg; ask.
prière, *s.f.* prayer; request.
primaire, *adj.* primary.
prime, *adj.* first, early.
primer, *v. a.* surpass, excel; award a prize to.
primeur, *s. f.* early vegetables *(pl.)*.
primitif, -ive, *adj.* primitive, original.
prince, *s. m.* prince.
princesse, *s. f.* princess.
principal, *adj.* principal.
principalement, *adv.* principally, mainly.
principe, *s. m.* principle.
printemps, *s. m.* spring(time); *au* ~ in spring.

priorité, *s.f.* priority.
prise, *s.f.* taking; capture, catch; ~ *de courant* (electric) plug.
prisme, *s. m.* prism.
prison, *s. f.* prison.
prisonnier, -ère, *s. m. f.* prisoner.
privation, *s. f.* privation.
privé, *adj.* private.
priver, *v. a.* deprive.
privilège, *s. m.* privilege.
prix, *s. m.* price, cost, charge; prize; *au ~ de* at the cost of; *~ de la course* fare; *~ par mille* mileage; *~ courant* market-price; *~ fixe* fixed price.
probabilité, *s. f.* probability.
probable, *adj.* probable.
probablement, *adv.* probably.
problématique, *adj.* problematic(al).
problème, *s. m.* problem.
procédé *s. m.* proceeding.
procéder, *v. n.* proceed.
procédure, *s. f.* procedure.
procès, *s.m.* (law-)suit, trial; *faire un ~ u* bring an action against.
procession, *s.f.* procession.
prochain, *adj.* near(est), next. — *s. m.* neighbour
prochainement, *adv.* shortly, soon.
proche, *adj.* near, neighbouring, close at hand.
proclamer, *v. a.* proclaim.
procurer, *v. a.* procure.
procureur, *s. m.* attorney.
prodigieux, -euse, *adj.* wonderful, prodigious.
producteur, -trice, *s. m. f.* producer; — *adj.* producing.
production, *s. f.* production.
produire*, *v. a.* produce, bring forth, yield.
produit, *s. m.* produce; product.
professer, *v. a. & n.* profess; teach.
professeur, *s. m.* teacher; professor; lecturer.
profession, *s. f.* profession.
professionnel, -elle, *adj.* & *s. m. f.* professional.
profil, *s. m.* profile.
profit, *s. m.* profit, gain.
profitable, *adj.* pro'itable.
profiter, *v. n.* profit (by).
profond, *adj.* deep, profound.
profondeur, *s. f.* depth; *dix pieds de ~* ten feet deep.
programme, *s. m.* program(me); scheme.
progrès, *s. m.* progress, improvement; *faire des ~* make progress.
prohiber, *v.a.* prohibit.
projecteur, *s. m.* headlight; searchlight; projector.
projectile, *s. m.* projectile, missile.
projection, *s. f.* projection.
projet, *s. m.* project, plan; scheme; *~ de loi* bill.
projeter, *v.a.* project throw; scheme, plan.

prolonger, *v.a.* prolong.
promenade, *s.f.* walk; promenade.
promener: se ~ *go* for a walk; *se* ~ *en voiture* go for a drive.
promesse, *s. f.* promise.
promettre, *v. a.* promise.
promotion, *s. f.* promotion.
prompt, *adj.* prompt.
pronom, *s. m.* pronoun.
prononcer, *v.a. &n.* pronounce; utter; deliver.
prononciation, *s. f.* pronunciation; delivery.
propagande, *s. f.* propaganda.
propager, *v.a.* propagate.
prophète, *s.m.f.* prophet.
prophétie, *s. f.* prophecy.
proportion, *s. f.* proportion; ratio.
propos, *s. m.* talk, remark; *à* ~ in good time; by the way.
proposer, *v.a.* propose, offer.
proposition, *s. f.* proposal, proposition.
propre, *adj* own, peculiar; proper, fit.
propriétaire, *s.m.f.* owner, proprietor; landlord, landlady.
propriété, *s. f.* ownership; property.
propulsion, *s. f.* propulsion; ~ *à réaction* jet propulsion.
prosaïque, *adj.* prosaic.
proscrire*, *v. a.* proscribe.
prose, *s. f.* prose.
prospectus, *s.m.* prospectus.
prospère, *adj.* prosperous.
prospérer, *v. n.* prosper, get on (well).
prospérité, *s. f.* prosperity.
protecteur, *s. m.* protector, patron.
protection, *s.f.* protection, support.
protéger, *v.a.* protect; patronize.
protestant, -e, *s. m. f. & adj.* Protestant.
protestation, *s.f.* protest(ation).
protester, *v. n. & a.* protest.
prouver, *v.a.* prove.
provenir, *v.n.* come (from), issue, arise.
province, *s. f.* province, country, district.
provincial, *adj.* provincial, country.
provision, *s. f.* provision.
provisoire, *adj.* provisional, temporary.
provoquer, *v. a.* provoke; stir up.
proximité, *s. f.* proximity.
prudence, *s. f.* prudence, caution.
prudent, *adj.* prudent, cautious.
prune, *s. f.* plum.
pruneau, *s. m.* prune.
prunelle, *s. f.* pupil.
psaume, *s. m.* psalm.
psychologie, *s. f.* psychology.
psychologique, *adj.* psychological.
public, publique, *adj.* public, common; — *s. m.* public, audience.

publication, *s.f.* publication.
publicité, *s. f.* publicity.
publier, *v. a.* publish.
puce, *s. f.* flea.
puer, *v. n.* stink.
puéril, *adj.* childish.
puis, *adv.* then, after that.
puiser, *v. a.* draw up, fetch up.
puisque, *conj.* as, since.
puissance, *s.f.* power, might, force.
puissant, *adj.* powerful, strong; *tout* ~ almighty.
puits, *s. m.* well; pit.
punaise, *s. f.* drawing-pin; bug.
punch, *s.m.* punch *(drink)*.
punir, *v. a.* punish.
punition, *s.f.* punishment.
pupille, *s.m.f.* ward, pupil; — *s. f.* pupil (of the eye).
pupitre, *s. m.* desk.
pur, *adj.* pure, clean.
purée, *s. f.* mash, purèe.
purement, *adv.* purely, merely.
pureté, *s. f.* purity.
purgatif, -ive, *adj.* & *s. m.* purgative.
purger, *v. a.* purge.
purifier, *v.a.* purify, cleanse.
puritain, -e, *adj.* & *s. m. f.* Puritan.
pyramide, *s. f.* pyramid.

Q

quai, *s. m.* quay; wharf; platform; *billet de* ~ platform ticket.
qualification, *s. f.* qualification.
qualifié, *adj.* qualified.
qualifier, *v.a.* qualify.
qualité, *s.f.* quality.
quand, *adv.* & *conj.* when; while; ~ *même* all the same.
quant à, *prep.* as for, with regard to.
quantité, *s. f.* quantity; amount; ~ *de* plenty of.
quarante, *adj.* & *s. m.* forty.
quart, *s.m.* quarter, fourth part; quart.
quartier, *s. m.* quarter; piece, slice; district; ~ *général* headquarters *(pl.)*.
quatorze, *adj.* & *s.m.* fourteen.
quatre, *adj.* &*s.m.* four; fourth:
quatre-vingt-dix, *adj.* & *s. m.* ninety.
quatre-vingts, *adj.* & *s. m.* eighty.
quatrième, *adj.* & *s. m.* fourth; fourth floor; — *s. f.* third form.
quatuor, *s. m.* quartet(te).
que, qu', *rel. pron.* whom, which, that; of which, at which; — *adv.* how much, how many; — *conj.* that; than; as; if; as though.
quel, quelle, *adj.* what, which.
quelque, *adj.* some, any; a few; ~ *chose* something, anything; ~ *part* somewhere; ~ *peu*

somewhat — *adv.* about, some.
quelquefois, *adv.* sometimes.
quelqu'un, -e, *pron.* somebody; anybody.
querelle, *s. f.* quarrel.
quereller, *v. a. & n.* quarrel with.
question, *s.f.* question; point, matter, issue.
questionner, *v.a.* question, interrogate.
queue, *s.f.* tail; rear; queue; handle.
qui, *rel. pron.* who, whom; which; that; *à* ~ to whom.
quille, *s. f.* keel, skittle.
quincaillerie, *s. f.* hardware (shop).
quintal, *s. m.* hundredweight.
quinze, *adj. & s. m.* fifteen; fifteenth; ~ *jours* fortnight.
quittance, *s. f.* receipt.
quitte, *adj.* quit, free.
quitter, *v. a.* leave, give up, quit.
quoi, *rel. pron.* what, which; *à propos de* ~ what is it about?; ~ *qu'il en soit* at any rate.
quoique, *conj.* (al)though.
quotidien, -enne, *adj. & s. m.* daily.

R

rabais, *s. m.* reduction in price, rebate.
rabaisser, *v. a.* lower.
rabattre, *v.a.* beat down, pull down; reduce.
raccommoder, *v. a.* mend, repair.
raccourcir, *v.a. & n.* shorten, abridge.
raccrocher, *v.a.* hang up again.
race, *s. f.* race; stock; breed.
racine, *s. f.* root; *prendre* ~ take root.
raconter, *v.a.* tell, relate.
radar, *s. m.* radar.
radiateur, *s. m.* radiator.
radiation *s. f.* radiation.
radical, *adj.* radical.
radieux, -euse, *adj.* radiant, beaming.
radio, *s. f.* radio.
radio-actif, -ive, *adj.* radioactive.
radiodiffuser, *v.a.* broadcast.
radiodiffusion, *s. f.* broadcasting.
radiogramme, *s. m.* X-ray photograph; radiogram.
radiographie, *s. f.* X-ray photograph(y).
radioreportage, *s. m.* running commentary.
radioscopie, *s. f.* radioscopy.
radioscopique, *adj. examen* ~ X-ray examination.
radis, *s.m.* radish.
raffermir, *v.a.* strengthen, fortify.
raffinage, *s.m.* refining.
raffiné, *adj.* refined.
raffinement, *s. m.* refinement.
raffiner, *v. a.* refine.
rafraîchir, *v. a.* refresh,

cool; se ~ cool down.
rafraîchissement, *s.m.* refreshment; *~s* refreshments.
rage, *s.f.* rage, fury.
ragoût, *s. m.* ragout, stew.
raide, *adj.* stiff, rigid.
raidir, *v. a.* make stiff.
raifort, *s.m.* horse radish.
rail, *s. m.* rail.
railler, *v.a.* mock, rail at.
raillerie, *s.f.* raillery, mocking.
raisin, *s. m.* grape(s); *~ sec* raisin.
raison, *s.f.* reason; judgement; *à ~ de* at the rate of; *avoir ~* be right.
raisonnable, *adj.* reasonable.
raisonnement, *s. m.* reasoning.
raisonner, *v. n. & a.* reason, argue.
ralentir, *v. a. & n.* slow down.
ramasser, *v.a.* gather up, pick up; take up.
rame, *s. f.* oar; prop.
ramener, *v.a.* bring back, take back.
ramer, *v. n.* row.
rampe, *s.f.* banister; footlights *(pl.)*.
ramper, *v.n.* crawl, creep.
rance, *adj.* rancid.
rancune, *s.f.* spite, grudge.
randonneur, -euse, *s. m. f.* excursionist, hiker.
rang, *s.m.* row, line; rank.
rangé, *adj.* tidy.
rangée, *s.f.* row, line, range.
ranger, *v. a.* put in order; arrange; range; se ~ settle down; make room.
ranimer, *v.a.* revive, restore to life, refresh.
râpe, *s.f.* rasp, grater.
râpé, *adj.* shabby.
rapide, *adj.* rapid, fast; steep.
rapidité, *s.f.* rapidity, speed.
rappel, *s.m.* recall.
rappeler, *v. a.* recall, call back; bring back; se ~ remember.
rapport, *s.m.* product, yield; report, account; connection, relation; reference; *sous ce ~* in this respect.
rapporter, *v.a.* bring back; produce, yield; report, state; se ~ relate to, refer to.
rapprochement, *s. m.* drawing closer.
rapprocher, *v. a.* bring closer; se ~ draw nearer.
raquette, *s. f.* racket.
rare, *adj.* rare.
raser, *v. a.* shave, graze; pull down; bore; *v.n.* se ~ shave.
rasoir, *s. m.* razor; *~ électrique* electric razor; *~ de sûreté* safety razor.
rassembler, *v. a.* gather, assemble, collect.
rassis, *adj.* settled; stale.
rassurer, *v.a.* reassure,

comfort.
rat, *s. m.* rat.
râteau, *s. m.* rake.
ratelier, *s. m.* rack; set of false teeth.
rater, *v. n. & a.* miss fire; fail.
ratification, *s. f.* ratification.
ration, *s. f.* ration.
rattacher, *v.a.* tie up again, join.
rattraper, *v.a.* catch again; catch up; overtake.
rauque, *adj.* hoarse.
ravager, *v. a.* ravage, lay waste.
ravir, *v. a.* delight.
ravissant, *adj.* ravishing, charming.
rayer, *v. a.* scratch (out); cross out.
rayon, *s.m.* ray, beam; spoke; radius; shelf.
rayonnement, *s. m.* radiation; radiance.
rayonner, *v.n.* radiate, shine.
razzia, *s. f.* raid.
réacteur, *s.m.* reactor.
réactoin, *s.f.* reaction.
réagir, *v.n.* react.
réalisation, *s.f.* realization; carrying out.
réaliser, *v.a.* realize.
réaliste, *adj.* realistic.
réalité, *s. f.* reality; *en* ~ in fact.
rebelle, *adj.* rebellious; — *s. m. f.* rebel.
rébellion, *s. f.* rebellion.
rebord, *s.m.* edge, brim.
rébus, *s.m.* riddle.
récemment, *adv.* recently, lately.
récent, *adj.* recent.
récepteur, *s. m.* receiver.
réception, *s. f.* reception, receipt; at-home.
recette, *s.f.* receipt; recipe.
receveur, *s.m.* receiver; conductor *(bus)*.
recevoir*, *v.n.* receive; admit, take in; accept; *v. n.* entertain; *aller* ~ *qn. à la gare* meet s.o. at the station.
rechange, *s. m. pièces de* ~ spare parts.
recharge, *s. f.* refill.
réchaud, *s.m.* dish-warmer.
réchauffer, *v. a.* warm up again.
recherche, *s.f.* research; inquiry.
rechercher, *v. a.* look for, search for; research into.
récipé, *s.m.* recipe.
réciproque, *adj.* reciprocal, mutual.
récit, *s. m.* recital, account.
récital, *s. m.* recital.
récitation, *s. f.* recitation.
réciter, *v.a.* recite.
réclamation, *s. f.* claim, complaint.
réclame, *s. f.* advertisement; *faire de la* ~ *(pour)* advertise.
réclamer, *v.a.* demand, claim.
recommandation, *s. f.* recommendation.
recommander, *v. a.* recommend; introduce; request; register.

recommencer, *v. a. & n.* begin again.
récompense, *s. f.* reward.
récompenser, *v. a.* reward, repay.
réconcilier, *v. a.* reconcile.
reconnaissance, *s. f.* recognition, gratitude.
reconnaître, *v. a.* recognize, know; acknowledge; explore.
reconstruction, *s. f.* reconstruction.
reconstruire*, *v.a.* rebuild.
record, *s.m.* record *(sport etc.).*
recourir, *v. n.* ~ *à* have recourse to.
recouvrir, *v.a.* cover again, hide.
récréation, *s. f.* recreation, amusement, pastime.
recrue, *s. f.* recruit.
recteur, *s.m.* rector, chancellor.
rectifier, *v.a.* rectify, correct.
reçu, *s. m.* receipt; *au* ~ *de* on receipt of.
recueil, *s. m.* collection.
recueillir, *v.a.* collect; **se** ~ collect oneself.
reculer, *v.a.* put back; *v. n.* draw back, recoil.
rédacteur, -trice, *s. m. f.* editor; writer.
rédaction, *s. f.* drawing up; composition; editorial staff.
rédemption, *s. f.* redemption.
rédiger, *v.a.* draw up; edit.
redingote, *s.f.* frock-coat.
redire, *v. a.* repeat, say again; *trouver à* ~ *à* find fault with.
redoubler, *v.a.* redouble.
redoutable, *adj.* formidable, dreaded.
redouter, *v.a.* dread, be afraid of.
redresser, *v. a.* & **se** ~ straighten (up).
réduction, *s. a.* reduction, cut.
réduire*, *v. a.* reduce, cut down.
réduit, *adj.* reduced.
réel, réelle, *adj.* real, actual.
réélection, *s.f.* re-election.
réélire, *v. a.* re-elect.
refaire, *v.a.* do (over) again.
réfectoire, *s. m.* refectory, dining-hall.
référence, *s. f.* reference.
référer, *v. a.* refer; **se** ~ *à* refer to; *nous référant à* referring to.
réfléchir, *v.a.* reflect; consider, think over.
réflecteur, *s. m.* reflector.
reflet, *s. m.* reflection.
refléter, *v. a.* reflect.
réflexe, *adj.* reflex.
réflexion, *s. f.* reflection, consideration.
reflux, *s. m.* ebb.
réformation, *s.f.* reformation.
réforme, *s.f.* reform, improvement.
Réforme, *s. f.* Reformation.
réformer, *v. a.* reform.
refrain, *s. m.* refrain.

refréner, *v. a.* bridle, curb.
réfrigérateur, *s.m.* refrigerator.
réfrigérer, *v. a.* refrigerate.
refroidir, *v. a.* chill, cool.
refuge, *s. m.* refuge; lay-by.
refugié, -e, *s. m. f.* refugee.
réfugier: se ~ take shelter, take refuge.
refus, *s. m.* refusal, denial.
refuser, *v. a.* refuse, deny; ~ *de connaître* ignore; *être refusé* fail.
regagner, *v.a.* regain, recover; return to.
regard, *s. m.* look.
regarder, *v. a.* look at; concern; regard.
régime, *s. m.* (form of) government; diet.
régiment, *s. m.* regiment.
région, *s. f.* region, area.
régional, *adj.* local.
régir, *v.a.* rule, administer.
régisseur, *s. m.* steward; stage-manager.
registre, *s.m.* register; record.
règle, *s. f.* rule; ruler.
réglé, *adj.* regular; punctual; steady; ruled.
règlement, *a.m.* rule, regulation.
régler, *v. a.* rule; regulate; time; settle.
règne, *s.m.* reign.
régner, *v.a.* reign.
regret, *s. m.* regret.
regretter, *v. a.* regret, be sorry for.
régulariser, *v. a.* regularize.
régularité, *s. f.* regularity.
régulateur, *s. m* regulator.
régulier, -ière, *adj.* regular; correct.
rein, *s.m.* kidney.
reine, *s.f.* queen.
reine-claude, *s. f.* greengage.
rejeter, *v. a.* reject, throw out.
rejoindre, *v.a.* rejoin; overtake, catch up; se ~ meet.
réjouir, *v. a.* give joy to, cheer up, delight; **se** ~ rejoice.
relâche, *s. f.* relaxation; respite.
relâcher, *v.a.* slacken, loosen; relax; **se** ~ relax.
relatif, -ive, *adj.* relative; ~ *à* relating to.
relation, *s.f.* relation, connection; report; *entrer en ~ avec* get in touch with.
relever, *v. a.* lift, take up, pick up; set off; *v. n.* recover.
relief, *s.m.* relief.
relier, *v. a.* bind (a book); hoop (casks).
religieux, -euse, *adj.* religious; — *s. m.* monk; *s. f.* nun.
religion, *s.f.* religion.
relique, *s.f.* relic.
relire, *v.a.* read (over) again.
remarquable, *adj.* remarkable, noticeable.
remarque, *s. f.* remark, observation, notice.
remarquer, *v. a.* remark,

notice, observe; *faire* ~ point out.
rembourser, *v.a.* repay, reimburse.
remède, *s.m.* remedy; medicine.
remerciement, *s. m.* thanks *(pl.)*.
remercier, *v.a.* thank *(de* for).
remettre, *v. a.* put back; put on again; postpone; **se** ~ recover (oneself).
remilitariser, *v. a.* rearm.
remise, *s. f.* remittance; delivery; allowance; revival, restoration.
remonter, *v. n. & a.* go up, remount; bring up again; set up again.
remords, *s. m.* remorse.
remorque, *s. f.* tow(ing), trailer.
remorqueur, *s. m. (bateau)* ~ tug-boat.
remous, *s. m.* eddy(-water), whirl.
remplacer, *v. a.* replace, substitute.
remplir, *v. a.* fill; fill up; fulfil; carry out.
remporter, *v.a.* take away, carry off; get, obtain.
remuer, *v. a. & n.* move, fidget about; **se** ~ be busy, move.
rémunération, *s. f.* remuneration.
renaissance, *s. f.* renascence; revival; *la Renaissance* the Renaissance.
renaître, *v.n.* be born again, revive.
renard, *s.m.* fox.
rencontre, *s. f.* meeting, encounter; collision.
rencontrer, *v.a.* meet, meet with; come across; run into; **se** ~ *avec* meet, be met with.
rendement, *s. m.* output.
rendez-vous, *s. m.* appointment, rendezvous.
rendormir: se ~ go to sleep again.
rendre, *v.a.* give back, return; yield; render; convey; ~ *un arrêt* issue a decree; ~ *compte* render an account, realize; ~ *visite* pay a visit.
renfermer, *v. a.* lock up again, confine; contain, include.
renfler, *v.a.&n.* swell.
renforcer, *v. a.* strengthen, reinforce.
renfort, *s. m.* reinforcement; help.
renier, *v. a.* deny.
renom, *s.m.* reputation.
renommée, *s. f.* renown.
renoncer, *v.n.&a.* renounce, give up.
renouveler, *v.a.* renew, renovate.
renseignement, *s. m.* information; indication; *bureau des* ~*s* inquiry office.
renseigner, *v. a.* give information to; **se** ~ inquire, ask *(sur* about).
rente, *s. f.* income; rent.
rentrée, *s. f.* return; reopening.
rentrer, *v. n.* reenter, go

in; get back, return home.

renversé, *adj.* reversed, upset.

renverser, *v.a.* upset; overthrow; turn upside down; **se** ~ be upset, tip over.

renvoi, *s.m.* return; (cross-)reference.

renvoyer, *v.a.* return; dismiss; refer.

réorganiser, *v.a.* reorganize.

·épandre, *v.a.* pour; spread, scatter, diffuse.

·éparation, *s.f.* repair, amends.

·éparer, *v. a.* repair, mend; make up for.

epartir*, *v.a.* answer.

epas, *s. m.* meal.

epasser, *v. n.* pass again.

épéter, *v. a.* repeat; say again; rehearse.

épétition, *s. f.* repetition; rehearsal.

éplique, *s. f.* retort, reply, answer.

épliquer, *v. a.* & *n.* reply, answer.

épondre, *v. a.* & *n.* answer, reply; respond to.

·éponse *s.m.* answer; response; ~ *payée* reply paid.

·eporter, *v. a.* carry back, take back.

:epos, *s. m.* rest; *sans* ~ restless.

reposer, *v. a.* lay again; *v. n.* rest, lie.

repoussant, *adj.* repulsive.

repousser, *v. a.* push back; repulse; drive back.

reprendre, *v.a.* & *n.* take back, get back; take up, go on; ~ *sa parole* go back on one's word.

représentant, -e, *s. m. f.* representative.

représentation, *s. f.* show, production; performance; display; representation.

représenter, *v. a.* represent; show, display.

reprise, *s.f.* renewal.

reproche, *s. m.* reproach, blame.

reprocher, *v. a.* reproach (with); blame for.

reproduction, *s.f.* reproduction.

reproduire*, *v. a.* reproduce.

républicain, -e, *adj.* & *s. m. f.* republican.

république, *s. f.* republic.

répulsion, *s.f.* repulsion.

réputation, *s. f.* reputation.

requête, *s.f.* request, demand.

réserve, *s.f.* reserve; reservation; caution; *de* ~ spare; *mettre en* ~ lay by.

réserver, *v. a.* reserve, lay by; book (in advance).

réservoir, *s.m.* tank *(petrol etc.)*.

résidence, *s. f.* residence, dwelling.

résident, *s. m.* resident.

résignation, *s. f.* resignation; submission.

résigner, *v. a.* resign; **se** ~ *à* resign oneself, make up one's mind.

résistance, *s. f.* resistance.
résister, *v. n.* resist.
résolu, *adj.* resolute.
résolution, *s. f.* resolution.
résonance, *s. f.* resonance.
résonner, *v. n.* resound, ring.
résoudre*, *v.a.* resolve; solve; settle; **se ~** resolve, make up one's mind (to).
respect, *s. m.* respect.
respectable, *adj.* respectable, decent.
respecter *v. a.* respect.
respectif, -ive, *adj.* respective.
respectueux, -euse, *adj.* respectful.
respiration, *s. f.* respiration, breath(ing).
respirer, *v. n. & a.* breathe.
responsabilité, *s. f.* responsibility.
responsable, *adj.* responsible.
ressaisir, *v. a.* seize again.
ressemblance, *s. f.* resemblance, likeness.
ressemblant, *adj.* like, similar.
ressembler, *v* emble.
ressentiment, *s. m.* resentment, grudge.
ressentir, *v.a.* feel; resent; **se ~** be hurt; feel still.
resserrer, *v.a.* tighten; bind.
ressort, *s.m.* spring; energy.
ressortir, *v. n.* come out again; stand out.
ressource, *s. f.* resource.
restaurant, *s. m.* restaurant; **~** *à libre service* self-service restaurant.
restaurateur, -trice, *s. m. f.* restorer; restaurant keeper.
restauration, *s.f.* restoration.
restaurer, *v. a.* restore.
reste, *s. m.* rest, remainder.
rester, *v. n.* remain, be left, keep; **~** *en arrière,* lag behind.
restituer, *v. a.* restore.
restreindre*, *v. a.* restrict.
restriction, *s. f.* restriction.
résultat, *s.m.* result, issue; *avoir pour* **~** result in.
résulter, *v. n.* result *(de* from).
résumé, *s.m.* summing up.
résumer, *v.a.* sum up.
rétablir, *v.a.* restore.
retard, *s. m.* delay; *être en* **~** be late; be overdue.
retarder, *v.a.* delay, retard.
retenir, *v.a.* keep back, hold back; hinder.
retirer, *v.a.* draw back, pull back; extract, get, derive; **se ~** retire.
retomber, *v. n.* fall again, fall back; relapse.
retour, *s. m.* return; *en* **~** homeward bound; *être de* **~** be back.
retourner, *v. n.* turn back; return, go back; **se ~** turn round.
retracer, *v.a.* retrace;

relate, tell.
retraite, *s.f.* retreat; retirement; *mettre à la ~* superannuate.
retrancher, *v. a.* retrench.
rétrécir, *v.a.* contract; make narrower; shrink.
retrousser, *v. a.* turn up.
retrouver, *v. a.* find again, recover.
rétroviseur, *s. m.* (rear-vision) mirror.
réunion, *s.f.* reunion.
réunir, *v.a.* reunite; join again.
réussi, *adj.* successful.
réussir, *v. n.* succeed.
réussite, *s. f.* success.
revanche, *s. f.* revenge; return match; *en ~* in return.
rêve, *s. m.* dream.
réveil, *s. m.* waking.
réveille-matin *s. m.* alarm-clock.
réveiller, *v.a.* & **se ~** wake (up).
révéler, *v.a.* reveal; **se ~** come to light.
revenir, *v. n.* return, come back; recur; cost.
revenu, *s. m.* income.
rêver, *v. n.* dream.
révérence, *s. f.* reverence; curtsey.
révérend, *adj.* reverend.
rêverie, *s.f.* reverie, fancy.
revers, *s. m.* back, reverse, wrong side.
revêtir, *v.a.* put on; clothe; cover.
révision, *s. f.* revision.
revivre, *v. n.* live again; *faire ~* revive.
revoir, *v. a.* see again, look over; *au ~* good-bye (for the present).
révolte, *s. f.* revolt.
révolter, *v. a.* revolt; **se ~** revolt, rebel.
révolution, *s. f.* revolution; turn.
révolutionnaire, *adj.* & *s. m. f.* revolutionary.
revolver, *s. m.* revolver.
revue, *s. f.* review; magazine.
rez-de-chaussé, *s. m.* ground floor.
rhétorique, *s. f.* rhetoric.
rhum, *s. m.* rum.
rhumatisme, *s. m.* rheumatism.
rhume, *s. m.* cold (in the head).
ricaner, *v. n.* sneer, grin.
riche, *adj.* rich, well off.
richesse, *s.f.* wealth, riches *(pl.)*.
ride, *s. f.* wrinkle.
rideau, *s. m.* curtain.
rider, *v. a.* wrinkle.
ridicule, *adj.* ridiculous; — *s. m.* ridicule.
rien, *pron.* nothing; not ... anything; trifle.
rigoureux, -euse, *adj.* rigorous, severe.
rigueur, *s. f.* rigour.
rime, *s. f.* rhyme.
rincer, *v. a.* rinse.
rire*, *v. n.* laugh; *pour ~* for fun; — *s.m.* laugh(ing), laughter.
risque, *s. m.* risk.
risquer, *v.a.* risk, run the risk of.
rivage, *s. m.* beach, shore.
rival, -e, *adj.* & *s. m. f.* rival.
rivalité, *s. f.* rivalry.

rive, *s. f.* bank, shore, beach.
rivière, *s. f.* river, stream.
riz, *s. m.* rice.
robe, *s. f.* gown, dress, frock; robe; *~ de chambre* dressing-gown.
robinet, *s. m.* tap, cock.
robuste, *adj.* robust; strong, sturdy.
roc, *s. m.* rock.
roche, *s.f.* rock, boulder.
rocher, *s. m.* rock, crag.
roder, *v. a.* run in.
rôder, *v.n.* rove.
rogner, *v. a.* clip, pare.
rognon, *s. m.* kidney.
roi, *s. m.* king.
rôle, *s. m.* roll; part, rôle.
romain, -e (R.), *adj. & s. m. f.* Roman.
roman, *s. m.* novel; *~s* fiction.
romançier, -ère, *s. m. f.* novelist.
romanesque, *adj.* romantic.
romantique, *s. m.* romantic.
romantisme, *s. m.* romanticism.
rompre, *v. a. & n.* break.
rond, *adj.* round; — *s. m.* round, circle.
ronde, *s. f.* round; patrol; *à la ~* round about, around.
rondelle, *s. f.* ring, collar, washer.
ronfler, *v. n.* snore; roar.
ronger, *v.a.* gnaw, eat.
rose, *s. f.* rose; — *adj.* rosy, pink.
roseau, *s. m.* reed.
rosée, *s. f.* dew.
rosier, *s.m.* rose-tree, rose-bush.
rossignol, *s. m.* nightingale.
rôti, *s. m.* roast (meat).
rôtir, *v.a.* roast; toast; *faire ~* roast, bake.
roucouler, *v. n.* coo.
roue, *s.f.* wheel; *~ de secours* spare wheel; *~ dentée* cog-wheel.
rouge, *adj.* red; — *s. m.* red (colour); *bâton de ~* lipstick.
rougeur, *s.f.* redness, blush.
rougir, *v.n. & a.* turn red, make red; blush.
rouille, *s. f.* rust.
rouiller, *v. n. & a.* rust, get rusty.
roulage, *s.m.* rolling; carriage (of goods); haulage.
rouleau, *s.m.* roll; roller; scroll.
roulement, *s. m.* roll(ing), rotation; *~ à billes* ball-bearings.
rouler, *v. a. & n.* roll; roll up, wind up; turn, revolve.
roulotte, *s.f. ~ (de camping)* caravan.
roumain, -e (R.), *adj. & s. m. f.* Rumanian.
route, *s. f.* road; highway; course; way; *en ~* on the way; *en ~ pour* bound for; *code de la ~* highway code.
routine, *s. f.* routine.
roux, rousse, *adj.* red(dish).
royal, *adj.* royal.
royaliste, -e, *adj. & s. m. f.* royalist.

royaume, *s. m.* kingdom.
ruban, *s m.* ribbon; band.
rubis, *s m.* ruby.
ruche, *s. f.* hive.
rude, *adj.* rough, rude.
rue, *s. f.* street; ~ *barrée* no thoroughfare; ~ *de traverse* crossroad.
ruée, *s. f.* rush.
ruelle, *s. f.* lane.
ruer; se ~ rush, dash.
rugissement, *s. m.* roar.
ruine, *s. f.* ruin; wreck.
ruiner, *v.a.* ruin, destroy.
ruisseau, *s. m.* stream, brook; gutter.
ruisseler, *v.n.* stream, run, flow.
rumeur, *s. f.* noise; rumour.
ruminer, *v. a. & n.* ruminate, chew (the cud).
rupture, *s. f.* rupture.
ruse, *s. f.* craft, cunning.
rusé, *adj.* cunning, sly.
russe (R.), *adj. & s. m. f.* Russian.
russien, -enne (R.), *adj. & s. m. f.* Russian.
rustique, *adj.* rustic, rural.
rythme, *s. m.* rhythm.
rythmique, *adj.* rhytmical.

S

s' see **se.**
sa, *adj. poss.* his, her, its.
sable, *s. m.* sand.
sablonneux, -euse, *adj.* sandy.
sabre, *s. m.* sabre.
sac, *s. m.* bag, sack; ~ *a main* handbag; ~ *de couchage* sleeping-bag.
saccager, *v. a.* plunder.
sacré, *adj.* sacred, holy.
sacrement, *s. m.* sacrament.
sacrifice, *s.m.* sacrifice.
sacrifier, *v.a.* sacrifice.
sacristain, *s.m.* sexton.
sage, *adj.* wise, well-behaved.
sagesse, *s. f.* wisdom.
saignant, *adj.* bleeding; underdone.
saigner, *v. a. & n.* bleed.
saillant, *adj.* projecting.
sailllir, *v. n.* stand out, project. .
sain, *adj.* sound; ~ *et sauf* safe and sound.
saint, -e, *adj.* holy, sacred; — *s. m. f.* saint
saisir, *v.a.* seize.
saison, *s. f.* season.
salade, *s. f.* salad.
salaire, *s. m.* wages *(pl.)*, pay, salary.
sale, *adj.* dirty, filthy.
saler, *v. a.* salt.
saleté, *s. f.* dirt.
salière, *s. f.* salt-cellar.
salir, *v. a.* soil, dirty.
salle, *s. f.* hall; assembly room; house; ~ *d'attente* waiting-room; ~ *de classe* schoolroom; ~ *(de cours)* auditorium; ~ *familiale,* ~ *de séjour* living-room.
salon, *s. m.* drawing-room; saloon; *petit* ~ sitting-room.
saluer, *v. a. & n.* bow to; greet.

salut, *s. m.* salvation; bow, greeting.
samedi, *s. m.* Saturday.
sanatorium, *s. m.* sanatorium.
sanction, *s. f.* sanction.
sanctuaire, *s. m.* sanctuary.
sandale, *s. f.* sandal.
sang, *s. m.* blood.
sanglier, *s. m.* wild boar.
sanitaire, *adj.* sanitary.
sans, *prep.* without.
santé, *s. f.* health.
sapin, *s. m.* fir(-tree).
sarcasme, *s. m.* sarcasm.
sarcastique, *adj.* sarcastic.
sardine, *s. f.* sardine.
satellite, *s. m.* satellite.
satire, *s. f.* satire.
satisfaction, *s. f.* satisfaction.
savoir*, *v. n.* know, be aware; be trained in; understand; be able to; — *s. m.* knowledge, learning.
savon, *s. m.* soap.
savourer, *v. a.* taste, relish.
savoureux, -euse, *adj.* savoury, tasty.
scandale, *s. m.* scandal.
scaphandre autonome, *s. m.* skin diver.
scaphandrier, *s. m.* diver.
scarabée, *s. m.* beetle.
sceau, *s. m.* seal.
sceller, *v. a.* seal; fix.
scénario, *s. m.* scenario.
scène, *s. f.* scène; scenery; *fig.* **stage;** *mettre en* ~ **produce** (a play).
sceptre, *s. m.* sceptre.
scie, *s. f.* **saw.**
satisfaire, *v. a. & n.* satisfy, please.
satisfaisant, *adj.* satisfactory.
satisfait, *adj.* satisfied.
sauce, *s. f.* sauce.
saucisse, *s. f.* sausage.
sauf, sauve, *adj.* safe; — *prep.* except, save.
saumon, *s. m.* salmon.
saut, *s.m.* jump, leap.
sauter, *v. n.* leap, jump; spring; *faire* ~ blow up.
sauvage, *adj.* savage, wild.
sauver, *v. a.* save, rescue; se ~ run away.
sauveur, *s. m.* Saviour.
savant, -e, *adj.* learned, clever; expert; — *s. m. f.* scholar.
saveur, *s. f.* savour, taste.
science, *s. f.* science, knowledge; *homme de* ~ scientist.
scientifique, *adj.* scientific.
scier, *v. a.* saw.
scolaire, *adj.* school; *année* ~ school year.
scooter, *s. m.* motor-scooter.
scrupule, *s. m.* scruple.
sculpter, *v. a.* carve, sculpture.
sculpteur, *s. m.* sculptor.
sculpture, *s. f.* sculpture.
se, s' *pron.* himself, herself, itself; each other.
séance, *s. f.* sitting, meeting.
seau, *s. m.* pail.
sec, sèche, *adj.* dry dried up.
sécher, *v. a. & n.* dry

(up).
sécheresse, *s. f.* dryness.
second, *adj.* second.
secondaire, *adj.* secondary.
seconde, *s. f.* second.
seconder, *v. a.* back.
secouer, *v. a.* shake.
secourir, *v. a.* help.
secours, *s. m.* help, succour, aid; *au* ~ help!
secousse, *s. f.* shake, jolt, jerk.
secret, -ète, *adj. & s. m.* secret.
secrétaire, *s. m. f.* secretary; — *s. m.* writing-desk.
secrétariat, *s. m.* secretariate.
secteur, *s. m.* sector, section; ~ *(de courant)* mains.
section, *s. f.* section
sécurité, *s. f.* security.
sédatif, -ive, *adj. & s. m.* sedative.
sédiment, *s. m.* sediment.
séduire, *v. a.* seduce.
seigle, *s. m.* rye.
seigneur, *s.m.* lord, squire.
seize, *adj. & s. m.* sixteen; sixteenth.
seizième, *adj.* sixteenth.
séjour, *s. m.* stay, visit; (place of) residence.
séjourner, *v.n.* stay, sojourn.
sel, *s. m.* salt.
selle, *s. f.* saddle.
selon, *prep.* according to; after.
semaine, *s. f.* week.
semblable, *adj.* (a)like.
semblant, *s. m.* semblance; appearance.
sembler, *v. n.* appear, look, seem.
semelle, *s. f.* sole *(footwear)*.
semer, *v. a.* sow.
semestre, *s. m.* half year; semester.
séminaire, *s. m.* seminary.
sénat, *s. m.* senate.
sénateur, *s. m.* senator.
sens, *s. m.* sense; judgement, opinion; direction.
sensation, *s. f.* feeling; sensation.
sensé, *adj.* sensible, reasonable.
sensibilité, *s. f.* sensibility, feeling.
sensible, *adj.* sensible, perceptible; sensitive.
sentence, *s. f.* sentence.
senteur, *s. f.* scent, smell.
sentier, *s. m.* path.
sentiment, *s. m.* feeling, sense, sentiment.
sentimental, *adj.* sentimental.
sentinelle, *s. f.* sentry, sentinel.
sentir*, *v. a.* feel, perceive; experience; smell; se ~ feel.
séparation, *s. f.* separation.
séparer, *v. a.* separate, divide; se ~ part.
sept, *adj. & s. m.* seven; seventh.
septembre, *s. m.* September.
septième, *adj.* seventh.
sérénade, *s. f.* serenade.
sérénité, *s. f.* serenity.

sergent, *s. m.* sergeant.
série, *s. f.* series.
sérieux, -euse, *adj.* grave, serious.
serin, -e, *s. m. f.* canary.
seringue, *s. f.* syringe.
serment, *s. m.* oath.
sermon, *s. m.* sermon.
serpent, *s. m.* snake, serpent.
serpenter, *v. n.* wind, meander.
serre, *s. f.* claw; hot-house.
serré, *adj.* tight, close, serried.
serrer, *v. a.* press, crush, jam, tighten.
serre-tête, *s. m.* crash-helmet, headband.
serrure, *s. f.* lock.
serrurier, *s. m.* locksmith.
servante, *s. f.* servant.
service, *s. m.* service, duty; favour; set; *être de ~* be on duty; *à votre ~* at your disposal.
serviette, *s. f.* napkin; towel; briefcase.
servir,** *v. a. & n.* serve; be in the service of; *~ à* be used for; *ne se ~ à rien* be of no use; *Mme est servie* dinner is ready; **se ~** use, make use of, help oneself.
serviteur, *s. m.* servent.
servitude, *s. f.* servitude.
ses, *adj. poss.* his, her, its; one's.
session, *s. f.* session.
seuil, *s. m.* threshold.
seul, *adj.* alone, single, sole, only.
sévère, *adj.* severe, hard.
sévir, *v. n.* punish; rage.
sexe, *s. m.* sex.
sexuel, -elle, *adj.* sexual.
shampooing, *s. m.* shampoo.
si, *conj,* if, whether; — *adv.* so, so much, such.
siècle, *s. m.* century.
siège, *s. m.* seat.
sien, -enne, *poss. adj.* his, hers; its; one's.
siffler, *v. n.* whistle, hiss.
sifflet, *s. m.* whistle.
signal, *s. m.* signal; *~ d'alarme* communication-cord.
signaler, *v. a.* signal.
signalisation, *s. f.* signals *(pl.); feux de ~* traffic-lights.
signature, *s. f.* signature.
signe, *s. m.* sign.
signer, *v. a. & n.* sign.
significatif, -ive, *adj.* significant.
signification, *s. f.* signification; meaning.
signifier, *v. a.* signify.
silence, *s. m.* silence.
silencieux, -euse, *adj.* silent.
silhouette, *s. f.* outline, silhouette.
sillon, *s. m.* furrow.
simple, *adj.* simple.
simplicité, *s. f.* simplicity.
simplifier, *v. a.* simplify.
simultané, *adj.* simultaneous.
sincère, *adj.* sincere.
sincérité, *s. f.* sincerity.
singe, *s. m.* monkey.
singulier, -ère, *adj.* singular, strange.
sinon, *conj.* (or) else.

otherwise.
sire, *s. m.* sir, lord.
sirène, *s. f.* siren; hooter, fog-horn.
site, *s. m.* site, place.
sitôt, *adv.* as soon; ~ *que* as soon as; ~ . . . ~ no sooner. . . than.
situation, *s. f.* situation; state; office, position.
situer, *v. a.* place, locate.
six, *adj. & s. m.* six; sixth.
sixième, *adj.* sixth.
ski, *s. m.* ski; *faire du* ~ ski.
skieur, *s. m.* skier, ski-runner.
smoking, *s. m.* dinner-jacket.
sobre, *adj.* sober.
social, *adj.* social.
socialisme, *s. m.* socialism.
socialiste, *adj. & s. m. f.* socialist.
société, *s. f.* society; company; ~ *anonyme* limited liability company.
sœur, *s. f.* sister.
soi, *pron.* oneself; himself, herself; itself.
soi-disant, *adj.* so-called.
soie, *s. f.* silk.
soif, *s. f.* thirst; *avoir* ~ be thirsty.
soigner, *v. a.* take care of, look after.
soigneux, -euse, *adj.* careful.
soin, *s. m.* care; *prendre* ~ *de* take care of; *aux bons* ~*s de* c/o.
soir, *s. m.* evening.
soirée, *s. f.* evening (party).
soit, *conj.* say; suppose; either . . . or; ~ *que* whether.
soixante, *adj. & s. m.* sixty.
soixante-dix, *adj. & s. m.* seventy.
sol, *s. m.* soil; ground.
soldat, *s. m.* soldier.
soleil, *s. m.* sun; *il fait du* ~ the sun is shining.
solennel, -elle, *adj.* solemn.
solennité, *s. f.* solemnity.
solidarité, *s. f.* solidarity.
solide, *adj.* solid.
solidité, *s. f.* solidity.
solitaire, *adj.* solitary.
solitude, *s. f.* solitude.
solliciter, *v. a.* solicit, entreat.
sollicitude, *s. f.* care.
soluble, *adj.* soluble.
solution, *s. f.* solution.
sombre, *adj.* dark; dim.
sombrer, *v.n.* founder, sink.
sommaire, *adj. & s. m.* summary.
somme, *s. f.* sum, amount.
sommeil, *s. m.* sleep; *avoir* ~ be sleepy.
sommeiller, *v. n.* slumber.
sommer, *v. a.* summon.
sommet, *s. m.* top, summit.
sommier, *s. m.* spring mattress.
somnifère, *s. m.* sleeping-pill.
somnolent, *adj.* sleepy.
son[1], **sa,** *adj. poss.* (*pl.*

ses) his, her, its; one's.
son², *s. m.* sound.
songe, *s. m.* dream.
songer, *v. n.* dream.
sonner, *v. a.* & *n.* ring, sound; *on sonne (à la porte)* there is a ring at the door.
sonnette, *s. f.* bell.
sonore, *adj.* sonorous.
sorcier, *s. m.* sorcerer, wizard.
sorcière, *s. f.* witch, sorceress.
sornette, *s. f.* nonsense.
sort, *s. m.* fate, lot.
sorte, *s. f.* sort, kind.
sortie, *s. f.* going out; way out, exit; *~ secours* emergency exit.
sortir*, *v. n.* go out, walk out, leave; *ne pas ~* keep indoors; *v.a.* take out, bring out.
sot, sotte, *adj.* foolish, silly.
sottise, *s. f.* foolishness, nonsense.
sou, *s. m.* sou, copper, penny.
souci, *s. m.* care, concern.
soucier: se *~ de* care for.
soucieux, -euse, *adj.* full of care, anxious.
soucoupe, *s. f.* saucer.
soudain, *adj.* sudden; — *adv.* suddenly.
soude, *s. f.* soda *(chemical)*.
souffle, *s. m.* breath.
souffler, *v. a.* & *n.* breathe; blow (out).
soufflet, *s. m.* box (on the ear); bellows *(pl.)*.
souffrance, *s. f.* pain, suffering.
souffrir*, *v. a.* & *n.* suffer, bear.
souhaiter, *v. a.* desire.
soulever, *v. a.* lift, raise; se *~* rise (in rebellion).
soulier, *s. m.* shoe.
souligner, *v. a.* underline.
soumettre, *v. a.* submit, subdue; **se** *~* submit.
soumission, *s. f.* submission.
soupçon, *s. m.* suspicion.
soupçonner, *v. a.* suspect.
soupe, *s. f.* soup.
souper, *s. m.* supper; — *v. n.* have supper.
soupir, *s. m.* sigh.
soupirer, *v. n.* sigh; *~ après* long for.
souple, *adj.* supple, flexible.
source, *s. f.* source, spring.
sourcil, *s. m.* eyebrow.
sourd, *adj.* deaf.
sourd-muet, sourde-muette, *adj.* & *s. m. f.* deaf and dumb (person).
sourire, *v. n.* smile.
souris, *s. f.* mouse.
sous, *prep.* under; beneath; before.
souscripteur, *s. m.* subscriber.
souscription, *s. f.* subscription.
souscrire, *v. a.* & *n.* sign, subscribe (to).
sousdéveloppé, *adj.* under-developed.
sous-marin, *s. m.* submarine.
soussigné, -e, *adj.* & *s. m. f.* undersigned.

sous-sol, *s. m.* basement.
sous-titre, *s. m.* subtitle, caption.
soustraction, *s. f.* subtraction.
soustraire, *v. a.* take away; subtract.
soutenir, *v. a.* support, sustain, maintain.
souterrain, *adj.* underground; — *s. m.* subway.
soutien, *s. m.* support.
soutien-gorge, *s. m.* bra.
souvenir*, *s. m.* remembrance; souvenir; memory; — *v. reflex.* **se ~** remember.
souvent, *adv.* often.
souverain, -e, *s. m. f.* sovereign.
spatial, *adj.* *vaisseau* **~**, *véhicule* **~** space-craft, space-vehicle.
speaker, *s. m.* announcer.
speakerine, *s. f.* lady announcer.
spécial, *adj.* special.
spécialement, *adv.* specially, particularly.
spécialiser, *v. a.* specialize.
spécialiste, *s. m. f.* specialist.
spécialité, *s. f.* special(i)ty.
spécifier, *v. a.* specify.
spécifique, *adj.* specific.
spectacle, *s. m.* spectacle, sight.
spectateur, -trice, *s. m. f.* spectator, spectatress, onlooker; bystander.
spéculation, *s. f.* speculation.
spéculer, *v. n.* speculate.
sphère, *s. f.* sphere.
spirale, *adj.* spiral.
spirituel, -elle, *adj.* spiritual; witty.
splendeur, *s. f.* splendour.
splendide, *adj.* splendid.
spontané, *adj.* spontaneous.
sport, *s. m.* sport.
sportif, -ive, *adj.* sporting; sportsmanlike.
squelette, *s. m.* skeleton.
stade, *s. m.* stadium; *fig.* stage.
stalle, *s. f.* stall; box.
station, *s. f.* **standing**; stay; station, **stop**; **~** *balnéaire* **watering-place, spa.**
stationnement, *s. m.* **stationing; parking; ~** *interdit* **no parking.**
stationner, *v. n.* **stop; park.**
station-service, *s. f.* service-station.
statistique, *s. f.* statistics; — *adj.* statistical.
statue, *s. f.* statue.
statut, *s. m.* statute.
sténographie, *s. f.* shorthand.
stérile, *adj.* sterile.
stimuler, *v. a.* stimulate.
stipuler, *v. a.* stipulate.
store, *s. m.* (Venetian) blind.
strabisme, *s. m.* squint(ing).
stratégie, *s. f.* strategy.
structure, *s. f.* structure.
studieux, -euse, *adj.* studious.
stupéfier, *v. a.* stupefy.
stupide, *adj.* stupid, dull.

stupidité, *s. f.* stupidity.
style, *s. m.* style.
stylo, *s.m.* ~ *à bille* ball(-point) pen.
stylo(graphe), *s. m.* fountain-pen.
suave, *adj.* soft, gentle.
subjonctif, *s.m.* subjunctive.
subjuguer, *v.a.* subjugate, overcome.
submerger, *v. a.* submerge, flood.
subordonné, *adj.* subordinate.
subordonner, *v. a.* subordinate.
subséquent, *adj.* subsequent.
subsistance, *s. f.* subsistence.
subsister, *v. n.* subsist.
substance, *s. f.* substance.
substantiel, -elle, *adj.* substantial.
substantif, *s.m.* substantive.
substituer, *v.a.* substitute.
substitution, *s. f.* substitution.
subtil, *adj.* subtle.
subvention, *s. f.* subvention, subsidy.
succéder, *v. n.* succeed *(à* to), follow; **se** ~ follow one another.
succès, *s. m.* success; result.
successif, -ive, *adj.* successive.
succession, *s. f.* succession.
sucer, *v. a.* suck (in).
sucre, *s. m.* sugar.
sucré, *adj.* sweet(ened).
sud, *adj.* & *s. m.* south; *du* ~ southern; *au* ~ southward.
sud-est, *adj.* & *s. m.* south-east.
sud-ouest, *adj.* & *s. m.* south-west.
suédois, -e, (S.), *adj.* Swedish; — *s. m. f.* Swede; Swedish (language).
suer, *v. n.* & *a.* sweat.
sueur, *s. f.* sweat.
suffire*, *v.n.* be sufficient, be enough.
suffisamment, *adv.* sufficiently, enough.
suffisant, *adj.* sufficient enough; conceited.
suffoquer, *v.a.* & *n.* suffocate, choke.
suggérer, *v.a.* suggest, propose.
suggestion, *s. f.* suggestion, hint.
suicide, *s. m.* suicide.
suisse (S.), *adj.* & *s. m.* *(f.* Suissesse) Swiss.
suite, *s. f.* retinue; suite, sequence, result; *à la* ~ after; *tout de* ~ at once, directly; *par* ~ consequently; *par* ~ *de* due to.
suivant, *adj.* following, next; — *prep.* according to.
suivre*, *v.a.* & *n.* follow; *comme suit* as follows; *ce qui suit* the following.
sujet, -ette, *s. m. f.* subject; *s. m.* subject.
superficie, *s. f.* surface, area.
superficiel, -elle, *adj.* superficial.

superflu, *adj.* superfluous.
supérieur, *adj.* superior, upper.
supériorité, *s. f.* superiority.
supermarché, *s. m.* supermarket.
supersonique, *adj.* supersonic.
superstitieux, -euse, *adj.* superstitious.
superstition, *s. f.* superstition.
suppléer, *v.a.* supply; substitute, do duty for; *v. n.* make up for.
supplément, *s. m.* supplement; extra charge; excess.
supplémentaire, *adj.* supplementary, extra.
suppliant, -e, *adj.* suppliant; — *s. m. f.* supplicant.
supplier, *v. a.* beseech.
support, *s.m.* prop; support.
supporter, *v.a.* bear, support.
supposer, *v. a.* suppose.
supposition, *s. f.* supposition, conjecture.
suppression, *s. f.* suppression.
supprimer, *v. a.* suppress, abolish, do away with.
suprême, *adj.* supreme.
sur, *prep.* on; over; concerning.
sûr, *adj.* certain, sure; secure, safe; *pour* ~! to be sure!
surcharger, *v.a.* & *n.* overload; weigh down.
sûrement, *adv.* surely, certainly.
sûreté, *s. f.* safety; security.
surface, *s.f.* surface.
surgir, *v. n.* arise, spring up, emerge.
surmonter, *v.a.* surmount, overcome.
surnaturel, -elle, *adj.* supernatural.
surpasser, *v. a.* surpass, outdo.
surpeuplé, *adj.* overcrowded.
surplus, *s.m.* surplus, excess.
surprendre, *v. a.* surprise.
surprise, *s.f.* surprise.
surseoir*, *v.n.* & *a.* postpone, delay, put off.
surtaxe, *s. f.* surtax.
surtout, *s. m.* overcoat.
surveillance, *s. f.* supervision.
surveiller, *v.a.* supervise.
survenir, *v. a.* arrive unexpectedly; happen, occur.
survivant, -e, *s.m.f.* survivor.
survivre, *v.n.* survive, outlive.
susceptible, *adj.* susceptible.
suspect, *adj.* suspicious, suspect.
suspendre, *v. a.* hang up; suspend.
suspension, *s. f.* suspension.
svelte, *adj.* slender, slim.
syllabe, *s. f.* syllable.
symbole, *s. m.* symbol.
symétrie, *s. f.* symmetry.
symétrique, *adj.* sym-

metrical.
sympathie, *s. f.* sympathy.
symphonie, *s. f.* symphony.
symptome, *s. m.* symptom.
synagogue, *s. f.* synagogue.
syndical, *adj.* trade.
syndicat, *s. m.* syndicate; trade-union; ~ *d'initiative* tourist information office.
synthétique, *adj.* synthetic(al).
systématique, *adj.* systematic.
système, *s. m.* system.

T

tabac, *s.m.* tobacco; *bureau de* ~ tobacconist's (shop).
table, *s. f.* table; board; food; ~ *des matières*, table of contents.
tableau, *s.m.* picture; scene; board, panel.
tablette, *s. f.* tablet.
tablier, *s.m.* apron; dash-board.
tabouret, *s. m.* stool.
tache, *s. f.* spot, stain; *sans* ~ spotless.
tâche, *s. f.* task, job.
tacher, *v.a.* spot, stain.
tâcher, *v.n.* try.
tact, *s. m.* touch.
tactique, *s.f.* tactics.
taille, *s.f.* cut; height, stature, size; waist.
tailler, *v.a.* hew, trim; cut.
tailleur, *s. m.* tailor.
taire*, *v.a.* be silent about, conceal; **se** ~ be quiet.
talent, *s. m.* talent, attainment(s).
talon, *s. m.* heel; counterfoil.
talus, *s. m.* slope, bank.
tambour, *s. m.* drum.
tamis, *s. m.* sieve.
tamiser, *v. a.* sift, sieve.
tampon, *s. m.* plug; tampon.
tamponner, *v. a.* plug.
tandis que, *conj.* whereas, while.
tangible, *adj.* tangible.
tant, *adv.* so much, so many, such, so.
tante, *s. f.* aunt.
tantôt, *adv.* shortly, by and by; ~ ... ~ now ... now.
tapage, *s. m.* noise, fuss.
taper, *v.a.* & *n.* tap, strike, knock; **type.**
tapis, *s. m.* carpet, rug.
tapisser, *v. a.* upholster.
tapisserie, *s. f.* tapestry.
tapissier, *s. m.* upholsterer.
tard, *adv.* late.
tarder, *v.n.* delay, put off; be long.
tardif, **-ive,** *adj.* late.
tarif, *s.m.* tariff, rate; price-list; fare.
tarte, *s. f.* tart.
tas, *s. m.* heap, pile; mass; crowd.
tasse, *s. f.* cup.
tâter, *v.a.* & *n.* feel, taste, handle.
tâtonner, *v.n.* grope.
taureau, *s.m.* bull.
taux, *s.m.* price, rate (of exchange); tax.

taverne, *s. f.* tavern.
taxe, *s. f.* tax.
taxer, *v. a.* tax, rate.
taxi, *s. m.* taxi; *station de ~s* taxi-rank.
tchèque (T.), *adj.* & *s. m. f.* Czech.
te, *pron.* you; to you.
technicien, -enne, *s. m. f.* technician.
technique, *adj.* technical; *s. f.* technique, technics.
technologie, *s. f.* technology.
teindre*, *v.a.* dye, stain.
teint, *s. m.* complexion; dye.
teinte, *s. f.* tint, shade.
teinter, *v. a.* tint.
teinture, *s. f.* dye; tincture.
teinturerie, *s.f.* dye-works, dyer.
tel, telle, *adj.* such, like, similar.
télécommunication, *s.f.* telecommunication.
téléférique, *s.m.* rope-way.
télégramme, *s.m.* telegram, wire.
télégraphe, *s.m.* telegraph.
télégraphie, *s.f.* telegraphy.
télégraphier, *v.a.* & *n.* wire.
télégraphique, *adj.* telegraphic.
télémètre, *s.m.* range-finder.
téléphone, *s.m.* telephone.
télescope, *s. m.* telescope.
téléspectateur, -trice, *s. m. f.* (tele)viewer.
téléviser, *v. a.* televise, telecast.
téléviseur, *s.m.* television-set.
télévison, *s. f.* television.
télex, *s. m.* telex.
tellement, *adv.* so (much).
témoigner, *v.a.* & *n.* testify; give evidence.
témoin, *s.m.* witness; testimony.
tempe, *s.f.* temple *(forehead)*.
tempérament, *s. m.* temper(ament), constitution.,
température, *s.f.* temperature.
tempête, *s. f.* storm.
temple, *s. m.* temple, church; chapel; lodge.
temporel, -elle, *adj.* temporal, transient.
temps[1], *s. m.* time; opportunity; *à ~* in time; *pendant ce ~ l* in the meantime; *en ~ voulu* in due time; *combien de ~?* how long?; *la plupart du ~* mostly; *de ~ en ~* at times.
temps[2], *s.m.* weather; *prévisions du ~* weather-forecast.
tenaille, *s.f.* pincers, pliers, tongs *(pl.)*.
tendance, *s.f.* tendency, trend.
tendon, *s.m.* tendon, sinew.
tendre[1] [1]*adj.* tender, soft.
tendre[2], *v.a.* stretch; strain; bend; hang.
tendresse, *s. f.* tenderness.
tendu, *adj.* tense, taut.
ténébreux, -euse, *adj.*

dark, gloomy, dismal.
tenir*, *v. a.* & *n.* hold; get hold of; hold on; take, contain; keep; se ~ stay, remain.
tennis, *s. m.* tennis.
tension, *s.f.* tension.
tentation, *s. f.* temptation.
tentative, *s. f.* attempt.
tente, *s. f.* tent.
tenter, *v.a.* attempt; try; tempt.
ténu, *adj.* thin, slender.
tenue, *s. f.* holding; session; behaviour.
terme, *s. m.* term; expression; goal, aim.
terminer, *v. a.* terminate, end, close; se ~ (come to an) end.
terminus, *s. m.* terminus.
terne, *adj.* dull, dim.
terrain, *s. m.* soil, earth; site; ground; ~ *de jeux* sports-ground.
terrasse, *s.f.* terrace.
terre, *s.f.* earth, land.
terreur, *s.f.* fear.
terrible, *adj.* terrible.
terrifier, *v.a.* terrify, frighten.
territoire, *s. m.* territory.
testament, *s.m.* will, testament.
tête, *s. f.* head.
têtu, *adj.* stubborn.
texte, *s.m.* text; type.
textile, *s.m.* textile.
textuel, -elle, *adj.* textual.
texture, *s. f.* texture.
thé, *s. m.* tea.
théâtral, *adj.* theatrical.
théâtre, *s.m.* theatre, stage; drama; *pièce de* ~ play.
théière, *s. f.* tea-pot.
thème, *s. m.* theme, topic; prose.
théologie, *s. f.* theology.
théologique, *adj.* theological.
théorie, *s. f.* theory.
théorique, *adj.* theoretic, theoretical.
thermal, *adj.* thermal.
thermomètre, *s. m.* thermometer.
thermos, *s. f.* thermos.
thèse, *s. f.* thesis.
thon, *s. m.* tunny.
tien, -enne, *poss. adj.* yours.
tiers, tierce, *adj.* third; — *s.m.* third party.
tige, *s. f.* stem, stalk.
tigre, *s. m.* tiger.
tigresse, *s. f.* tigress.
timbre, *s. m.* bell; sound; (postage-)stamp.
timbre-poste, *s. m.* postage-stamp.
timide, *adj.* timid, shy.
timidité, *s. f.* timidity.
tir, *s.m.* shooting.
tirage, *s.f.* draught, pull(ing); impression; issue.
tire-bouchon *s. m.* corkscrew.
tirer, *v. a.* & *n.* draw, pull, drag; extract; derive; fire, shoot; print.
tiroir, *s.m.* drawer.
tison, *s.m.* brand.
tisonnier, *s.m.* poker.
tisser, *v.a.* weave.
tisserand, *s.m.* weaver.
tissu, *s. m.* texture, fabric; tissue.
titre, *s. m.* title; heading;

right.
titrer, *v.a.* give a title to.
toast, *s. m.* toast.
toi, *pron.* you.
toile, *s. f.* linen; cloth.
toilette, *s.f.* dress, clothes *(pl.)*; dressing-table; *faire sa* ~ dress; *cabinet de* ~ dressing-room.
toison, *s. f.* fleece.
toit, *s. m.* roof.
tolérance, *s. f.* tolerance, toleration.
tolérer, *v.a.* tolerate, bear.
tomate, *s.f.* tomato.
tombe, *s. f.* tomb, grave.
tombeau, *s. m.* tomb.
tombée, *s.f.* fall.
tomber, *v.n.* fall, fall down; tumble; decay; ~ *sur* meet, run into; *faire* ~ push down; *laisser* ~ drop.
tome, *s. m.* volume.
ton[1], **ta,** *poss. adj. (pl.* **tes)** your.
ton[2], *s. m.* tone; colour; manner.
tondeuse, *s.f.* lawn-mower.
tondre, *v.a.* shear, clip, mow.
tonnage, *s. m.* tonnage.
tonne, *s. f.* barrel, tun; ton.
tonneau, *s.m.* barrel.
tonner, *v.n.* thunder.
tonnerre, *s.m.* thunder-(bolt).
toqué, *adj.* crazy.
torche, *s. f.* torch.
torcher, *v.a.* wipe, rub.
torchon, *s.m.* duster; dish-cloth.
tordre, *v. a.* twist, wring (out).
torpille, *s. f.* torpedo.
torrent, *s. m.* torrent.
tort, *s. m.* wrong, harm, injury; *avoir* ~ be wrong.
tortue, *s. f.* tortoise.
torture, *s. f.* torture.
torturer, *v. a.* torture.
tôt, *adv.* soon, quickly; early.
total, *adj.* total, whole.
totalement, *adv.* totally, entirely.
touchant, *prep.* about.
touche, *s. f.* touch; key; hit.
toucher, *v. n. & a.* touch; feel; strike, hit; concern; — *s. m.* touch; feeling.
touffe, *s. f.* tuft.
toujours, *adv.* always, ever; still.
toupet, *s. m.* tuft, lock.
tour[1], *s.f.* tower.
tour[2], *s.m.* turn; tour, trip; feat, trick; (turning-)lathe; revolution; ~ *à* ~ in turns; *à son* ~ in turn; *faire le* ~ *de* go round.
tourelle, *s. f.* turret.
tourisme, *s. m.* tourism; touring; *faire du* ~ *à pied* hike.
touriste, *s. m. f.* tourist, hiker.
tourment, *s. m.* torment, torture.
tourmenter, *v. a.* torment; **se** ~ worry.
tournant, *adj.* turning; — *s. m.* turn(ing).
tourné, *adj.* turned; sour.
tournée, *s. f.* tour, walk;

circuit.
tourner, *v. a.* turn, twist, wind; turn round; *v. n.* turn, revolve; turn out; turn sour.
tournevis, *s.m.* screw-driver.
tournoi, *s.m.* tournament.
tournure, *s.f.* shape, figure; turn; cast; appearance.
tous *see* **tout.**
tousser, *v.n.* cough.
tout, -e, *adj.* *(pl.* **tous, toutes)** all, every, any, whole, full; ~ *le monde* everybody; ~ *son possible* one's utmost; *à* ~ *e force* at any cost; — *adv.* wholly, entirely; ~ *coup* suddenly; ~ *fait* thoroughly; ~ *de suite* directly; ~ *à l'heure* just now; ~ *au moins* at least; — *pron. & s.m.* everything, all; *pas du* ~ not at all.
toutefois, *adv.* yet, nevertheless, however.
tout-puissant, *adj.* almighty.
toux, *s. f.* cough.
tracas, *s. m.* bustle, stir; worry.
tracasser, *v. n. & a.* worry, bother; fuss; se ~ worry.
trace, *s. f.* trace, track; footprint.
tracer, *v. a.* trace, draw; lay out.
tracteur, *s. m.* tractor.
traction, *s.f.* traction, pull.
tradition, *s. f.* tradition.
traditionnel, -elle, *adj.* traditional.
traducteur, -trice, *s. m. f.* translator.
traduction, *s. f.* translation.
traduire*, *v. a.* translate.
trafic, *s. m.* traffic; trade, commerce.
trafiquer, *v.n.* traffic; trade, deal.
tragédie, *s. f.* tragedy.
tragédien, -enne, *s. m. f.* tragedien.
tragique, *adj.* tragic.
trahir, *v. a.* betray; deceive, mislead.
trahison, *s. f.* treason, treachery.
train, *s.m.* pace, rate; train; ~ *couloir* corridor-train; ~ *direct* through train; ~ *de marchandises* goods train.
traîne, *s.f.* train (of a dress).
traîneau, *s. m.* sledge.
traîner, *v.a.* drag, draw; lead (to); delay; *v.n.* drag; lie about; lag behind.
train-poste, *s.m* mail-train.
traire*, *v.a.* milk.
trait, *s.m.* arrow; dart; flash; line; trait, feature.
traite, *s.f.* journey; stretch; export; draft, bill.
traité, *s. m.* treaty.
traitement, *s. m.* treatment; usage; reception; salary.
traiter, *v.a.* treat, use,

deal with; call; entertain.
traître, *s. m.* traitor; — *adj.* treacherous.
trajet, *s.m.* passage, journey, course, crossing.
tram, *s.m.* tram(-car).
trammer, *v. a.* weave; plot; devise.
tramway, *s. m.* tram.
tranchant, *adj.* sharp, keen.
tranche, *s. f.* slice, chop, steak.
trancher, *v.a. & n.* cut; cut off; carve; break off.
tranquille, *adj.* quiet, calm; *soyez ~!* don't worry!
tranquilliser, *v. a.* soothe, calm; se ~ keep calm.
transaction, *s. f.* compromise, transaction.
transalpin, *adj.* transalpine.
transatlantique, *adj.* transatlantic; — *s. f.* deckchair.
transfert, *s. m.* transfer.
transformation, *s. f.* transformation, change.
transformer, *v.a.* transform, convert.
transfusion, *s.f.* transfusion.
transistor, *s. m.* transistor.
transit, *s.m.* transit.
transition, *s.f.* transition.
transmettre, *v. a.* transmit; forward; pass on.
transmission, *s. f.* transmission.
transparent, *adj.* transparent.
transpiration, *s.f.* perspiration.
transpirer, *v. n.* perspire.
transport, *s. m.* transport, conveyance; *enterprise de ~* forwarding agency.
transporter, *v.a.* transport, convey; transfer; enrapture.
trappe, *s. f.* trap; trapdoor.
travail, *s. m.* (*pl.* **-aux**) work, job, employment; task; piece of work; workmanship; *petits travaux* odd jobs; *sans ~* unemployed.
travailler, *v.n. & a.* work, labour; take pains.
travailleur, -euse, *s. m. f.* worker, workman, workwoman.
travers, *s. m.* breadth; *à ~* across, through; *au ~ de* through; *en ~* across.
traverse, *s.f.* traverse; obstacle; crossing.
traversée, *s.f.* crossing, passage.
traverser, *v. a.* traverse, cross, go through; run through.
trayeuse, *s. f.* milking-machine.
trébucher, *v. n.* stumble; turn the scale.
tréfle, *s. m.* clover; club *(cards)*.
treille, *s. f.* vine arbour.
treize, *adj. & s.m* thirteen;
tremblant, *adj.* tembling

shaky.
tremblement, *s. m.* trembling, shaking; *~ de terre* earthquake.
trembler, *v. n.* tremble, shake.
tremper, *v. a.* soak, wet; dip; *il est tout trempé* he is wet through.
tremplin, *s.m.* spring-board.
trentaine, *s.m.* thirty.
trente, *adj. & s. m.* thirty; thirtieth.
très, *adv.* very, most, very much; *~ bien* very well; all right.
trésor, *s. m.* treasure.
trésorie, *s. f.* treasury.
trésorier, *s. m.* treasurer.
tresse, *s. f.* plait, tress, braid.
trêve, *s. f.* truce, rest; *faire ~* stop, cease.
triangle, *s. m.* triangle.
tribu, *s. f.* tribe.
tribunal, *s. m.* tribunal, law-court.
tribune, *s.f.* tribune, platform; grand-stand.
tributaire, *adj.* tributary.
tricher, *v. n. & a.* cheat; trick (s.o. out of).
tricot, *s.m.* (knitted) jersey.
tricoter, *v. a. & n.* knit.
triomphant, *adj.* triumphant.
triomphe, *s. m.* triumph.
triompher, *v. n.* triumph.
triple, *adj.* triple.
tripot, *s.m.* gambling-den.
triste, *adj.* sad.
tristesse, *s. f.* sadness.
trivial, *adj.* trivial.
trois, *adj. & s. m.* three; third.
troisième, *adj. & s. m.* third.
trolley, *s.m.* trolley (-pole).
trolleybus, *s. m.* trolley-bus.
trompe, *s.f.* trumpet, horn.
tromper, *v. a.* deceive, cheat, take in; *se ~* mistake, be mistaken; be wrong; *se ~ de train* take the wrong train.
trompette, *s. f.* trumpet; trumpeter.
tronc, *s. m.* trunk; stock; collecting box.
trône, *s.m.* throne.
trop, *adv.* too; too much.
trophée, *s. m.* trophy.
tropical, *adj.* tropical.
tropique, *s. m.* tropic.
trot, *s. m.* trot.
trotter, *v. n.* trot.
trottoir, *s. m.* pavement; footway.
trou, *s.m.* hole; gap; opening.
trouble, *s. m.* disorder; confusion; misunderstanding; dispute; — *adj.* troubled; muddy.
troubler, *v.a.* stir up, disturb; make muddy; muddle; confuse, perplex; upset; trouble.
troué, *s. f.* opening, gap.
trouer, *v. a.* make a hole in; pierce; bore.
troupe, *s. f.* troop, band.
troupeau, *s.m.* herd, drove; flock.
trouvaille, *s. f.* find(ing).
trouver, *v. a.* find, discover; find out; think;

contrive; **se ~** be, be found to be, prove; turn out, happen; *je me trouvais là* I happened to be there.
truite, *s. f.* trout.
trust, *s. m.* trust.
T.S.F., *s. f.* (*=télégraphie sans fil*) wireless (set).
tu, toi, *pron.* you.
tube, *s. m.* tube; pipe; **~** *de télévision* TV tube.
tuberculose, *s. f.* tuberculosis.
tuer, *v. a.* kill; slay.
tuile, *s. f.* tile.
tumeur, *s. f.* tumour.
tunnel, *s. m.* tunnel.
turbine, *s. f.* turbine.
turbopropulseur, *s. m.* turbo-prop aircraft.
turboréacteur, *s.m.* turbo-jet engine.
turc, turque (T.),*adj.* Turkish (language), Turk.
tuteur, -trice, *s.m.f.* guardian, trustee.
tutoyer, *v. a.* to 'thee-and thou' s. o.
tuyau, *s. m.* pipe, tube; flue; **~** *d'échappement* exhaust-pipe.
tympan, *s. m.* ear-drum.
type, *s. m.* type.
typique, *adj.* typical.
typographie, *s. f.* typography; printing.
tyran, *s. m.* tyrant.
tyrannie, *s. f.* tyranny.
tyranniser, *v. a.* tyrannize (over); oppress.

U

ulcère, *s. m.* ulcer.
ultérieur, *adj.* ulterior; further.
ultime, *adj.* ultimate, last, final.
ultra-violet-, -ette, *adj.* ulra-violet.
un, une, *art. & pron.* a, an; any, some; one; *l'~ ou l'autre* either one or the other; *ni l'~ ni l'autre* neither one; *l'~ et autre* both; *~e fois* once; **~** *à* **~** one by one.
unanime, *adj.* unanimous.
uni, *adj.* smooth, even, level; united.
unification, *s. f.* unification.
unifier, *v. a.* unify; unite.
uniforme, *adj.* uniform.
union, *s. f.* union; agreement: match, marriage.
unique, *adj.* unique, sole, only.
uniquement, *adv.* solely, only.
unir, *v.a.* unite; level, smooth; **s'~** join.
unité, *s.f.* unity; unit.
univers, *s. m.* universe.
universel, -elle, *adj.* universal; world-wide.
universitaire, *adj.* academic, university.
université, *s.f.* university.
urbain, *adj.* urban.
urgence, *s.f.* urgency; *d'~* urgent; *en cas d'~* in case of emergency.
urgent, *adj.* urgent, pressing.
uriner, *v. n. & a.* urinate.
urne, *s. f.* urn.
usage, *s. m.* use, custom;

habit, way; wear; *d'*~ usual, habitual; *en* ~ in use.
usé, *adj.* worn-out, shabby.
user, *v. n. & a.* use, make use of; wear out; use up; — *s.m.* wear, service, use; *être d'un bon* ~ wear well.
usine, *s. f.* factory, works.
ustensile, *s. m.* utensil; implement, tool.
usuel, -elle, *adj.* usual, customary.
usure¹, *s. f.* usury.
usure², *s. f.* wear (and tear).
usurper, *v.a.* usurp.
utile, *adj.* useful, of use, profitable; *être* ~ ( ) be of use.
utilisation, *s.f.* utilization.
utiliser, *v.a.* utilize.
utilité, *s. f.* utility, use.

V

va *int.* agreed!, indeed.
vacance, *s. f.* vacancy; *(pl.)*, holiday(s), vacation; *être en* ~*s* be on holiday.
vacant, *adj.* vacant.
vacarme, *s.m.* noise, uproar.
vaccin, *s.m.* vaccine.
vacciner, *v. a.* vaccinate.
vache, *s.f.* cow.
vaciller, *v.n.* vacillate; reel; waver.
vacuum, *s. m.* vacuum.
vagabond, *s. m.* trampe.
vague¹, *adj.* vague.
vague², *s.f.* wave.
vaillant, *adj.* valiant.
vain, *adj.* vain; empty; *en* ~ in vain.
vaincre*, *v. a. & n.* conquer, defeat.
vainqueur, *s.m.* conqueror, victor; — *adj.* conquering, victorious.
vaisseau, *s. m.* vessel; ship.
vaisselle, *s. f.* plates and dishes, table-service; *laver la* ~ wash up the dishes; *lavage de* ~ washing-up.
valet, *s. m.* valet; knave, jack.
valeur, *s. f.* value, worth; price; courage; ~*s* securities.
valide, *adj.* valid; able-bodied.
validité, *s.f.* validity.
valise, *s. f.* valise, (travelling-)bag; suitcase; ~ *diplomatique* dispatch-box, diplomatic bag.
vallée, *s. f.* valley.
valoir*, *v.n. & a.* be worth, be as good as; deserve; procure; yield.
valse, *s.f.* waltz.
vanille, *s.f.* vanilla.
vanité, *s.f.* vanity.
vaniteux, -euse, *adj.* vain, conceited.
vanter, *v. a.* extol, cry up; *se* ~ boast.
vapeur¹, *s.f.* steam; vapour.
vapeur², *s.m.* steamer.
vaporeux, -euse, *adj.* vaporous.
vaquer, *v. n.* be vacant.
variable, *adj.* variable,

changeable.
variante, *s.f.* variant.
variation, *s.f.* variation.
varier, *v. n.* & *a.* vary; ~ *de* ... *à* range from ... to.
variété, *s. f.* variety.
vase, *s. m.* vase; vessel.
vaseline, *s. f.* vaseline.
vassal, *s. m.* vassal.
vaste, *adj.* vast; spacious.
vautour, *s. m.* vulture.
veau, *s. m.* veal; calf.
vedette, *s.f.* mounted sentinel; motor-boat; (film) star.
végétal, *s. m.* vegetable; plant.
végétation, *s. f.* vegetation.
végéter, *v. n.* vegetate.
véhémence, *s. f.* vehemence.
véhément, *adj.* vehement.
véhicule, *s. m.* vehicle.
véhiculer, *v. a.* transport.
veille, *s. f.* waking; vigil; eve.
veiller, *v. n.* sit up, keep watch; *v.a.* watch.
veine, *s. f.* vein; luck.
vélo, *s.m.* bike.
vélocité, *s.f.* velocity.
velours, *s.m.* velvet.
velouté, *adj.* velvety, soft.
velu, *adj.* hairy.
venaison, *s.f.* venison.
vendange, *s.f.* vintage, grape-harvest.
vendeur, -euse, *s. m. f.* salesman, shop assistant; saleswoman.
vendre, *v. a.* sell; *à* ~ for sale.
vendredi, *s. m.* Friday; *le* ~ *saint* Good Friday.
vénéneux, -euse, *adj.* poisonous.
vénérable, *adj.* venerable.
vengeance, *s. f.* vengeance, revenge.
venger, *v.a.* avenge, revenge; **se** ~ avenge oneself.
venin, *s.m.* poison.
venir*, *v. n.* come, arrive; grow; occur; arise; ~ *de* come from; ~ *à bout de* manage.
vent, *s. m.* wind; *grand* ~ gale; ~ *alizé* trade-wind.
vente, *s. f.* sale; auction; *en* ~ for sale.
venteux, -euse, *adj.* windy.
ventilateur, *s. m.* ventilator.
ventilation, *s. f.* ventilation.
ventre, *s. m.* belly.
venue, *s.f.* coming, arrival.
ver, *s.m.* worm.
verbal, *adj.* verbal, oral.
verbe, *s.m.* verb.
verdeur, *s.f.* greenness; harshness.
verdict, *s.m.* verdict.
verdure, *s.f.* verdure; greenness.
verger, *s.m.* orchard.
vergue, *s.f.* yard.
vérification, *s.f.* verification; check(ing).
vérifier, *v.a.* verify; check; confirm.
vérité, *s.f.* truth.
vermicelle, *s.m.* vermicelli.
vernir, *v. a.* varnish; pol-

ish.
vernis, *s.m.* varnish; polish.
verre, *s.m.* glass.
verrou, *s.m.* bolt.
verrouiller, *v.a.* bolt.
vers[1], *s.m.* line; verse.
vers[2], *prep.* towards, to; about.
verser, *v. a.* pour (out) spill, upset; *v. n.* overturn.
version, *s. f.* translation; version.
vert, *adj.* green; hearty; sharp.
vertical, *adj.* vertical, upright.
vertige, *s. m.* dizziness.
vertu, *s.f.* virtue.
vessie, *s.f.* bladder.
veste, *s. f.* coat, jacket.
vestiaire, *s. m.* cloakroom.
vestibule, *s.m.* lobby, hall; *grand* ~ lounge.
veston, *s. m.* coat; *complet* ~ lounge-suit.
vêtement, *s.m.* clothes *(pl.)*; *~s de dessous* underwear, underclothes.
vétéran, *s.m.* veteran.
vétérinaire, *s. m.* veterinary surgeon, vet.
vêtir*, *v. a.* clothe, dress.
véto, *s.m.* veto.
veuf, *s.m.* widower.
veuve, *s.f.* widow.
vexer, *v. a.* vex, annoy.
via, *prep.* via.
viaduc, *s. m.* viaduct.
viande, *s. m.* meat; ~ *réfrigérée* chilled meat.
vibration, *s. f.* vibration.
vibrer, *v. n.* vibrate.
vicaire, *s.m.* curate.
vice, *s.m.* vice, evil.
vice-, *prefix* vice-
vicieux, -euse, *adj.* vicious; faulty.
vicomte, *s. m.* viscount.
victime, *s.f.* victim.
victoire, *s.f.* victory.
victorieux, -euse, *adj.* victorious.
victuailles, *s. f. pl.* victuals.
vide, *adj.* empty; void; vacant; — *s.m.* space.
vider, *v. a.* empty; drain.
vie, *s.f.* life.
vieillard, *s.m.* old man.
vieillesse, *s.f.* old age.
vieillir, *v.n.* grow old.
vierge, *s. f.* virgin, maid.
vieux, vieil, vieille, *adj.* old.
vif, vive, *adj.* live; quick; lively; full of life; bright, vivid; fiery, ardent.
vigilant, *adj.* watchful.
vigne, *s.f.* vine; vineyard.
vignoble, *s.m.* vineyard.
vigoureux, -euse, *adj.* vigorous.
vigueur, *s.f.* vigour force.
vilain, *s. m.* villain, ca[illegible]
village, *s.m.* village.
ville, *s. f.* town, city; *hôtel de* ~ town hall.
vin, *s. m.* wine.
vinaigre, *s. m.* vinegar.
vingt, *adj.* & *s.m* twenty; twentieth.
vingtième, *adj.* twentieth.
violation, *s.f.* violation.
violence, *s.f.* violence.
violent, *adj.* violent; excessive.

violer, *v. a.* violate, ravish.
violette, *s.f.* violet.
violon, *s.m.* violin.
violoncelle, *s. m.* (violon-) cello.
violoniste, *s. m f.* violinist.
vipère, *s.f.* viper.
virgule, *s.f.* comma; *point et* ~ semicolon.
virtuose, *s. m. f.* virtuoso.
vis, *s. f.* screw.
visa, *s.m.* visa, visé.
visage, *s. m.* face.
vis-à-vis, *prep.* opposite; facing.
viser, *v.a.* aim (at); aspire to.
viseur, *s. m.* view-finder.
visibilité, *s. f.* visibility.
visible, *adj.* visible.
vision, *s.f.* sight.
visite, *s. f.* visit; *faire* ~ *à* pay a visit to, call on.
visiter, *v. a.* visit; ~ *les curiosités* go sightseeing.
visiteur, -euse, *s. m. f.* visitor.
visser, *v. a.* screw (down, in).
visuel, -elle, *adj.* visual.
vital, *adj.* vital.
vitalité, *s.f.* vitality.
vitamine, *s. f.* vitamin.
vite, *adj.* fast; swift; — *adv.* fast, rapidly.
vitesse, *s. f.* speed; rate (of speed); gear; *à toute* ~ at top speed; *boîte de* ~ gear-box; ~ *de croisière* cruising speed.
vitrail *s. m.* church window.
vitre, *s. f.* pane.
vitrier, *s.m.* glazier.
vivant, *adj.* alive, living; full of life; *de mon* ~ in my lifetime.
vivement, *adv.* quickly, fast.
vivre*, *v. n.* live, be alive.
vocabulaire, *s. m.* vocabulary.
vocation, *s.f.* vocation, calling.
vœu, *s. m. (pl.* **-x)** wish, desire; vow.
vogue, *s. f.* vogue, fashion; *avoir la* ~ be in vogue.
voici, *prep.* here (is); *le* ~*!* here he is!
voie, *s.f.* way, road; route; line, track; means, channel.
voilà, *prep.* there (is).
voile[1], *s.m.* veil.
voile[2], *s.f.* sail.
voiler, *v.a.* veil, cover, hide.
voilier, *s. m.* sailing-ship.
voir*, *v. a.* see; look at; view; *faire* ~ show; *ne pas* ~ miss.
voire, *adv.* even.
voisin, *adj.* neighbouring, adjoining, next (door).
voisinage, *s.m.* neighbourhood.
voiture, *s.f.* vehicle, conveyance; carriage; car; coach; van; wagon; *aller en* ~ drive.
voiture-ambulance, *s. f.* ambulance(-car).
voix, *s. f.* voice; sound; *à haute* ~ aloud.
vol[1], *s. m.* flying, flight.
vol[2], *s. m.* theft, robbery.

volaille, *s.f.* poultry, fowl.
volant, *s.m.* steering-wheel.
volcan, *s.m.* volcano.
volée, *s.f.* flight.
voler[1], *v. n.* fly; run at top speed.
voler[2], *v. a. & n.* steal, rob.
volet, *s.m.* shutter.
voleur, *s. m.* thief, robber.
volontaire, *adj.* voluntary; — *s. m. f.* volunteer.
volonté, *s. f.* will; *à* ~ at will.
volontiers, *adv.* willingly.
volt, *s.m.* volt.
voltiger, *v.n.* flutter about, fly about.
volume, *s. m.* volume; bulk.
voluptueux, -euse, *adj.* voluptuous.
vomir, *v. a. & n.* vomit, be sick.
vos, *adj. poss.* your.
vote, *s. m.* vote; voting.
voter, *v. n.* ~ *& a.* vote.
votre, *adj.* yours.
vouer, *v. a.* vow; dedicate.
vouloir*, *v. a.* want, require, demand; ~ *bien* be willing; *je voudrais + inf.* I should like to; *comme vous voulez* as you please.
vous, *pron.* you; to you.
vous-même, *pron.* yourself.
voûte, *s.f.* vault, arch.
voyage, *s.m.* journey; voyage; *bon* ~*!* a pleasant journey (to you)!; *partir en* ~ set off on a journey; *fair un* ~ make a journey.
voyager, *v.n.* travel, make a trip.
voyageur, -euse, *s. m. f* traveller, passenger.
voyelle, *s.f.* vowel.
voyou, *s.m.* hooligan.
vrai, *adj.* real, true, right *être* ~ hold (good); — *s. m.* truth; *être dans le* ~ be right.
vraiment, *adv.* truly, really; indeed.
vraisemblable, *adj.* likely, credible, probable.
vu, *prep.* considering.
vue, *s. f.* sight; vision; view; *à* ~ at sight; *en* ~ *de* with a view to; *point de* ~ point of view; *avoir la* ~ *courte* be short-sighted; *être en* ~ be in the limelight.
vulgaire, *adj.* vulgar; common; coarse.

W

wagon, *s. m.* coach, carriage, car.
wagon-lit, *s. m.* sleeping-car.
wagonnet, *s.m.* tub; truck.
wagon-poste, *s. m.* mail-van.
wagon-restaurant, *s. m.* dining-car.
water-closet, *s. m.* W. C.
water-polo, *s. m.* water-polo.
wattman, *s.m.* tram-

driver.
week-end, *s.m.* week-end.
whisky, *s.m.* whisky.

X

xérès, *s. m.* sherry.
xylographie, *s. f.* xylography.
xylophages, *s.m. pl.* xylophages.

Y

y, *adv.* here, there; *il ~ a* there is, there exists; *s'~ connaître* well informed.
yacht, *s. m.* yacht.
yeux *see* œil.
yogourt, yoghourt, *s. m.* yoghourt, yaourt.
yougoslave, *adj.* Yugoslav.
youyou, *s.m.* dinghy.

Z

zèbre, *s.m.* zebra.
zébrer, *v.a.* stripe.
zèle, *s.m.* zeal.
zélé, *adj.* zealous.
zénith, *s.m* zenith.
zéro, *s.m.* zero.
zézayer, *v.n.* lisp.
zigzag, *s.m.* zigzag.
zinc, *s.m.* zinc.
zone, *s.f.* zone, belt.
zoo, *s.m.* zoo.
zoologie, *s.f.* zoology.
zoologique, *adj.* zoological.
zut, *int.* *~!* damn it!